Anthropology of Contemporary Issues

A SERIES EDITED BY

ROGER SANJEK

Farm Work and Fieldwork: American Agriculture in Anthropological Perspective
EDITED BY MICHAEL CHIBNIK

The Varieties of Ethnic Experience: Kinship, Class, and Gender among California Italian-Americans
BY MICAELA DI LEONARDO

Chinese Working-Class Lives: Getting By in Taiwan
BY HILL GATES

Accommodation without Assimilation: Punjabi Sikh Immigrants in an American High School and Community
BY MARGARET A. GIBSON

Praying for Justice: Faith, Order, and Community in an American Town
BY CAROL J. GREENHOUSE

American Odyssey: Haitians in New York
BY MICHEL S. LAGUERRE

From Working Daughters to Working Mothers: Immigrant Women in a New England Industrial Community
BY LOUISE LAMPHERE

State and Family in Singapore: Restructuring a Developing Society
BY JANET W. SALAFF

Children of Circumstances: Israeli Emigrants in New York
BY MOSHE SHOKEID

City of Green Benches: Growing Old in a New Downtown
BY MARIA D. VESPERI

Renunciation and Reformulation: A Study of Conversion in an American Sect
BY HARRIET WHITEHEAD

Upscaling Downtown: The Tangled Engagements of a Varied Community
BY BRETT WILLIAMS

Women's Work and Chicano Families: Cannery Workers of the Santa Clara Valley
BY PATRICIA ZAVELLA

State and Family in Singapore

RESTRUCTURING A DEVELOPING SOCIETY

Janet W. Salaff

Cornell University Press

Ithaca and London

A GRANT FROM THE UNIVERSITY OF TORONTO–YORK UNIVERSITY
JOINT CENTRE FOR ASIA PACIFIC STUDIES HAS HELPED
TO DEFRAY PUBLICATION COSTS FOR THIS BOOK.

First published 1988 by Cornell University Press.

International Standard Book Number 0-8014-2140-3
Library of Congress Catalog Number 87-47962

Printed in the United States of America

*Librarians: Library of Congress cataloging information
appears on the last page of the book.*

*The paper in this book is acid-free and meets the guidelines for
permanence and durability of the Committee on Production Guidelines
for Book Longevity of the Council on Library Resources.*

To Aline

Contents

Acknowledgments   xiii
Author's Note   xv

Part I   Background
1. Introduction: Development and the Fabric of Life   3
2. State, Economy, and Social Services   19

Part II   The Early Development Stage
3. Introducing Poor Families   41
4. Poor Families in the Early Development Stage   79
5. Introducing Secure Families   103
6. Secure Families in the Early Development Stage   144

Part III   The Second Development Stage
7. Poor Family Lives Evolve   163
8. The Lives of Secure Families   193
9. Singapore Society in the Advanced Development Stage:
    Two Families or One?   226
10. Conclusion: Restructuring an Industrial Society   261

Notes   271
Index   295

Illustrations

Unskilled peripheral-sector vegetable seller 9
Political slogans 22
A kampung home, 1976 29
An HDB highrise 31
One-room rented flat in Toa Payoh housing estate 32
Hawker with child 81
Unskilled laborers in a core-sector shipyard 83
Semiskilled workers in a peripheral-sector garment factory 85
Skilled workers in a core-sector shipyard 147
Skilled worker in a peripheral-sector garment factory 150
High-density living in Chinatown 154
Religious procession 233
A family of modest means in their new home 241
Children of the secure try out their new toys 245
Breakfast at traditional hawkers' stalls 258
Men lounge in the shade of an HDB building 259
Singapore, crossroads of the world 267

Tables

1. Socioeconomic group of respondent couples, phases 1 and 2 *12*
2. Industrial sector and skill level of respondent men, phases 1 and 2 *13*
3. Occupations of Singapore Chinese men, phase 1 respondents and National Labour Force Survey, 1975 *14*
4. Percent of mothers engaged in full-time wage work, phase 1 respondents and all Singapore married women aged 25–34, 1973, by number of children born alive *14*
5. Occupations of Singapore Chinese women, phase 1 respondents and National Labour Force Survey, 1975 *15*
6. Average earnings of poor men in peripheral and core sectors, phase 1 *80*
7. Number of poor couples who intended to have and did have specified numbers of children, phase 1 *98*
8. Average earnings of secure men in peripheral and core sectors, phase 1 *145*
9. Number of secure couples who intended to have and did have specified numbers of children, phase 1 *158*
10. Average earnings of poor and secure men, phases 1 and 2 *227*
11. Average earnings of poor men in peripheral and core sectors, phases 1 and 2 *228*
12. Average earnings of 17 secure men in peripheral and core sectors, phases 1 and 2 *231*
13. Percent of poor and secure couples who desired specified levels of education for their children, phases 1 and 2 *246*

Acknowledgments

This book was long in the making and I have incurred many debts in the process. First, I acknowledge my great debt to my coresearcher and friend, Aline Wong, without whose years of input and informed enthusiasm the study would not have been launched or completed. Because Dr. Wong was unable to work on the final manuscript, none of the opinions expressed there is necessarily held by her, but I hope she likes the outcome of the work we shared.

Many people read parts of this manuscript and provided fine critical comments that were very helpful. Among them are Chan Heng Chee, Fred Deyo, Nancy Folbre, Pauline Kling, Harry Makler, Paul Rosenblatt, Lillian Rubin, Stephen Salaff, Roger Sanjek, James C. Scott, Marnie Wasserman, Aline Wong, Irving Zeitlin, and several anonymous reviewers of earlier drafts of the manuscript. I thank them all.

Generous financial assistance to conduct the research was provided by the International Development Research Centre (Ottawa), the Social Sciences and Humanities Research Council of Canada, the Social Science Research Council (Committee on Southeast Asia) (New York), and the Structural Research Programme (Department of Sociology, University of Toronto). The University of Toronto–York University Joint Centre on Asia Pacific Studies helped defray publication costs. I am very grateful to these bodies and to the people associated with them for their support.

JANET W. SALAFF

Toronto, Ontario

Author's Note

The lives explored in this book are those of ordinary people, without fame or fortune. Only their names are fictitious. As is customary, the Chinese family name precedes the given name. The equivalent of the Chinese Mandarin is spelled in Pinyin.

The monetary unit used in this book is the Singapore dollar. The exchange rate in 1975 was about 2.25 Singapore dollars to 1 U.S. dollar. In 1980 the rate was around S$2 = U.S.$1.

J. W. S.

To look at the institution of the family in the context of development processes and development policy is to see clearly that it is not possible to insulate the moral order from the technical order. The development process will make use of existing family institutions and will reshape them. The family, our most private of institutions, is also enormously malleable by state economic forces, and affected by public policies, even if these do not always intend the effects they have.

LISA PEATTIE

PART I

Background

[1]

Introduction: Development and the Fabric of Life

A Third World proletariat has been created in the growing manufacturing centers of the Asian Pacific Rim. In factories and workshops of Singapore, Hong Kong, Taiwan, and South Korea, where workers make low-cost goods for the export market, families maintain subsistence economies and forge kin and community ties to survive. That the rapid expansion of the world capitalist system has created urban poverty has been well documented.[1] Yet the first wave of entrants to the world manufacturing system are now experiencing considerable change. As additional nations join their ranks with even cheaper labor and other incentives, competition for investment forces the early entrants to embark on a second development stage. Investment in this second stage is geared largely to the manufacture of commodities with a high-technology component for regional and world markets. Thus Asian workers who one or two decades ago printed T-shirts are today assembling aircraft engines and computer circuits. In such a process, social life is bound to undergo deep change. The social structure of the second stage, which has received less attention than that of the first, is the topic of this book.[2]

By following the personal experiences of a number of families over time, this book examines how the society of the Republic of Singapore was transformed by state-sponsored social policies. This new nation has engineered the shift from first- to second-stage development at a remarkable rate. Many Singapore families I met for the first time in 1974–1976 exhibited the profile of Third World poverty. Since then, the Singapore state has launched a second development stage that is driven by the capitalist market within the strictures of foreign investment and trade dependency. The government expects the work force to strike deep roots in this economy. The entire population is to be integrated into a single class system, sloughing off social bonds and sharing a common industrial culture. So integrated, the work force can be mobilized to work in the advanced technical industries of what is called the "new economic order."

Central to the new economic program are two types of state social services that greatly affect family lives.[3] Both types, whether by design or by chance, extend the scope of the market economy. They also strengthen state agencies that fulfill many family needs and reduce reliance on personal ties. The first set of services directly invests in labor, providing job training and technical education. Such programs, if fully carried out, can open channels of income upgrading which are independent of kinship connections. Amenities, the second type of services, include public housing for rent or purchase and family-planning services to raise and equalize living standards. Again, such services stimulate the market and enhance the nuclear family at the expense of bonds with neighbors and kin. When it is no longer feasible for families to trade services and barter goods within long-established local communities, the nuclear family must shoulder all burdens itself. The state's role will be further enlarged as it restructures the economy and society for the second development stage.

This new nation's attempt to upgrade the economy and forge the people into an advanced labor force within a generation raises many practical and theoretical issues. As a city-state, Singapore differs from developing nations with a rural sector that encompasses the majority of the people. But a study of this dynamic area has wider significance, and other states have explored features of it, in particular its public housing program and its family-planning measures. What kind of life will emerge from the massive social programs advanced by the Singapore state? Will its programs in fact unify social groups into a single lifestyle? Or will they fail to close the deep divisions based on access to wealth and personal ties? Is there a sweep of modernity? A sinking into tradition? Some observers would put the question in another way: Can contemporary social institutions advanced by a centralizing state homogenize families and individuals? Will these institutions overcome the cleavages that separate social groups and economic classes as a result of the nation's international standing, especially its dependence on foreign economies for capital, products, and markets?

Any investigation of the impact of development on social life thus must address the sociological tradition within which societies are seen in terms of polarities: underdeveloped versus developed, traditional versus modern.[4] Modernization theory posits the gradual spread of industrial society, in this case from the "advanced" nations of the West to a "backward" nation of the Third World. Technology and consumer goods lead the way and introduce new ideas and cultural dispositions. As the underdeveloped society crumbles, inherited class, caste, religious, and ethnic groups are integrated into a single modern social system, and the old divisions disappear. As education becomes widespread, poverty declines and living standards rise. A meritocracy emerges as the best talents flow to their proper jobs. Families at all class levels assume the isolated nuclear form and become increasingly alike.[5]

Dependency theorists see the situation of the Third World in quite different terms; they argue that homogeneous modernization of a society is not possible. Third World capitalist economies are bound into the world economic system by relations of unequal exchange with the metropolitan industrial nations. The developed economies provide the new nations with capital and markets for only a narrow range of products. Through their economic power, foreign investors reinforce the role of these peripheral nations as suppliers of low-wage labor in the manufacture of goods for export. When foreign investors extract profits, they doom sectors of the new nations to crushing poverty.[6]

Both theories tend to view development as a set of forces that impinge on people mainly from outside. When we view development in this way, we transform both the state and its people into passive actors. I believe it is a mistake to expect uniform and massive social change without exploring the continued strength of social bonds, kin and ethnic groups, and local culture. Thus I follow still another structural tradition, one that focuses on types of states as actors that can forge structures to alter the society even as they depend on the world economy.[7] This structural approach looks at the impact of the state on society. Writers of this tradition also look to social structures that mediate economic and cultural forces and prevent uniformity in a society. Families' relationships with the market economy vary, and social class differences will persist and shape other lifestyle differences. Some writers have even documented the intensification of primordial ties and link the loss of previous levels of advanced culture with the emergence of new forms of "tradition."[8]

My special focus is on the place of the family in the development process, as seen through in-depth ethnographies of lives over time. The family is an important unit of study in the newly developed economy. The family, with the household, quasi-kin groups, and neighborhood around it, shapes the supply of labor and generates capital for the economy. The family reproduces labor power, channels its members into the job market, and imbues them with a work ethic. The people, too, are themselves active members of the social groups, as the current concept "family strategies" suggests.[9] I believe we can study the kinds of penetration effected by new institutions and the variations in their meanings to people through their family lives.

As we begin to learn about changes in family lives and look more closely into the ways in which people choose among the new resources available to

[5]

them, we find a richly textured set of responses. Many family-change patterns cannot be fitted into a modern/traditional or have/have-not framework. It is true that the people studied here act within a framework set largely by the state, in the context of the world economy. Further, they can meet their needs only in ways shaped by their economic, social, and cultural positions. Yet, as we focus on the variations in people's responses as they alter their way of life, we must also look at the ways such variations are organized on a local level.

Historical and cross-cultural studies suggest that we focus closely on economic and social structures, social bonds, and culture to determine the types of resources and constraints of the second-stage development program and to learn more about the structural limits to the actions of families. The rise and fall of individual, family, and group fortunes in the class hierarchy are one concern. As the industrial mix changes, old occupations disappear and new ones emerge. One master trend is the proletarianization of labor, and theorists predict widely differing outcomes. As wage labor spread in North America, the status of craft occupations and other self-taught and self-financed trades declined. The expansion of the market transformed goods and services into commodities, sold mostly by corporations instead of by itinerant workers or family firms.[10] Modernization scholars believe this process homogenizes the labor force in old and new nations alike. As people become wage laborers subject to the same market forces, distinctions between skill levels disappear. Structural theorists, in contrast, stress that the capitalist market in the West did not incorporate families evenly at all social levels. They anticipate that the income gap between occupational groups may widen even further in the new nations.[11] We therefore must look for differences in income, or stratification, among occupations in Singapore.

Industrial stratification can be seen as well. As capitalism matured in the West, a stratum of highly capitalized, union-organized "core-sector" firms emerged. Most were monopolies, which controlled the market. Because such firms earned high profit margins, their workers received relatively good wages, and higher prices for products were passed on to consumers.[12] Firms in the "peripheral sector," usually poorly capitalized, had to compete for a narrow share of the market. As they lacked the assets to exploit the economies of scale in research and development and in production, their workers earned lower wages. These divisions in workers' wages reflect industry differences, not workers' education. Yet workers cannot easily move from core-sector to peripheral-sector firms in search of better wages.[13]

Are skills and job sectors stratified also in the newly industrializing nations? A recent study of South Korea suggests that they are.[14] We must then look at the wages of men and women in different types of jobs in core and periphery industries in Singapore, and at their opportunities to improve their skills. Will workers' unequal economic standing persist unchanged? Or will new inequalities emerge with the second-stage industries? If solid earnings are enjoyed only by favored industries, which are they, and which industries decline under the new economic program?

The state, through public services, can propel families into the capitalist market economy to sell their labor and thereby can alter the stratification system. Studies of urban renewal programs in Puerto Rico and in Venezuela find that before people were physically relocated, large shantytowns contained both poor and better-off families. These workers helped each other by bartering and exchanging services.[15] But when urban renewal dispersed residents into housing projects, families had to buy most of what they needed. Laborers were forced into wage labor at a more intensive rate, and could afford fewer goods and services than the middle class, beginning with the new housing bills they had to pay. The populace not only became deeply stratified by class, determined by their wage labor, but also became subject to the new goals of the regimes.

Gender structures options within the development regime. As countries industrialize, the places of both women and men in the family and economy undergo change. One debate centers on whether women lose or gain by development. Both social-class position and the prevailing family structure condition the impact of development programs on women's options.

In their search for cheap labor for the manufacture of electronic devices, textiles, and garments, the new export industries in the Pacific Rim draw on women. Firms impose ceilings of pay and promotion and encourage high turnover among women workers to keep wages low. The family roles of Chinese women shape them to be a prime source of labor for such jobs. Unmarried women can accept low wages because they are supported by their families in return for their contributions to the household economy.[16] Married women can also perform wage work, but they are at a disadvantage in this labor-intensive regime. Low-cost day care and labor-saving devices are often lacking. Women, everywhere the mainstay of the home, can be released from household duties only if they earn enough to repay the members of their extended families who shoulder these burdens.

Meanwhile, their alternatives have vanished. On the eve of industrialization, married women could often engage in subsistence activities and contribute to the family economy without leaving their local community. But as urban living spreads, women no longer have access to the products once made and traded in the neighborhood.[17] When petty vending is no longer viable, often under the pressure of civic authorities, many female venders cannot make the transition to wage earning.[18] Married women who wish to work now must compete with the unmarried for the same narrow category of low-wage industrial jobs. This situation depresses the earning levels of all

[7]

women and discourages those married women who cannot strike a good bargain from seeking wage employment in such firms. To understand the impact of development on women, we must explore their family roles.

Both modernization and dependency theories stress that neither men nor women with little education, or "human capital," can get good jobs.[19] But women's position differs from that of men, as women of all classes must have family support to be able to work. Married women of lower-class backgrounds, with limited marketable skills, usually command less support from their kin than those with industrial skills or some education, whose families may urge them to add their wages to the household economy. These skilled women, often of better-off backgrounds, are likely to enter the capital-intensive, transnational core-sector firms that pay higher wages than the peripheral-sector firms. Women in such firms can help their families further improve their solid class standing.[20]

In these ways, families closely evaluate the "cost" of the employment of their members, but in ways that vary by social class, gender, and life-cycle stage. Since these factors shape opportunities for women, we must learn what women gain and lose by a development program such as Singapore's and what factors figure in these changes.

Political economists argue forcefully that the state increases power by weakening locally controlled ties, including self-help ties. I approach the quality of social bonds, hard to study in the abstract, through the exchange of needed goods, services, and information.

Among studies that describe how state welfare and social services intervene in the lives of the poor, Michael Young and Peter Willmott find that post–World War II government housing projects, which moved people from their traditional family settings, disrupted family ties in London's East End. Jane Humphries believes that the British welfare system broke up working-class community bonds of mutual help. Similarly, Jacques Donzelot maintains that nineteenth-century French welfare schemes were deliberately built at the expense of social ties.[21]

Singapore's social services, too, appear to mold a public that turns from kin ties. The social services are interlaced with the new ideology of individual merit and responsibility for one's own poverty. They extol self-help, individualism, and competition. The educational, family-planning, and housing policies move people around. Such mobility in living arrangements, social class, and flow of ideas tends to atomize people and devalue reliance on kin.[22] Will the family become isolated and the community destroyed as a result? Will other, looser social ties emerge?[23] Or will families be pulled toward close dependence on the state through its offerings of uniform social services?[24] How does the state social service system control the populace?

Changing social bonds will have repercussions on the jobs people can get and hence on their class position. Mark Granovetter found that men with

An unskilled woman in the peripheral sector sells vegetables. Photo by Eric Khoo.

[9]

"strong ties" to narrow circles of kin and friends sought them out when they needed work. The information that such people provided about the job market, however, was limited to the kinds of work the job seekers already knew about. Men with wider and dispersed "weak ties" to a range of aquaintances profited much more from their advice in the search for good jobs. Such weak ties were class-linked.[25] Thus I will explore the extent to which social class dominates job-seeking channels and the ways in which Singapore development programs replace community or class-linked ties with other channels to jobs.

Finally, new types of marriage and family life emerge as the community bonds of the early industrial society give way. Elizabeth Bott discussed the "segregated" marriage of working-class British couples, characterized by separate spheres of work, leisure, and communication for husband and wife. She linked segregated marriages to close-knit networks of strong kin and community ties, in which friends and relatives know each other well. To such marriages Bott contrasted the "joint" marriage, in which the partners, having moved far from their traditional homes, must share activities and draw their friends from diverse circles. But why did the British marriage change? Was the cause geographical movement, as Bott thought? Change is partly class-based, according to Christine Oppong, who has found career mobility most important in the forging of strong marriage bonds. Similarly, Hannah Gavron described the plight of the isolated working-class London wife who lost touch with her kin but did not gain a partner in her husband.[26] Changing marriage ties reverberate back on the political-economic program. Thus studies of the emergence of modern French and American society suggest that the new joint marriage contributed to the spread of the mass market, to the growth of the middle-class consumer society, and ultimately to an expansion of the state.[27]

An important part of family change is the regular progress of the life cycle, such as the transition from the early to mid-childbearing stage. This cycle has its own dynamic.[28] Will a family's progress though the life cycle shape its goals in ways that vary by social class, or are all families now constrained by similar forces? We can approach these questions by looking at the goals of families at two points in their life cycle.

In an early developing nation that is riven by poverty, the major class groups are rarely integrated into a single culture. Therefore, some writers look to public service programs (what political scientists refer to as "political goods") to incorporate people of all classes into a single industrial culture. Then people can be mobilized behind the development program, and even behind the state and leading political parties.[29] In this manner, the Singapore public services will enlarge the party-state's popular base of support. Others doubt whether even a concerted state program of social services can alter the typically divided pattern of life of first-stage development. Will

Singapore's public service program alter the "culture of poverty" and reach the poor?

I construct indices in order to distinguish the level of use of social services by people of different groups and the meaning of the services to them. On the one hand, the centralized party-state regulates access to political goods. People's use of the state-proffered social services forms structures that reproduce a way of life, whose powerful forces shape family goals. Thus state social services become cultural objects that unify the industrial society, incorporating people into its sphere, and redividing them along new lines. On the other hand, people mesh their own lines of action with a set of social services that seems uniform in content. We will see how families organize to attain the key services and interpret the services in their own distinct manner. They may even attempt to gain control over their lives through the use of services. In the process, families become active participants in the construction of an industrial culture by means of these cultural objects.[30]

This study was conducted at two points in time. In the first period, I chose for study 100 young married Singapore Chinese couples from a range of class backgrounds. The period in which I first met these couples, mid-1974 to mid-1976, I designate as "phase 1." During the next few years the government elaborated many of the programs of the second development stage. I term this intervening period, 1976–1981, the "interphase." In "phase 2," in 1981, I met for a second set of interviews with 45 of the original families. I call these 45 families the panel sample, and it is mainly from them that we learn how the development program affects family lives.

Eight years may be a short period, but much can happen to a young nation and to young families in this time span. Because of Singapore's compact size and the power of the centralized state, the economy was transformed. And the young panel families, who were in a dynamic period of their life cycle, also experienced great change. Moreover, because the period was so short, I was able to locate many of the original families again, and they could readily recall their earlier aspirations and compare them with their later experiences.

I studied Chinese from the range of speech groups. The Chinese comprised 77 percent of the Singapore population in 1980[31] and fill a wide range of jobs in all industries and at all social-class levels. Whether poor or well off, the Chinese are noted for their reliance on family and kin in their economic dealings.[32] Thus any set of public programs that attempts to change the political economy must contend with the strong group ties of the Chinese. Moreover, as a student of the Chinese family in Hong Kong, the People's Republic of China (PRC), and the Republic of China (Taiwan), I was long interested in Chinese populations. In an in-depth study of this type, I decided to limit variation across racial groups. Singapore has large Malay and

Tamil Indian minorities, but only one Tamil Indian, married to a Chinese wife, entered my sample, and he had adopted the Chinese style of living.[33] It is hoped that other research will address the multiethnic features of Singapore in development.

The couples were young parents. The wives were in their twenties in phase 1. Their husbands' ages ranged from twenty-two to thirty-nine and averaged thirty. Respondents ranged from poorly educated men and women with low-paid jobs to college-educated couples with high status and well-paid jobs. Over half of the wives worked full-time, three-quarters as operatives in factories or workshops.

I distinguish the respondents throughout the study by socioeconomic class. I derive the class position by assigning scores based on the occupational status of the parents of both husband and wife and the average educational level, occupational status, and combined earnings of the husband and wife. I divide the couples into two main socioeconomic groups: the poor, subdivided into the very poor and the semipoor; and the secure, among whom are couples of modest means and the affluent.[34] This division results from computations internal to the data, but other large-scale surveys of social class in Singapore arrive at similar class distributions.[35] As I kept constant this social-class ranking in phase 2, I could trace changes in the education, earnings, and experiences of each class group as the development program proceeded to its second stage. The percentages of respondents in each socioeconomic group in both phases are shown in Table 1.

I also distinguish the couples by the skill and industrial sector of the husbands, factors found to be of key importance in North American studies of the labor process. "Skill" refers here to resources that are recognized on the job. Workers who have none (laborers, hawkers) are designated "unskilled"; "some resources" designates workers with capital or higher "arts" education; "industrial skills" is self-evident. Poor and secure socioeconomic groups contain men who have skills of all these types.

Table 1. Socioeconomic group of respondent couples, phases 1 and 2 (percent)

Socioeconomic group	Phase 1 (N = 100)	Phase 2 (N = 45)
Poor		
Very poor	17%	13%
Semipoor	41	49
Secure		
Modest means	19	20
Affluent	23	18
Total	100%	100%

The terms "core" and "periphery," as I noted earlier, are drawn from analyses of labor processes in the West. In the Singapore context the peripheral sector consists of industries that are not highly capitalized, have low profit margins, and for these reasons are not favored under the Singapore development program. These sectors, which include both family firms and formally organized companies, are defined by their products, profits, and clients, not by their size. All the "shadow economy" labor is included here; but so are textile industries, among others. Core industries have higher value added and are more profitable, and for these reasons are favored under the state program. Shipbuilding and ship repair industries are among those in the core industrial sector. Men of both class groups are found in both sectors, and their jobs are typical of those of Chinese men in Singapore, as Tables 2 and 3 indicate.

I obtained the names of half of my 100 couples from the files of five maternal and child health clinics, where nearly all new mothers who live in surrounding districts register to receive well-baby care. The clinics serve a range of communities: resettled households of the very poor, semipoor, those of modest means, the affluent, and a partly rural, partly poor suburban community.[36] Clinic records list the husband's occupation and age and the couple's ethnicity. I interviewed the first ten cases in each clinic which fitted my specifications. I obtained the names of the remaining fifty couples from eight factories that employ mainly women. As few young married women with small children were employed at that time, I often took a factory's entire contingent of such women.

In order to get enough cases for analysis, I oversampled married women in the labor force, and more of my full-time working women worked in factories

Table 2. Industrial sector and skill level of respondent men, phases 1 and 2 (percent)

Sector	Phase 1 (N = 100)	Phase 2 (N = 45)
Periphery		
Unskilled	13%	9%
Some resources[a]	32	31
Industrial skills	15	18
Core		
Unskilled	9	7
Industrial skills	31	36
Total	100%	101%[b]

[a]Occupation requires some capital, a nonindustrial skill, or an academic degree.
[b]Percentages total more than 100 because of rounding.

Table 3. Occupations of Singapore Chinese men, phase 1 respondents and National Labour Force Survey, 1975 (percent)

Occupational category	Phase 1 (N = 100)	National Labour Force Survey (N = 447,339)
Professional, technical	15%	11%
Administrative, managerial	5	4
Clerical	13	11
Sales	10	19
Service	7	6
Farm	3	3
Production, transport equipment operators, laborers	46	37
Unclassifiable	1	9
All categories	100%	100%

Source: Ministry of Labour and National Statistical Commission, *Report on the Labour Force Survey of Singapore, 1975* (Singapore, December 1975), Table 34, pp. 60–64.

than the proportion of Singapore Chinese women who held such jobs in 1975 (see Tables 4 and 5).

I had intended to interview only intact couples, but one couple separated during the interview process and two husbands were absent, one in jail, the other on a long business trip. The Singapore divorce rate is low.[37]

Flats in highrise public housing projects housed 73 percent of the sample. This proportion exceeded that in the city-state as a whole at the time (43 percent in 1973–74) because I contacted couples through clinics and factories affiliated with the Housing and Development Board (HDB). I discuss their housing as a type of residence, and do not view the sample as represen-

Table 4. Percent of mothers engaged in full-time wage work, phase 1 respondents and all Singapore married women aged 25–34, 1973, by number of children born alive

Number of children	Phase 1 respondents	All women
1	95%	29%
2	52	18
3	40	14
4	25	19

Source: Singapore Family Planning and Population Board and National Statistical Commission, *Report of the First National Survey of Family Planning in Singapore, 1973* (Singapore, 1974), Table 9, p. 30.

Table 5. Occupations of Singapore Chinese women, phase 1 respondents and National Labour Force Survey, 1975 (percent)

Occupational category	Phase 1 respondents (N = 55)[a]	National Labour Force Survey (N = 206,460)
Professional, technical	5%	11%
Administrative, managerial	7	1
Clerical	4	24
Sales	0	14
Service	4	16
Farm	5	3
Production, transport equipment operators, laborers	75	31
Unclassifiable	–	1
All categories	100%	101%[b]

[a]This figure differs from that in Chapter 4 because I include here three farm wives who are not considered as wage earners in Chapter 4.

[b]The total is more than 100% because of rounding.

Source: Calculated from Ministry of Labour and National Statistical Commission, *Report on the Labour Force Survey of Singapore, 1975* (Singapore, December 1975), Table 34, pp. 60–64.

tative in this respect. Nearly half of the couples lived with kin, most with the husband's parents.

The Singapore government extends its many services mainly to citizens. Only citizens, for example, can buy public housing. I therefore concentrated on citizens: in 93 of the 100 cases, both spouses were citizens. In each of the remaining seven couples, one Chinese spouse was a Singaporean and the other held Malaysian or Indonesian citizenship.

The sample couples averaged 2.3 children. To explore the impact of the state's population-limitation measures, which affect most parents beginning with the third pregnancy, I chose more women with two children (53 percent of the sample) than their proportion in Singapore at the time (34 percent of Chinese women aged 20–29). Parents with one child and with three to six children are also represented (20 and 25 percent, respectively, compared with 35 and 29 percent for all Singapore Chinese women aged 20–29), to show the range of effects of the measures on all women.[38] Two husbands had been married previously, and the children of their earlier marriages are included in my calculations, as is a son adopted by a third couple.

I located the couples for phase 2 by visiting their homes and the homes of kin, contacting them at their places of work, and searching through telephone books. The records of the Family Planning and Population Board and of the HDB were helpful. By these means I was able to locate 75 of the original 100 couples. From these couples I selected 45 to reinterview.

The husbands in this panel held jobs that I had found to be theoretically

[15]

significant in phase 1. They worked in industries of both core and peripheral sectors and had a broad range of skills, from lowest to highest classifications. My goal was to learn how men of particular economic characteristics fared under the development regime. Thus the phase 1 classification was kept constant, to aid such comparison over the interphase. In comparison with the phase 1 sample, men with industrial skills were slightly oversampled in phase 2 and the very poor in the periphery were undersampled (see Table 2) because they were hard to locate after the passage of years. The very poor usually had lived in homes listed under the names of other family members and had been resettled under their own names. The affluent, in contrast, were easy to find, but because they had done well over the interphase, they presented little mystery. I therefore devoted my resources to understanding the complex situation of semipoor families and those of modest means.

Forty-four percent of the panel women worked full-time; 80 percent had been employed throughout the study.

By phase 2, the proportion of couples that lived in HDB flats had risen to 93 percent, still in excess of the Singapore population (with 67 percent in HDB homes, 1978–80). Couples who had lived in kampungs in phase 1 were somewhat underrepresented because all had been resettled since then and were difficult to find. Consequently I discuss families by their living environment rather than by their proportion in each housing type.

The panel couples averaged 2.5 children in phase 1, slightly more than the entire phase 1 sample. By phase 2, their families averaged 3.0 children.

The key issue that must be addressed is whether the increased proletarianization and similarity of lifestyles of the two class groups along several indicators over the interphase is an artifact of second-stage sampling. Specifically, have I, because it was hardest to locate the families in outlying kampungs, and the poorest HDB housing that was torn down, underestimated the marginalization and impoverishment of Singapore life? I am unable to assess the wider processes in Singapore with my small sample, and thus I have tried to relate changes to types of people in types of social structures over time in the two phases under study. The panel couples that were poorest in phase 1, and there were many, did experience considerable change. Not all improved their lives, but many did. Further, no new couples joined their ranks. I base my conclusions on the couples I could locate over time. But ultimately I cannot assess the wider society from a small subsample, and I look forward to other studies that may turn up the crucial life-history data of individuals over time. Then we can all better understand the processes of the penetration of state into society under the impact of a forceful development program.

Interviews, conducted in the respondents' native dialect, took nearly ten hours spread over five weekly sessions. When details of the couple's livelihood, such as the husband's wage, changed over the period of the interview, as a rule the first set of data is used for tabulation purposes. The life histories, however, can use a fuller span of the data. The phase 1 interviews were conducted from late 1974 to early 1976, with the bulk in 1975. The phase 2 interviews took about five hours, in three sessions. They were conducted from December 1980 to December 1981.

In both phases I asked each couple about their (1) family background and household structure, (2) household budget, (3) work experiences, (4) educational plans and job aspirations for their children, (5) marriage and kin relations, and (6) contraceptive practices and family-size plans. I covered this set of topics in phase 1, usually in four sessions with each wife, and interviewed the husbands once on the same topics.[39] Many of my queries were open-ended and couples could elaborate on their responses. When possible I observed family interaction in visits with couples. I met twenty-five couples at least once and revisited a dozen of them often, to keep immersed in the family life changes. My interviewing team also tried to interview respondents' kin to obtain their views on the couple's family lifestyle.

I trained my interviewers to carry the bulk of the interviews. The interviewer plays a paramount role in the study. In addition to the high level of rapport needed for the lengthy interviews, she gave us a deeper understanding of the situation in each family. In each case the interviewer suggested and pursued new lines of inquiry from the material she had gathered.

I have chosen twelve families to represent the main social class groups, skill levels, and industrial sectors. Their life sketches, presented in Parts II and III, reveal vividly how lives are changing under the development program.

I approach the families first from an ethnographic perspective, in order to focus on their strategies and goals. I then describe the structural sources of variation among them. I find in their responses much that was not anticipated by the development system. The Singapore families I met certainly work within the constraints of the system, but they also extend and reshape the system by their practical choices. The outcome is a nuanced framing of and answer to the question: What changes with development?

To reach families at all class levels effectively, state agencies that provide social services must overcome opposition from powerful interest groups. Chapter 2 traces the postindependence history of Singapore's development program, focusing on the key structures of the state and economy which enabled state bodies to become efficient conduits of social services. It describes how social service agencies replaced local groups that delivered amenities, and their efforts to reach families at all levels.

Part II discusses the 100 poor and secure families studied in phase 1. Ethnographies of twelve typical couples in the main industrial, occupational, and skill sectors (Chapters 3 and 5) show that their lives vary greatly by class position. I focus on the structures that shape their life chances in Chapters 4 and 6, which discuss their limited access to social services and their goals and aspirations. That their economic worlds affect not only their access to state services but also their marriages and kin ties is the conclusion drawn from phase 1.

Part III updates the overall picture of the economic and social positions of the forty-five poor and affluent panel couples met again in phase 2. Here we learn how their structural positions shaped their uses of the main services that upgrade labor and amenities over the interphase. Chapters 7 and 8 show the personal approaches to these forces by the twelve typical couples. Chapter 9 then compares the forty-five couples' access to resources to learn the extent to which they approach a single family type under the impulse of the state social services. Chapter 10 locates areas of family lives which have changed the most and the least under the state development program and asks: Has the spread of state services given rise to a society that is more homogeneous than it was in phase 1? How do the various social groups differentiate themselves? How do the families imprint their personal signatures on their lifestyles and goals?

[2]

State, Economy, and Social Services

National data show that the major policies by which Singapore sought to restructure its society to meet the needs of its economic programs unfolded in two main waves. In the first phase, social class cleavages were marked; in the second stage, industrialization narrowed some gaps. Nevertheless, these data suggest that differences in family opportunities are still associated with social class.

The State Restructured

A small city-state of 225 square miles off the southern tip of the Malay peninsula, Singapore has a population of 2.4 million. Over three-quarters are Chinese; among the various dialect groups, Hokkien, Teochiu, and Cantonese predominate. Malays and Indians account for the remainder of the population. Founded by Britain in 1819, the settlement grew rapidly as a commercial trading station, or entrepôt, where rubber and tin were exchanged for Europe's manufactured products. The ruinous Japanese occupation during World War II left behind a legacy of unemployment, starvation, and broken families, and the 1950s were dominated by the Malayan struggle for independence from Britain.[1] When Singapore gained independence in 1959, it faced active political opposition, a weak economic infrastructure, considerable unemployment, inadequate housing, and a high population growth rate. The state forged its social policies to cope with this heritage.

Of the various approaches to the formation of state social policy, the most clearly applicable to Singapore is corporatism. Corporatism gives special attention to organizational interests and their relations to the state. Philippe

Schmitter's definition stresses the "intermediation" function that groups play in a corporatist social system: "the constituent units are organized into a limited number of singular, compulsory, noncompetitive, hierarchically ordered, functionally differentiated categories, recognized . . . by the state and granted a deliberate representational monopoly within their respective categories in exchange for observing certain controls on their selection of leaders and articulation of demands and supports."[2] What makes the Singapore political system special is the state's substitution of new, controllable corporate units for traditional units that it could not control. In doing so it established the foundations of its development program.

The Singapore government is headed by the People's Action Party (PAP), founded by Lee Kuan Yew and others as a coalition of political movements. In the elections of 1959 the PAP won a sweeping mandate to form the first independent government. From the outset the PAP expanded party-state institutions and sharply curtailed the activities of its left-wing opposition. Early on the PAP retrained the top civil servants inherited from the colonial era to gain their allegiance to its programs. Paternalistic colonial rule by authoritarian decision makers bequeathed a legacy of noncompetitive politics. The PAP added its own hallmark: an "increasing merger of Government and party at the local constituency."[3] By strengthening the links between the ruling party and mass organizations, the regime undercut the opposition's potential recruitment sources.

Using such inherited legislation as the Preservation of Public Security Ordinance and the Internal Security Act of the Federation of Malaysia, the party-state suppressed opposition by political parties and trade unions. Since around 1968, the government and parliament of Singapore have been formed almost entirely of PAP members. In control of the party and the government, the Lee Kuan Yew caucus secured a free hand to implement its development policies.[4] The first decade of reforms in the political and administrative organs of the republic laid the groundwork for the delivery of social services.

The technocratic state continues to change its development program to cope with shifts in Singapore's position in the world economy. The party-state's activist approach to engineering the political economy makes it impossible to follow up each change over the years. My review of state structures therefore encompasses the period through the early 1980s.

Through its new vertical bureaucracy, the state eclipsed many of the long-standing local interest groups on which Chinese society was built, including lineage and clan associations. These heterogeneous guilds, or *hui guan*, drew mainly on family, kin, ethnic, and other parochial allegiances. Generally based on dialect, they advanced their members' welfare by introducing men to jobs and providing mutual aid, burial, education, and other services. Leaders sought to mediate the disputes of their constituents with members of other dialect groups. The powerful Hokkien hui guan, a major private landowner with assets of S$100 million, founded Nanyang University in 1956 and established five Chinese primary and secondary schools. The PAP regime took over such social services, weakened the strong hui guan, and coopted their leaders. Political competition by such communal organizations is not permitted. In 1963 the Hokkien hui guan leader was accused of supporting the left-wing opposition and deprived of citizenship. Control tightened on the eve of the second industrial phase. In 1980 the Nanyang University was closed, and the following year it was reorganized as part of the National University of Singapore.[5]

The party-state mobilizes and coopts interest groups in support of its development policies by reorganizing the major social and economic factions into large corporate collectivities.[6] Tripartite bodies of labor, management, and state representatives are expected to eliminate discord and divisions among social classes and to maintain the political stability needed for the inflow of foreign capital.[7] The tripartite National Wages Council, part of the conciliatory labor policy, suggests guidelines for yearly wage increases, and so has become a key actor in the collective bargaining arena. The trade unions encompass one-quarter of Singapore's labor force; 90 percent of their membership are affiliated with the PAP-led National Trades Union Congress (NTUC). The NTUC leader concurrently holds a ministerial portfolio, and many of his colleagues are also government officials. The NTUC sits with the other main sectors of management and the state on key state councils and boards of enterprises. The Employment Act and the Industrial Relations Act, both promulgated in 1968, limit NTUC power to challenge management policies on recruitment, retrenchment, transfers, and promotions. An Industrial Arbitration Court within the Ministry of Labour resolves most labor disputes. There are few work stoppages. Singapore exhorts labor and capital to cooperate in a system of "enlightened capitalism" which can provide for workers' basic needs while promoting rapid economic growth.[8]

The key to state leadership in Singapore's development program is the extensive network of semiautonomous statutory boards and state corporations responsible to the Cabinet. For example, the Economic Development Board (EDB), under the Ministry of Finance, holds wide powers to extend loans and tax concessions to companies, construct industrial parks for the location of new factories, and promote investment in the high-value-added goods crucial to the New Economic Program. The EDB is staffed by young technocrats and professional civil servants. The regulatory and revenue-generating activities of this board and of related public bodies spearhead economic growth. And these boards provide widespread social services.[9]

The government effectively acts as a gatekeeper for entry to the higher professions.[10] Professional groups cannot freely recruit new members and are restrained from promoting causes or lobbying in opposition to state

Political slogans. Photo by Dominic Yip.

policy. Students at the government-administered National University of Singapore are channeled into designated fields of study, including engineering and medicine. The incorporation of swelling numbers of new technical and professional graduates into the civil service further enforces the development programs. Government employment accounts for 20 percent of the work force.

Student associations lost an autonomous voice as a result of protests over inequities in the early industrialization program. In mid-1974, activists at the University of Singapore and Nanyang University sought to increase student consciousness of poverty and injustice, and advocated alternative development policies. Within months, a number of student leaders were arrested or deported and campus dissent was suppressed. Since that period, university associations have been reorganized under administration auspices.[11]

Despite control of dissent, there is still an active, if restrained, political life in Singapore. Political sovereignty has imparted a sense of national identity and purpose and a popular commitment to development. The state has utilized this national spirit to extend its sway over the elites and the general population. Government-sponsored youth and neighborhood organizations serve as its chief vehicles to mobilize the populace.[12] The state has created a value structure designed to legitimize its development program, strengthen loyalty to the People's Action Party, and integrate the populace into its social program.

The effort to forge a new identification with the development program peaks at the annual National Day Celebration, August 9. This fete features parades of schoolchildren and floats of the major organizations and statutory boards. The pageantry vividly portrays well-appointed highrise housing, contented two-child families, and flourishing Post Office Savings Banks. The gala climaxes with a major policy address by the prime minister on progress and problems in the managed economy, and an appeal for mass support.

Restructuring the Economy

In the mid-1960s, Singapore's development program centered on creating a potentially skilled but labor-intensive and low-wage industrial sector to produce for foreign corporations and absorb the many unemployed.[13] Overseas enterprises in shipbuilding and ship repair, petroleum and petrochemicals, electronics and electrical machinery produced for the world market. They coexisted with local firms that catered mainly to the retail needs of the city-state and its environs, although they also exported textiles and apparel, footwear, sawn timber, wood products, and other commodities. The proportion of workers in manufacturing rose (from 19 percent in 1966 to 27 percent

in 1977) and the number of firms employing ten or more workers increased.[14] Within a decade there was a labor shortage, and wages had begun
to rise.

The Second Development Program: Capital-Intensive Industry

As the 1970s drew to a close, the leadership took an increasingly dim view
of the country's future as a regional outpost for low-wage and low-skill manufacturing. Singapore actively solicited knowledge-based, capital-intensive
industries from abroad and launched the New Economic Program. Older
heavy industries are being joined by new firms that exploit advanced technology in chemical processing, machine tools, heavy engineering, computer
microtechnology, technical services, and industrial research and product
development, mainly for export goods. The finance and banking industry,
which includes offshore fund management, is also a leading growth sector.[15]

The large economic changes since independence can be summarized by
the following quantitative indicators: entrepôt trade, which comprised 33
percent of the gross domestic product (GDP) in 1960, declined to 30 percent
in 1970, and to 27 percent in 1979. Manufacturing, which contributed only
13 percent of the GDP in 1960, grew to 20 percent in 1970, and 24 percent
by 1979.[16]

Singapore's export-led industrial strategy widened divisions between local
and foreign-owned firms and their work forces. Wholly foreign-capitalized
firms and joint ventures (mixed foreign and local capital) in 1979 comprised
36 percent of all manufacturing enterprises, 71 percent of manufacturing
employment, 84 percent of total output value, and 93 percent of direct
export value.[17] The foreign sector thus dominates Singapore industry, and
its grip is strengthening. To help domestic firms compete, the Economic
Development Board (EDB) subsidizes the use of advanced technology by
firms that produce high-value-added goods for export. The EDB also encourages local firms to manufacture parts and provide services under contract to international firms operating in the republic. Nevertheless, the market share, profits, and percentage of the labor force employed by firms that
produce mainly for the home market are likely to diminish. Employees of
local firms not tied to foreign capital will then suffer a decline in their wages
and in demand for their labor.

Investment in Labor

The state has organized a battery of programs to raise workers' skills to
meet the many new demands of second-stage industrialization. The National
Wages Council recommended three years of wage increases for less skilled

workers to induce employers to mechanize and eliminate their labor-intensive occupations. With trade union support, the National Productivity Board conducts campaigns to increase productivity and output. The Vocational and Industrial Training Board (VITB) runs centers for preemployment technical training for secondary school leavers. Centers also provide short- and long-term continuing education courses for workers, mostly in the key growth industries, who are nominated by their firms for skills upgrading. By extending technical training widely throughout the population, the government hopes to reduce dependence on foreign firms to provide the skills for advanced industrial development.[18]

The National Trades Union Congress is concerned, however, that inferior English and mathematical skills disqualify the majority from these training programs.[19] In exploring the impact of state economic programs on some of the work force we will ask: Which class, skill, and industrial sectors have access to the retraining programs and which are excluded from them?

Wages

Wages have responded to the new development policies. One study shows that, deflated by increases in the Consumer Price Index, real average weekly earnings of workers of all ethnic stocks and both sexes rose 22 percent, from S$39.40 in 1975 to S$48.26 in 1980.[20] I calculated median wage rates for Chinese men from 1975 and 1979 national data, which approximate my two-stage sequence. In 1975 (my phase 1), the median gross monthly wage for all Chinese men was about S$319. Earnings of the top 16 percent exceeded S$600, nearly twice the median wage. By 1979, the median gross monthly wage of Chinese men had risen nearly 70 percent. Yet in that year the earnings of the top 15 percent of all male Chinese workers had increased only about 33 percent, to over S$800.[21] This finding suggests a decline in wage inequality among male workers. In the chapters that follow, I measure the earnings of the Chinese men in my 1975 (phase 1) sample against that year's national median for Chinese men of about S$319. I peg the national median wage for Chinese men in 1981 at S$600, 188 percent of the 1975 median wage. I evaluate the wages of the panel men in phase 2 against this estimated median.[22]

The first industrial revolution drew unmarried and young married women from their home- or cottage-based tasks into the burgeoning light industrial sector. By the mid-1970s, Singapore had become one of Asia's leading centers for electronics assembly and the stitching of inexpensive garments for the world market. In this export-based industrial regime, women toil at low-skill jobs with few chances to advance. Their wages are too small to commit them to a lifetime of factory labor.[23] While the young women workers contributed their wages to the family, other household women had to stay home to sustain the family and community. In 1957, 22 percent of Chinese women aged fifteen and over had joined the enumerated labor force, and this contingent increased to 35 percent in 1975, and to 42 percent in 1979. The proportion of married women who earned wages was lower but also doubled, from 14 percent in 1957 to 27 percent in 1979.[24]

In 1975 the median national monthly wage for Singapore Chinese women was under S$200 (approximately 63 percent of the median for men), while earnings of the top 15 percent exceeded S$500. Studies have shown that a worker could not support a family on S$200 a month.[25] Hence the average woman worker depended on her husband or parents. This situation depressed overall female wage levels. As the tightening labor market exerted upward pressure on the pay of women workers, the median monthly wage for all Singapore Chinese full-time working women reached S$379 by 1979. The top 18 percent of Chinese women workers received over S$600 in 1979. I estimate that by 1981 the median wage of Chinese women rose to S$400. The median women's wage also increased slightly, to about 67 percent of the male median in 1981.[26]

The massive foreign-financed electronics firms pay more than firms in textiles and garments. Women's wages also vary by skill level.[27] But few receive on-the-job training.[28] As Singapore enters the second stage of industrialization, however, the electronics, textile, and garment industries are upgrading their facilities in an effort to improve product lines and quality.[29] The ensuing demand for skilled workers has helped female high school graduates and women with English-stream schooling become lower-level supervisors, especially in foreign electronics companies that print employee instructions in English. Nevertheless, electronics firms in the process of upgrading their technology hire mainly men with formal training to operate the more complex machinery, and women with practical experience but no diplomas have so far not qualified for these positions.[30]

In 1979, 29.3 percent of the students enrolled in technical and vocational institutes and 20.5 percent of the students training at the diploma-conferring technical colleges were women, an upsurge over the past.[31] In 1975–76, three relatively small joint government-industry training programs placed 100 female technical school graduates in shipbuilding and ship repair positions. These figures may appear significant by North American standards, but Singapore's supply of such training programs is still inadequate to meet the demands of many mature women who wish to enter the labor force or to upgrade their qualifications.

Singapore's high average growth rate and full employment have led to a modest reduction in overall income inequality. The Gini ratio, a measure of income inequality, registered a decline from 0.498 to 0.448 between 1966 and 1975.[32] However, the two-stage creation of an industrial labor force in Singapore occurred during a relatively short segment of the life cycle of the work force. Older men and women—especially housewives, over half of whom are illiterate—are the least likely to compete for jobs in the new knowledge-based industries.[33] The outcome of structural inequality among mature workers can be seen in my interviews.

Social Services and Development: Equal Access?

The social services directed toward raising family living standards—pensions and savings plans, housing, education, maternal and child health, and family-planning services—are not social welfare or social security programs.[34] Indeed, the Singapore government, like the governments of most new nations, maintains that its limited resources should not support public assistance programs that may undermine the work ethic.[35] Instead, state services enmesh citizens in the money economy and speed the tempo of the industrial way of life. As services gradually reach all class levels, they provide new consumer goals that spur families to work harder to pay for increased purchases. Moreover, most of the social services help to accumulate investment capital.

Savings and the Central Provident Fund

Poor urbanites the world over, traditionally without access to bank credit services, establish less formal lending agencies.[36] Singaporeans have joined revolving credit associations (also called "tontines"), burial societies, and other cooperative groups for long- and short-term help. Some of these associations were organized as benevolent funds of clans, unions, and other local groups, others as less formal arrangements among friends. The Singapore government criticizes such rotating credit societies and has even disbanded several of the larger ones, on the grounds that it cannot properly regulate informal credit institutions and so cannot protect members from fraud. Government policy encourages citizens to amass capital instead in state accounts, which it draws upon for development. Many people place their funds voluntarily in tax-exempt Post Office Savings Bank (POSB) accounts, and employers are required to place pension contributions in the Central Provident Fund (CPF).

The POSB casts a wide net through promotional campaigns, extended banking hours at local branches, and savings schemes for primary school students. The 1979 POSB Annual Report claimed deposits of over S$2.5 billion in more than 1.7 million accounts (or one for every two Singaporeans).[37] But our interviews suggest that many accounts are only nominal.

About 20 percent of each employee's salary is deposited directly in the CPF in a compulsory savings plan. Employers match this sum. The funds accumulate interest and are released to the employee at retirement age. Before retirement these funds can be withdrawn only for a down payment and monthly fees for the purchase of a public-sector flat. Unlike pension plans in many other developing nations, the CPF is vested and covers domestic servants and all service-sector employees.[38] With the trend away from self-employment, nearly the whole local work force will soon be enrolled in the CPF. In fact, this coverage is considered an attractive feature of wage labor by workers forced out of ill-paid self-employment.

The CPF is expected to free retired people from close dependence on their kin for support. Moreover, it can help couples buy homes of their own. Still, neither goal is likely to be universally realized. James Malloy has argued that contributory pensions in general are regressive, because they tax people proportionately and do not redistribute income. Furthermore, employers can pass on their contributions in the form of higher prices for their products.[39] This argument applies in Singapore. CPF benefits reflect the class standing of their recipients, since contributions are a fixed percentage of income. Low-paid men and most women workers may not accumulate enough CPF revenue to subsist on when they retire. Moreover, home purchase through the CPF narrows the balance, as only the affluent can buy a home and save for the future as well. These considerations suggest that the CPF and its home-buying options, despite their present benefits to individuals, may reinforce class divisions in future retirement years.

Public Housing

The construction of large blocks of rental housing and the Home Ownership for the People Scheme are government programs designed to stimulate the market in construction and finance and to promote the industrial way of life. The nation inherited inadequate housing stock, mainly in the forms of kampung and tenement structures. A kampung hamlet consisted of single-story wooden houses with zinc or palm-frond roofs and dirt or concrete floors. Occupants often constructed their own homes, although they could not own the land. Running water was frequently lacking; residents used wells and outdoor toilet and bath sheds. Many cultivated fruit and vegetable plots and kept barnyard animals to supplement their diets. Although devoid of basic amenities, kampungs were spacious and usually not slums. They housed extended families, whose members pooled their resources to reduce expenses. Surrounded by neighbors of long standing, these families extended their ties of exchange to the wider community.

Worse off in 1960 were the more than 250,000 Singaporeans crowded into cubicles in a central core of pre–World War II tenements. Originally constructed for a single family, these structures had been divided into as many as seven units. All of them lacked adequate privacy, lighting, ventilation,

A kampung home, 1976. Photo by Fred Salaff.

and sanitation. An estimated 350,000 other residents lived in small wooden huts wedged into empty urban spaces. Middle-income families, in contrast, built spacious semidetached or detached houses with terraces, both in the urban center and on the outskirts.[40]

To rationalize the use of Singapore's limited physical space, the government had allotted half of all land to development by phase 1. Kampung and squatter housing was seen as wasteful consumption of valuable plots. For this stated reason, the Housing and Development Board (HDB) has demolished such quarters and replaced them with multistory highrise buildings. Each development accommodates several tens of thousands of families in units of from one to five rooms. By the outset of my study, 63,347 kampung and squatter households had been resettled, 65 percent of them in highrise buildings. The rest (farmers, small business people, and the like) moved elsewhere, but rarely formed new squatter communities.[41]

The state housing program thus propels HDB residents into the wage labor force and consumer economy, with wider impacts on social bonds. In the shift from kampung housing and small farms to HDB quarters, families lost their home garden plots and their food bills increased, as did their outlays on utilities.[42] Many farm bungalows and kampung houses that were torn down housed several married couples, both related and unrelated, while few of the HDB flats do.[43] Before resettlement, these family units often shared appliances; now they must buy their own appliances, furnishings, and other consumer durables. When they have no need to borrow these things from other people, their exchanges with kin and neighbors decrease.[44] Deployment of women into the wage labor force, overtime work, and moonlighting help pay for the more costly and elaborate HDB lifestyle, with implications for women's position in the society.[45]

However, the first industrial stage, based on low wage labor, could not guarantee a strong wage-earning position. Although many households moved into low-cost HDB units and were wage earners, they often continued subsistence production and petty trading in their highrise flats. Low-income families could not give up their exchanges within the community of the impoverished. Poverty was thus "modernized" into highrise housing blocks.[46] Further, in the early 1970s one's position in the labor market greatly affected one's housing options. Families with below-average housing before their relocation occupied the smallest HDB flats afterward. In 1973 the average per capita annual income in HDB households was S$947, but it varied widely by housing development—from S$750 in lower-class Bukit Ho Swee up to S$1,318 in middle-class Queenstown. Bukit Ho Swee families consisted mainly of resettled slum dwellers, while middle-class families applied for the more spacious and expensive Queenstown flats.[47] Furthermore, families that purchased their own HDB flats earned more than the renters.[48] Although the monthly purchase payment could be as low as the

An HBD highrise. Photo by Eric Khoo.

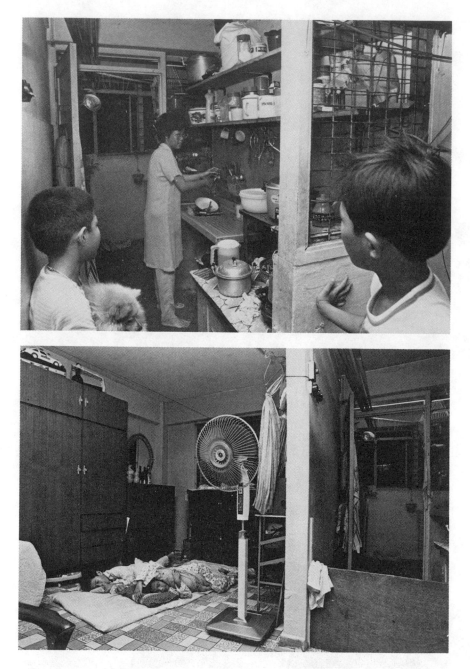

One-room rented HBD flat in Toa Payoh. The boys sleep on the floor. The family is saving to buy a flat of their own. Photos by Eric Khoo.

rent on a comparable flat, other expenses, including the $100 cash registration fee, down payment, and furnishings, were more costly. HDB home-ownership perpetuated the division of the population into haves and have-nots.

By phase 2, however, a spurt in HDB construction, the accumulation of CPF savings by maturing workers, secure employment, and higher average wages have decreased visible class differences in housing. Parts of the poorest developments have been demolished. The policy of mixing flats of various sizes in new developments further loosens the link between address and class position. In 1973–74, HDB units accommodated 43 percent of the population, and 37 percent of them lived in flats owned by their families. By 1979–80, in contrast, 67 percent of all Singaporeans resided in HDB quarters, and 59 percent of these homes were their own. Engaged couples and families of any size are entitled to buy or rent an HDB flat, subject to a monthly family income ceiling of S$2,500 in 1980. All of the families of my study met this qualification, and most of them exercised this option. In this short interval, Singapore took a long step toward becoming a society of small homeowners.[49]

Consumer financing of HDB housing through the CPF strengthens the involvement of families in the labor force over the entire life cycle as they commit themselves to regular monthly wage checkoffs.[50] When they save enough for a down payment, couples can improve their housing by buying their first public-sector flat; later they may sell it and buy a larger one. In 1973, one-room, "one-room improved," and two-room dwellings accounted for 58 percent of all HDB households; few larger flats were built. (A one-room flat consists of a single room, usually referred to as a "hall," which residents can partition into smaller areas; a "one-room improved" flat is an L-shaped room, slightly larger; a two-room flat contains a bedroom and a hall. Kitchens and bathrooms are not counted as "rooms.") By phase 2, only 31 percent of all HDB households lived in one or two rooms.[51] It appears that the occupants of the larger flats have advanced to the later stages of their family cycle and have achieved greater earning power.[52] Provisions for moving from smaller to larger apartments and from renter to ownership status demarcate the Singapore proletariat from their counterparts in many older industrial cities with inadequate housing stock and weak home-financing arrangements.[53] Singapore working-class families are not forever doomed to the flats they move into when they marry, as we shall see.

Education for All: The Pathway to Advancement?

Singapore inherited a variety of schools run by Christian missionaries, guilds, and other local groups. Instruction was offered in English, Malay, Tamil, and the various Chinese dialects; the British authorities had trained in English only the relatively few people needed to staff the civil service and the trading firms.[54] After independence, a literate populace with a technical English-language education was needed to contribute its skills to the industrializing, cosmopolitan economy. The new republic placed private schools under the direction of the Ministry of Education and subsidized their operation as "government-aided" schools.[55] The number of all schools has increased, and tuition fees have been reduced and equalized. Principals, teachers, and Ministry of Education officials now are securely educated professionals. They espouse the norms and values of the meritocracy, the scientific-technological revolution, multiculturalism, and egalitarianism.

The schools have a unified admissions policy, a common core curriculum, and a bilingual language system. Children begin with one or two years of kindergarten. Chinese pupils may choose either English-medium or Mandarin-medium primary school, and course work is also introduced in the second language. Increasingly, however, Chinese parents place their children in English-medium schools. The proportion of primary school students enrolled in Chinese-medium schools dropped from 50 percent in 1959 to 11 percent in 1978, although not all perform well in the English language.

Entrance to schools is competitive. First priority in admission to a particular primary school goes to children in small families, especially if one parent was sterilized before age forty, in accordance with current birth control policies. Next come children whose parents or siblings attended the same school. Finally, parental choice and neighborhood location are considered. Secondary school admission is even more competitive. Parents tend to rank a secondary school by its pupils' success in the major national school-leaving examinations. Places in secondary schools are determined both by choice and by the pupil's scores on the primary school-leaving examination (PSLE). Candidates who attend a primary school attached to a secondary school gain first priority. This arrangement gives an edge to the mainly middle-class parents who have the savvy and the organizational ties to stream their offspring through these feeder primary schools.

The schooling experience turns on common examinations. In phase 1, promotion to grade 6 was automatic; at the end of the year, pupils sat for the PSLE. Those who failed were allowed to repeat grade 6 and the PSLE twice. After that they were shunted into vocational school, or quit school.[56] The first two years of academic secondary school offer both academic and technical subjects, after which students are streamed by their exam scores into academic or trade courses. Science subjects leading to better-paid jobs in engineering and high technology are most popular. Secondary school pupils generally sit for the Cambridge ordinary-level (O-level) examinations. Two years of further study lead to the Cambridge advanced-level (A-level) exams, which decide admissions to the university.

[34]

Despite its expansion, however, the school system was criticized in the late 1970s for its inability to produce enough high-quality, technically skilled bilingual students for the new economic program. "Educational wastage" was extensive. Out of a cohort of 1,000 first-grade pupils, typically only 440 graduated from secondary school ten years later. The rest repeated courses or dropped out of the academic stream without acquiring any of the skills required by the advanced hi-tech industries.[57] Therefore sweeping educational reforms accompanied Singapore's second-stage economic program. The revamped instructional system in place at the time of my reinterviews featured continuous testing, starting with a language test in grade 3. Examination-based streaming within each grade separates students of different language, technical, and academic abilities.[58] The new scheme allows around 40 percent of the primary school cohort to succeed at O-levels. Only 14 percent, however, will pass at A-levels. Only 9 percent of their age group were enrolled in university or polytechnic institutions in 1982.[59] Most significant, those who do not advance along the preuniversity path will attend the Vocational and Industrial Training Board's certificate- and diploma-conferring institutions.

Although Singapore's meritocratic development program claims to reduce the role of class origins in educational advancement, the desired equality of opportunity has not been achieved. Pupils in government-aided private schools have higher social-class backgrounds and perform better on the key exams than their peers in state schools.[60] Middle-class parents devote much more time and money to preparing their children at home for success in school. As exams are as likely to measure pupils' familiarity with schoolroom concepts and techniques as their inherent intelligence,[61] streaming and early testing of students cannot help the poor. The battery of tests designed to identify superior pupils has given rise to widespread tutoring to improve children's performance. Again, parents with money and knowledge have an edge. The tuition fees at the local university and polytechnic institutes are low, but degree-seeking students who fail to gain admission to the sole university, the National University of Singapore, must go abroad at considerable expense.

As parents devote time and effort to their children's education, the nuclear family has become deeply involved in the educational system. The outcome is seen not only in economic opportunities for youth but also in political commitment.[62] The ideology of the Singapore meritocracy labels those who cannot continue on in school as lacking qualifications. Richard Sennett and Jonathan Cobb report that the poor American families they studied refrained from directly challenging the political system because they "felt personally responsible for the labels of ability they bore."[63] In these ways the educational system reproduces the class-structured society.

[35]

Health and Population Policies

The ratio of physicians and beds in government-run hospitals to population has improved, while small clinics run by midwives for the poor have been labeled "below standard" and closed. Maternal and child health services in phase 1 were delivered by 24 hospitals, 13 of them public, and an associated network of 46 clinics.[64] Over 80 percent of all registered births take place at public hospitals, and over 90 percent of all newborns are enrolled for comprehensive postnatal care at a neighborhood clinic. This extension of state medical care enables the public to enjoy a better quality of life and reduces occupational time lost to illness. It also lays the groundwork for what Michel Foucault has called the medicalization of social control.[65]

Population grew rapidly in postwar Singapore, and the government resolved early that such growth would slow capital formation. After independence, the Ministry of Health provided contraceptive services through its network of public health facilities. In the late 1960s the state overrode the opposition of interest groups in the medical, religious, and professional communities and liberalized abortion and sterilization laws. The crude birth rate declined in response to fertility-limitation services and first-stage industrialization. From 44.4 per 1,000 population in 1956, the crude birth rate fell to 21.8 in 1969 and on to 16.6 in 1977.[66]

In the early 1970s, however, the government became alarmed by evidence that family size was still relatively high among the working poor. A 1973 survey by the Family Planning and Population Board (FPPB) revealed that fully 35 percent of the blue-collar workers studied, but only 11 percent of the clerical workers and 7 percent of the professional and technical workers, considered four or more children "ideal."[67] The FPPB then vigorously popularized its tenet that numerous children undermine efforts to upgrade the family, because they keep the family too poor to afford their own flat, mothers cannot work, and children cannot receive a good education. Mass media presentations on population control created an atmosphere of crisis and identified large families as an imminent threat to the limited resources of the city-state. Thus the national family-limitation campaign aimed to convince the people that rapid population growth endangered both their present livelihood and their future prospects.

Amid much fanfare, the economic and social "Disincentives against Higher Order Births" were enacted in 1973 in an effort to attain the FPPB's goal of zero population growth by the year 2030, at a level of 3.6 million persons.[68] Disincentives linked negative sanctions against large families to social services. Public hospitals' obstetrical fees increase sharply with the number of living children to whom the mother has already given birth, but the fees are waived if the mother is sterilized (usually by means of tubal ligation) within six months of the birth.[69] Though no child is denied schooling, the fourth child receives lower priority in choice of elementary school than children of small families, especially those whose parents have been sterilized. Though public housing is available to all, large families no longer have priority in access to HDB flats as hardship cases, nor can families with three or more children rent out one of their rooms. A female civil servant or union member obtains two months' paid maternity leave for each of her first two deliveries, but not for subsequent births. She is, however, given paid medical leave for sterilization.[70] Finally, all individuals whose annual income exceeds S$3,000 must pay income tax, and couples can claim no more than two children as deductions.

These measures do not actually deny citizens services, for it is in the state's interest to expand public goods. They do, however, raise the price of needed social services for parents of large families, and further reinforce the view that these people are poor because they have too many children. The measures shore up the ideology of the Singapore meritocracy: only planners will succeed in raising their families above poverty. Prime Minister Lee Kuan Yew has explained that a system of disincentives was needed "so that the irresponsible, the social delinquents do not believe that all they have to do is to produce their children and the government then owes them and their children sufficient food, medicine, housing, education, and jobs. . . . Until the less educated themselves concentrate their limited resources on one or two to give their children the maximum chance to climb up the educational ladder, their children will always be at the bottom of the economic scale."[71] Lee's government justifies the measures as a means of helping the poor help themselves, and of reducing conflicts engendered by competition over social services.

Yet such measures quickly come to be seen as a means to blame the victim. Chua Sian Chin, minister of health in 1973, when the accouchement fees were raised for higher-order births, stated:

> In an industrialized and highly urbanized Singapore of the 1970s, a large family is a tragedy for the children, a burden to their parents, and a drag on the whole society. . . . As our economy expands, wages will go up. But the rise in wages will not bring a better life to those families who increase their burdens by having more children to feed, clothe, and nurture. When parents have more children than they can adequately feed and care for, these children will have poorer diet and health. Their education and training will suffer and they will remain at the lower levels of incomes and unskilled jobs. No amount of subsidies by the Government can remedy the lack of adequate food and care at home. . . . In fact, the greater the feather-bedding of large antisocial families, the greater will be the numbers of large families. . . . Moreover, social friction and tensions will increase because [children in large families] will do poorly because they are deprived of adequate food and care. It is a vicious circle which we must

[37]

break. It is kinder in the long run to put disincentives on large families. Certainly it will carry less danger of social tensions, overcrowding, and generally lower standards in the very limited space of Singapore. . . . To bring each child to his or her full potential, we must break this vicious cycle.[72]

Zero population growth was attained on the eve of the new economic policy, and pressures on mothers to be sterilized abated. Indeed, such tendencies had gone so far that the policies were temporarily reversed for sections of the educated population.[73]

In sum, the first industrial phase saw considerable social-class variation in family size, owing largely to the felt need for children by the proletarian poor. As the national birth rate declined in the 1970s, the social-class differences in family size narrowed. Yet the continued cleavage in life options is likely to be reflected in the diverse meanings of children to families along the spectrum of class backgrounds.

PART II

The Early
Development Stage

[3]

Introducing Poor Families

The couples I portray here are typical of those with low education and wages and difficult family backgrounds, those I designate as "poor." In phase 1, the husbands worked as peripheral-sector hawker, bus conductor, stationery store clerk, and tinsmith, and as laborer and fitter in a core-sector shipyard. We will meet the same families again in Chapter 7, in their phase 2 lives.

Ng Family: Hawker and Homemaker (I)

Ng Kong Chong came from a family of street vendors, people known in Southeast Asia as hawkers. Both he and his wife, Wee Ping, were Hokkien, members of the largest Chinese dialect group in Singapore. They had two children. Kong Chong sold steamed pastries of rice flour filled with sweetened shredded coconut (*tutu*) on pieces of leaves from a pushcart in a large parking lot at night. He was unable to get a license and was repeatedly fined by the authorities. Vending, once valued among overseas Chinese for its income opportunities, under these circumstances provided low and uneven earnings.

Kong Chong was born in 1942 in Singapore and his family returned with him and his siblings to their native village in Fujian Province in the late 1940s. There, in the People's Republic of China, his father continued to ply the hawker's trade, while Kong Chong went to primary school. He reemigrated with his family to Singapore at age 17. The family expected him to continue the family practice of petty vending. In late 1974, he estimated his net income at S$250 a month, and assured me that he could put nothing aside for the future. He could not find a better-paying job because he was not qualified for any.

"What kind of work can I do? I have so little education. All my family have been hawkers, and my older brother vends cakes too. Only my younger brother had more schooling and a better type of job. If I went to work in a factory, the best I could get would be an unskilled job. At least now I can feed my family." He punctuated this and other responses with an expression of resignation: "Oh, I don't know!"

Kong Chong in fact realized he was a "small businessman," but took no pride in his independent status. He knew his job had no future. "People are not allowed to sell in the daytime unless they're over forty years old. The government is always after us—what can a person do?" He felt quite helpless and despaired of improving his circumstances. "My family makes it with my earnings because we are thrifty. We live day by day; no extras, no chance to save."

Wee Ping, a plain-spoken woman of twenty-eight was the only surviving daughter of twelve children born to an impoverished Singapore family. Seven of her siblings perished during the Japanese occupation. Owing to the family's poverty, Wee Ping was required to remain at home to care for her brothers; she never attended school. In her early teens, she took a job as a packer in a peanut factory. She gave half of her S$70 monthly earnings to her family. She never considered changing jobs because her lack of education made it hard to find alternative work. When she was twenty-four, her family arranged for her to meet Kong Chong, and the couple courted a year before they married. She then felt there was no longer any point in working because she would not be able to earn enough to pay for child care. Nevertheless, Wee Ping was uncomfortable with her status and bored with life. She spoke directly, in a bare-boned way: "Life before marriage was much better than now 'cause I have to look after the kids. Looking after children is very tiring. No one can possibly enjoy that. It's much better to be a working wife. But I have no choice." In addition to her housework, she helped prepare the coconut for the tutu peddled by her husband.

Wee Ping was unaware of the possibilities for women outside her narrow neighborhood circle. Like her neighbors, she dressed in inexpensive pajamas at home and used no cosmetics. The interviewer admired the halterneck dress that her two-year old daughter was wearing. Wee Ping reflected on the restrictive mores of her domestic milieu. "You know, even girls of twenty wear halter dresses. But I'd never dare wear one. It's shocking, and all the neighbors would talk. My husband would scold me, too. It's not so bad if people don't comment, but in this building people will talk, and you'd bring embarrassment to the family. My husband has really 'old brains.' He comments on my clothing if my dress is too short. But sometimes I tell him that if he complains too much about my short dresses, I'll make them shorter so my backside can be seen!"

Wee Ping and Kong Chong had married because of their mutual poverty and because, at twenty-five and twenty-nine, they were running out of time to find marriage partners. Kong Chong acidly compared his lot with that of better-off people. "Poor people marry late," he said. The interviewer rejoined, "But late marriage is now a trend. Do you know that?" Kong Chong retorted, "Where'd you get that idea? Don't all rich people marry young? Of course it's not good to marry late because your children are young when you're getting old. It's better to have children when you're younger so that when you're old they are grown up. But poor people depend on luck when they have children." Kong Chong could hope to retire from his arduous job only when his children were mature workers, and his comments reflected this dependence on the upcoming generation.

Wee Ping did not differentiate boys' and girls' jobs at home. She said boys should sweep the floor and wash the dishes, and there was no such thing as "girls' work" in the home. But Kong Chong's attitude and schedule did not permit him to share the housework. He sold cakes from 5 to 11 P.M. daily, then retired until 11 the next morning. After breakfast at noon, he relaxed over the paper at home and visited with his friends in their homes. He doted on his daughter and often took her along on his social calls. His presence in the kitchen was limited to preparing the tutu ingredients.

Wee Ping did not know her husband's chums and confined her social life to her own neighborhood circle. Without Kong Chong she occasionally took the children to a nearby cinema and a neighborhood park. Every Sunday afternoon she took them to a family gathering at her mother's home. The couple's ties on Kong Chong's side were weak. He had two brothers in Singapore, and only the youngest was salaried. His mother resided with this youngest son, a primary school teacher, some distance from the Ngs' residence. Wee Ping visited there infrequently and got little help from her mother-in-law.

Wee Ping told us that she and her husband had little to talk about. "But what can you do? If you don't get married, people gossip. They say, 'How come she's so old and hasn't married?' I have a girl friend who is over thirty and not married. Maybe she can't find a husband, or isn't interested in marriage, but people do chatter. I don't like people to talk."

She considered sexual intercourse an obligation. "I don't like sex. Even though I haven't told him, that sticky thing frightens me. He doesn't know how I feel. Most women I know don't like sex either. I suppose that's why men look for a 'second wife.' What can you do when he wants sex? If you don't give it to him, he may go to a prostitute and not only spend a lot of money but come home with all kinds of diseases. I know a man who that

[43]

happened to. I think sex is for having children. If you don't want children, why bother to get married?"

The Ng family lived in a simply furnished "one-room improved" flat in one of the poorest HDB buildings. They had partitioned it into living, sleeping, and cooking areas. Their only amenities were a rice cooker and a radio. Large containers of flour and broad sword-shaped pandan leaves (from the textile pine tree) in which the tutu was steamed filled the living area. Rent and utilities totaled S$40, 16 percent of their net income; expenditures on food exhausted most of their remaining income, leaving little for other household and personal needs. Wee Ping had no hope of owning a home of her own, and denied she needed to buy household appliances. "We don't need a refrigerator since the market is nearby and I can go every day. My husband thinks we don't need a television. He prefers to watch it in other people's homes."

Kong Chong's pessimism kept him from setting goals for his children. He declined to forecast their education or job prospects. In response to questions on education, he laughed and shook his head. "Look at our baby son over there sleeping in his sarong, and our daughter, who is only two years old, playing in the corner. What's going to happen to me and them tomorrow? I don't even know that, so how can I tell you what will come up in three years?"

I nonetheless continued to seek information about the children's education. "What can parents do to help their children study when they reach school age?" He replied, "If the parents want a child to study and he refuses, what choice do the parents have? If they don't have ability, there is really nothing you can do!"

Wee Ping did not think there were many differences between her child-raising practices and those of her mother except for her mother's much larger brood. While she had a vague awareness that Singapore was changing, she did not know how to prepare her children for the future. She looked to her neighbors for guidance in choosing jobs and planning for her children's later occupations. "I can only hope that my children will study hard and be clever," she affirmed. Because the Ngs' economic situation was marginal and they depended strongly on their children's labor power for security in their old age, her views revealed considerable conflict. She first stated her intention to enroll her infant son in an English-stream primary school in order to increase his chances of finding work. In a subsequent interview, however, she hinted that she would instead send him to a Chinese primary school. Some neighbors told her that English-stream pupils became "spoiled." "They end up different from what is expected of sons. We want our children to support us when we're old, but children are different these days, and have to be taught to do so. Maybe it's not so hard to get jobs after all if you're Chinese educated."

[44]

Her daughter's academic path was "not important." Children should go to school "as far as possible"; without education, they would be "blind cows" (illiterate). However, she could not specify the amount of schooling she planned for her children. The interviewer asked, "What kind of jobs would you like your children to have?" Wee Ping replied, "A good job for a girl is in a clothing factory, but I wonder if such factories will be around when my daughter grows up. I'd like my son to be a printer. They make a lot of money. My upstairs neighbor works in that trade and that's what he told me."

The interviewer then asked, "What do you think about your children becoming teachers?" She answered, "How can they? I doubt if they'll be so clever!" She hoped that her children would have a better life than she did, but she was already resigned to their possible lack of achievement.

The Ngs had hoped that their first child would be a son. When a daughter was born a year after their marriage, they decided to try again for a boy, and their son was born the following year. After this birth, Wee Ping began to use contraceptive pills. She thought that four children would be the right number, but resolved to wait four or five years before she became pregnant again. She thought Singapore was overpopulated, "judging by all the houses, cars, and people we see." She disapproved of very large families. "My neighbor in the flat opposite has ten children. She had to give one of them away." Wee Ping believed that low-income families should plan their births for economic reasons, as she was doing. "More children, more food needed. Long ago people had such big families, ten or twelve kids, but that's not right nowadays, three or four is just right." She thus endorsed the spirit of official population policy but disagreed with its ceiling of two children.

Kong Chong seemed to share Wee Ping's views. But when I queried him directly, he merely laughed and shrugged. He felt that his life was being frustrated by the authorities. "If the government wants people to have two children, everybody has to stop at two or they'll be fined. Two isn't enough. Three or four are about right. Boy or girl, all the same. Of course, the disincentives discriminate against the poor. If you're rich, dollars are no problem. You can have as many as you like." Just as he thought that mon-eyed people married earlier, he thought they had more children. He could not imagine a well-off couple voluntarily curtailing their family size if their income was adequate, unless they were charged high fees in the state hospi-tal for childbirth. He ended on a note of despair. "It's hard to earn a living nowadays. If you're lucky, things will be a bit better. But if the laws are against you, what can you do? If the government wants to do something, you can't stop it."

His lack of future earning options and low education gave him scant hope. The Ngs worked and lived in the industrial economy of the city-state and all their actions were affected by the development program. They felt buffeted by this program, and used its services at a minimal level. The daily harassments suffered by an unlicensed vender prevented this family from entertaining higher aspirations for their children. The Ngs rented the poorest form of government housing and used the facilities of the neighborhood birth-control clinic, but hoped for more children than the clinic sanctioned. Without help from neighbors, they could not survive. The Ng family did not expect their lives to improve significantly in the foreseeable future.

Chua Family: Bus Conductor and Electronics Factory Worker (I)

The Teochewnese bus conductor Chua Kay Yong, aged thirty-five, was married to the Hokkien electronics assembler Siew Gek, aged twenty-seven. The couple had a two-year-old son whom they called Robert, in anticipation of his English-stream schooling. Siew Gek was pregnant with her second child when I interviewed the couple in December 1974. This couple's life was also circumscribed by poverty and hardship. Kay Yong felt his grade 2 education and lack of industrial skills limited his opportunities to advance. "When I was young, my father was a labor contractor on construction jobs. He neglected me because he had a second wife, whom we called 'young aunt.'[1] Father and she had a son together. My real mother didn't even live at home, she had a job somewhere else. Young Aunt used to make me carry water and do chores until late at night. I went to work as a hawker's helper when I was thirteen. No matter how carefully I hid my earnings, she was sure to find them and use them to gamble. She saw to it that Stepbrother completed primary school. If father had known how to think, I wouldn't have any financial problems today. But he used to turn down jobs that paid fifteen dollars a day. Back then it was good money." As first son, Kay Yong expected at least as much education as Stepbrother. His childhood deprivation, which limited his education and job chances, generated his pessimistic outlook. He was an argumentative man, and his wife ascribed this shortcoming to his childhood experiences.

As a late teenager, Kay Yong became a construction worker. His boss loaned him the small sum required to establish himself as an independent subcontractor, but he found this regime too demanding. "In construction you have to wake up before dawn to get the laborers and tradesmen started. And most of the day you stand in water up to your knees. So I said to myself, 'This is not the life for me! Not only that, the money I earned helped pay the doctor bills for Young Aunt's illness. She had cancer for the three years before she died. She saw an expensive private doctor and bought costly special foods. Altogether it took my savings of a few thousand dollars. Father wasn't working at the time."

[46]

He then became a low-paid office boy at the police station in the Queenstown district, near his home. "You know how low civil service pay can be, and I was a married man. So four years ago my father-in-law got me a job with the Singapore Bus Service, where he's been a conductor for a long time. I work night shift for two weeks and day shift for two weeks. I normally take home two hundred dollars a month, but recently I've been working overtime and this brings me an extra fifty. But overtime is hard to come by because so many people want to do it."

The interviewer asked, "Are you thinking of looking for a better job?" Kay Yong replied, "No, I won't change. This job is secure and I'll stay with it. But I've got a language problem. When a rider asks me in English for directions on the route, all I can say is 'What?' In Singapore, English is very important. Everywhere you go, English is spoken, and a worker just can't get ahead without it. If I had more education I could do better. Also, the company fines me every time I get to work late. It bothers me!"

Siew Gek admonished him, "It's a good job. Better not change!"

Siew Gek, the first of eight children born to a hard-working washerwoman, had managed to complete the fifth grade, but when she failed the sixth-grade exams, she went to work as a domestic servant and gave all of her S$120 monthly earnings to her parents. After marrying, she worked for a time on the assembly line of a knitwear factory. She disliked this occupation, and left it to bear her first child. When her son was six months old, she acquired her present position as an assembler at the Hewlett-Packard plant, a large, U.S.-based electronics firm, in Queenstown.

Siew Gek's next younger sister, a home seamstress, lived nearby with her husband and family. Second Sister cared for Robert, and Siew Gek lingered to visit with her when she dropped off her son on the way to work. Kay Yong picked him up in the evening. Then Kay Yong's father died, and they invited his mother to live with them and care for their child during the day.

In contrast to her morose husband, Siew Gek was a lively extrovert. She enjoyed factory work and was one of the few poor women in my sample who considered that factory work could expand her horizons. She had a keen social intelligence and used all the resources in her social setting. Her husband, however, did not want her to return to the factory after the birth of their son. Haunted by the unhappiness of his own broken family of origin, he was determined to be the only breadwinner in his family.

Siew Gek recalls, "I explained to him that he just doesn't make enough money for me to stay home. So in the end he accepted my return to work. Father-in-Law was very old-fashioned, and he also objected to my factory job. My own mother didn't like my working. She's old-fashioned too. She's bothered that I have to work so hard. Before I got married things were different. I was expected to help support the family. But now she doesn't see our financial problems and asks, 'What for?' Mother-in-Law, for her part, is

[47]

really a very nice old lady who doesn't say much." Despite the doubts of her elders, Siew Gek stressed that everyone would continue to benefit from her employment. "Prices and inflation are so high nowadays that we need my wages to feed our family. I really like chatting with the other girls at work and learning from them about the job, and I like getting out of the house. We talk a lot about modern gadgets for the home. I like the afternoon shift best because I can get most of my housework done in the morning, spend time with my son at noon, and still have a chance to rest before the shift begins. I'm lucky that my mother-in-law helps with the chores. I'm a very active person and I couldn't bear wasting my time at home all afternoon. I prefer to earn some money. It's important for us to save for our children's education and for social occasions. We also need to put cash by for old age. So I bank fifty dollars every month. We just got a one-compartment refrigerator. It's a brand-new Acma model that cost over four hundred dollars. We paid for it by using my last month's bonus and the bonuses Kay Yong and I received from our factories at the Chinese lunar New Year. I've also started to buy things for the new baby." She gestured toward the layette accumulating in the corner.

After she went to work at the factory in 1972, Siew Gek had three months of training, then began to work her way up the incremental wage ladder from the novice category A to the level of a grade B worker. She did not expect to become a lead girl (the worker who supervises the output of her section of workers). Only two of her large section of 160 workers were designated as lead girls. "Lead girls have a lot of responsibilities. They have to deal with a lot of workers who don't want to cooperate. If you scold them, they can get funny with you. Some of them have boyfriends who are gangsters. They talk back at their lead girls and supervisors. It's not easy for a lead girl in that situation. I personally never try to talk back and be funny, but I wouldn't like the lead girl's job, even though it pays over three hundred dollars. Besides, I've heard you need to have a good education to get a lead girl position. Promotions also depend on whether the management likes you or not."

Siew Gek was ambivalent about seeking promotions and felt uncertain about her prospects for continued employment in the electronics factory. She described the factory management's problems. Like her fellow workers, she was forced to wait passively for the outcome of her firm's financial crises. "Our manager called a meeting last month and told us about the difficult situation the company's in. They then cut us to four days a week. The girls accepted this cut in hours and wages. In fact," she laughed, "the boss told us that otherwise we wouldn't be the only ones out of a job—he'd be unemployed himself." Since she was hoping for the revival of the factory business, she did not seek another position. Besides, "I'm pregnant now, and who wants to hire a pregnant woman? I'll wait until after the baby is born and then maybe start looking around for another job. I thought of taking in a child to care for, but now I think I'd prefer factory work because it's a regular job with shorter hours."

She was determined to continue working and had to make plans for the care of her child and herself during the first several weeks of her confinement. She had expected Mother-in-Law to help her during her confinement, but now Sister-in-Law (the wife of Kay Yong's stepbrother) was expecting a baby at the same time. This coincidence meant that Siew Gek might lose the help that she depended on in order to work. "I wouldn't know what to do if Mother-in-Law had to help Sister-in-Law during her one-month confinement instead of me. It's no use discussing this with Mother-in-Law. She's the type that doesn't express her preferences. You just ask her to do something and she'll do it. It would be a pity for me to give up such a good job if I had to care for my baby and myself."

Siew Gek turned to her mother for advice. "My mother told me to hire an amah [domestic servant] to help Sister-in-Law after her birth, so that Mother-in-Law will be free to help me. I'm willing to sacrifice, even though it may cost two hundred and fifty dollars, so I can continue working later on. But I don't know if Sister-in-Law would accept this arrangement."

Siew Gek needed to plan kin help to support her dual role of homemaker and factory worker. "I can manage to get my housework done in the morning before I leave for the factory. Every morning I get up at seven, go marketing, come back to wash clothes, feed the baby, clean the flat, and cook lunch. Now that I'm pregnant, though, Mother-in-Law does the washing, cleaning, and cooking. It used to be worse when I didn't have her help. Then I had the extra task of delivering my baby to Second Sister. Since I have to be at work at three, there's no time to spare. I have to move quickly." Kay Yong had never assisted Siew Gek with housework. But since he gave her S$6 a day—most of his income—to run the house, she did not complain.

Even though Kay Yong had difficulties in relation with his workmates and family members, he gave much to his home. The couple shared their leisure-time activities, and they discussed their jobs, the management of the household, and large purchases. For these reasons I call theirs a "joint marriage." The characteristics of their common world were shaped by their individual personalities and access to kin. Whereas morose Kay Yong was limited in his kin life by his interrupted childhood, outgoing Siew Gek was blessed by an abundance of family and friends.

She explained that the hours she spent in the factory, even though she worked the night shift, did not detract from her relationship with her husband. "We see each other when I come home from work at eleven and on the weekends. Sometimes he even comes to the factory to get me and we walk home together. Or if I come home and find him asleep, he doesn't mind if I'm naughty and wake him up. On his day off, he just stays home. Occasionally we leave Mother-in-Law behind when we take Robert to the movies or to eat out. We took her with us to the movies only once. She didn't seem to grasp much about the movie." Siew Gek often visited her relatives. "I take Robert with me to see my mother every week. Sometimes my husband comes along with me. If not, he always comes to walk us home."

Siew Gek found the temporary four-day workweek allowed her more time "to go shopping and visit my friends and family." But she acknowledged that she had to restrict her social activities because they cost money. When she had worked as an amah for European families in her teens, she had learned that walking was considered good exercise for expectant mothers. Therefore she and Kay Yong took many strolls together.

The Chuas felt they communicated with each other satisfactorally. When Siew Gek returned home from work in the evening, "I tell him all the funny day's news, every little thing on the job. He also tells me what happens on his job during the day." I asked her, "Do you think he confides completely in you?" Siew Gek replied, "I don't think so. After all, most men don't tell everything to their wives." She went on, "All couples have conflicts some-times." Examples of Kay Yong's opposition to her activities abounded. He was distressed when she went back to work after Robert's birth, and when she socialized with her mother. He felt that once a woman marries, she should separate from her relatives.

Siew Gek disagreed. "For example, my eldest brother is getting married, and I wanted to give him two hundred and fifty dollars. But Kay Yong reminded me that if I were to give one brother two hundred and fifty, I'd have to give the same amount to the other three when they got married. He feels that we couldn't afford that much. In the end we compromised. I donated a hundred and twenty to my mother for her to spend on my broth-er's wedding expenses. And I suppose I'll do the same for the others. But still I bought some gifts for his new home. I use my own earnings for these purchases, and that's a good reason for a person to have her own income."

Siew Gek's substantial financial contribution strengthened her domestic decision-making role. Kay Yong, for his part, did not hold his wife back from her kin alliances. His wife's dominant role was reinforced by the meekness of his mother. This long-suffering elderly woman had lost considerable status when her husband took a consort. In a reversal of generational expectations, she was invited into the home of her offspring. Siew Gek explained, "Moth-er-in-Law doesn't know much about the world. She's been confined to her family all her life. When the price of rice or sugar goes up, she doesn't find out until I break the news to her. I tease her about her stupidity." Her choice of commodity prices to illustrate Mother-in-Law's ignorance reflects the Chuas' preoccupation with the necessities of life. Siew Gek told me about a significant family incident. "Mother-in-Law used to side with my husband whenever we had a quarrel. Then one day I told my sister-in-law [the wife of Kay Yong's stepbrother] that Mother-in-Law should avoid taking sides. You see, sometimes he's in the wrong. Sister-in-Law must have told her how I felt, because Mother-in-Law has stopped joining our quarrels. She just stares out of the window when we have words. That cuts our arguments short, too!"

The Chuas rented their present one-room HDB flat four years ago, when they got married. They wanted a home of their own, but Kay Yong confessed that their family income would probably remain too low ever to support the purchase of a flat. His pessimism was born in part of his mistrust of the Housing Development Board. "All housing officials are dishonest!" he claimed. He told us of his difficulties in renting his present quarters. Several weeks before the marriage, he complained at the HDB office: "I'll have to move out of my rented room at the end of the month, and if you don't give me a flat by then, I'll hire a truck to bring my furniture to your community center. I'll leave it there until you give me a new place to live." He believed that the HDB's decision to allow him the present flat was due to this threat.

Siew Gek had given thought to improving their small flat. She had draped an attractive yellow curtain around their double bed in the bed-sitting room. She explained, "It's better this way, because Robert sleeps here." Before retiring, Mother-in-Law and Robert removed a thin mattress from the corner and unrolled it for their bed. In the morning, this mattress was returned to the corner. In another section of this room stood the refrigerator, a cupboard that stored ornaments, an electric sewing machine, an electric fan, and a television set. A small kitchen accommodated a raised cement area for a one-ring gas burner and a coal stove, a sink, an electric blender, and two small tables for meals and storing provisions. There was a small bathroom and shower area off the kitchen.

Siew Gek had learned about using the blender to prepare infant food from her European employers. She had also absorbed other kitchen practices from them. She proudly announced, "I prepared fresh fruit and vegetables for Robert in the blender, not just rice gruel, like my mother fed us. Robert really grew. At the checkup, the nurse at the Maternal and Child Health Clinic couldn't believe he was only three months old, and asked what I had been feeding him!"

Kay Yong wanted Robert to have a good education, but was uncertain of the details and prospects. "I want Robert to advance as far as he can go. Like my cousin's son. That boy even won a scholarship to study in Japan. But if Robert doesn't learn well, it can't be helped."

The couple did not budget funds for Robert's future education. Kay Yong explained, "That will have to wait until we're better off." The Chuas nevertheless wished to instill proper study habits in Robert. I asked them, "Where do you plan to educate Robert?" Kay Yong replied, "I'll send my son to an English school, because English is widely used and will give him better job prospects. I sure don't want him to do 'buffalo work' like me. As a

[51]

parent, I naturally want him to achieve more than me. One thing I've noticed as a bus conductor, some students use their time after school for dating instead of studying. I don't mean students shouldn't socialize, but there must be a time for study and a time for play. We'll have to be selective about his friends." When I sought specifics, he was unable to name a suitable profession, except to say that Robert should obtain a lighter job with higher status. For her part, Siew Gek was aiming at a white-collar profession for the children.

The Chuas wished to have three children. Siew Gek wanted at least one daughter who would take on family responsibilities as she had done. Siew Gek's mother also hoped for three or more Chua grandchildren; Kay Yong's mother had expressed no preference to them. Though Kay Yong yearned for a second son, he nevertheless agreed with the government's two-child policy. "If the government doesn't do this, people will have too many children! After all, Singapore is already overcrowded. No matter how high the new housing is built, all the flats are taken. I've noticed that the women boarding my buses are usually pregnant, or are leading a handful of children." He drew on his everyday experiences to make his point. He felt that the short-term expenses of feeding and clothing more than three children would require him to limit the size of his family. This stress on budgetary restrictions could not explain why a more affluent family would seek to limit its offspring. He resolved this anomaly by reasoning that workers more affluent than he, even the wealthy, are aware of the instability of their income. "Some rich people also know how to think and plan. They are aware that their fortune may change. Today they may be prosperous, tomorrow they can fall."

Siew Gek said that she had once hoped to have four children, but she had lowered her sights to three. One reason was the disincentives program promulgated by the Singapore government in 1973. "I've been influenced by the policy of lower educational priority for the fourth child. I also heard that the fourth child will have difficulty in getting government jobs."

Siew Gek was the hub of her family's domestic life. Kay Yong's job lacked prospects for advancement, but Siew Gek's was more promising. Her earnings gave her a measure of esteem and status on both sides of the family. She banked close to 10 percent of their joint income and looked forward to buying a few more consumer goods. Moreover, her experience as a factory worker, and before that as a domestic servant, gave her insights into urban Singapore life which could serve her well in bringing up her children. Her kin networks provided a minimum of resources for them. Nevertheless, Kay Yong's poor earnings and prospects fundamentally limited the Chua family's ability to utilize the Singapore government's social service programs. They were too poor to buy an HDB flat, to accept fully the two-child ethic, or to save money for their children's education.

Loy Family: Store Clerk and Homemaker (I)

Loy Heng Yeo, who spoke the Hainanese dialect, was married to Mei Po, a Cantonese speaker. The couple had two sons when I interviewed them in late 1974. Heng Yeo was my only poor respondent who had studied for and passed the Cambridge O-level examination. He was employed as a salesclerk by the Chung Hwa Trading Company, a small peripheral-sector import-export firm that dealt in stationery. This enterprise, with a staff of ten, was located in the densely populated district known as Chinatown, the area north and south of the Singapore River where immigrants from China, most of them men, had settled in Singapore's early years as a trading post. Most of the buildings in this area were narrow, two- or three-story structures that were gradually being demolished during my phase 1 interviews. The Chung Hwa Trading Company was owned and operated by the husband of Heng Yeo's elder sister, who had hired him when he completed his education.

Heng Yeo's family had emigrated to Indonesia from the Chinese island of Hainan. There Mother gave birth to a daughter and then to Heng Yeo in 1941. Father died during the Japanese occupation of World War II. After the war, Mother remarried and Heng Yeo was sent to Mother's sister in Singapore. Stepfather, a businessman, financed Heng Yeo's secondary education.

When anti-Chinese feelings in Indonesia caused difficulties in the early 1960s, Mother and Stepfather sought refuge in Singapore. Stepfather's loss of his business abruptly ended Heng Yeo's prospects for postsecondary education, and Mother suggested that he approach his sister's husband for a job. In December 1974, when I first interviewed him, he was earning S$250 monthly. Three months later, when my visits to this couple were ending, Mei Po happily reported that her husband had just received a S$100 monthly raise. He was now earning S$350, just above the median wage of Singapore men. Heng Yeo stressed the positive features of his family employment and pointed out that his contribution was central to the prosperity of the firm. "I help my brother-in-law take orders from foreign countries, since he doesn't know English at all. I also travel in Malaysia, where I enlist new customers and fill their orders. Some of my regular clients ask to do business with me personally."

He was proud of fulfilling his family and business obligations through the hard work and long hours he dedicated to the firm. At the time of these interviews, his parents were living with four younger stepbrothers in a small flat. His elder sister and brother-in-law lived nearby. He accompanied Brother-in-Law after work each evening for a visit with his mother. He usually ate dinner there and returned home later. These visits further strengthened Heng Yeo's bond to the firm.

[53]

Heng Yeo held more responsibilities than others in the firm with the same nominal rank and income. He stated, "My boss is my brother-in-law, and I must therefore be more responsible and work harder than my colleagues."

However, Mei Po criticized Brother-in-Law's treatment of her husband. "Being a close relative of the boss, my husband works very hard for the store, but his brother-in-law doesn't seem to treat him accordingly. After working for his brother-in-law for nearly fifteen years, my husband earns only two hundred and fifty dollars. He hasn't had a single raise in the six years since we married. My husband is too good and too shy to ask for one. Brother-in-Law is certainly a peculiar person. He doesn't mind that his wife takes in washing to earn a bit of extra income. Maybe he expects people to work hard even if their wages are low!"

She told us that Brother-in-Law gave presents to his employees instead of raising their salaries. Thus Heng Yeo received an annual Chinese New Year's bonus worth several months' salary. When the couple moved into their present flat, they received a black-and-white television set worth approximately S$300. They received a S$200 cash gift at the birth of each of their two children. Heng Yeo counseled his wife to be patient and essentially dismissed her complaints. His sense of family obligations prevented him from requesting higher wages or from seeking a better-paying position. His sense of satisfaction with his good job performance obscured the inadequacies of his job. His close links to a family firm in the small Hainanese-speaking community discouraged any attempts to gain the wage customary for a person of his educational attainment in Singapore today.

Workers who are employed by members of their own ethnic group, to whom they owe ritual or familistic obligations, and who serve mainly their ethnic community, are ensnared in what has been called the "ethnic mobility trap."[2] Frequently the wages of such workers do not match their education, but the individuals affected have few or no links to jobs outside their community. Heng Yeo was clearly ensnared in such a trap.

Mei Po, aged twenty-six, daughter of a carpenter, was one of six children. She was very close to her siblings. Elder Brother took over her father's small furniture workshop. He remained in his parents' home and supported them. Mei Po, however, had few skills. After finishing primary school, she learned to operate a sewing machine and worked as a seamstress in a small neighborhood garment factory until the birth of her first child, three years after her marriage to Heng Yeo. At that point, Mei Po took in piecework from the same factory. From her gross monthly earnings of S$170 she paid a neighbor S$50 for help with child care. She left the labor force completely after her second son's birth. "When you are sewing uniforms for the factory, you are expected to send back each batch of goods right on schedule, so it was impossible for me to continue piecework sewing when my second son came along. He was very active and needed my full attention. I don't think I'll ever go back to the factory. Even when the kids reach school age, they still need a mother to take them to school, fix meals for them, and be around when they get home in the afternoon."

Lack of kin support contributed to Mei Po's decision to remain a house-wife. "It's very difficult for any mother to work full-time unless she has a mother-in-law to look after her kids. For one thing, you don't have to pay Mother-in-Law too much money for babysitting, and for another, you can be sure your mother-in-law will take good care of your children. Unfortunately, Heng Yeo's mother is already watching her own daughter's children, while my mother takes care of my brother's kids. Sister-in-Law works in the office of the furniture workshop and pays Mother a hundred and seventy dollars for caring for her child all week long." Mei Po had less cash and could not command Mother's help.

One of Mei Po's childhood neighbors was a washerwoman who had done Heng Yeo's bachelor laundry, and the couple had met on his trips to collect his clean clothes. Since Mei Po's parents set strict limitations on her social life and wished to influence her choice of a husband, she hesitated to tell them of their friendship. Six years after the couple met, they decided to get married, and only then did she take Heng Yeo home to meet her parents. After inquiring about the young man among their acquaintances, her parents acquiesced in the match.

Mei Po regretted that her husband earned so little, and poignantly de-fended her marriage choice as fated. "I guess I was destined to marry Heng Yeo. At the beginning of our courtship my mother asked me to meet another man she had picked out for me. He was quite nice and even owned a business. Even though Mother didn't know it, I was already committed to Heng Yeo at the time, so I refused him. I've heard that he's since gotten married and his business is doing quite well. They say he has two sons, just like me." She was pleased that Heng Yeo helped with the housework and child care. "He prepares breakfast for himself, and boils water for our morn-ing Ovaltine. On weekends when he has time, he does some of the cleaning. When our kids were young, he occasionally got up with them at night."

The Loys paid a visit to Heng Yeo's mother each Sunday, but otherwise they seldom went visiting or shared entertainment together. They had gone to the movies only once in the year and a half since the birth of their second child. Mei Po socialized with her neighbors and played mah-jongg with them regularly, but Heng Yeo claimed he had nothing in common with the neigh-bors. The couple elected to live near Mei Po's mother and visited her frequently with the children. Mei Po told us that although Heng Yeo was emotionally close to his mother and she herself had a cordial relationship with the woman, his mother appeared to favor her other sons, the offspring of her second husband.

Mei Po was resigned to her way of life. "I had more freedom before the children came along. Then my husband and I often went to the movies, but now we very seldom go anywhere. It's just too much trouble to carry all those bottles, diapers, and baby supplies around. Sometimes my children are very good, but occasionally they can be very naughty. I guess this is just how life is after you have children."

I learned in the course of our conversations that Mei Po discussed some of her personal problems with Heng Yeo before she mentioned them to her mother. She had sought medical treatment when she failed to become pregnant during the first two years of her marriage, and her physician had advised dilatation and curettage (D and C), a procedure that enlarges the cervix as the uterus is scraped to remove diseased tissues. After discussing his advice with her husband, Mei Po decided to go ahead. After six more months of infertility, the physician performed a second D and C. The couple then conceived their first son. Only then did Mei Po tell her mother what she had done. After two sons were born, Mei Po longed for a daughter, and they considered adopting one, but at the time of my interviews they had neither adopted nor conceived a third child.

A sore point that limited their full communication was Heng Yeo's habit of visiting his mother every evening. "My husband is a good-natured man. We seldom quarrel. Still, I can't help scolding him when he repeatedly comes home late at night from his mother's house. I reasoned with him that it's not necessary to see his mother every night, but he keeps on going there. I found that these quarrels are useless, because he becomes silent. How can I keep on scolding him when he doesn't fight back? So Mother has advised me to stop nagging him."

Before they moved into their present flat, the Loys had had another tiny dwelling of their own. Heng Yeo's parents lived with their younger sons and had no room to shelter the Loys. One of my standard questions to women who did not live with their kin was "Would you like to live together with your mother-in-law?" Mei Po answered frankly, "I don't think I'd like that! We get along, and I visit there once a week with the children, but that's enough."

The Loys lived in poverty in a one-room flat in Toa Payoh, one of the new Singapore housing developments with 17,500 units. Their monthly bill for rent and utilities was S$30. Their appliances included an old refrigerator and their small portable TV. They acquired their other furniture as gifts as well. Their sofa and chairs were produced in Mei Po's father's furniture workshop. An electric clock was a gift from her mother; their electric fan and rice cooker were gifts from her sisters. One of their storage cupboards was handed down to them by her sister. It contained some toys for the children, which were gifts of the two sets of grandparents. One wall of their neat and sparsely furnished apartment contained a large map of China. The second storage cupboard was filled with books on Chinese culture and history. The Loys' collection of publications devoted to Chinese culture was somewhat unusual; the cupboards in most other homes I visited held bric-a-brac and other common household items.

Mei Po felt that this dwelling was adequate for the raising of her two children, and she prized the nearness to her mother's residence. Heng Yeo, however, wanted to buy a larger flat elsewhere. This hope, like his ambition for the postsecondary education of his sons, was not supported by the family income.

Owing to their stress on Chinese culture, the Loys planned to send their sons to Mandarin-language primary schools. Heng Yeo explained, "Chinese is our mother language, and it is also very difficult. The younger you learn it, the better. When they reach secondary level, they must then learn English to get a good job. If they continue in Mandarin-language school, we will hire private tutors for them. However, we may decide to send them to English-language secondary school. Of course, we hope they will go on to university and will have the chance to study abroad. I must admit that it won't be easy to pay for this training. But if the boys are clever and hard-working enough, I hope they'll win scholarships. I learned from some of my middle school classmates that many students in the United States support themselves with summer jobs."

Heng Yeo spoke of the employment prospects for his sons. "Singapore is a crowded place. It would be good if my children could get training in engineering or in some other profession, so that they could always find a job." He expected his sons to live with him after he retired from the stationery trade. Despite Mei Po's views on living with her own mother-in-law, he did not expect generational differences between his wife and his sons' future wives to impede this ambition. "It is good for grown-up children to bring their wives to live in the homes of their parents. Their wives can rely on Mother-in-Law for help with child care and household duties, and they can even go out for entertainment with their husbands once in a while." I took his comments to imply that he wished that Mei Po's responsibilities could be eased by help from the older generation.

They had hoped that their second child would be a girl. During a hospital visit in her second pregnancy, the nursing staff asked Mei Po to sign a form authorizing her gynecologist to perform a postpartum tubal ligation to sterilize her. Such requests were a key part of the government's family-limitation policies. Mei Po was in sympathy with those policies, but she did want a daughter. Therefore she agreed to undergo sterilization provided her baby was a girl. Heng Yeo also signed with this proviso. Eighteen months after her second son was born, she said, "We're going to practice contraception until our toddler is about five years old. Then we'll try again for a girl." The interviewer asked, "If you got pregnant in the meantime, what do you think you would do?" "I suppose I might have an abortion. If only I could know whether I was carrying a girl," she replied. The interviewer, suspecting that Mei Po might carry a pregnancy to term in the hope of getting her girl, pressed her further: "Is it possible a third child would be a burden on your family resources?" Mei Po's reply reflected some common gender stereotypes. "I think it will be easier to raise a girl baby because girls are usually not as naughty as boys. My first son was a difficult infant and it was a lot of trouble raising him. But now with the hundred-dollar raise in my husband's salary, I think we're in a position to support a third child of either sex. Besides, Brother-in-Law always gives us a bonus when I have a baby." Extrapolating income and prices, she optimistically concluded that she could meet all costs of another baby.

Heng Yeo disagreed. "Mei Po is still hoping for a daughter, but I don't think we can afford it. If we have a third baby, there will be less for the first two."

Their approach to the population disincentives was shaped by Mei Po's wish for a daughter. She said that people reduced their family size because of income pressures. "The disincentive measures are good because Singapore is very crowded, and people will find it hard to get jobs if the population keeps rising. But it's a pity that some parents will be denied the chance to have at least one son and one daughter."

The Loys' limited use of social services was consistent with the short-range planning horizon imposed by their low income and restricted prospects of job advancement. Heng Yeo derived considerable satisfaction from fulfilling meaningful if prosaic responsibilities in his brother-in-law's firm. While Heng Yeo entertained optimistic educational and employment goals for his sons, it appeared to me that he might comfortably accept somewhat lower and more realistic levels of achievement for his boys.

Tan Family: Tinsmith and Domestic Servant (I)

Tan Poh Wah worked as a tinsmith in a small peripheral-sector firm owned by Singapore-Chinese capitalists. This Hokkien worker, aged thirty-two in mid-1975, had acquired his skills as a smith in an informal apprenticeship. As he lacked formal educational qualifications, his wages and job prospects were limited. Poh Wah's father, a truck driver, had deserted his wife and three children when Poh Wah was a small boy and gone to live with another woman. The family saw little of him after that. Poh Wah attributed his lack of education and job prospects to this early breakup of the family. "My father walked out on us when I was just five years old. My elder sisters both had to go to work before they were twelve to support the family. I got only a few years of school before I also had to quit to go to work. Mother hated Father for leaving us, but she worked like a dog to bring us up. When I married

Giok Bee, Father attended the wedding banquet, but apart from that, we don't keep in touch. I blame Father for giving me a hard life, but I can't change the history of another generation. After my broken childhood, I know the value of solid family life, and I would certainly never repeat his mistakes. My children are lucky, they can enjoy life."

He got a succession of jobs through friends and workmates. Only one of his jobs paid well. "After I left school I took a job at piecework wages in a factory that made tin cans. In my neighborhood many of the fellows were entering this kind of work. Our rates were low, and frequently there was no metal to cut. I married Giok Bee in 1963. She worked as an amah in the home of a British family. Her employer was on the staff of the British army base at Ayer Rajah Road. He recommended me for a position as a general worker. I was given the task of repairing small metal ships. I looked forward to promotion, but just two years later they let me go when the British withdrew some of their troops. In 1969 I was back as a tinsmith in another small Chinese company. Now I am again receiving piecework wages to cut out and fit together tin kettles. Sometimes I have to wait until the materials arrive, and I am forced to sit idly. No overtime is ever paid on a piecework job like this. I can seldom earn more than two hundred fifty a month."

The interviewer asked, "Have you tried to find a better job?" "I'm used to this work. Anyway, since I can't speak English, I doubt if I can do any better. You see, all Chinese firms offer about the same general conditions to their workers." The interviewer mentioned a large firm: "What about Metal Box?" Poh Wah shook his head. "Metal Box just installed lots of labor-saving machinery, and I don't think they need people like me anymore." In fact, he feared that his present firm would be forced off the market by mechanized competitors.

Giok Bee was thirty-two years old and also a Hokkien speaker. Her father, a salesman, had died in 1965; her mother was a domestic servant. They had had eight children. After I had gotten to know her, Giok Bee revealed that her mother was Father's legitimate wife, but he had had two other women, the third of whom had had five children. Giok Bee had received only four years of primary schooling, then quit to care for her five younger siblings. When she was seventeen she entered domestic service, like Mother and her older sister. She found employment first with British families and then in Japanese homes. Her basic wage in mid-1975 was S$180 a month. She learned English and some Japanese at work. When her three daughters were born, she left temporarily to care for them. After the first birth she tried another line of work. Giok Bee spent a year making joss sticks in an incense factory, but found that she could not fit factory hours into her demanding regime of household tasks. The Tans' first daughter was subject to epileptic seizures, and the care of this child imposed an added burden on her. "I prefer to work as an amah because I don't have to keep strict hours on this job. Sometimes I can go home early or choose my own day off, when I have to take my daughter to the hospital on a working day. I cook lunch for my mistress and do most of the housework. Usually by two-thirty I'm finished and I'm free to leave. Actually, I could work even faster and leave a little earlier, but I don't want my employers' neighbors to gossip that I'm taking advantage by leaving early."

Each expatriate family for whom Giok Bee worked introduced her to another employer when they left the republic. At the time of our early interviews with her, her current mistress, from Tokyo, was pregnant. Giok Bee said, "With children of course there is more work for me to do, and I may have to look after the infant when it arrives. I dare not ask now what raise I'll get after the baby's born, but I'll do so nearer the time. The Japanese people are all right. Recently I went shopping with my mistress to help her carry home her parcels. In one of the stores I admired a six-dollar bathing cap and thought that it would suit my daughter very well. So my mistress bought it for me on the spot." During later interviews, Giok Bee told me more about her work. "My mistress increased my wages twenty dollars a month after the baby was born, but I have to work at least an hour a day longer. Actually, taking a job is like braving the wind and the rain [a saying for enduring hardship]. Ideally, I should stay home to care for my three children. But I have to work to pay the grocery bills. Even if my husband earned more money, I'd still work. I'm used to being an amah, and it's probably less demanding than some other jobs. Now that I think about it, I suppose that when my children are grown up and have left home, I'll keep on working. We'll need money to retire on."

Giok Bee was barely literate and was unable to read newspapers. Owing to her lack of education and contacts on the job, she was virtually isolated from events around her. "I don't talk with the neighbors or the other amahs in my mistress's apartment house. Employers don't like their amahs to get into long conversations." I discussed family finances with Giok Bee. "Our budget is very tight," she said. "My husband is thrifty. He only spends one or two dollars a day on his personal needs. So he gives me between one and two hundred each month to manage on. He increases this amount if he happens to earn more that month. We both put cash in a drawer and take it out for household expenses. It's a matter of I trust him and he trusts me." The Tans spent S\$100 a month on housing and utilities; food expenses amounted to S\$200 a month. Their incidental expenses included as much as S\$6 a week for sweets for their two school-age daughters and S\$3 for trishaws to take them to school. In exchange for her assistance with child care, Giok Bee gave Mother-in-Law S\$20 a month. Poh Wah also helped his mother with occasional cash gifts.

Poh Wah and Giok Bee had lived in the same apartment building as children. They became friends when they were fifteen years old and married five years later. Giok Bee then moved into the two-room fourth-floor HDB flat rented by Poh Wah's mother. Mother-in-Law was aging, but she managed to help Giok Bee with the housework. Giok Bee laundered and marketed every morning before leaving for work and cleaned the flat thoroughly each weekend. She and Mother-in-Law alternated at cooking supper.

Middle Daughter attended a neighborhood primary school during the morning session, and the youngest and eldest girls attended school in the afternoon. Mother-in-Law cooked and served lunch to the three children. After returning home from work each afternoon, Giok Bee walked to the school to fetch her daughters. She imposed strict discipline on them. "I never let the girls play outside the apartment because they might be influenced by rough children. I won't send them on errands, either, even if it means I have to make an extra shopping trip. I'm the one who disciplines them. My husband is often absent at work or with his friends. I sometimes use a cane [a rattan switch about eighteen inches long] to punish them. They don't take it seriously enough. Middle Daughter often takes the canes out and throws them away!" She chuckled. Though Poh Wah left the disciplining to her, he took the girls on walks on the weekends.

Mother was her closest companion. She received much advice and practical assistance from this woman. "Sunday is the day when I join all my brothers and sisters at Mother's place. We have a grand time there." She was barely acquainted with her husband's friends, however. "My husband and I seldom go out visiting as a couple, not even for Chinese New Year's festivities. His friends usually meet without their wives, who are home with their children. Since Poh Wah and I don't socialize together, he goes to ceremonial affairs like dinners without me, especially when they are given by workmates and their families."

It was largely poverty, it developed, that limited the Tans' joint social life. "When an invitation comes to us from my husband's friends," she explained, "I don't accept and he may go alone. If I went we'd have to put eight or twelve dollars more in the *ang pow* [red envelope for a gift of money]. For that money, I can buy a lot of food to cook at home. Poh Wah goes to the movies with these same friends of his. Besides the fact that I don't know these people very well, it would be costly for me to buy a ticket. He and I go to the movies with the girls only once or twice a year. Fortunately, there are good programs on the TV for us to watch. He rarely comes shopping with me. The last occasion I can remember was the time we bought our bridal suite. It was important for us to pick out the bed and chest of drawers together. But my husband went with his sister to buy our television set so he could choose a model just like hers."

Most of the couple's remaining household furnishings were obtained through family exchanges. "Recently Mother gave us this red vinyl couch and matching chairs. She had just bought her own new settee. It cost her

[61]

over a thousand dollars. So we gave our old sofa to my husband's sister." I sensed that Giok Bee was willing to discuss her financial situation further, and I asked her, "How do you manage when you're short of funds?" She replied, "I borrow from my mother left and right. She and four other people in her household are working, and I can always count on her help."

Although Giok Bee preferred family life at home, she and Poh Wah had little to discuss. "We just talk about how to handle the children when they are naughty. We have to discuss our choice of TV programs. Then we might just sit and watch the TV without talking at all." The Tans rarely discussed such troublesome matters as Eldest Daughter's epilepsy, the low school grades of First and Third Daughters, and their financial straits. Giok Bee told us about her marital quarrels. "Sometimes Poh Wah stays out and drinks with his friends after work. I scold him because he comes home so late and talks nonsense. Naturally, he apologizes because he's in the wrong and we make up. He is a neat person, and he criticizes me when I don't clean the house as well as he expects. He probably thinks I'm lazy, but he never lifts a finger to help. Frequently I worry because there's no more cash in the money drawer, and I complain to him about this. Somehow we manage to get through the month and our quarrel ends."

The Tans seemed to resolve their financial problems without much acrimony even though Poh Wah earned less than the male median wage, perhaps because Giok Bee's independent source of income and the occasional assistance of her family helped keep them solvent. I asked her how she got along with her mother-in-law, and she told me, "I've ironed out most of the conflicts a woman usually has with her mother-in-law during the twelve years we've been living here. True enough, we argued a lot in the beginning, before I got used to her, but now it's ok. I'm more tolerant now, and also we've settled down with our three children and have accommodated our differences." The adjustment had clearly been Giok Bee's.

The Tans thought their flat was too small and too close to the neighboring apartments. They were uncomfortable with the noise, disorder, odors, and insufficient natural light in these crowded quarters. Giok Bee told me in 1975 that some years earlier the couple had considered getting a three-room, better-appointed flat, one that was also within walking distance of her mother's home and close to the children's schools. But even after several years they were still unable to file an application to buy such an apartment because they could not save or borrow the S$100 cash deposit. Moreover, their combined Central Provident Fund savings account totaled only S$4,000, less than one-third of the cost of a three-room flat. Afraid to use up their nest egg, they abandoned the hope of buying a flat and instead petitioned the HDB to rent the three-room apartment they wanted. They were distraught when the HDB rejected their application. Intensifying their efforts, they persuaded their family doctor to write a supporting letter explaining that

Poh Wah's mother was too frail to walk up the four floors of stairs to the Tans' apartment. In fact, the woman had a terminal illness. They obtained another letter of support from their member of Parliament, of the ruling People's Action Party, who asked that new quarters be granted quickly, on compassionate grounds. These efforts brought results, but not the ones they wanted: the board offered the Tans an apartment in Telok Blangah, two kilometers from their present home. Although this flat would have been more suitable for Poh Wah's mother, its location was extremely inconvenient for the rest of them, and they declined the offer. They were still trying to obtain an apartment that met all of their requirements.

The two older girls attended an English-language primary school. The Tans chose English education to improve the girls' chances for well-paying employment. Giok Bee pointed out, "English is used in all government departments. I will send all my daughters as high as they can go, even the university. But if one of the children fails the exam to the next grade and has to drop out of school, then she should go to work and then get married." Her appraisal of the job market for her daughters was clearly limited. "I think that dressmaking would be a fine occupation for my daughters. The teacher writes lots of red marks on the test papers that Eldest Daughter brings home from school. Since she makes so many mistakes, we paid ten dollars a month to hire a tutor for her. The tutor coached my daughter three times a week for two months, and her schoolwork did improve. Unfortunately, this tutor had to quit and I couldn't find a replacement for less than thirty a month. So I don't bother, and she has to manage on her own. I'm afraid my daughter will not advance much beyond the fifth grade." Her ambitions to advance her daughters' education were frustrated by poverty.

Giok Bee knew that girls could help the family out when they were older, as she had done. But she was partially swayed by the view that only a son could carry forward the family line. When her third child was born, she recalled sadly, "I cried my heart out at the hospital because I didn't get a boy. My husband comforted me and said that he didn't mind having a third daughter. At first I considered undergoing a sterilization operation. But I decided not to, for two reasons. First, I heard a woman needed to take a long convalescence after a sterilization operation. Second, my mother-in-law wanted us to have a son. In fact, she went to see a fortune-teller and was told I would have four daughters before bearing a son. This is what happened to my own mother. Poh Wah agreed with his mother. For the last three years I've been taking the pill."

The Tans could not afford to feed another mouth. Moreover, Mother-in-Law's serious illness prevented her from assisting with the upbringing of another infant. Giok Bee earned too little to pay an outsider for help with a fourth child, and she could not stop working herself. Apart from these economic motivations, she was uncomfortable with the prospect of being housebound with an infant. She thus had to postpone her fourth pregnancy. Later in 1975, the couple's ambivalence about a new baby had deepened. Giok Bee said, "No, I don't want to try for a son because everything costs money. I suppose it doesn't matter after all whether we ever have a boy. People certainly have boys hoping that these sons will make offerings to them after they die, but with me it's different. I don't care once I close my eyes!" Poh Wah added, "Naturally we would like a son. But in our current economic situation, three is enough."

I sought the couple's views on the Singapore disincentive program. Giok Bee said, "I know that the government wants people to stop at two children. In my opinion, one or two children, if they are good, is enough to carry on the generation. There's no point in having more children than you can care for, otherwise the young ones will run wild. In my opinion, we ourselves should know how many children we can feed and bring up properly." Poh Wah remarked, "I think it's a good idea for the government to discourage people from having three children. But I know other people may disagree." He was aware of the official formulation of the population policy. "Singapore is a small island with just over two million people, and we depend on import and export trade, but we have no raw material of our own except our labor force. It's true that foreign companies invest in Singapore, but after they make money here, they send their profits home." Though he understood that Singapore remained a poor country and needed to limit its population, his personal feelings were ambivalent. "For me the ideal family size is four children. Couples should be allowed to have four children. Then the government can encourage them to be sterilized. Families who want to have more children won't heed the government policies. But with today's high inflation, parents also don't want to have too many children. Most of my friends have two or three children only."

Hemmed in by their low wages and lack of training, the Tans felt their economic situation was quite circumscribed. The Tan family's hopes for future betterment were slender.

Lim Family: Shipyard Worker and Homemaker (I)

Singapore is separated from Malaysia by the kilometer-wide Johore Strait. Near this border lies Sembawang, a farming and fishing village, where Lim Joo Koon was born and brought up. Sembawang was originally constructed to serve a British naval base, and Joo Koon, who was thirty-five in 1975, was employed in the Sembawang shipyard as an unskilled maintenance man and general dockworker. He and his wife, twenty-nine-year-old Peck Hoon, lived in Sembawang with their four girls, aged two, three, four, and six, and a newly adopted infant son. Joo Koon told of his upbringing as the youngest of four sons. "My parents were poor villagers. In order to survive the hardships of the wartime Japanese occupation, my parents had to go into bootleg operations. My father became an opium trafficker and my mother sold wine illegally. Father died in 1943, when I was only three years old, and I had to fend for myself from an early age. Mother sent the four of us boys to school but no one finished the primary level. I was lazy and skipped school. Poverty doesn't scare me now. When I was a teenager I wasn't making much money, but somehow I managed to scrape by. Poor and uneducated men make it to the top in the shipyard. If I get a lucky break, I might also succeed."

Eldest brother was a foreman at the Sembawang shipyard, Second Brother was a laborer at the Sembawang naval base, and Third Brother was a construction laborer. Joo Koon learned the rudiments of electrical wiring as a helper at the naval base but was never formally apprenticed in a trade. He was hired as an electrician with the Ministry of Defence for nearly a decade, but was eventually laid off. Around 1971 he began a succession of subcontracting jobs at the shipyard. His tasks included general repair work, painting, and maintenance on ships. He was paid by the job and earned a basic rate equivalent to S$250 monthly. His work gang earned bonuses for their considerable exertions in completing the job on time or ahead of schedule. These emoluments could total 50 percent of the flat rate. In this way he was able to buy and maintain a motor bike, which he drove on weekend pleasure jaunts with a group of workmates to Johore Bahru, just across the Malaysian border. He was a carefree person who took each day as it came. Indeed, his shipyard work routine contained no incentives for planning.

Peck Hoon was the third of thirteen children. Her father was a road sweeper, and her mother cultivated a vegetable plot for family consumption. She dropped out of school after four years because of poverty. Then she helped raise her younger siblings until she was seventeen, when she went to work as a domestic servant. Her employers were British families stationed with the British navy. She was paid S$150 monthly for cooking and general housework. "I learned to cook European meals for them, but I wouldn't serve it in my home. It's tasteless. It's like eating pig food!" She gave her mother S$50 from her wage each month until she married. "I enjoyed working life, because I could save and buy things. I bought the refrigerator and the rice cooker. My husband shared the costs of other purchases with me. Money wasn't the only reason for working. Life gets monotonous here at home and it's easier to pass the day if you have a job. However, my husband asked me to leave my job when our first daughter was born. If I became an amah, or even a factory worker, I couldn't earn enough to hire someone to take care of my family. It's true that my mother-in-law comes over almost every day to help with the laundry. But she doesn't love children and only

[65]

knows how to beat them. I wouldn't feel happy leaving my kids in her care. Maybe when my son is eleven or twelve, then I'll consider going back to work."

The Lims courted for two years after they were introduced by mutual friends. They married when she was twenty-three. She said, "It's better for a couple to marry even earlier. Then their children can support them for a longer period later."

They rented a kitchen and a bedroom in a small wooden building on a narrow lane in Sembawang, at a cost of S$56 with utilities. They shared water and toilet facilities with neighbors. They carried cold water in buckets from the spigot in the washroom into their quarters. Their two-room flat was filled with baskets and utensils, some of which hung from hooks in the ceiling. The kitchen space was taken up by a gas burner, a refrigerator, a small dining table, a storage cupboard, and a shelf with a small TV perched on it. The bedroom was just as crowded with a double bed and double-decker bunk bed, the top bunk of which was used for storage. The three eldest daughters shared Joo Koon and Peck Hoon's bed. Fourth Daughter and the adopted son slept in hammocks suspended from the ceiling. Peck Hoon observed, "If you think this flat is tight, our first apartment was even smaller! We only had one room for our growing family."

In 1973 Joo Koon paid S$100 of his bonus to the Housing and Development Board for a three-room flat that was under construction some distance away, in Ang Mo Kio. While Peck Hoon was anxious to relocate to more comfortable quarters, he was in no rush to move. He spent little time at home and did not experience domestic discomfort as intensely as his wife. His income was clearly insufficient to meet the payments on the new apartment. In any case, he was not eager to move to a new neighborhood. "My husband likes this place," Peck Hoon said, "and thinks we can put up with the cramped quarters."

Joo Koon's mother did most of the marketing for the Lim household. She walked from her home to a nearby market, bought a day's supply of produce, and continued the short journey on foot to the Lims' home. "I leave the choice of vegetables and other staples to Mother-in-Law. I just cook what she brings us. Then she stays most of the day to help mind the children and do some of the housework," Peck Hoon said. Mother-in-Law's marketing provided the family's lunch and supper; for breakfast Peck Hoon bought steamed buns (*pao*) and hot coffee at a nearby hawker's stall. Her husband ate at seven o'clock and then left for work. While the children still slept, Peck Hoon began her laundry in a basin at the common household spigot. She returned to her household when the children awoke and supervised their breakfast at eight. When Mother-in-Law arrived with the groceries, she returned to the laundry area to wash another batch of clothes. She scrubbed clothes for the third and last time after the children retired at night.

Her neighbors sometimes watched her youngest children while she prepared lunch between nine-thirty and ten. She served the five children
around eleven. After washing the dishes and cleaning the kitchen, she
bathed the children and put them down for a nap. While the house was
quiet, she enjoyed her first hour of free time. She then assembled dinner
from Mother-in-Law's shopping basket, and served it at five. Joo Koon was
seldom home for this meal. "My husband frequently works overtime. He
also stays out until the children are nearly ready for bed. By that time the
children are impatient for him and create a racket. This irritates him, but he
doesn't show his annoyance. He should discipline them more. Actually, he
spoils them and lets them sit on his head [take advantage of him]."

She was deeply fond of her children and enjoyed talking and sharing jokes
with them at all times. She was lenient and patient with their misbehavior.
When a daughter broke a small porcelain cup, she shrugged and picked up
the pieces. "Well, that girl has broken three cups already this year. There's
no point in beating her. One of my sisters-in-law always beats her children,
but what good does it do? The cup won't mend." On some afternoons, Peck
Hoon taught Chinese characters to the older girls. "I don't believe in forcing
them to learn anything, but I'm glad when they ask me to teach them."

She was interested in and communicative about the education of her
children. Like most of the poor mothers in my sample, she was influenced
by her friends' accounts of the educational system and lacked the means or
motivation to form independent critical judgments. I noted in her views on
formal education the same permissiveness I observed in her handling of her
children. Peck Hoon had enrolled Eldest Daughter at a neighborhood English-language school for the following semester. "Since most of the kids
around here attend that English school already, my daughter asked to join
them, and I agreed. I'll let the other children go to school with their playmates, too. The other evening we were watching a ballet program on TV
after dinner, and Eldest Daughter asked if she could have ballet lessons.
When my daughter made that request, I was keen on the idea. I've heard of
a well-off woman who lives nearby sending one of her daughters to ballet
lessons downtown on Orchard Road. She pays thirty dollars a month. But
maybe it's just wishful thinking. I haven't yet done anything to enroll her in
ballet classes." Throughout my discussions with Peck Hoon, she punctuated
her statements of fact and personal observation with references to actions
and views of her neighbors.

During one visit to the Lims' residence, Peck Hoon was preparing food as
part of local religious rites. In the courtyard she was plucking a chicken and a
duck whose necks she had just cut and whose blood was drained into con-

[67]

tainers. She would then clean and steam these fowl and offer them at an altar to deities before serving them at a family dinner. Alongside Peck Hoon, Mother-in-Law was hanging washing on the line to dry. A neighbor was holding Younger Daughter and conversing with the pair. When she had completed her cleaning tasks, Peck Hoon washed in a bucket of water, took Younger Daughter from the neighbor, and carried her into the kitchen. There she held her on her lap while we continued our conversation. "It's such a job plucking the feathers from those birds!" she exclaimed.

"Do you prefer life before marriage or after?" she was asked. She retorted, "How can I know? If you had asked me when I was single, I'd say it's better to be married, but now I feel the opposite. I'm married and it's better to be single!" They seldom socialized as a couple outside the home. Joo Koon fraternized with his workmates regularly in the evenings and on the weekends. He attended any celebratory banquets to which they were invited by himself. Peck Hoon shrugged. "Those dinners are very boring. They're always the same!" Joo Koon took responsibility for major household purchases; Peck Hoon bought all the other articles needed in the home without him. "I don't like shopping with Joo Koon. We always end up quarreling. So I buy all the children's clothes alone or with my girlfriends. Family shopping is a pleasant custom for me at New Year's time, and Joo Koon isn't really interested in those trips. He just rushes through, so I just leave him out of those excursions."

The couple never discussed the employment conditions at Joo Koon's place of work or his wages. "I don't talk much with my husband," Peck Hoon said. She knew little about his friends and the places he went on afternoons and weekends.

When the interviewer entered for her last visit, Peck Hoon was in the washroom scrubbing her laundry. A neighbor was holding the youngest Lim daughter; the infant was asleep. The neighbor had just permed Peck Hoon's hair for S$2.50 plus the cost of the lotion. After Peck Hoon finished her laundry, she and her visitor sat in the kitchen. While she held her youngest daughter and the others played nearby, she discussed family size and childbearing.

The Lims had adopted their boy at the urging of his parents, who were friends of Joo Koon. The Lims had given the parents S$500; they expected the legal transfer to cost S$1,000 more.[3] Peck Hoon spoke of the adoption as a gesture of reciprocity common in their kampung, but it was clear that they sorely wished a son. "His mother is only twenty-one, but his father is forty-six. She was raped and had no choice but to marry a widower with several kids. When this man begged my husband to take the boy, he agreed. Joo Koon is softhearted and can't bear to see other families suffer. I don't really want to raise him, but I'm doing it for Joo Koon. If he prefers to acknowledge his real parents when he grows up, I'll accept his decision." Despite her reservations about the added responsibility, Peck Hoon did not see the infant as making any great change in her daily routine. The Lims did not plan to change their way of life much in the future.

They still wished for a son of their own, however, and intended to try again. Peck Hoon explained, "If only I had a son and a daughter, I'd have been sterilized long ago. Now, after five children, all the noise and problems they make have become a habit with me. If I wait too long before my next birth, I may lose this habit and starting again would be a headache. But I'll wait until he's a little bigger before trying again. If the next one isn't a boy, there's nothing to be done." Peck Hoon said she had considered a tubal ligation after the birth of Younger Daughter, "but I didn't dare go ahead with it because I was afraid Mother-in-Law would scold me. You see, several years ago, First Sister-in-Law [the wife of Joo Koon's older brother] was sterilized after her third birth, and Mother-in-Law really criticized her, and that scared me." But she gave the impression that she was not convinced that she should do it herself. "I know a silly girl whose tubes were tied after her first child. Now she regrets it. She can't even lay an egg, let alone have another baby. How stupid can people be? Even Ah Kim [one of my respondents and an acquaintance of hers, who was sterilized after bearing four daughters and a son], I hear, regretted doing it. I heard she may want to adopt a child too! What happens if you have no sons? You know Chinese people don't like that. Best, of course, is to have two sons and two daughters. It is very reasonable to expect that people should give adequate food and shelter to their children, but then if you have no sons, it can't be helped. You have to try. My husband loves the children. Boy or girl, it's all the same to him. But next time we'll try for a son, so he can have someone to carry on the surname." Peck Hoon gave the impression that a fifth birth would be her last. While she intended to have another child, she did not value sexual relations for their own sake. "I didn't mind sex at first, but not after so many children. I'm tired of it. I'm not afraid of getting pregnant. We're taking precautions now—Joo Koon uses condoms. My husband knows I don't enjoy sex, but we never discuss it."

The interviewer was a young married woman. During their discussion about childbirth and motherhood and the population policies, Peck Hoon advised her to try for her first child right away. "The pill is no good and I don't believe in it. One of my neighbors took the pill for several years. She stopped and hoped for a baby, but she hasn't had one yet. I wonder if she'll always be childless. Pills also make a woman as fat as a pig. The IUD is no good, either. Another neighbor used one and it came out and she got pregnant. Imagine, her youngest child is in his teens, and the mother is having another baby! The condom is the best. It works!"

Peck Hoon was only vaguely aware of the population disincentives. Joo Koon paid without complaint what the couple called "the fines" (higher accouchement fees), rising to S$180 for the fourth birth. Peck Hoon was indifferent to the antinatalist arguments of the government nurses. "The government wants people to stop after two children. The TV is always saying this, but who wants to listen? Even after Fourth Daughter was born, the doctor didn't ask me to have my tubes tied. He was understanding. But the nurses always pester people. They didn't bother me, but they tried to persuade other women I know, even those with just two children. Some of these nurses have four children themselves. Have they decided to have their tubes tied? They talk a lot! Every family wants to give birth to one son. Look at the member of Parliament for this district. He has four children, and the youngest is a boy about the same age as my third child." She continued her argument against the contradictions that in her eyes vitiated the official population limitation policy. "The government probably wants family planning to avoid building too many more HDB apartment houses, but although people say the waiting list for HDB homes is long, I see by the classified ads that lots of HDB apartment owners are advertising their flats for sale." With such arguments she bolstered her plan to have another child.

Lack of education and Joo Koon's low pay and unskilled position provided limited opportunities for the Lims to look beyond their daily needs. Only overtime pay and occasional bonuses enabled the Lims to pay their bills. The down payment on an HDB flat was their only financial investment in the future. Peck Hoon drew considerable enjoyment from interacting with her five children, and the couple seemed intent on adding a son to the burden. They depended closely on relatives and neighbors, who were themselves faced with the dilemmas of poverty.

Cheong Family: Shipfitter and Electronics Factory Worker (I)

Thirty-six-year old Cheong Tan To, tall and dark, of serious demeanor, was employed as a shipfitter in 1974. A Cantonese speaker, he was married to a Teochew speaker, Soo Hiang, aged twenty-six. Plump, talkative, and jovial, she worked on the assembly line of an electronics factory. The couple had a six-year-old boy and a two-year-old daughter. Tan To was the eldest of six children; his father worked variously as a rubber tapper and pig wholesaler in Malaysia and as a carpenter and newspaper vendor in Singapore. Tan To was raised by his grandmother in Malaysia, then helped Father vend newspapers in Singapore after he finished primary school. Later he was apprenticed as a shipfitter, and by 1970 had gained employment in the trade at the Far East Levington Shipyard. In 1974 the firm's order book had shrunk, and Tan To had been laid off. He had been proud of his work performance at the shipyard, but he declined the offer of a promotion in order to remain alongside his mates in the rank and file.

Tan To was able to get a job repairing ships at another yard for S$15 a day (for an average basic wage of S$420 a month). On some days he was able to increase his pay to S$20 by overtime work. On other days, though, he stayed away from work altogether. On one of my afternoon visits to the Cheongs, I encountered Tan To. "Today I overslept and I decided to stay home. There was no time to catch the launch for Pulau Bukum, where my job is. The contractor gets mad at men who show up late."

"So you'd rather not to go work at all?"

"Yes, that's right," he replied.

Tan To had recently suffered a serious accident at the workplace. Ever since, he had considered his job unlucky. "My mate and I were standing on a wooden platform, and it fell through. My jaw was broken, and I received only partial compensation. When the doctor certified me unfit for work, I was paid ten dollars a day. I'd rather set up my own business, because ship repair work is very dangerous. Besides, I'll never be able to continue as a fitter after I'm forty-five."

He occasionally gambled after work until nearly midnight. "Why should I save, when we don't know what's going to happen tomorrow?" Tan To contributed only S$30 weekly to the household budget. Expenses were met mainly through Soo Hiang's earnings.

Soo Hiang was the eldest of eleven children. Her mother worked in a laundry while she was growing up, and Soo Hiang had to watch her brothers and sisters after school. When Mother fell sick, Soo Hiang had to take her place at the washbasin. She also ironed to earn extra income. Thus her school marks suffered, and she left school after junior high to help Mother full-time at home. Soo Hiang's driving force helped keep the family together.

In 1974, none of Soo Hiang's younger siblings had a job. A brother two years her junior had been a house painter but was now incapacitated as a result of a fall from a scaffold several years earlier. Second Sister, twenty-two in 1974, had worked for two years in an electronics factory and returned to home when her plant was closed. Second Brother had just completed his two-year compulsory national service in 1974. Seven youngsters were still in school. The youngest was a four-year-old boy, born the year before Soo Hiang had her first child. Soo Hiang's mother had worked until 1973 as an ironer in a laundry, then managed to obtain a license to sell food at a stall in a military base. Father, who played a lesser role in the home, was a night watchman in a warehouse. He earned S$300 a month, most of which, according to Second Sister, "he drinks and gambles away." Mother was the mainstay of the family economy, and Soo Hiang became her prime source of support.

At eighteen Soo Hiang married Tan To and took her first full-time job, alongside Mother at the laundry. After Soo Hiang's second child was born, she went to work at Hewlett-Packard, near her home. She was assigned to the assembly line in the transformer section at a daily wage of S$10.

Soo Hiang acquired skills rapidly, and often helped newcomers with their tasks on her own initiative. She told us proudly that the management considered her a conscientious operative. At the time of the interviews, she was being considered for promotion to a leadership post. A downturn in the electronics market in the early 1970s led a number of multinational firms to lay off workers in Singapore. In 1973, Soo Hiang and Mother jointly applied for an additional hawker's permit. When the permit was granted, in December 1974, Soo Hiang was better able to plan against the contingency of mass layoffs at Hewlett-Packard. She at once withdrew S$1,000 from her bank account and her tontine funds (a revolving chit fund) and bought the equipment and furnishings for a small hawker stall, which she established in the large market near her home. She sold *mee* (fried noodles) and *laksa* (a spicy noodle stew). She learned the recipes for these dishes from Mother, who was already offering them to her customers at the army base. Mother lent two of her sons as helpers.

Although Hewlett-Packard managed to remain solvent, Soo Hiang persisted at her soup kitchen. She awoke at 5:00 A.M. to fry coconut with peppers and pungent spices as a base for the laksa. Soo Hiang's brothers left their flat before dawn to set up the stall and remained to help her serve a steady stream of customers until midday, while her father and Second Sister cared for her two children in their home. Soo Hiang arrived at the stall around 6:00 A.M. to cook the laksa in a large *guo* (Chinese frying pan) on a small burner fueled by bottled gas. She managed the stall until after lunch and then returned to Mother's to rest before her afternoon shift at three. At the end of the day the two lads cleaned and closed the shop. Second Sister soon joined Soo Hiang and the two brothers at the laksa stand. Some of the youngest brothers and sisters came to wash dishes during their school holidays, and Soo Hiang paid them each S$30 a month.

Soo Hiang felt close bonds to her family. They looked to her for continued help, and every month she donated S$100 of her salary and more from the earnings of the laksa enterprise to their household budget. In addition, she offered S$30 pocket money to her father. Soo Hiang's importance to her parental home was enhanced by the success of the laksa business. This venture aided the economies of two families and also brightened the prospects for the schooling of her younger siblings. Soo Hiang became the family representative, and it was she who saw through the compensation claim for First Brother's accident.

Soo Hiang told us that at one time she had had little influence in her parents' family. She described a highly emotional situation that showed how vastly her power had increased. "Several months ago when I was at the factory, my youngest brother pushed my son down on the floor. When I heard about this incident, I scolded Brother for pushing my little son. I packed my children's clothing and prepared to move out. Mother knelt before me and begged me to stay. This frightened me." When Mother pleaded with Soo Hiang on her knees to remain in the home, she was departing from a cultural norm. This acknowledgment of her dependence on Soo Hiang's earning power was unique in the families of my sample.

Soo Hiang claimed she would never have freely chosen an irresponsible husband like Tan To. In her eighteenth year, however, Mother had arranged the marriage for her. Most of the women I interviewed married people they had gotten to know, but Soo Hiang had to accept an arranged marriage with a total stranger. "I never saw him before, let alone got to know him. My family was growing too rapidly and my parents couldn't hold it together. What mother intentionally causes her children to suffer? Mother was only trying to marry me off to someone she thought would support me." Mother had probably chosen Tan To, who patronized her laundry, because he was available, apparently healthy, and lived nearby. "I was too afraid of Mother to refuse Tan To. When I hesitated, she'd pinch me until I was black and blue. At eighteen I hadn't yet learned to think for myself. Mother controlled me then, but you might say I control her now!"

Soo Hiang was still somewhat bitter when she recalled her difficult marital relationship. "Tan To had always gambled, but soon after my daughter was born, his habit became worse. He sometimes gambled away his entire month's pay in one evening. I begged him to stop, but he wouldn't listen. To avoid me, he came home after I had gone to bed at night and left the house early the next morning. For a while there I had to maintain the household from my own salary, and hardly got to see him. After some months of this, I complained to his parents, and they agreed that he was at fault. I told them of my plan to return to my parents' home and they accepted it. So I went back to Mother's home right away. Our departure shocked Tan To and he came to take us back, but my parents wouldn't let him in the door. While he was standing outside, Mother grabbed a bamboo stick and was ready to beat him if he entered. I believe that Tan To has never forgiven Mother for this threat. Tan To turned next to the neighbors of our one-room flat. He warned them that he was about to jump off a high building because I had deserted him. The neighbors rushed over with news of this threat, and so I decided to give him a second chance. I brought the children back to our flat the same evening. After that day, he began to reform. Gambling is a terrible addiction, and the effort to break it must have been difficult for him. But now he advises all his friends also to quit playing cards and dice. He says, 'There's no point slaving weeks for your money and giving it up in an hour.'"

Soo Hiang was not well acquainted with his friends and gambling companions. But after their marriage had mellowed, she and her husband shared entertainment outside the home, until her second job left little time for common leisure. "We sometimes went to the movies together. Tan To likes Westerns. He wants to see every new one that comes along, though I prefer to wait for a good one. We couldn't leave our two children with my parents. My mother would pull a long face—at least I think she would—so we took them along with us to the show." Indeed, a number of grandparents among the poor families were in fact willing to care for the children of working mothers but were reluctant to babysit while parents went out for a costly evening's entertainment.

Soo Hiang revealed that she seldom discussed family affairs with her husband. She did not tell him of her intention to begin factory work until after she had been hired by Hewlett-Packard. Since the Cheongs badly needed a regular second income, he could not complain. Neither did he object when she established her hawker stall, even though she could now spend little time at home. "I'm working as a hawker for my own family, not for any employer. As long as I stay healthy, he doesn't complain about my busy life. But he criticizes me for endangering my health, and becomes upset when I get sick. I'm free to give the income from the laksa shop to my parents because they're my very own earnings!"

Soo Hiang's objections to Tan To's occupational instability led to quarrels. Her mother also looked askance at Tan To's irregular job pattern. Tan To defended himself. "You women don't know how tough it is to hold down a job of outdoor labor! Our foremen are rough people, and it's hard to get along with them!"

Although Soo Hiang and Tan To frequently quarreled, she seemed to believe her marriage was better than her mother's. "Mother's youth was passed in years of poverty and pain. Mother was brought up by a couple who had a young son, but no other child. This couple expected Mother to become his bride.[4] Unfortunately, Mother was dark-skinned and quite thin, and suffers from a skin disease. So he found her unattractive and refused her. And her adoptive parents treated Mother quite badly. She didn't sit at the family dinner table, but was fed alone afterward, with the leftovers. Her adoptive parents beat her without reason. They regarded Mother as being in their debt. One of the reasons was an incident regarding a revolving credit society organized by my adoptive grandmother and her sister. Adoptive Uncle absconded with the cash accumulated in the fund, and Mother, who apparently was entrusted with the money, was unfairly blamed for the loss. In the end, her adoptive parents married Mother off to my father, but continued to demand cash payments from her. Father was another one who ill-treated Mother. From the beginning he scolded her, although she was already working very hard to raise the family. Today, whenever Father quarrels with Mother, we defend Mother, and after it's all over, we take her out for a walk alone to cool down, away from him. We can't stand his nagging!"

Upon their marriage in 1967, Tan To and Soo Hiang rented a one-room HDB flat near the two sets of parents. Thereafter, the Cheongs changed their household arrangements several times in rhythm with Soo Hiang's work patterns and economic needs. In 1968 they sent their infant son to live with Great-Grandmother Cheong in Malaysia to enable Soo Hiang to work in the laundry. When the boy reached kindergarten age, he returned to Singapore and lived with Tan To's parents while he attended school. In 1972 the Cheongs' daughter was born, and Soo Hiang's mother cared for her while Soo Hiang went to work in the electronics factory. In early 1975 the laksa venture had gotten under way, and Soo Hiang's family took on the care of both Cheong children during the day. The couple ate most meals with Soo Hiang's family. In early 1976, Soo Hiang's family rented a larger two-bed-room flat to accommodate their now combined household. Then in May 1976 the Cheongs informally sublet their one-room flat to Tan To's brother, who was about to be married, and moved in with Soo Hiang's parents. They shared one bedroom while Soo Hiang's parents and siblings slept in the other bedroom and the living room. Their family budgets were then virtually combined.

Soo Hiang felt confident of the child-care help of her in-laws and her mother. She spoke of the considerable care and discipline her children could receive, which she lacked time and skill to impart. "I didn't know how to care for a baby, and I couldn't send my son to Mother because there were already too many small children in Mother's home. Tan To's grandmother, however, felt lonely and welcomed her grandson in her home. Later she couldn't care for him anymore, so Mother-in-Law volunteered to help. Now he is very attached to his great-uncles and -aunts. Father-in-Law Cheong takes him to the PAP kindergarten each morning at ten. It's only a short walk from his home, and Father-in-Law returns at noon to bring him home for lunch. Next January we will take my son back here and send him to primary school. You see, Father-in-Law Cheong sleeps late in the morning and can't take the boy to school at seven."

Later on, however, Soo Hiang did complain that her child had been overprotected. "When Mother-in-Law Cheong was looking after him, our son was often sick. That's because, before bathing him, she'd close all the windows, undress him in the bedroom, wrap him up in thick towels, and then wash him in hot water. As a result, whenever the weather turned a little chilly, he'd catch a cold! Mother-in-Law insisted that this was the best way to bring up a child." Soo Hiang also complained, "Mother-in-Law Cheong doesn't give her children or mine the right kind of nutritious food. That's why I think my husband is so thin today!"

[75]

In 1975, when Soo Hiang's family was entrusted with the care of the two Cheong children, Second Sister told me that she took an approach sharply different from that of Soo Hiang. She mentioned the poor eating habits of her niece and nephew. "Sometimes I quarrel with Soo Hiang about their behavior. They are very naughty. Soo Hiang gives her son a dollar every day to spend on cakes and other sweets at school. Her daughter wants to drink four or five bottles of soda pop every day. When Soo Hiang is eating a meal and she wants some of it, she'll carry on dreadfully until she's given what she wants. Elder Sister sometimes gives her the whole bowl of what she's eating. We've told Soo Hiang she shouldn't be so lenient, otherwise the kids will grow up with bad manners."

Second Sister did think that Soo Hiang was a better companion to her children than her husband was. "Soo Hiang helps her son with his homework, and she takes the children to the playground whenever she sells out the laksa early." She felt Tan To was much better at disciplining the children. "I've seen him punish them for misbehaving by forcing each of them to bend their knees for a long time. The children are frightened by their father's stern treatment, and as a result they obey his commands."

Second Sister was referring to a form of symbolic punishment sometimes used by parents and teachers. Full squatting is common in Chinese society, and it is not surprising that Tan To would ask them to assume a partial squat as a form of punishment. Soo Hiang and Tan To did not discuss better ways to improve their children's behavior, however. Soo Hiang objected to Tan To's method of corporal punishment as a means of discipline, but was unable herself to develop a consistent approach to their upbringing.

According to Soo Hiang, "Tan To has a hot temper. If our son doesn't learn the right answer to a homework problem after Tan To tells him twice, then my husband beats him." Soo Hiang was also unhappy about Tan To's indifference to saving for the children's education. "Nowadays things are so expensive. I ask him to save money in a bank account especially for the children's education after primary school. But he cuts me off, saying, 'By that time I'll have died already!' So far I've persuaded him only to take out a life insurance policy." Tan To's willingness to pay life insurance premiums may be due to the riskiness of his occupation.

Tan To clearly hoped the children would progress in school, but he made no concrete plans to assist them. I asked him how far he thought his children could progress in the school system. "That depends on their abilities. It's difficult at this point to say how far they can rise. With inflation, things are so expensive that we're only earning enough to get from one day to the next. I leave it to Soo Hiang to save." Although Soo Hiang was the major earner in both families, Tan To still thought that boys should have more education than girls. "Boys work for their families all their lives, but girls marry out of their families."

Soo Hiang held similar views on educational planning. "Education depends on the children. No use planning too far. Some children's minds don't work well. I myself left secondary school because I had too many red marks. Sixth Sister has been in school for a year but she can't even write her name. She just doesn't speak much, so we don't know what's wrong and find it hard to help her." Soo Hiang was also critical of what she took to be the prevailing mores in the public schools in her area. I detected in her response a note of uncertainty about her children's educational prospects. "Some children who don't do well in their class will develop bad habits. Many of them smoke cigarettes and take pills."

Soo Hiang sacrificed for her kin, and she expected her own offspring to do the same. "Why have kids? Why give birth to children at all if you don't expect a lot of help from them? I hope our kids will support us in our old age." Tan To's attitude was colored by his fatalism. "When my children grow up, I don't know if I'll still be among the living." Neither parent, then, entertained the view, increasingly held by better-situated Singapore families, that grown-up sons and daughters should fashion their own lives and plans. Tan To told us that he liked girls and hoped to have another daughter. "To my way of thinking, three children would be ideal." I probed further, asking why he chose this number. "In case one child should turn out to be useless, or die of illness, then at least we have two others." Soo Hiang at once disagreed. "If your children are good, then two are enough. But if your children turn out poorly, then even having ten of them won't help."

In 1967, Soo Hiang's mother had given birth to her last child. A Caesarian section was required and Mother was in critical condition for many days. She then underwent a tubal ligation, to which Father reluctantly agreed. In 1968, after Soo Hiang's son was born, the nurses at the hospital explained the oral contraceptive technique to her. Soo Hiang then followed this method for several years, until she decided to have another child. In 1972, just before the birth of her daughter, she quit her job at the laundry. After the birth, Mother urged Soo Hiang to have a tubal ligation. She told her daughter, "Two children are enough for you." Mother's views led family opinion. Second Sister told us somewhat later, "Soo Hiang should stop at two, because her children are very naughty."

In offering this antinatalist advice, Mother was more concerned about Soo Hiang's well-being and her ability to work than about a succession of grandchildren. Soo Hiang was prepared to follow Mother's advice, but Tan To wanted another daughter. Therefore, Soo Hiang postponed a decision. She did, however, resume oral contraception.

Soo Hiang told me that pregnancy did not impede her working life, and that her confinements were uneventful. She agreed with her mother, however, that her responsibility for the welfare of her numerous younger siblings was great. Therefore, she hesitated ("feared") to get pregnant again.

Finally, she suggested that Tan To have a vasectomy. He refused. "I'm afraid sterilization will weaken me." Soo Hiang was on the way to taking the pivotal family-limitation decision by herself. Thus in this critical area the views and actions of Soo Hiang, the family leader, reflected her desire and ability to impose order on her strenuous and demanding existence.

[4]

Poor Families in the
Early Development Stage

For most families, a life of poverty meant close dependence on kin and minimal use of social services, which were available only to people with some money to invest. The lives of the poor were affected by the type of work they did, the past course of their family life, their material resources, and the presence or absence of wider kin ties. Let us now see how these features shaped variations in the families of the poor.

Work

Men's Jobs

The husband's job was at the root of the low standard of living. The average earnings of poor husbands were higher than the 1975 national median of Chinese men's monthly earnings of S$319; half of the group earned less than the national median.[1] I have divided the group into the very poor, with the least education and most family hardships, and the semipoor. The earnings of the very poor averaged S$282, 76 percent of the S$347 earned by the semipoor.

All of the poor men had had impoverished childhoods. Their parents had gone through the Depression years, the Japanese occupation, World War II, and the struggle for independence as poorly paid, often unemployed breadwinners. Before my respondents reached their teens, nearly half of them had lost their fathers to the high mortality of the wartime period or to second "wives." As few of the fathers had managed to accumulate any savings, the sons entered the work force early. Most of the fathers who survived this period were unskilled, holding such jobs as that of rubber tapper or hawker. A few worked in secure trades as construction labor contractor, truck driver, pig wholesaler, or clerk, but many were irresponsible and provided little support to their families.

Most poor men ended their education, barely literate, at primary level.[2] A few recalled that while funds could have been found to support them through one more school term, they had not performed well. Moreover, they were intent on earning money like others their age. The difficult class backgrounds that sent these men to wrestle for a wage at an early age placed most at the outset in low-paying, unskilled jobs.

Two-fifths of the poor men worked in the core sector, the rest in the periphery, including the civil service.[3] There was no difference at all between their average wages at this time. In sharp contrast, wages varied widely within each industrial sector by type of skill and the extent of other resources (see Table 6).[4]

Unskilled laborers in the peripheral sector were the least well off, with the dimmest prospects. State urban renewal programs threatened the workplaces of petty vendors and workers in small shops, and vendors had trouble getting licensed. Since mass-produced versions of the goods they made had entered the market, demand for their trade had passed. Others at the lower levels of state statutory boards, such as bus conductors, were just as poorly paid.

Men with nontechnical resources of education or petty capital earned the highest wages among the poor. Capital was more important than education. Men with a small amount of money to invest in their own shops—vendors

Table 6. Average earnings of poor men in peripheral and core sectors, phase 1

Sector	Average earnings[a]	Number
Periphery		
Unskilled	S$248	11
Resources[b]	433	16
Skilled	319	8
Average peripheral-sector poor male worker	349	35
Core		
Unskilled	300	8
Skilled	378	15
Average core-sector poor male worker	351	23
Average poor male worker, both sectors	350	58

[a]Pre-overtime gross monthly wage, before withdrawal of CPF.
[b]Occupation requires some capital, a nonindustrial skill, or an academic degree.

Hawker with child: traditional work combined with child care. Photo by Dominic Yip.

and cooks in their own market stalls, a taxi driver who could afford the license fee and a car—could make ends meet. So could those who catered to foreign visitors, such as a tailor who plied his trade when the ships of the British navy docked in Sembawang and a carpenter in a small Chinese hotel. These petty businessmen raised the average wage of the peripheral-sector men with nontechnical resources to a level well above that of others. They provided vivid proof that the traditional effort of overseas Chinese men in Southeast Asian cities to start their own small businesses paid off.[5] In contrast, the educated clerk in his brother-in-law's tiny stationery store earned low wages.

Men with technical skills in peripheral-sector firms with limited capital averaged only the national median wage, and some earned very little. For example, we have met the tinsmith who welded kettles by hand for a small firm for about S$250 a month. Thus the earnings of workers in the peripheral sector varied greatly with the type of their resources.

Unskilled construction and shipyard laborers in the core sector earned less than the national median but more than their unskilled counterparts in the peripheral sector. Better off were skilled men in the core sector, whose basic wages were second highest of the group as a whole, and who also earned overtime pay. These men with technical skills outearned their core-sector unskilled brothers by 26 percent. The skilled core-sector men also outearned their peripheral-sector skilled counterparts, but by a smaller margin of 18 percent. Skills, then, were a greater determinant of earnings than industrial sector.[6]

All the same, skilled workers could not always count on steady work in the core sector. And while demand for workers had begun to increase in the shipyards, they still had jobless days. Their way of life forged close ties. The all-male setting, their low levels of education, and the prevalence of sub-contracting, which often sent workers to new jobs together, bound them together as peers. When the job ended or bad weather halted work, their income stopped. On the job, workmates banded together to protect themselves from the dangers of shipyard work or construction, and many gambled or drank together after work.[7] So, although the skilled core-sector shipfitter did better on the average than his unskilled brethren, we have seen that their stories differed only slightly.

Men made individual efforts to add to their basic wage by working longer hours and taking second jobs. Overtime work could raise their basic wages from 20 to 50 percent. These men were still young and willing to put in "buffalo effort," but none expected to maintain this arduous pace through middle age. Yet workers rarely upgraded their job skills through adult education courses or self-study. Their level of education was too low to permit them even to begin a trade course. The few who pursued elementary En-

Unskilled laborers in a core-sector shipyard. Photo by Eric Khoo.

glish or other basic school courses at night found that they never qualified for higher-level jobs, and soon stopped attending.[8]

Most had entered the labor force as teenagers, and by phase 1 they had already held an average of three jobs; a fifth had held five or more. Nearly all of their most recent job changes had been unplanned: their firm had gone out of business, or they had been laid off for lack of work, or they had been injured, or they had walked out after a quarrel with the foreman. A few had quit entry-level jobs for slightly better-paid work. Since they rarely upgraded their skills between posts and few could transfer their on-the-job training, these forced job changes did not greatly increase their earnings.[9]

Narrow social networks further constrained efforts to get better jobs. When they first sought work, no formal labor exchanges or agencies helped them. They started working with kin or friends, and learned the skills they needed from them.[10] They found later jobs the same way; all men about whom I have information found their phase 1 jobs through close personal ties.[11] This seemed a natural process to them. All the low-level jobs that were potentially open to them paid about the same, so they saw no reason to look further afield. As they said, "all jobs are the same." As their kin had no more schooling than they did, most people they knew had the same kind of jobs.[12] Such strong ties among like-placed people greatly constricted job information.[13] Poor men thus had few prospects other than overtime work to improve their family's standard of living.

Women's Jobs

Wives aided their families with their earnings as wage workers and as homemakers. Their wage levels, like those of their husbands, were determined by their class position and industrial sector. Their sex further reduced women's options, even within the narrow range of jobs available to the poor.

Forty-three percent worked full-time for a wage, mainly as factory workers but also as domestic servants or waitresses.[14] Two-fifths earned no more than the 1975 national median monthly wage for women (around S$200).[15] All of these low earners worked in the peripheral sector. Domestic servants and other service workers earned the least; operatives in local firms earned somewhat more. In contrast to the men, women in core-sector firms, such as the two we have met in foreign-capitalized electronics assembly factories, earned the highest wages (all earned more than S$200). A recession in the trade, however, cut the wages of many of these women in 1974–75. The cuts were later restored, but core-sector workers remained vulnerable to fluctuations in the world economy. Thus the women workers, like the men, faced uneven demand for their labor in all sectors.

Singapore firms paid women relatively low wages, expecting their families

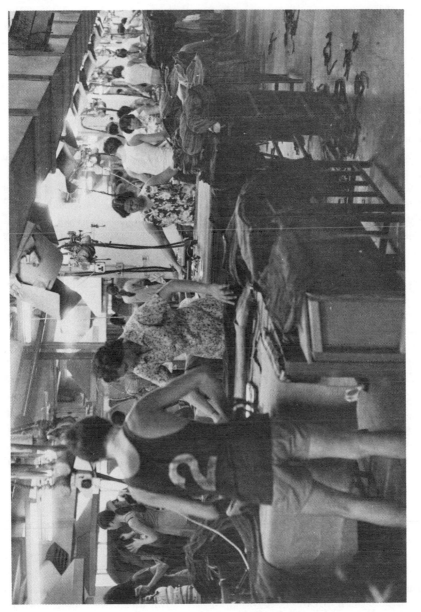

Semiskilled workers in a peripheral-sector garment factory. Photo by Fred Salaff.

to make up the difference between their earnings and the cost of living. Most women earned less than their husbands and none attained the average men's wage. When asked why they worked when they earned so little, they replied that they worked first to make ends meet, second to invest in a better future for their families, and only last for self-interest. We have seen that the wives of the low-paid bus conductor and tinsmith went to work when they lost hope that their husbands' income would improve. We have met an electronics worker whose skilled shipyard-fitter husband gambled away most of his paycheck. In addition to sheer needs, inflation and rising expectations in this developing society drew other women into the labor force.

Of the thirty-three poor housewives, all but two had once earned wages. They spoke of their weak market position as the reason for quitting after they married. They had, at most, primary school education, and the peripheral-sector jobs they had held, such as putting peanuts in packages, disqualified them for the better-paid women's jobs in the core sector. Many had worked only intermittently, and were often called back home to mind younger siblings so that their mothers could work in shops and stalls. Many served as domestic servants between factory stints, and few had accumulated seniority. Others were unpaid workers in the family's hawker store or vegetable plot, or in other areas of the natural economy. Economics, not prestige, determined their work choices. For these reasons, few housewives could qualify for a job that would pay above the woman's median wage, and so most refused to work. Only two with some secondary education and a higher earning potential stayed home because that was what their husbands wanted them to do.

Some homemakers who could not command the median wage sought informal work that helped them care for their children at the same time. Five took in sewing or washed clothing for neighbors, taking their places in the low-paid shadow economy that is not reported in Singapore's work force statistics. Some women hoped to get better-paying hawkers' jobs when their children were older, but as the government was phasing out this avenue of self-help, social mobility for poor women was not likely.

It was in any case often hard for young mothers to manage even part-time wage labor from their homes, because they attended to many household and community tasks that helped poor folk survive. Women who did not do wage work performed the housework for their families and often released higher-earning female kin from domestic tasks to work outside the home or in a family firm. Here we see the reason that the majority of my poor female respondents earned more than the median female wage: most low earners had already been forced out of the labor force. But often even the low wages commanded by wives could lift household income above the poverty line. As a result, when we add the full-time wage of the wife to that of her husband, the joint income of very poor families was often higher than that of many semipoor men and their nonworking wives.

The life-cycle stage of these women kept them close to their kin, and caring for and raising their children was easier when others helped out. Young employed mothers especially depended on a network of women to take over their parenting and household tasks. Living in an extended or stem household helped a great deal.

In the early stages of their family cycle, couples were expected to live with their elders, usually in the home of the husband's parents.[16] In the patrilocal household favored by the Chinese, all sons contributed their labor or a portion of their pay packet.[17] The household head, once the manager of inherited family property, had the authority of the patriliny. He or his wife, who represented him, still collected, budgeted, and redistributed the household income. Income was shared in the form of food, clothing, and other essentials and cash for expenses, including school and medical fees. Ideally, all members of the household were supposed to consume the same amount. When more than one nuclear family unit lived under one roof, those with more dependents and expenses received a larger allowance. Elders exerted pressure on the household to keep expenses low. This factor, plus the economies of scale achieved when several family units lived under one roof, reduced living costs. Cultural expectations, combined with the need to cut costs, explain why as many as two-fifths of the poor lived with kin.

The willingness of these coresident women to relieve our young mothers of their household chores and child-care tasks was the condition of their entry into the labor force. In exchange, the women added their wages to the family purse. The importance of this division of labor for their employment is seen in the fact that working women were more than twice as likely as homemakers to live with kin. Further, women flexibly expanded their circle of helpers with a mixture of paid and unpaid kin and neighbors. Some couples lived near one or both sets of parents to avail themselves of grand-parenting services. They dined daily at the homes of elders and thereby reduced their own homemaking chores. Others left their infants at the homes of grandparents or other kin during the week. Grandparents who could not take in their grandchildren would visit the care-giving family to ensure that the youngsters were content. There were few isolated wives and even fewer isolated women who earned wages: 92 percent of the women wage earners interacted with kin frequently.[18]

But family support was not always easy to come by. One effect of the rapidly expanding housing program was to uproot village-style housing and separate young couples from their community of kin. Kampung housing could accommodate complex extended families—two married brothers and their families, for example, as well as the senior parents. Public housing held stem families at most.[19] The constraint of housing did not in itself isolate people from their elders. Young couples often went to great lengths to find a flat near their relatives, since without help of in-laws, working mothers could not enter the labor force. In exchange, the older generation obtained some economic support for watching their grandchildren, and they performed a useful social role that was highly valued in the Chinese family.

When an older woman had more than one working daughter or daughter-in-law, she had to decide which one to help. Her decision turned partly on affective ties, partly on the young woman's marketable skills and earning power. Women who earned less than S$200 a month had trouble persuading kin to help them care for their children when the senior women had other claims on their time. Thus social class position—the household's need for the woman's income and her earning power—shaped the kind of support she could get for her efforts to work outside the home.

Living in a low-income extended household forced many women to enter the labor force in order to earn petty cash. A young daughter-in-law who needed money often found either that there was too little in the till or that the family head had spent the household money without taking her needs into account. The struggle over money typically took place between the young wife and her mother-in-law, with the youthful husband acting as ineffective go-between. This was particularly the case when the total income was small and husbands were most beholden to their kin for jobs and other forms of help. When wives came into conflict with their husbands' parents, they rarely got support. Thus some women escaped the tensions of the extended household by going out to work.

Once in the labor force, women could more easily control a portion of their earnings. They spent their wages first to buy clothes and toys for their children and then for their own clothing and household essentials. Their earnings also helped them to maintain their kin networks, for now they could buy gifts on the occasions of visits, marriages, birthdays, and religious festivities.[20] We have seen the cases of the electronics workers, who expressed their filial desire to help their aging parents and other kin with sums of money. For such help it was essential to have a private income. Among the poor, unless a wife worked full-time, it was impossible to budget S$100 a month to support a needy mother or aunt. Employed mothers paid between S$50 and S$100 for child-care services, and kin were the prime beneficiaries. The women used any remaining funds to enjoy a modest social life with workmates and other peers. They increasingly spent their leisure time and money in the city's shopping complexes and cinemas. In that way, even low-paid labor brought women into contact with the mass consumer culture. Thus the low wages of women who worked outside the home contributed to the family's survival and provided the extra margin that allowed them to enjoy their rather narrow social and cultural milieu.

The Marriage Bond

Poverty, limited education, and lack of a secure job or future career created financial dependence on kin which diluted the marriage bond. We see this in the work that men and women did at home, their use of leisure time, and their talk about family issues. Looking at their patterns of leisure activities and discussions, I distinguish "segregated" and "joint" marriages. Those husbands and wives with segregated marriages spent their leisure time apart (mainly with friends, peers, and kin of the same sex) and enjoyed few confidences with their spouses. They did not share domestic tasks. Such segregated marriages were the majority. In contrast, couples with a joint conjugal bond shared leisure time and discussions of family affairs, and a very few shared household chores as well.[21] Joint marriages were found only among those with above-average job security, wages, or schooling.

Although some husbands helped out, only a few did regular housework. Since this was the case, husbands' help in the home did not seem closely related to other features of the family experience, and was thus excluded from the measure of segregated and joint families. However, there were a few patterns worth noting.

Men with little education did the least housework. The less schooling a man had had, the more he tended to regard certain tasks as natural to one sex or the other. Further, as the jobs of such men forced them to obey the commands of a supervisor, they tended to adopt rigid views of the tasks people could do.[22] In addition, the tightly knit personal network of kin, workmates, and close friends, all with equally minimal education, provided no support for the treatment of spouses as equal partners.[23] Peers and kin thus reinforced conformity.[24]

Wives tended to excuse their husbands from housework when the men toiled a long workweek that included overtime or a second job to add to their paychecks. They returned home each day exhausted, convinced their long hours and arduous work were sufficient family contribution.[25] Women relied instead on help from their female kin and neighbors. Neighbors might rotate shopping chores and mind a sleeping child while its mother went to market. Indeed, women without close kin, such as the wife of the tutu hawker, often voiced the wish that they had a mother-in-law to help them with their daily routine. Because of their minimal education, most wished to raise their children as their mothers had raised them. This desire to carry forward tradition added to their concern to get help from experienced older wom-

[89]

en.[26] These personal networks were crucial in helping poor mothers cope with homemaking, but they hindered men and women from sharing household tasks. As a result, the very poor and many semipoor referred to the division of labor by sex in the home as "natural."

Robert Winch has pointed out that the more functions the family fills, the more need it has for a strict definition of roles by age, sex, generation, and lineage.[27] The urban Singapore Chinese family still performed many functions, from serving as an income-earning unit to caring for all its members and on to helping each other find jobs. The senior generation in many homes set the division of labor: men earned the income while young wives performed most home tasks and relieved their mothers-in-law of much work. These young couples deferred to their elders' view of family roles.

The life course of poor couples added further to their unwillingness to divide home chores equally. The sociologist Lillian Rubin has found that U.S. working-class men whose families had dissolved in their youth longed for a more protective marriage.[28] As many of my couples had come from broken families and their mothers had had to work outside the home to sustain them, some men wanted their wives to care for them in a more solicitous way. They created the ideal breadwinner families, in which the men earned the living and the women ran the home. Wives, for their part, vowed not to repeat their own bitter childhood experiences. Although circumstances did not always permit them to limit themselves to the home, such wives did not urge their husbands to do housework.

In six households, however, there was an above-average sharing of tasks. Some wives lacked female kin, and their husbands stepped into the breach. They prided themselves on the small domestic contribution they could make. Too, several employed women stated that their husbands relieved their "double day," while others looked forward to going out to work when their children were older, relying on a promise of help. But in general, employed women got no more help than the others. Few expected long-term employment, and therefore lacked a basis to renegotiate home tasks, and their wages were too low to overcome their husbands' resistance to housework.[29] So they, too, relied on other women to help them.

Men with a bit more earnings and schooling and skilled core-sector work were most likely to help their wives.[30] Five of the six men who helped their wives "a lot" were skilled core-sector workers. Three of the six men with full secondary schooling helped their wives "a lot." Further, such men whose jobs did not directly pass through kin were best able to challenge their families' definition of sex roles. Even so, none shared an equal burden of tasks with his wife.

Only a minority of ten husbands and wives shared leisure activities. They were found solely among semipoor couples, of whom they formed 25 percent. This had not always been the case. Five-sixths of the couples had known each other well and had come to care for each other before they married. The rest of the marriages were arranged. Even among couples who had chosen each other, however, long working hours and separate work and social circles drew husbands and wives apart. Their work roles spilled over into home activities. Women who could add little to the family wage if they returned to work might escape their homemaking tasks in outings with friends. They created a women's sphere. Neighbors visited, women bought breakfast for each other at the nearby market, played mah-jongg, and joined excursions to temples on the gods' birthdays. Many men compensated for their heavy work burdens by socializing with their workmates before journeying home. Others sought escape from their low-paying jobs in gambling. The outcome was their chronic absence from home.

Life-cycle stage contributed to sex-linked leisure patterns. The birth of children divided husband's and wife's circles, as the mother had then especially to depend on other women to do household tasks. Many women believed that they and their husband's men friends "naturally" had few interests in common. Their main desire was for their husband to become a close companion to their children. Living with kin also put an end to shared socializing. Women who married into their husbands' households often stopped all outside social activities with their own friends, whereas men were not so constrained. Women's ties with their own mothers and sisters centered on children and the home, and their husbands rarely shared these relationships. On the few occasions when they did visit, such as during major festivals, the men were "quiet." This imbalance distressed their wives. Only when a wife's kin took part in the couple's daily routine, such as by caring for their young children, did husbands visit those in-laws more often.

Nevertheless, a minority of ten couples—a few were the same as those that shared tasks—did join their circles of friends. Eight of these men held secure and mainly white-collar jobs, which they had not gotten through kin. Four of them had some secondary schooling. Only two couples lived with the husband's parents. Finally, childhood circumstances (being orphaned or raised by distant kinfolk) had loosened the ties of these men with their kin. But such sharing was unusual.

Nearly half of the poor—and nearly all the very poor—talked over few matters with their spouses. Many marriages had never become satisfactory to the women, especially the one-sixth that had an arranged match. In any case, the poor believed they could find no way out of their poverty, and that frequent discussions helped very little. Indeed, such discussions often erupted into arguments, which alarmed them, for they seemed to have no solution. When they feared that to express themselves was to trigger a fight, silence became a weapon. Men who gambled with their workmates also became secretive, aware that their losses damaged their family's livelihood. Such furtive behavior deepened cleavages in the marriage.

[91]

Close economic ties with kin further inhibited discussions with mates. Men who worked in family firms, especially the low-profit ones of the poor, exercised little control over their livelihood. They were especially reluctant to discuss their work with their wives. Yet few of the rest discussed their jobs, either. Often they had little control over the conditions of their work, and long hours reduced the time that could be spent in such talks. The exclusion of discussions of jobs, while grounded in their class setting, itself limited any help they might have gotten by working out problems with their mates. This reticence made it even harder to chart a course of economic betterment to overcome the difficult circumstances of the poor.

Loyalty to one's spouse was rare in the extended household. Wives were sometimes dismayed to find that the confidences they shared with their husbands quickly became known to their mothers-in-law. Thereafter, they hesitated to discuss with their husbands such sensitive matters as giving money to their parents, which was frowned upon in the poor households.

While 37 percent discussed "some issues" with their spouses, the examples they gave revealed the limits of such exchanges. Wives said that they did not disclose "everything," and did not expect that their husbands would listen to them if they did. Nor did they think that their men told them everything, either. Women reserved their most intimate discussions for the ears of mothers or sisters, because they held limited expectations of a husband. A good husband was one who did not gamble regularly, but sharing intimacies was not part of the definition.

The ten poor couples who disclosed inner feelings were the same ones who shared leisure activities. They were not tightly bound to their kin economically, and they expected future careers. Their release from parental control over their purse strings, in fact, helped them enjoy outings together, expanding common interests and topics to talk over. An important topic was plans for the family: where to live, whether or not to buy a home, what school to choose for their children. They saw a close marriage as one in which both spouses discussed the future, especially how to use the newly available social services. These couples were in a minority precisely because most working-class couples lacked a secure economic base and could not realistically expect to upgrade their lifestyle. Communication was thus closely related to economic prospects.[31]

Public Housing

Couples relied on subsistence economies, social exchanges, extended family living, and economies of scale to lower their costs of living. Four couples rented tenement rooms, while twelve lived in kampung bungalows or on farms. Although kampung dwellers earned wages, they paid little or no rent, grew subsidiary crops, and raised barnyard animals to extend their diets. They thus were partly outside the money economy. Even those in suburban tenements often grew some of their food, and they bought few consumer goods. They were aware that the government's urban renewal plans called for their housing to be torn down, and they dreaded the anticipated increase in rent when they had to move to a highrise flat. Finally, 42 couples lived in HDB flats, nearly all of which were rented; in many cases relatives paid the rent. They, too, exchanged goods and services with kin and neighbors and thereby reduced their living costs. Close reliance on others hindered efforts of the poor to move into a home of their own.

Couples that lived with their parents spent less per capita on rent and utilities than they would have spent in their own homes. For instance, the joined family units shared a single refrigerator, stove, television, electric iron, electric fan, and living room furniture, and were discouraged from freely buying consumer goods. Although cultural expectations combined with poverty to slow the move to their own home, couples did plan to move into their own flats as their families grew. Releasing their room to a younger brother who was ready to marry, they received wider family agreement to separate their budgets. When they moved, their costs rose sharply. Now they became much more deeply enmeshed in the market economy as workers, consumers, and debtors. Given their limited finances, poor couples were saving mainly to rent and furnish a flat; they did not envision buying a home of their own.

Most couples depended on the husband's earnings to pay rent and on his pension (the Central Provident Fund, or CPF) if they bought a home. Because of their poverty, most couples in single-family households lived in minute one-room "improved" flats, with a hall in addition to the main room, kitchen, and bath.[32] Such small flats were not for sale, and few could afford the two-bedroom flats that were the smallest that could be purchased. For, they reasoned, if they were without work, they would receive no CPF and would have to finance this larger home out of pocket. Uncertain employment, whether in core or peripheral jobs, thus kept the poor from commitment to years of high monthly payments. Even with an above-average income, the shipfitter on a contract could not depend on the steady work needed to buy a flat through CPF installments. Low-paid pieceworkers, such as the tinsmith, were worse off. Self-employed workers, such as the tutu hawker, had no CPF accounts, and noncitizens were not allowed to draw on theirs to buy a public flat. Even with steady work, most of the poor feared they had too little coming in each month to afford a larger flat. Nor, with their children still tots, did most feel they needed more room. The earnings of the poor were thus too unsteady a basis for homeownership.

The twenty-five women who worked full-time used their earnings for daily expenses. Their CPF funds were too small to finance a home.[33] Most required the agreement of others to go on working, and could not count on long-term work.[34] Therefore families could buy a flat only if the husband worked steadily and had a sizable sum amassed in his CPF account, not usually the case among the poor.

There were other economic obstacles, beginning with the S$100 registration fee to enter their names on the waiting list to buy a home. Then all homeowners wanted to make some improvements—change the shape of a doorway from a rectangle to an arch, build kitchen counters, lay mosaic or marble tiling on the floors, paint walls. They counted these renovations as part of buying a house, and could not afford them.

There were exceptions. Four couples lived in their own flats, and four others had registered for one. These early home buyers differed from the rest. The husbands held solid working-class posts: a clerical worker in a warehouse, a technical assistant in a soil-testing firm, a joint owner of a canteen at an oil rigging station, and a postman. Two had above-average education and three of the four had close marriage bonds. A strong marriage was thus an additional resource that helped these couples buy homes of their own. Their accounts of the home-buying process stressed their talks and savings over the years and their willingness to tell their reluctant parents that they wanted to live apart. Yet we should not overestimate their independence in buying a flat, because three of the four borrowed heavily from employers and relatives to do so. Thus early home purchase was helped by job stability and a career ladder, solid education, a strong marriage, and support from a social network. Few of the poor could boast of all these assets.

Education: The Pathway to Advancement

To meet the needs of early industrial capitalism, families were urged to adhere to the performance principle. A key area of performance was the school system. As progress through school became highly competitive, parental intervention remained crucial at many points along the children's educational pathway.[35]

Low hopes for their children emerged from my questions on the kind of education and jobs that parents desired for their children. Nearly half lacked clearly defined goals. While the remainder wished their children to complete at least secondary school, they qualified these ambitions. They doubted their offspring's ability, and few knew how to boost them through the selective school system.[36]

As these parents had little control over their own livelihood, they rarely made long-term plans for their children. Mothers hoped that their daughters would get a better factory job than they once had, and that their sons would enter a technical trade. But while somewhat aware of the rapid job changes in Singapore, few parents knew how to prepare their children for the future. Moreover, depending on close personal ties to locate jobs, they assumed that their children would also get jobs in this way. In a world of personal connections, education did not loom very large. Parents drew on their own experiences and those of friends and kin for direction in raising their youngsters' school performance and choice of school or job. Their lack of familiarity with the school system and with people who had such information short-circuited their use of the system.

Some were aware that a university degree was required for many jobs and hoped that their children would show promise and receive state support. Beyond this vague hope that their children would win a scholarship, few made concrete plans. They relied on the school system to teach the children what they needed to know to pass exams. As they left career choices to the youngsters, the parents could not guide them to seize the few postsecondary places. Thus the limited job prospects and education that reduced the parents' earning ability would be reproduced in the younger generation.

Those who believed in nature before nurture believed that children's characters were set at birth. They attributed poor school performance to lack of ability, and the ideology of meritocracy reinforced this view. The parents then reasoned that since such egalitarian admissions policies were in force, their children's school problems were caused by lack of intelligence. They overlooked the likelihood that talented children of poor families would be derailed from the educational pathway. This personal attribution of blame, the hidden injury of class, hindered parents' efforts to prepare their children for higher education.

I asked parents how they prepared their children for school. As most worked in jobs that required outward obedience to work rules, they voiced their confidence in strict discipline.[37] Many said they admonished their children to do their homework, and applied a rattan switch to them when they got bad grades. The poorest saw toys as a frivolous expense and not as educational aids. They had little time to monitor their schoolwork, nor did they know how to do so. They rarely read educational materials or kept up with the discussions of the changing school system in the newspaper.[38] Parents' low expectations for their children's future were seen in their answers to questions on their intention to send their children to one or two years of kindergarten, and the language stream and locale of the primary school of their choice.

They had trouble planning ahead. Plans for their children's education were intertwined with the mother's daily routine. Two years of kindergarten were available, but busy mothers chose only one year, because they lacked the time to take them to school and fetch them home. Since few parents taught their children at home, the delay in school entry might later affect the youngsters' learning.[39]

They also had to choose a primary school. Most chose a school because of proximity and the opinions of others close to them. The majority of parents and their close associates had attended Chinese-stream primary school. They were disappointed in their own low level of achievement and attributed their poor earning power to their limited facility with English. Many then hoped to enroll their children in an English-stream primary school. Nevertheless, parents expressed certain reservations about the lax discipline commonly associated with English-stream education. Since some, such as the tutu seller, needed a son to support them in later years, they were genuinely worried that an English-stream education would weaken filial piety. Also, as they usually could ensure only primary education, they had to decide which of the two imperfectly mastered languages—English or Mandarin Chinese—would provide access to better jobs. Some parents decided to send their youngsters to a Chinese-language school because they did not believe that their children could learn enough English in primary school to help them land good jobs. Others came to the opposite conclusion. Most found the range of choices bewildering, and were prepared to follow the advice of people around them.

Parents lacked the background to help with homework or studying for tests, but few could afford to hire a tutor. At the most they sent their children to group classes, which were less expensive but provided little individual attention. Still to come was the decision of whether to support their children through high school, at an age when they could be earning wages.

Men with unsteady jobs had the greatest trouble saving for education. Working wives more easily helped their families save, but most already budgeted their wages for other vital necessities. Couples whose income was not supplemented by any earnings by the wife found their already problematic educational plans hardest to meet. Thus most had to decide each month whether to allot a given amount of income for school costs or for the purchase of household goods to make their lives more comfortable. If parents managed their slim budget inefficiently, they had even less chance to meet their minimal educational bill. Half saved small sums of money for their children's schooling, on an irregular basis. Some couples put money aside in a tin can or drawer for these purposes, but none could save more than S$20 a month. Since they already spent to the limit of their weekly wage, they often had to draw on this small nest egg for family events or an unanticipated crisis.

Unable to plan more than "one step at a time," as a truck driver put it, parents could not place their children in an elite secondary school. Parents who intended to enroll their children in government-aided (mission) or elite government schools had to plan carefully from their child's infancy. Entry into an aided school came easiest for those with an "old school tie," which gives a child priority. Entry into an elite secondary school was determined largely by test scores, and children in neighborhood schools rarely competed successfully. Entry into such schools was somewhat easier from the ground up, from a kindergarten that funneled students into a primary school whose graduates then went on to an attached secondary school. But the kindergartens charged high fees, they were not local, and parents had to pay for a school bus. Few poor parents dreamed of sending their children beyond the neighborhood and the local knowledge of their kin and acquaintances. Their main chance of entering their child in either type of school at a later stage was for one of them to be sterilized when they had no more than two children. But no poor couple took this step.

A few couples with some secondary education stressed the importance of instilling good study habits in their youngsters. They tried to think ahead to what the children would need to help them learn, and what the problems might be. Such parents bought plastic alphabet letters and other learning toys for their toddlers to teach them at home. They later contacted the school to learn how their children were doing.[40] In these and other ways, parents with better education could supplement the teacher's role. But the majority could not go beyond their own limited background to make far-off plans for their children's educational pathway.

Planning Families

Most couples had two children, and the average was 2.4. Only a minority (19 percent) had been sterilized. We asked each couple their "intended family size."[41] Their responses referred to the children they expected to have, taking into account their economic situation, opinions of kin, and the sex of the children.

Poverty was reflected in their wish for many children, and also dominated their reasons for deciding on a family of a particular size. Some expected to draw on their children's labor for the household economy. Singapore still had farmers, who traditionally wanted sons to labor beside them and daughters to help in the home. Thus farmers had at least four children and intended to have more. Indeed, one respondent, who lived with her married sisters-in-law on a small farm, remarked that they did not even set a limit to the size of their family. "We'll have babies until we drop!" she commented. A respondent who worked in a small traditional family store also wished for several sons.

Most, however, were wage earners without property. They were anxious to ensure themselves support in their old age, beyond what would be available through their slim pension savings. They expected, further, that their children would need to help each other look for jobs and exchange goods and

Table 7. Number of poor couples who intended to have and did have specified numbers of children, phase 1

Family size	Number of children				
	1	2	3	4+	Average
Intended	0	8	27	23	3.4
Actual	9	30	10	9	2.4

Note: The specified numbers of children include surviving children born to couples, children of former marriages, and adopted children; they exclude children adopted out permanently but include those temporarily living with other families as a form of child care.

services, much as they did themselves. So each child needed brothers and sisters. Thus dependence on personal ties for security underwrote acceptance of and even a need for many children.

Low wage earners found many children an expense, but they had in mind what demographers call the short-term costs of raising children: their food, clothing, housing, and school fees.[42] Young children also may be liabilities during the frequent crises of the poor, such as job loss. But poor parents sought to reduce these costs by family-wide child-care arrangements, and some children were left with kin on weekdays, or even throughout their early years. If the kinship network can be called on to help in normal times or emergencies, then individual parents need not bear all the responsibility of having children by themselves. The costs of children are thus redistributed among the poor.[43] For these reasons, a family of four children was not considered overly expensive.

Childbearing plans also turned on the sex of the children. All parents wanted a son, and many wished two. But children of both sexes could help the family, and so couples also wanted daughters.[44] They sometimes used gambling analogies to justify having another child. They "took a chance" on the pregnancy in the hope that the child would be of the desired sex.[45] Parents frequently bore many children in the process of reaching the desired sex ratio.

Nevertheless, despite traditional motives to bear children, parents felt their childbearing plans represented a great change over those of the past. They termed their own intended families "small" when they compared them with the larger families of the older generation. Many used the full range of birth-control methods, and many wives had had abortions. Even those who hoped for four children felt they were reducing their family size below some higher ceiling.

Parents who intended to limit their family to three children considered, in addition to the short-term expenses of feeding and clothing them, the time constraints for the mother—the opportunity costs of childbearing.[46] Economic and time costs weighed heaviest on full-time working women, who realized that large families were incompatible with their participation in the labor force. If they could not care for their children themselves, they had to earn enough to reimburse kin for their support, and they foresaw difficulties. The few mothers who devoted themselves to educating their children at home also considered the time constraints of large families costly.

Several women joined the labor force after their children entered school. Some of them had borne large families at an early age, when work opportunities were few. When their children were older, demand for unskilled assembly-line workers increased, and these women arranged for inexpensive or free child care and went out to work. As full-time employment made it difficult for them to care for an infant, they ended their childbearing at that point.

Working at home did not affect family size goals in the same way as did full-time labor in factories.[47] Home labor was the refuge of lower-class women who lacked alternative means to make money and had no child-care help. Many had left the labor force upon marriage or motherhood because they earned too little to warrant help in home tasks. They could not return for the same reason, and could expand their husband's wage only by means of their home sewing machines. Because of their limited economic options and horizons, these women could not plan far ahead, and rarely planned on small families. Thus it was hope for a better economic future that reduced family-size goals.

Kin who performed important economic and social roles exerted influence on the number and timing of children.[48] Young parents who worked on a family farm or in a family store felt the elders' desire for offspring most strongly. Their marriages had been contracted to further the kin group and pass on property. Their childbearing decisions began with one or two sons; if daughters were born, their total intended family size often rose past three. Such parents were dependent structurally on their kin: they shared an economic fate with relatives with whom they lived. As they interacted with few people of significantly different views, it was hard for them to separate their views from those of their kin or find support when they did not agree with them. Parents who shared a near-total world with their kin might be all but coerced to have more children. Therefore, most, like the tinsmith and domestic servant, stressed their relatives' views concerning contraception, abortion, sterilization, and the decision to bear an additional child.

Relatives often made their wishes felt by extending or withholding child-care help. Some working women who had borne only daughters found their in-laws offering to help watch another newborn. The in-laws of other employed women, expressing reluctance to care for a granddaughter, pressed the woman to quit her job and have yet another child, this time the long-wished-for son. Elders might go to greater extremes to see a grandson born.

The mother of the unskilled shipyard worker forbade her daughter-in-law, who had given birth only to girls, to let herself be sterilized.

A few, in contrast, felt that large families were only burdens, and urged their daughters to limit their family size, as in the case of the electronics worker married to a shipfitter. Finally, there were those elderly women who had seen their headship role eroded and withdrawn from the family decision-making process, such as the mother of the bus conductor married to the electronics worker.[49]

A very few couples intended to have small families. These exceptional parents had relatively good working-class jobs, above-average education, and strong marriage bonds. The wives had well-paid core-sector factory jobs. Their parents were not pressing them for more grandchildren; either the mothers themselves worked or the husband and wife were not emotionally close to either set of parents. But these were the exceptions.

Parents were urged to base their family-size decisions on the needs of the nation. The answers given by my respondents showed that many had absorbed the message that "Singapore is overpopulated." The policies known as the social disincentives against higher-order births had just come into effect. When asked their opinion of the disincentives, over half approved, and many more of the remainder registered qualified endorsement—the qualification being that people had the right to bear children of both sexes.[50]

But acceptance of these measures was not dictated by patriotism. The measures themselves added to the short-term cost of rearing children. As most parents felt that their own low income required them to have fewer children than their parents had had, the disincentives mainly reinforced this decision. Many were already in conflict over having a large family, and the disincentives tipped the scales toward a smaller one. Therefore, most interwove the policies with decisions already made on material grounds. They felt the high hospital fee for a third or fourth birth would increase the incentive for Singaporeans like themselves to reduce their family size. The measures were not solely responsible for family limitation, but they were mentioned by couples in conflict over family size as one of several reasons not to have a large family.[51]

The few relatively well-educated couples with hope of advancing on the job claimed to take little account of the disincentives, because they strongly assessed the costs of having a large family as too high even without such measures. They believed that parents like themselves made such decisions without regard to government policy. These couples admitted that the measures were useful to put pressure on others, but they wondered if they would have any effect on couples that "just don't care."

Coercion—from the perspective of the couples—comes into play for the few parents who either would have borne more children if it had not been for the measures or, to the contrary, openly resented having their family size monitored by the authorities and tried to evade the sanctions. One couple had to comply with the wishes of their kin, who urged them to bear at least two sons, and to conceal her actions the wife entered a private maternity home to have her fourth child. In order to ensure that they could try again if they had another daughter, they had to bypass the hospitals and state social security apparatus that enforced state policies and put pressure on parents like them to have no more children. Few, however, felt so coerced.

In sum, most poor parents took into account both their economic circumstances and the state policies in setting their family-size goals. Many who intended a sizable family to protect themselves against an insecure and uncertain future did not feel that several children would further affect their already limited horizons, and their kin bore the brunt of the costs. But at some point, when the disincentives increased costs to the already overburdened household economy even further, they considered ceasing childbearing.

Conclusions

In the first development stage, poverty shaped the lives of many families. With limited education, having entered the labor force at an early age, and with social resources entirely within the same class group, men and women could not break out of their early impoverished job status. Work in the core industrial sector boosted the wages of both men and women. The highest wages accrued to men with a skill or entrepreneurial resource, especially a sum of capital. Wives who earned money helped their families eke out a minimal living but they earned less than the men.

Poverty and their life-cycle stage placed families in close dependence on their relatives to make ends meet. They looked to their relatives for help with their early family building. Caring for and educating their numerous children was far easier when their relatives helped out. Most remained partly outside the market economy, because of close dependence on help and handouts from others.

The closeness of poor couples to their families and to their peers of the same sex, which was fostered by their jobs, competed with the husband-wife relationship. Most marriages were segregated. Since the couples had to take into account the views of kin in many spheres of their family life, they were not independent decision makers. Poverty and close kinship ties limited access to the state housing and educational services, and they could not plan far ahead. Their relatively high family-size goals balanced the costs of raising children in the short term against their limited hopes for the future.

The few exceptions to this norm had hopes of advancing in their jobs, had above-average schooling, or for some reason were not deeply integrated into their kin community. They enjoyed joint marriages and tried to use the social services to a fuller extent. Sad to say, few of the poor couples I met in phase 1 enjoyed such hopes for improved family life.

[5]

Introducing Secure Families

Couples with above-average education, a skill, or another asset did far better under first-stage Singapore industrialism. As they held solid jobs and their futures seemed bright, I refer to them as secure, but they include couples of relatively modest means as well as the affluent. Secure couples worked in both core and peripheral sectors. By looking at some details of their lives, we can see how their position in the labor market affected their family styles and personal relationships. A focus on representative couples also shows that the well-off based their strategics for advancement on their family assets early in the developing order. I begin with peripheral-sector workers: a meter reader and a wholesale grocer have education and capital as assets; a sewing machine mechanic has skills. Core-sector men include a computer technician, a quality control foreman, and a draftsman in an oil company.

Goh Family: Meter Reader and Garment Factory Worker (I)

Goh Tee Tong, aged thirty in mid-1974, read electric meters for the Public Utilities Board, a quasi–civil service post that was secure and well paid and hence a desirable working-class job. Of Teochew background, Tee Tong was married to a Hokkien speaker, Bee Tim, and had a two-year-old son. Bee Tim counted the piecework output of seamstresses in her section in a garment factory. Taken together, the Gohs' joint income was nearly twice the Singapore male median wage. Their income provided them with a solid start in married life, although it was not high enough to free them from their kin.

Tee Tong owed his secure job to his above-average family background. His parents were from merchant families. Father Goh had owned a cargo boat and Mother's brother was a shopowner. Father had lost his property to the Japanese and had received S$10,000 as compensation after the war. He then became a house painter, but sometimes lacked work and relied on his children's earnings for support. There were twelve Goh children, ten of them still living at home. Tee Tong was the eldest.

Despite Father's business setback, Tee Tong was able to complete secondary school and passed his O-level exam. During his compulsory army service, a classmate who was serving with him coached Tee Tong as he wrote to his member of Parliament to request help in locating a job. The appeal had the hoped-for effect and got him his position as a meter reader. He held this job for nine years. He earned S$500 monthly and believed that his work suited his educational level. Tee Tong prided himself on getting his own job, which is how he interpreted the introduction by his M.P., and he claimed to need no help from well-placed kin: "The richer they are, the farther I stay away from them," he reported.

Tee Tong was ambitious and hoped to expand his earnings. "Have you ever thought of changing your job?" I asked him. "Yes, but where else can I get such a good deal, five hundred with short working hours? I have a few sidelines. Not doing business—that takes capital. I'm thinking about going into sales on commission. It doesn't take much money to start." Tee Tong had friends in this line of work and he thought of getting help from them.

Tee Tong also joined the volunteer police force as a community service. He later complained that he was paid only 70 cents an hour for this service, and should have gone instead to evening school to study "management" and better himself. But he greatly enjoyed the authority conferred by the rank of sergeant and the brotherhood of the others. He was keen on contributing to the common weal. And throughout our long acquaintance, Tee Tong saw himself as a guardian of that civic life which had so benefited him.

Bee Tim was the eldest of four children. Her mother, widowed young, then married a man in construction subcontracting, good work at the time. Mother had never gone to school or earned a wage, and now busied herself tending fruit trees and a flock of chickens and geese in her courtyard at home, on the outskirts of the city. Bee Tim attended an English-stream primary school but failed to pass into secondary school, although her family could have managed to pay for her studies. Bee Tim said sadly, "Mother really couldn't teach me how to study, and she didn't discipline me either. Now I regret it. I will certainly make sure my son studies well."

Soon after graduation, Bee Tim went to work in a nearby garment factory, a branch of a Chinese firm in Hong Kong. One of the early entrants into the garment export industry, Bee Tim earned only S$200 a month, the median women's wage. Believing she could never earn much in this peripheral-sector firm, she considered quitting. There was some tension in the family over Bee Tim's continued employment, but it was contained and did not lead to open disputes.

At times Bee Tim spoke wistfully of being able to spend full days with her son. "In Singapore, women drop out of the factory when they marry. Seamstresses and so on stop work. Office workers keep on. It's a question of income. We don't earn enough to make it worthwhile," she explained. She was under some family pressure to quit because of her low wages, but the Goh family used her wages to upgrade their standard of living.

Bee Tim was not keen to quit her job. Her comments on her desire to quit were spurred more by the image of a homemaker who can afford to care for her son and husband than by an actual desire to stay home. Employed in the firm for over ten years, she very much liked her colleagues and was proud of being able to walk around the floor as part of her job. She was frequently praised. "I'm often told I'm a fine worker. That makes me feel good." To justify her failure to quit, she reported on the improvements in working conditions during her tenure in the firm. "When I started we earned fifty cents an hour and had to work ten hours every day. Now we earn nearly a dollar twenty-five an hour." The only thing she disliked was compulsory overtime. As a low-level clerk, she had no chance to advance. To become a section leader, she would have to learn how to sew, as she had to be able to demonstrate all the features of the work. She's have to take responsibility for the work, and if it were not done on time, she would "receive a scolding," so she did not think she would advance to this post.

Tee Tong was also ambivalent about his wife's working. If she insisted on working, then she should "stick up for her rights. She should tell them, 'You can't force us to work overtime.' I wanted her to argue for the rightful day off, but she was too submissive. If we had a strong labor union, they couldn't lock the girls up and make them work overtime," he protested. Tee Tong was a firm believer in demanding one's rights.

Her mother understood that the Gohs needed money and that today's married women differed from those of her own generation, who did not work in factories. She fully supported Bee Tim's work. Bee Tim gave token gifts of money to Mother, but Mother had a son and husband to support her and was not badly off. Bee Tim then used her earnings mainly for herself and her family. Her mother-in-law received S$50 monthly for child-care help, and Bee Tim gave most of the rest of her income to Tee Tong to deposit in her separate savings account.

She got along with her co-workers, but as most were single, she seldom joined in their activities. "I come right home after work. But we do enjoy talking with each other during work. We often discuss cosmetics, and show each other how to put on makeup." Bee Tim also created new social ties in the plant. She found work there for her second sister-in-law as a seamstress and for her brother as an apprentice tailor. As a married woman, she considered that her main interest was her husband. Yet she clung tightly to the right to work.

Marriage did not impose a heavy double day on Bee Tim. She looked to her husband's family for help. The household took advantage of everyone's labor in a way that allowed Bee Tim to continue working without strenuous objections from other members.

The eldest four Goh siblings were sons, all of whom worked and gave part of their earnings to the household. Then came two daughters, the one who was working in the same factory as Bee Tim (and who also contributed money to the home) and another who had lost an unskilled factory job and now did the housework. The remaining six were sons, the youngest four years old. Father, five of his children, and Bee Tim therefore supported the household, while Mother Goh and her daughter did most of the housework.

Only one other besides Tee Tong had married, his next brother, who lived elsewhere. Mother Goh cared for all the children—her own, Tee Tong's son, and her other married son's infant daughter, who was left with the family during the week—and did the daily marketing. Her second daughter cleaned the house, washed the family's clothes, and took turns looking after the children in the evening. Tee Tong, who often completed work by mid-afternoon, liked to return home early and cook the evening meal. Sometimes he cooked for everyone, sometimes only for Bee Tim and himself. Tee Tong also ironed his and his wife's clothes and cleaned their bedroom. "She's lucky," he said with a grin, and indeed his willingness to do housework was unusual. Even on her day off, Bee Tim had no pressing tasks to perform in the home.

The Gohs had met through mutual friends. A fellow volunteer policeman, a friend of Bee Tim's brother, introduced them. Tee Tong chuckled when he recalled how the mutual friend drove him to Bee Tim's house as a practical joke. The couple dated, and when they married Bee Tim was several months pregnant. Their main regret was the financial burden of raising a child so soon after marriage.

The Gohs enjoyed each other's company and liked to shop together on weekends. In the street markets they chose bright-red satin-finished cloth for Bee Tim's frocks and clothing for their toddler. Tee Tong usually made the final choice. They strolled through the outdoor marketplace looking for bargains and then stopped at a hawker's stall for a bowl of noodles. The couple might cap these late-afternoon excursions with a movie. Tee Tong and Bee Tim went out together several times a week, leaving their child at home.

Mother Goh did not want the couple to go out together so often, and sometimes she insisted on joining them at the movies. Bee Tim unburdened herself about her mother-in-law: "That old woman is not a bad person, but she doesn't understand that I want to be alone with my husband. I don't like the idea of Mother-in-Law coming along with us to the movies." Tee Tong was sensitive to his wife's feelings, and eventually stopped including his mother on their outings. Like many other young salaried husbands, Tee Tong was torn between loyalty to his mother and Bee Tim's claim on his attention. He placated his mother but gave first place to his wife.

Bee Tim considered Tee Tong her closest companion, and they discussed many issues. Tee Tong made most decisions. He decided the monthly sum of money to give to his family for food and rent. He decided on the location, size, and price of the flat that they applied for. He arranged their outings and bought Bee Tim's clothing. When they used the rhythm method of birth control, he counted the days of her monthly cycle. Tee Tong treated Bee Tim almost like a doll to look at and care for.

Bee Tim informed us, "Tee Tong likes me to dress up. If I want something, I just ask. After all, he took me as a wife. He should be willing to spend money on me. The other day he gave me a hundred twenty dollars for clothes and I've already used it up." I once joined them on a shopping expedition. Bee Tim tried on dresses while Tee Tong told her which ones were pretty and accurately guessed the prices. Indeed, they influenced each other. Tee Tong revealed, "A few years ago I couldn't care less about clothes. Bee Tim persuaded me to dress more fashionably. Now I go for expensive material and design my outfits myself. The other day I spent a hundred dollars on several pieces of material for pants. I have so many pairs that I could never wear them all!"

Next to her husband, Bee Tim felt closest to her mother, whom she visited every Sunday. Bee Tim also found Mother-in-Law quite easy to talk to. Mother-in-Law confided in Bee Tim that the pain of childbearing was so intense that she had unsuccessfully appealed to her husband to stop having sex. "My own mother is too traditional to talk to me openly like that," Bee Tim confessed. Yet Bee Tim often referred to the tensions of living with her in-laws, "I get along all right with my sisters-in-law, but I don't really have anything special to talk to them about. I don't even ask them to sew my clothes for me. The less I ask for, the fewer problems."

Tee Tong felt their combined earnings of S$700 were more than adequate, and stressed the importance of saving. "When you keep your money in a box at home, there's a temptation to open it up and take it out. There must be a reason to go to the bank. It makes you think twice." Yet they spent large amounts on consumer goods. While Tee Tong often voiced his hope that Bee Tim would quit her low-paying job in favor of spending more time with their son, they would have found it difficult to live at the same level if she had actually quit. Bee Tim, who did not really know what she could do with her time if she quit, stressed that since her help was not needed in the home, she had no reason to do so. "Tee Tong said I could rely on him to support me. But how can I stay in the flat all day? I'd be so bored. And it's chaotic here. So I told him if I don't work, I'll just sit down, stick up my feet on a chair, and take it easy. He was so mad!" Her continued input was a compromise that gave them extras but also required them to live with his family.

Upon their marriage, the couple was awarded the main bedroom in the Goh flat, and the former kitchen was converted to a second bedroom. Father slept on the raised platform that once had held a wood-burning stove, while Mother and her two daughters slept in a double bed in the same room. The sons slept on mats on the floor of the living room and on the sofa. The small storeroom became the kitchen.

Despite the prized bedroom, Bee Tim resented the close family living. She wanted her own home, to buy more consumer goods and "be free" of the constraints of the family. Her wish to be "free" was class-based, and rested on the Gohs' above-average living standard. I asked Bee Tim, "Whose idea was it that you should move into your in-laws' flat when you married?" Bee Tim expressed her unfilial views in a low voice, as if someone might overhear. "I wasn't for the idea. I wanted to live apart, but we didn't have much money. Besides, we thought we might be able to get a flat pretty soon after our wedding—we didn't realize it would take so long. So my husband said we might as well move in with his parents. His mother also wanted us to stay with her. But I find it inconvenient. I have to lock up my closet when I leave for work in the morning. Otherwise my seven-year-old brother-in-law will mess up everything inside. There's never any peace at home. Everything is so confusing and noisy!"

Bee Tim gestured around the bedroom. "It's so crowded here that I just haven't redecorated our room at all," she explained, although the room was quite neatly arranged. Her voice rising with excitement, "We really look forward to having a place of our own, so we can be free of the restraints of living together. I'd be free to have more room, to fix up our home the way I want. Free of the family. I'd be free to care for my own children."

They faced economic difficulties in taking this step to a home of their own. Tee Tong therefore thought the lower expense of their extended household living was a practical means of saving money. He was also concerned to maintain a proper balance in his relations with his wife and his family of birth as eldest son. "I earn five hundred, my wife earns two hundred. Altogether we pay my mother a hundred sixty every month for food, rent, and utilities. My next brother and his wife, who live elsewhere but leave their daughter here during the week and eat with us, pay the same. Third Brother, who isn't married yet, gives a hundred. The total is quite enough. Anything else we add to the household is up to us. But we do buy things. I paid for the TV, for example, but when we move we won't take it with us because it wouldn't be nice. Otherwise you're no longer like a family. In fact, my wife and I are now discussing how we can continue to contribute to the household after we move out. I think we will, otherwise it sets a bad example. When all my brothers and sisters are grown up and everyone leaves home, who will care for our aging parents?"

While depending on his parents and siblings, Tee Tong made plans for his own family. "We put our name on the list for our flat four years ago. HDB offered us a place in Toa Payoh two years ago. That area had a reputation for crime and it's far from Mother's, so I wouldn't move there. So the HDB put our name at the bottom of the list again. Now I really regret it, because Toa Payoh has become quite stable, and we've waited such a long time. We've also put our name down to rent an HDB flat while we're waiting to buy one. Privacy is really important to us. We plan to use my CPF to buy a home, and it will take almost twenty years to pay it off. No need to put money in the bank for a home."

He had already begun to save money to furnish the home of the future. Tee Tong showed us the kitchenware set he had purchased for the event. "We bought these Tupperware things for twelve hundred on installment. We're getting ready for our new flat!" Bee Tim added, "We keep them all under our bed. They're stuffed with things! Now and then my husband takes them out to dust and cleans the floor. I think he likes to look at them."

Tee Tong told us, "My mother is willing to take care of the grandchildren because she belongs to the older generation. She feels grandmothers should take care of grandchildren as a matter of duty." Yet Bee Tim voiced a common complaint of secure women: "Mother-in-Law absolutely spoils my son. There's no way for me to control him. He only fears his father, not me, although I discipline him sometimes. When I hit him, Mother-in-Law pulls a long face, because she loves the kid so much. But that absolutely spoils the child. He's wild! Sometimes I complain about the misbehavior of my two youngest brothers-in-law to my husband's second brother and he will hit his younger brothers for me. Then Mother-in-Law gets mad, and it looks like all the household troubles started after I joined the family!" Although she depended on the wider family for help with child care, Bee Tim complained that she could not raise her children her "own way."

Tee Tong also reflected on generational differences in raising children. "I'd like to be friends with my father rather than hold him in awe. I argue with him about his old-fashioned ideas. Of course, Father doesn't like me to talk back! I also treat my son like a friend. I play with him and take him with me to the police station when I'm doing night duty. It's better when your children listen to you out of mutual respect, and there is no need to punish them." Such leniency was appropriate to his circumstances, for Tee Tong did not expect his son to contribute to his support in later years, "This is a different generation from my father's. Nowadays we want to take care of our own finances."

Although two elder Goh sons had received secondary education, four younger children had already stopped at primary school. Only one son now in secondary school could be counted on to continue. The Gohs expected to send their own son to an English-stream primary school, "of course! Nowadays no jobs are available for the Chinese-educated." And then Tee Tong hoped their son would become a doctor. However, they had no funds specifically earmarked for the boy's later years. Indeed, Bee Tim did not seem to be fully aware of the competition for higher education. She referred instead to the Buddhist cycle of retribution to explain why five of her in-laws quit school after the sixth grade. "We must have done something wrong five hundred years ago. Now we have the money for them to study, but they just can't pass the course." Thus, although she held higher hopes for her son's schooling, it was not clear whether she knew how to channel his energies.

They hoped for three children. I asked Bee Tim if she had practiced birth control before their son was born. "Yes, we did. But we miscalculated. We used the safe-period method. My husband knows how to count the days, I don't. He reads about the methods in books." Their new baby did not greatly inconvenience her, as the Goh family took care of him. "Why don't you use a more reliable method?" I asked. "I'm scared of them. All kinds of harmful side effects. But my husband has been telling me to try the IUD."

They were postponing their second child until they had more time and money. Bee Tim again spoke of her hope for more privacy when she had her next child. She recalled that during her first pregnancy, she could not relax. "I had very little trouble with childbirth. Little pain. I wasn't sick or clumsy, either. I worked at the factory throughout. But when I felt tired and sleepy, I couldn't lie down, because my little brothers-in-law would come in and disturb everything. I wouldn't be able to rest at all."

"Would your mother-in-law say anything against you if you stayed in bed?" I asked her. She nodded. "She wouldn't be happy. That's why I didn't dare lie down much. My husband came home every afternoon when I was on maternity leave to keep me company. He cooked me something to eat. Mother-in-Law also cooked for me. We'll wait a long while before having a second child. The reason we want a small family is not government pressure but the need to finance their education. We really want our child to study hard and succeed. You have to watch over them and make sure they study, train them in their lessons, and don't let them go out to play so often. You can't bring up your children properly if you have too many."

Tee Tong was in accord with the population disincentives, although he based his family-size plans on his own analysis of his family's needs. "I think the disincentives are fair. Singapore is too overcrowded. It's for the good of the families themselves. If they have a small family, parents can afford to bring up their own children and educate them. It's also fair because everyone can have a place in school." "How about the measure regarding the fourth child's difficulty in getting a place in school?" Tee Tong reasoned, "It's not that the child won't have a place in any school. It's just that parents can't pick the schools they like. We've had some discussions with friends about this, and we don't particularly agree with this measure. And then we concluded that the government must have a reason for doing this. They must have thought about these things very carefully before they would pass such a law. I tell you, the Lee Kuan Yew government has done a lot of good for our society. I really admire that man!"

As a worker in a job more secure than most, with a solid family income and a public-sector flat, Tee Tong put his trust in the state. He reasoned that the government knew what was good for people in general, and for his family, too. Proud of his public service position, he was proud of his ability to aid the progress of the nation. He had great faith in the place of his family in the future order of Singapore.

Ong Family: Vegetable Stall Proprietors (I)

The Ongs managed the Good Year Vegetable Market, a peripheral-sector wholesale vegetable firm in densely settled Chinatown. Although Ong Nan Seng earned well above average, the Ongs' family plans were limited by their deep material and structural ties to the family. Nan Seng and his wife, Siew Hwa, worked in the family firm. Siew Hwa was not paid for her work, and her talents were channeled to helping the firm behind the scenes. Because of their economic ties to the family firm, the Ongs had little capital that they could use, but their aspirations were high. Nonetheless, these constraints shaped a more segregated marriage style and allowed less freedom to maneuver than I found in other secure couples I met.

Nan Seng, of Hokkien Chinese background, was thirty years old in 1975 and had worked in the family business since he left primary school. He was the sixth child and third son in a family of eight children. It is common for the oldest son to run the family business, but Nan Seng took charge. Siew Hwa explained why her husband had more authority than any of the four brothers: "Eldest Brother-in-Law is an adopted son. Mother-in-Law had three daughters and then many miscarriages, and thought she would never have a son of her own. So she adopted him to bring some luck. When he grew up, he went to work for another company as a truck driver. That's probably because as an adopted son he had to put up with jealous comments by relatives that he was after the family's money." (It is widely believed that an adopted son will remain loyal to his own blood line.)[1]

"Four years after Eldest Brother-in-Law was adopted, my parents-in-law bore a true son, Poh Seng. They spoiled him, and he became the black sheep of the family. Poh Seng works in the Good Year Market sometimes, but he's unreliable. He works in an illegal lottery at other times. He frequents bars and is a womanizer." The Chinese view a person who has been raised leniently as one who will not endure hardship. Such a person will squander the family's capital. "When Nan Seng wasn't doing well in school, Father-in-Law was afraid he would go astray like Poh Seng. Father-in-Law brought him to help with the business and paid special attention to him. After that, father and son got along quite well. Now my husband works there full-time, and is helped occasionally by his next younger brother and sometimes by Poh Seng."

Siew Hwa came from the same market background as her husband and was deft at helping to run the complicated family firm with its many personal demands. Her widowed mother maintained a small provision shop in Chinatown, catering to customers who sent parcels to relatives in China. Mother believed that as the shop made little money, she could not afford to employ a staff reliable enough to deliver the goods. Siew Hwa was the fourth of seven children. When she turned twelve, her eldest brother was employed as a teacher and her elder sisters had married. Mother turned to Siew Hwa, who left school to work in the shop. When Siew Hwa married and turned her attention to her husband's vegetable firm, Mother had to close the provision shop. Nan Seng then helped Siew Hwa's younger brother obtain a clerk's job in a nearby Chinatown bookstore.

With the aid of kin, Nan Seng had attained the pinnacle of traditional dreams: a family business. The firm imported 600 kinds of vegetables from Malaysia, Indonesia, and the People's Republic of China to meet year-round customer needs. They supplied Singapore restaurants and provisioned ships from Indonesia and the Republic of China. Sales expanded with the flourishing of the restaurant business. They also had some retail sales. The monthly turnover of the firm was between S$10,000 and S$20,000.

Nan Seng took home S$600 and put nothing into CPF. His wage was enough for family expenses, but he was unable to save because the firm plowed back profits into the company as working capital. Nan Seng thus found it hard to make distant plans for his own family, but he held high hopes for the firm.

Siew Hwa wished to help out, but each of her moneymaking projects encountered problems. "We used to glue together Kotex boxes. I did this with the second wife of my husband's older brother. But she had recently undergone an operation and her husband objected that it was tiring for her to sit down all day, so we had to stop. We were paid two dollars for a thousand boxes. And even though we sometimes worked all night to finish them on time, my husband didn't object to this kind of work."

But Nan Seng did not want Siew Hwa to work for strangers. "I was considering taking in the four-year-old child of a friend who is working. She'd bring the child here for the day and take him back after work, and she'd pay me seventy dollars every month. Nowadays servants are expensive and it's hard to get one to come to your home, so a lot of working women board their children out. But my husband objected to the idea. He said it's a lot of responsibility. Otherwise, next year, when my youngest will be going to kindergarten, I thought I'd have the time." Siew Hwa then considered turning her cooking talents into a profit-making venture. She hoped to take cooking lessons at a nearby community center to upgrade her skills and then go to work with a relative in a stall or restaurant. Nan Seng did not object in principle, but Siew Hwa's relative did not proceed with his part of the plan. Siew Hwa also remarked that Mother-in-Law relied on her for help and would not want her to work full-time. This was a case of a wife's complete submission to the needs of the family enterprise.

The Ongs met through friends in the community. They had known each other for two years before they married. Their division of household tasks was governed by their close ties to the family business and by the young age of their children. Siew Hwa did her own housework and helped at the family store. She had experienced many problems in the early years of her marriage because of this double burden, but she learned to put the needs of the wider family first. At that time, Siew Hwa and Nan Seng rented a room near the family store.

"I used to cook both for our family at home and for the market staff. Even when I was expecting my first child, I had to go to Mother-in-Law's place and cook the noon lunch, wash up, and then start cooking again at three o'clock for the five-o'clock dinner. If Mother-in-Law returned home from the store and saw that I hadn't started to cook, she'd scold me. I was so upset by my obligations that on many days I couldn't even eat. Whenever I returned home for a visit to Mother, Elder Brother used to ask me why I was so thin! You see, living with the old folks means accommodating them in all sorts of ways. It's no good complaining to your husband about how his mother treats you. It would just put him in a difficult position. He wouldn't know what to do about my unhappiness. After all, it's his mother! In my eight years of marriage, I never once answered her back. When we first married, Father-in-Law, who is very nice to me, told me that Mother-in-Law had a bad temper, and I should give in to her. Since the old man put it this way, how could I go against the old lady? Before we got married, my husband warned me that Mother-in-Law was different from my own mother. My mother has been most helpful to her own daughter-in-law, looking after the grand-children and cooking for her instead of the other way around."

After they rented a flat farther away, Siew Hwa still had to help during family gatherings. "With a large family like this, someone has to offer to cook. Otherwise, if this person doesn't want to and that person doesn't want to, nobody at all will do the work. So we all have to give in a little. I'm more easygoing than my husband's sisters, and more willing to work for the family. Elder Sister-in-Law only knows how to prepare one kind of dish. My younger sisters-in-law have long manicured fingernails and don't want to spoil their hands. The firewood for Mother-in-Law's stove gets your hands dirty. So she calls me over to cook whenever she feels she needs help." Only when she had three children to care for did Siew Hwa stop cooking for the family store. Fifth Brother's wife took over while Mother Ong, over seventy years of age, still went to the market to help with the business.

Unable to earn money, Siew Hwa reduced her household expenses. She dismissed the family launderer to save S$30 monthly and did the washing herself. She was used to frugality, having grown up at a time "when girls were more straight. They didn't expect a regular allowance from their parents. Nowadays, girls are smarter. They demand pay whether they're working for their parents or someone else." Nan Seng did not need to oversee Siew Hwa's budget; he trusted her, she said. Without his explicit command, for example, Siew Hwa turned down invitations to play mah-jongg in a nearby apartment that catered to card-playing neighbors, "because I also come from a thrifty family, and I understand my husband's situation." Siew Hwa managed to save S$30 of her housekeeping allowance each month in a tontine started by her sisters. Apart from this sum, she had no access to funds.

The couple's discussions mainly concerned their children. Nan Seng reserved his concerns about work for his father. The Ongs often could not act upon their decisions, because obligations to the family store and kin precluded economic and marital independence. They could not change jobs or buy a home without wider family agreement. Siew Hwa, however, accepted these constraints as legitimate.

Siew Hwa was satisfied to visit her mother every other week. She spoke to her sisters and friends on the phone. Most of her friends were childhood acquaintances, and she arranged to meet them at her mother's home. The Ongs' few weekly outings were limited to taking the store's van to go shopping, and occasionally Nan Seng took the children for evening walks in the neighborhood. Siew Hwa did not join Nan Seng when he took wholesale buyers to dinner. Nan Seng spent most of his time at work, and he took New Year's Day as his sole holiday.

Siew Hwa spent much more time with the Ongs than with her own family. She prided herself on being the family peacemaker. Nan Seng's elder brother had taken a second wife. Siew Hwa sympathized with her. "My first sister-in-law can't look after her children properly and has no interest in the home. We think she badgered Elder Brother-in-Law to marry her. He didn't have much affection for her and so he got 'married' again, to a woman he really cares for. When my two sisters-in-law are at each other's throats, I'm the one who talks them into getting along with each other." The interviewer asked, "Does your elder brother-in-law's having two wives cause your other sisters-in-law to worry about their own husbands?" She replied, "It does make them a little nervous sometimes. As for me, I think if a man wants to look for other women, then the wife can't do anything about it!" She was resigned to the family structure dictated by the male family head or his parents.

Siew Hwa explained how the family business constrained their living arrangements. "Because of our ties to each other and to the business, it's not proper for our own family to put away earnings for our own home. Nevertheless, whenever I had the chance, I told my husband that it would be nice to have our own home. When we'd been married three years I finally persuaded Nan Seng to rent our own HDB flat, and we moved away from his mother's neighborhood."

The Ongs' one-bedroom flat was decorated modestly. "It's clean but simple," Siew Hwa reflected. They had bought the basic consumer durables for their social circle: an Acme refrigerator, black-and-white television set, and telephone. Green linoleum covered the floors. Their living room was dominated by a huge altar with incense burners and pictures of the god of peace, Kwan Yin, and the god of luck and prosperity, Tai Sin Yeh, to protect the family's business fortunes.

The Ongs paid a registration fee to buy a three-bedroom flat, and after another three-year wait were offered a new apartment. However, Siew Hwa felt that Nan Seng's filial obligations outweighed the benefits of home-ownership and they did not go through with the purchase. They offered their place at the head of the waiting list to Nan Seng's youngest brother, who had just become engaged. Siew Hwa explained the transaction: "It was my idea to give up the new flat to my husband's youngest brother and his bride. If we had taken it, people might have said, 'You're being greedy. You already have a flat to live in. Do you really need to buy another at a time when your elder brother is getting married and has no home at all?' Also, if we borrowed money from the business to buy it, then we'd have been obligated to offer a room to Nan Seng's brother and his new wife, and there's always the chance that I might not get along with her. And in addition to the family arrangements, we're not sure when urban renewal will come here and pull down more Chinatown shops. When that happens, we'll move the business. It will be better to know where the new location will be before we buy a home. All in all, there's no point in buying a flat now. Now that Fourth Son is engaged, Fifth Son will give their extra bedroom to the new couple. The brothers in the family are all very close."

Siew Hwa explained that if she had not been willing to give up their home-buying option, Nan Seng would have gone ahead and placed the down payment on the flat. She was so used to complying with the family's wishes that she anticipated complaints before they could be uttered.

Mother-in-Law held strong opinions on Siew Hwa's methods of raising her two daughters, aged four and eight, and their five-year-old son. Siew Hwa was cautious in the older woman's presence: "I'm the one who disciplines the children. If I really get angry, the children fear me. When the children are naughty, I tend to scold them and beat them, but my husband doesn't like to see me do it. Men spend so little time with their children that they're very precious to them. The kids are especially naughty when they've spent the whole day with me at Mother-in-Law's place, because I don't like to reprimand them there. Otherwise people will say that I'm too hard on them. Grandparents naturally dote on their grandchildren."

Siew Hwa had given thought to her own child-rearing methods, and stressed not abstract values of independence but practical methods of feeding and clothing them; even their moral training was approached from a concrete reference point. "There is considerable difference in child-care methods between Mother's and Mother-in-Law's generation and mine, and our new method is better. Before, people used to give children rice gruel with soya sauce, but we feed them milk, fish, vitamins, and other nutritious foods. The older generation scolds us when we dress our babies in thin clothing. They feel that babies should be wrapped with socks, bonnets, and blankets. We have to explain patiently to them that it's different now. When our children are older, we mothers will have to instruct our children in sex education. But one of my old-fashioned relatives, when her children asked her about something they'd learned in school about reproduction, scolded them for asking. I feel mothers must teach their children about sex. Otherwise, if the children are ignorant, they'll be easily led into doing something wrong." Siew Hwa tried to provide guidance for her children in this and other educational matters.

The Ongs sent their eldest daughter to a neighborhood English-stream primary school. Although the parents did not know English, they made an effort to improve their children's study habits. Siew Hwa reported that she made most of the child-rearing decisions. "I always tell Nan Seng when he buys toys not to get tea sets, but instead to get educational toys for the children, to increase their knowledge. I see to it that the children do their homework every night. I tell Nan Seng not to take them out for walks at night because they need to do their homework. My second child now needs my help because he has to learn the alphabet and numbers from one to twenty. My first is studying for her third-grade term exam. I seldom let the kids play outside the flat because if you let them roam freely in the corridor they'll imitate their playmates and go wild."

She combined strict and liberal child-rearing methods. "I sometimes scold the kids and beat them when I teach them, because it's most annoying when they still don't learn after an hour. But I also try to seek the cause of their difficulties. I've even gone to visit my elder daughter's teacher to see how I can help her review her lessons for the exam this year." The Ongs did not pay for a private tutor, but turned to better-educated kin for help. "My husband's sisters' daughters are all very bright, and they live nearby. I usually take my daughter to their homes so that her cousins can tutor her in English and help her with the rest of her homework." They hoped their children would rise above their own station. "I always tell the children to study hard so they can get a genteel kind of job and an easier life, and won't have to work as hard as their father." They used moral tales to encourage the children to take responsibility for their own future and to study harder.

They discussed their children's education. The children had a savings account into which they deposited their New Year's gifts. A friend had told Nan Seng about an educational insurance policy, and he was considering taking one out for the children. The Ongs believed that sons and daughters should receive the same level of education. Nevertheless, their occupational goals for their children were based on their sex. "For girls, jobs such as office clerks, and boys, engineering."

Their tight links to the family business and to Chinese tradition influenced most of the Ongs' decisions. Siew Hwa bore her three children in a Chinatown maternity home so that her husband could visit her during the slack time in the store rather than be confined to fixed visiting hours at the public Kandang Kerbau Maternity Hospital. Birth-control practices received the imprint of both state and local cultures. "My husband and I discussed family planning and agreed to space the children, so there was a wide gap between the first and second children. I took pills. I felt dizzy at first, but I switched brands and then I was all right. After the second child was born, I took Chinese medicine as a contraceptive. The herbalist said that taking the medicine for three months would be sufficient to prevent conception. But unfortunately he neglected to include the herb that would stop childbearing altogether. After taking the medicine for three months, I stopped and got pregnant. I wanted to have an abortion then, because it was difficult to cope with small children, but my husband wouldn't sign the consent form. My mother-in-law got to know about my intention and prevented me as well. We had only one son and she felt that that wasn't enough."

After the third birth, Nan Seng did not permit Siew Hwa to have a tubal ligation. "He said, 'Wait and see.' He also said, 'No one can look after the children.' But actually my mother could have come to help me." Siew Hwa acquiesced in the situation, but she planned to have no more children and was taking contraceptive pills again. Her ideal family size was two children, one boy and one girl. "If I didn't have a son, I'd try to have one. In this kind of family it's expected of me. But since we already have a son, I can stop now."

The Ongs knew about the government disincentives. They stressed, however, that they decided on their family size without reference to the measures, Nan Seng said, "I think three children is enough. I'm not affected by the government policy on population limitation. I plan for myself." He had in mind the short-term costs of supporting his family. "Nowadays people don't think the way they did in the past. They don't want large families. You need nearly six hundred dollars a month to support a family. Although the rich can pay for servants and for education, they also have to think of their children's future, about how they'll get jobs."

Nan Seng's responses to the cost of children reflected his mixed economic position. He was aware of the need to plan for his own family's future but was unable to set money aside. Funds for his own family's use were limited by the family firm, and his wife could not act as an independent economic actor either. The lack of money limited the Ongs' use of the social service package at the time, yet they had hopes for the future. Nan Seng and Siew Hwa were confident that their firm would grow and prosper, and that their own family would flourish with it.

Teo Family: Sewing Machine Mechanic and Garment Section Leader (I)

Teo Hiang Hong was a Teochew Chinese sewing machine mechanic in the Singapore branch of a Hong Kong peripheral-sector garment firm. Aged twenty-seven, Hiang Hong had worked in the firm for eleven years. In 1974 he was earning S$400 a month, which he felt was enough for his family. His wife, Lee Kim, aged twenty-six, was also a Teochew speaker. She had been a section supervisor in the same garment firm for eight years. The couple had a five-year-old son and a three-month-old daughter. The Teos' marriage was segregated because Lee Kim was very close to her kin, who were better off than her husband. Through them, Lee Kim had access to resources that helped her define and plan her family's future. Hiang Hong played a minor role in these plans.

Hiang Hong was the fourth child and third son in a family of one girl and five boys. Father Teo, a construction laborer, could afford to send Hiang Hong only through primary school. Hiang Hong began work as a messenger in the neighborhood garment firm, then transferred to the warehouse. He described his search for work as a personal effort, independent of his kin and friends. "I only earned a hundred dollars as an unskilled worker and felt there were no prospects. I decided to change my line of work. My boss liked me because I worked hard. I approached him and asked if I could learn sewing machine repair. He apprenticed me to a Hong Kong technician in our firm for three years before I was given full responsibilities for the job. It was tough. I had to work very hard to gain his confidence. In addition, the American Singer Company held a three-day course in Singapore, and my boss sent me, and paid the fee."

The garment company founder was also surnamed Teo, but Hiang Hong denied that this common "clan" tie gave him special treatment. "We just happen to have the same name. If there is any blood relation, it would be from ancestors long ago. He just happens to be a very good boss. I like him, and he looks after me. That's why I feel obligated to him."

Few men worked in the garment factory, and Hiang Hong caught the eye of management and was promoted. However, the narrow range of products, low level of technology, and small profit margin set limits to his future. Company policy required mechanics to leave when they reached their mid-forties because, Nan Seng explained, "they think your productivity will decline beyond that age, mainly because your eyesight goes. This work is hard on the eyes!"

After he had learned his skill, Hiang Hong was content to remain where he was. He worked in two other branches of the garment firm but in the same capacity, and did not expect further promotions. Hiang Hong was a dutiful worker, loyal to his employer and comfortable in the paternalistic arrangement. The employer's plan to terminate him in his mid-forties did not shake this loyalty.

Lee Kim was the fourth and youngest child in a family of three girls and one boy born to a farmer, now deceased. As a section leader, Lee Kim earned S$240, less than she had earned as a skilled pieceworker. Hiang Hong wanted to maintain good relations with his employer and urged Lee Kim to leave piecework and accept this position to give him "face."[2] Maintaining his standing was important to his career, so Lee Kim acquiesced. She, too, enjoyed the personal features of the informal work setting. "It's a friendly place. We aren't closely supervised and can chat, go to other sections, receive phone calls. We can even eat snacks at work. We talk about makeup, clothes, and other things. The only person we're a little afraid of is the big boss. The only thing that's wrong with our factory is that right now there's not enough work for us to do, not enough orders," she complained.

"I'd be bored if I didn't work. Even on Sunday I feel restless. I couldn't stop working. Prices are high, so I need to work," she added. Lee Kim gave half her monthly wage to her mother-in-law and neighbor for the care of the two children. Hiang Hong gave her S$80 every month for family expenses. She spent some of the remainder on outings and put the rest in the bank. Hiang Hong favored his wife's employment for the income and because Lee Kim enjoyed it.

Lee Kim anticipated that when she, Hiang Hong, and her children moved to an apartment of their own, she would leave the factory, because she would then lack help for her children. "After your children are older?" "Factories don't rehire women who are over thirty-five years old. I'll probably do outwork. Factories like ours send trucks to deliver goods to housewives who work at home."

Living with Hiang Hong's family relieved Lee Kim of some housework, but she still did some tasks, because her husband and his brothers did not help. Every morning Lee Kim made rice porridge and washed the clothes for the entire household. She cleaned her bedroom in the evening and ironed clothing for the household. Mother-in-Law prepared the evening meal. And on Sunday, Lee Kim cooked lunch.

Although the family freed her to work, tense relations in the household drove Lee Kim out of the house. Relations with First Sister-in-Law were especially difficult. Hence Lee Kim also chose to work "so I don't have to see all those sour faces."

Lee Kim and First Sister-in-Law, the only two daughters-in-law, competed for Mother-in-Law's attention. Lee Kim and Hiang Hong together earned more and had borne a son, whereas First Sister-in-Law was a full-time homemaker who cared for her three daughters. As the eldest son's wife, she was under pressure to bear a son. Lee Kim recalled: "Our youngest babies were born a week apart. When we were still carrying them, First Sister-in-Law proposed that if I had another son and she had a third daughter, we should trade children. I didn't say anything, but I didn't go for the idea. But anyway I had a girl, too."

First Sister-in-Law believed that Mother-in-Law Teo looked down on her. She detailed the rivalry over shares of the family purse. "There's too much gossip around and too much work for me to do in this big household. If you so much as eat an extra mouthful of rice, people will say something! Actually, my oldest daughter eats very little and Lee Kim's son eats twice as much!" she protested.

In turn, Lee Kim complained that First Sister-in-Law gossiped about her. There was also ethnic rivalry. "First Sister-in-Law won't say anything directly, but she talks about me to the neighbors, and they like me and so they tell me what she says. She gets jealous if Mother-in-Law treats me nice. You know, she's Cantonese, and those Cantonese!" To reduce tensions, Lee Kim turned outside for some of the help she needed. "Instead of asking Mother-in-Law to take care of my baby daughter, I hired our neighbor to babysit, because I'm afraid First Sister-in-Law might complain. Mother-in-Law helps Sister-in-Law with her kids so she can get her housework done." Lee Kim also sought refuge in the nearby home of her mother and her brother.

Her ties with her kin, which gave her a base independent of the Teos, had never been fully accepted by her in-laws. Lee Kim revered her brother's family for their generosity and criticized her in-laws for being tightfisted. Lee Kim tried to raise this problem with Hiang Hong, but he preferred to maintain harmony in the family, and discounted her accusations as women's gossip. The tension between mother- and daughter-in-law flared in 1972 when Lee Kim's father died. Lee Kim contributed S$200 to her brother toward the funeral costs. At the time, Mother-in-Law Teo said openly, "She gives money away as if her husband's money belongs to her own family!" Lee Kim recalls: "I was awfully hurt by that." Lee Kim believed that after this row, Hiang Hong saw the family situation more clearly, and he no longer faulted her for her poor relationship with his mother.

Hiang Hong and Lee Kim first met at work, but after their children were born, they rarely joined workmates on outings as a couple. Instead, Hiang Hong enjoyed excursions with his workmates and friends, while Lee Kim joined her own relatives. Their photo album contained many snapshots of Hiang Hong surrounded by young men and women from his workplace. He was photographed on picnics and dancing at parties with his friends, with Lee Kim nowhere in sight. Lee Kim was noncommittal when asked about his outings. "He likes dancing and I really don't," she said shortly.

Lee Kim's snapshots showed restaurant luncheons with workmates and various scenes with her elder brother's family and her mother. Lee Kim greatly admired her elder brother for his success in the family import business. She spent her time with them, and sought their advice on most matters.

Lee Kim and Hiang Hong sometimes went to the movies and took their son on strolls along kampung lanes in the evening. Even then they frequently ended up in Lee Kim's brother's home. Though she had never taken a vacation with her husband, Lee Kim had gone with her brother and his wife on a business trip to Indonesia during a week-long unpaid company layoff when the plant was being expanded. In 1974, Brother asked Lee Kim to join his family on a trip to Hong Kong. But Lee Kim had just given birth and was compelled to remain at home. They generously brought back many fine gifts for her. After that Lee Kim, who is athletic and sturdy, enjoyed swimming and rowing with them. While these activities were modest, they exceeded those she shared with Hiang Hong. The divided leisure pattern resembled that of poor couples, but Lee Kim retained significant areas of independence because of her spending money from her job and support from her well-off brother.

Hiang Hong and Lee Kim discussed some matters, but their communication was shallow. Hiang Hong was even-tempered, a devoted son and lenient father, but indecisive. Lee Kim liked to plan ahead, and she became irritated when Hiang Hong quietly withdrew. Generally she was the family decision maker, and her decisions were influenced by her well-to-do kin. Lee Kim applied for a new home, while Hiang Hong was not keen on moving from the kampung of his childhood. Lee Kim chose for her son the primary school that her brother's son attended.

The Teos lived in a roomy wood home and adjacent outbuildings built by

Father Teo twenty years earlier, on government land that they rented. The household contained fourteen members: Father and Mother Teo; Eldest Brother, a bus driver, and his wife and their three daughters; Hiang Hong, Lee Kim, and their two children; and three unmarried brothers. The compound contained several small adjoining buildings: an outhouse, a shed for bathing and washing clothes, two storage sheds, and a garage. Flower beds and mangosteen trees (bearing fruit that tastes like a blend of peach and pineapple, with purple skin and white flesh) circled the house. A kitchen lean-to attached to the house contained a refrigerator and wood-burning stove. The hall, with polished cement floor, held the family altar and two stereo speakers: its wall was adorned with family photographs, the largest picturing the five Teo sons arrayed by age. The hallway was flanked by three bedrooms, one for the senior Teos, a second for Hiang Hong and his family, and the third for the three unmarried sons. Behind the house was a one-room extension for Elder Brother and his family. Each evening the family members rested and chatted on the breezy, roofed front porch, furnished with a sofa, plastic dining table and chairs, and a large tank of tropical fish. The fourteen household members shared the refrigerator, stove, television, electric iron, stereo, telephone, and porch furniture. The only items that the family units bought separately were the beds and dressers in the bedrooms.

Until 1972 the household had functioned as a single economic unit. Father planned the budget and the amount each son would contribute, mainly on the basis of the number of family members and earnings in each unit. Then he retired and passed control over the budget to First Son. First Daughter-in-Law and Lee Kim took turns washing clothes and making breakfast and dinner. When First Daughter-in-Law gave birth to her third girl, however, she found her housework too time-consuming. It was inconvenient to prepare family meals and tend to her baby, although her husband helped at night. The conflicts that arose between the families of First Son and Hiang Hong precipitated a division. In 1973, First Son added two small rooms at the back of the house and moved into them with his family. They still shared the refrigerator and television of the main house, but his wife now prepared their own food on a gas burner. Thus the division of the household, which reduced tensions, could be managed under one roof in the kampung setting, and was inexpensive.

With no rent to pay but the small land rent, the family could live moderately well on low wages. Hiang Hong gave S$140 every month to his mother for household expenses. With few other major outlays, Hiang Hong and Lee Kim banked much of their income.

Then the government gave notice that the kampung would be leveled for a new airport to be built in the area. When they moved, each family would buy its own apartment. They applied for four HDB flats for First Son and his family, Hiang Hong and Lee Kim and their children, Second Brother (who had become engaged and was eligible for his own flat), and the older parents with their two unmarried younger sons.

Eager to live apart, Lee Kim took full responsibility for the move. "I won't wait until we're relocated to a place chosen by the government. I want to choose our new home," she said proudly. Hiang Hong, however, expressed regret at leaving the home where he had been born. Fearing to appear unfilial, he took no initiative in the move that would separate him from his parents. Lee Kim applied for their flat in a housing development. She was proud of her advance planning. "A fortune-teller told me my husband is the kind of person who doesn't think ahead and make plans for the future, but I'm just the opposite!" Although she contributed to the furnishings and helped buy the household television, Lee Kim did not expect to take it with her. She waved her hand airily, "They can have it all! We'll buy new things." She welcomed the opportunity to start a new and separate life in her own home.

Neither had yet given much thought to the education of the children. When asked whether he expected his children to support him in his later years, Hiang Hong replied, "I never bother to think too far ahead. My wife is different from me. I always tell her, 'Why think about things so far away? I don't even know whether I'll live that long or not!'" He thought, however, that he himself should respect and support his parents: "My parents are quite old now, and so they don't have many years left. I should do my best to make them happy."

Lee Kim had not yet started planning for the education of their children, and she had no special job in mind for them. She felt only that her children should study in the English stream. "Chinese is useless in Singapore; you can't get a decent job!" Lee Kim disciplined their children, and applied a rattan switch when their son did not obey. Hiang Hong was more lenient. "I've never beaten my son. Well, I think it's enough for my wife to discipline the child. A child also needs someone to love and comfort him."

Hiang Hong wished for a second son, but Lee Kim was not keen on a third child. She took contraceptive pills before and after the birth of her daughter. Hiang Hong gave economic reasons for spacing their children five years apart: "It's very difficult and expensive to raise a child. I don't mind working hard for the kids, but I don't think it's right to let the children suffer because we can't given them enough." He was nevertheless influenced by his mother's wishes; he had intended to wait even longer before having his second child, but his mother convinced him it was better to have the second sooner.

In this as in other life events, Lee Kim was influenced by her own mother: "After my daughter was born, I thought of having a tubal ligation. But Mother said I was still young and I should wait in case something should happen to one of the children."

Hiang Hong set his family size with an eye to his own needs, not the nation's. As one who regretted state housing relocation, he saw the population disincentives as just further state interference. He argued, "In all my life I've never heard of anything like such policies. You won't find them in Malaysia or any other country. People know whether they've had enough children and when to stop. Those politicians ask others to stop at two, but who knows how many kids they have!"

Although together the Teos earned a solid living, Hiang Hong's short career ladder and his close ties to his natal family pulled at his marriage tie and possibly limited his full participation in plans for the future. He allowed Lee Kim to make the family plans, aided by her kin and her wages. The Teos thus formulated medium-range family plans, which included HDB housing, probably three children, and no further job advancement by Hiang Hong.

Ramakrishna Family: Computer Technician and Homemaker (I)

Workers in high-technology core-sector firms on career ladders found it easier to plan for a future that fully used public services. And their access to resources strengthened the marriage bond, which also helped them to plan. Such a man was Ramakrishna Mani, my sole non-Chinese respondent, supervisor of shift operations for an American-owned computer firm that processed data for oil companies. Mani, aged twenty-six in 1974, was married to Wong Far Eng, aged twenty-nine and of Cantonese descent. The couple had a three-month-old son and were raising him in the Chinese culture.

The second of eight children, Mani was born in southern India and came to Singapore at the age of seven with his father, a barber without formal schooling, and his mother and brother. Plunged into the Singapore English educational setting and without parental guidance, the Tamil-speaking boy did poorly in school. "The change was a big shock. I was like a blind man," he recalled of his primary school years in Singapore. He managed to complete three years of junior high school, then joined the police force. After his National Service stint, a friend informed Mani of a job opening at the computer firm. Mani did not know how the friend heard of the opening, "possibly through friends of friends. He suggested that I go for it."

Mani started at S$200 a month in 1971, crossed the S$500 line by 1973, and earned S$560 in 1974. He felt his prospects were good, and he was a committed worker. "My company is very strong. The current inflation and depression won't have any influence on my company. I get quite good pay, and promotion in this firm is fast if the boss likes you. I intend to stay here for a while." Though Mani's lack of an engineering degree put him at a disadvantage, the small size of the company enhanced his chances for promotion, and he received recognition for his work. Mani would change companies only if he were sure of higher wages.

Short, plump, and lively, Far Eng worked as a junior mechanic in a locally owned color television firm, which sold to the local market. (It was thus a peripheral-sector firm.) Father Wong had cleaned ships in the dockyards for a low wage, and died when Far Eng was in primary school. Far Eng was the third of three daughters, the first of whom became a seamstress after primary school. Owing to financial hardship and the influence of relatives, who thought it was useless to educate girls, as they would inevitably marry, Second Sister and Far Eng nearly left school just as early. But Elder Sister took over and paid for their education. Second Sister became a nurse and Far Eng completed four years of high school but then failed the school-leaving exam. She became a factory assembler, but her above-average education made her eligible for technical courses, and after that she was promoted. Far Eng felt important as a junior mechanic: "I'm responsible for the final checking work on color TVs. You have to know almost everything about a color TV!"

In 1974 her monthly salary was S$200. Their above-average income, education, and jobs placed the Ramakrishnas among the affluent couples. Far Eng was convinced that considerable generational change had occurred and that women's roles differed from those of the past. "Women like my mother are usually shortsighted, simple-minded, and superstitious. Being a working woman with more education, I tend to think things through more, and think farther ahead." But she admitted, "Modern women have more problems and burdens, trying to be a good mother and wife and keep their careers going at the same time." She nevertheless liked working, and feared it would be dull to stay at home and unbearable to depend on her husband for every penny she spent. Mani wanted Far Eng to quit work and care for their baby, but she refused. "Besides, when a wife has her own income, the husband will treat her differently. And in case the husband should leave his wife, it wouldn't be too bad if the wife could earn her own living."

"Is equality between men and women possible?" I asked her. "No, not really. Since men and women are physically different, women just can't take certain jobs. It's good for a wife to have some kind of career and her own income, but it's better if her income is less than her husband's. Otherwise people might say something."

Mani and Far Eng met when both studied English in night school. When Mani's parents opposed their courtship, Mani left home and rented a room in Far Eng's home. One year later they married. Mother Wong's relatives were also critical, but Mother came around when the couple showed willingness to raise their children in the Chinese tradition. (Mani's elder brother also took a Chinese bride, a Christian, and converted to her religion.) They

[125]

named their son Ramakrishna Jonathan Wong, drawing on both husband's and wife's names. They did not give the boy a Chinese personal name so as not to offend Mother Ramakrishna. By the time of our 1974 meeting, Mother Ramakrishna had acquiesced in her children's mixed matches. Father Ramakrishna, however, had not fully accepted his Chinese daughters-in-law, and had not yet come to see the couple's infant.

Mani and Far Eng held a Chinese-style wedding banquet, and Mani observed the Chinese folk religious festivals. He accepted most of the customs that were daily practiced in Mother Wong's home. Mani recalled with a grin, "After living here for four years, I'm used to Chinese food, but when Mother-in-Law first prepared steamed chicken with chicken blood dripping from the bones, I was nearly sick to my stomach. I had to force myself to stay at the table." Mani and Far Eng spoke English at home, and planned to teach their son English, Cantonese, and Mandarin Chinese. Mani was not wedded to either the Tamil language or Hindu traditions. "Actually, my parents are sort of modern. We didn't even celebrate the Indian New Year when I was growing up. I'm a free thinker," he explained; he held to no specific religious belief.

Yet Mani was superstitious and freely drew on both cultures to protect his family. His baby wore a colorful loose circlet of linked cotton thread around his waist: "Several years ago someone used a charm on me and made me very ill. I was afraid the same thing might happen to my son, so I asked an Indian woman to make this special belt for my son to keep evil away."

They lived with Mother Wong in a two-bedroom HDB flat owned by Elder Sister, who lived elsewhere. Their flat also housed Eldest Sister's three-year-old son, whom Mother Wong cared for. The Ramakrishnas paid the housing installments and bought the groceries. Even after they gave a neighbor S$80 monthly to care for their infant, they were still able to save. They thus helped support Far Eng's mother. Mani did not need to contribute to his parents' upkeep, leaving this task to his older brother, who earned a substantial salary as an army officer.

The couple shared household tasks with Far Eng's relatives. Far Eng did the household shopping every week, and Mani sometimes mopped the floor. Mother Wong cooked, and everyone helped with the cleaning. Far Eng usually washed clothes, and sometimes Mani filled the washing machine. Both were responsible for their infant's night feeding when Mani wasn't working on the night shift.

Mani spent as much time with his son as he could. "My child is a happy child. Everyone likes him. He makes a lot of noise, not crying but laughing and giggling. I try not to let my mother-in-law look after our child because I don't like the way she spoils Elder Sister-in-Law's son, whom she's looked after since he was a baby. And my wife isn't very happy when I criticize her mother."

Mani and Far Eng had a close relationship. One weekend in 1973 they traveled to the Cameron Highlands for a delayed honeymoon. "No money for a honeymoon before," Mani recalled. They knew each other's friends and discussed all family problems. It was not common for the people I met to show their intimacy in front of me, but this couple was friendly and full of humor. They kidded and teased each other, exchanged knowing glances, and then broke into laughter.

Before the birth of their son, they frequently went to see Hollywood films and Chinese martial arts movies. They strolled around night markets in parking lots and along main thoroughfares. After the birth they rarely went out together, and occasionally Mani accompanied his friends. Far Eng, who expected her husband to be a homebody, laughed off this touchy point. "He doesn't go out with his friends every week. If that were the case, I'd be worried. It might mean he has a girl friend if he went out that often!"

Far Eng had lost touch with her classmates, but she maintained contact with her workmates and phoned them often. She was close to her sisters. The baby in the family, Far Eng had been spoiled and usually given her own way. She recalls that she was bad-tempered until she was in her twenties. She was also watched carefully—was not allowed to go swimming, for example. "Once Second Sister dreamed that I drowned. After that I couldn't swim because most of Sister's dreams turned out to be true."

Mani was close to his elder brother, who had taken most of the photographs in the family album. The two couples with mixed marriages often visited on weekends and holidays.

Upon their marriage, they first lived in Far Eng's mother's home in Queenstown, then moved to the one-room flat of Far Eng's second sister, where they lived for six months. Second Sister, who was pregnant, had moved in with her mother to have help close at hand. A month after her baby was born, they again exchanged homes. Far Eng and Mani had not liked the one-room flat. "It was too small."

While their current living conditions were relatively uncrowded, they still yearned for privacy, and they put a deposit on a three-room HDB flat of their own. They would pay the estimated S$12,000 for their flat over time, using Mani's CPF fund, and were saving for the moving costs and the expected S$6,000 for renovations and fixtures. They were choosy about their new neighborhood. Mani explained, "Queenstown has one of the lowest crime rates; that's why I like to live here. I wouldn't choose Toa Payoh, which has a bad reputation."

They had already decorated their present home attractively. Their washing machine must have cost about S$350, their Sanyo refrigerator S$400, their black-and-white television set S$900, their large secondhand transistor radio S$150, their stereo S$500. Mani indulged his hobby of stereo equipment and wanted to buy the latest model tuner-amplifier, which cost

S$1,500. But Far Eng persuaded him to wait until they had moved into their new flat and had paid for the basic fixtures. "I reminded him we just had a baby and we don't know when we'll need the money. He was unhappy but finally agreed to wait."

At the same time, Far Eng complained that Mani should buy a car. But Mani objected, "What for? Too much traffic in Singapore already and we can get around by bus."

Far Eng: "It's still nice to have a family car."

Mani teased: "She wants me to buy a Jaguar."

They planned to fix up their new flat even more elegantly than their present home. Mani said, "Some people like to save more money. But life is so short, why not live more comfortably? Besides, after my son grows up and gets married, if he wants to live with us, he can also enjoy the better living environment."

Mani to Far Eng: "I'd like to have everything new in our own flat."

Far Eng: "Yah, you can have a new wife too!"

They planned to send their son to an English-medium primary school. Mani thought that since most firms in Singapore were run by Chinese, Mandarin would also be important. Tamil, however, was "not at all useful." Far Eng wished their son to learn English in order to communicate with his father. They had few concrete plans for their son, but Mani stressed flexibility.

Interviewer: "What do you want your child to be when he grows up?"

Mani: "It depends on the child. I hope he's not as stupid as I used to be! To tell you the truth, I was really dumb in school. But since I left school I've been trying to improve my English by reading newspapers and books. I also like futuristic English-language television programs, like 'Toward the Year 2000' and 'Here Comes the Future.'"

Interviewer: "In that case, how are you going to prepare your child for the future?"

Mani: "Well, I'll try my best to let him know the new things and bring him up in the new ways." He gave a concrete example: "During our childhood, babies only lived on milk, but now we feed them Heinz baby food." Later he mentioned another example of flexible child rearing: "Parents in the older generation didn't know how to educate their children. They would never allow children to ask questions about sex or listen to conversations about it. By doing this, they were only making the children more curious. Actually, it's better for the parents to teach their children than to let the children try to find the answers somewhere else. I've seen a very nice film teaching parents how to give sex education to their children—for instance, taking the children to the zoo to observe animal behavior."

Mani, who compared himself with the engineers in his firm, felt he suffered from ending school early. "I won't repeat the mistakes of my parents."

He hoped to send his son to high school, but worried that the wealthy families would maintain the edge in admission to the university. Therefore, Mani wished to limit his family size to educate the children for a changing society. The couple had delayed the first pregnancy until Mani's pay had passed the S$500 mark. Mani's economic concerns and his close bond with Far Eng supported the goal of a small family. Indeed, he encouraged Far Eng to have only one child.

Mani insisted: "One child is enough, because my wife had complications. She was in labor twenty-four hours and then had a Caesarean. When she came out of the operating room she looked just like a dead person to me, and I got such a scare. For the second child you must go through the operation again. I dread to think what may happen to her, and I don't know whether these operations will leave any bad effects on her. She may suffer when she gets old. But my wife doesn't seem to understand my concern for her. She still wants one more."

Bringing up children took considerable time and money, Mani explained: "Another reason for having one child is that we're both working. We have to leave the baby with another family. Unavoidably, the babysitting family will influence the child in many ways. Then if the child is taught differently at home, there will be confusion and problems. Take language, for instance. My wife speaks Cantonese, I speak English, and the babysitting family speaks Teochew. How can you expect a small child to learn so many languages all at once? And the other thing is that the babysitting family can feed and watch the baby but they can't give the baby enough affection. Nothing is like parents' love. So no matter how tired we are after coming back from work, we have to make an effort to make up what the child misses during the daytime. I think one child will give us enough problems to deal with."

"I've seen many people supporting children with a much lower income," the interviewer pursued. Mani insisted, "Although there are many ways to bring up a child, the right way isn't easy, and sometimes it can be quite expensive. I was rather dull at my schoolwork, but my elder brother was different. He was university material, but because of our family's economic situation he couldn't go that far with his studies. Income is very important in deciding to have two children. What is even more important is the matter of understanding. Before one makes a decision on the number of children to have, he must first understand himself and his situation today, and a few years into the future too. He simply can't insist on trying for a son, just because he has only daughters, without considering his own ability and the educational problems his children are facing in the future. Raising children is different from raising pigs!"

But Far Eng wanted a daughter as a companion for her son. "It's too lonely for my son if he's the only child in the family. He might grow up with an odd temperament because of lack of company. But I don't know if my husband will agree or not." She figured out the best year to have her daughter. "Nineteen-seventy-six is a good year to have the second child, since it's the year of the dragon." Mani teased her: "Seeing how busy you are with this child, don't you think with a second child you'll be even more busy?" She replied, "I can do it. Imagine, people used to have many more!" She planned to stop after the second birth so she would have enough time to raise the children properly. As a child needed a mother's love and care, she would probably leave her job when she had two.

The couple's reasons for limiting their family were personal and economic, but Mani approved of the family planning policies for the good of the people. "Some people insist that they must have a son and end up with many kids. Both adults and children suffer because of this."

Far Eng was also well versed in the disincentive policies because she wanted another child. She was concerned mainly about the clause limiting the large family's choice of primary schools while providing easier access to the small family. She believed that such policies were good, although the method of reporting children's births should be improved. Falsification was a matter of concern to Far Eng, who hoped to send her children to good government schools. Far Eng thought people who bore their children before the policies were announced should not be penalized; strict controls should be enforced to ensure that parents did not deliberately claim a lower birth order to facilitate a child's access to school.

Their response to the population limitation measures was consistent with Mani's career goal. His family already enjoyed the full range of services, from job retraining to the amenities of home and family planning. On a career ladder, Mani organized his family's resources to obtain even more for them in the future.

Chan Family: Quality Control Supervisor and Homemaker (1)

Chan Lam Lee, aged twenty-seven in 1976, supervised the quality control division of a core-sector American-capitalized firm of 400 workers. The firm, located in the Jurong Industrial Zone, made parts for oil rigs. Lam Lee was married to Sock Boon, a twenty-eight-year-old homemaker, and they had five- and two-year-old sons. Lam Lee got this skilled core-sector job at an early age and advanced with the state programs in the early 1970s.

Lam Lee's father was a fitter at Sembawang naval base. His mother remained at home, but she was a disturbed woman who could not manage the care of Lam Lee and his older sister. After he reached the age of eleven, he alternated between visits to his better-off grandparents in Malaysia and care by his father, who consequently had a strong influence on him. Father often took Lam Lee along to his workshop, and this eldest son soon developed a keen interest in mechanics.

He left his studies in an English-stream primary school because he "lacked the motivation to study," and at fourteen became a contract painter at the naval base. Father, fearing that his son was in danger as he climbed the slippery and unsteady scaffolding, forced Lam Lee to quit. Lacking a skill and with no introductions to other workplaces, the boy could get only dead-end jobs. He quit a job as an ironer in the Malayan naval barracks in the same area because he preferred more meaningful work. "I got no satisfaction from that job. Work means a lot to a man, though not to a woman, who finds it secondary to a home." Lam Lee, who believed that the work roles of men and women were different, though complementary, stressed that men must have scope to advance themselves on the job. At the age of sixteen Lam Lee went to work at the Sembawang shipyard as a messenger, and he was still there when the government began to upgrade the shipbuilding industry two years later. He responded to a flier distributed at the base, offering room, board, and pocket money to boys willing to be apprenticed at the HMS Dockyard Technical College.

Lam Lee studied the rudiments of mechanical engineering for three years at this college, then joined the ranks of shipyard workers at a monthly wage of S$200. He began to advance in job category and salary as he accumulated on-the-job experience. Lam Lee characterized himself as ambitious and as a self-made man. He was impressed by the rapid penetration of the market economy. "In this world, you can't go far without money!" He worked as a mechanical and then electrical engineer, then was transferred to quality control.

Lam Lee, who wished to move forward rapidly, thought his prospects were limited in this sizable division, and saw that he must cultivate personal relationships to advance. He quit and joined his present private-sector firm in 1972, and after a year of hard work became a supervisor of fitting for a monthly wage of S$1,100. He traveled to offshore rigs to service them, and felt he could still learn a lot. Lam Lee felt he understood workers, having himself learned his trade from the bottom up. He criticized the American managers of his firm for their insensitivity to the Chinese need to maintain face. "Some of the American managers don't know how to treat the workers. They shout at them in front of others. They praise the workers openly, too, but people remember the scolding more. Some expats [expatriates] treat the locals like they must treat their blacks. But we are sensitive. If you make a worker mad for no reason, he's likely to walk out on you and then you're the loser. In Singapore, workers don't worry that they won't find a new job—the only problem is the salary. The worst that can happen is that he becomes a road sweeper."

An attractive woman with her hair rolled in a crown around her head, Sock

Boon wore a pink-and-white flowered dress. Soft-spoken, she seemed even-tempered. But underlying this slow-paced manner was a strong determination to control her life. After completing three years of primary school, Sock Boon helped her mother perform domestic service for European families in Sembawang. By sixteen she was on her own. She gave S$80 of her S$120 pay to her mother every month. At eighteen she began to date Lam Lee. They married five years later, when Lam Lee, then earning S$200 a month, could just manage to support a family.

With no alternative because of her lack of education and industrial work experience. Sock Boon was content with married life. She fixed lunch at home for Lam Lee every day, and happily quit work when she became pregnant the following year. She did not expect to return to work. "I don't really like the idea, now that I have children to take care of."

Lam Lee and Sock Boon were Hokkien speakers who had grown up in the same small rural community. When I first met them, they lived in a wooden three-apartment house owned by Sock Boon's parents. In one apartment lived her mother, a home seamstress, and her father, a retired fishmonger; her younger brother, a naval base employee, and his wife and three children; Sock Boon's "younger sister," a cousin, whom Mother had informally adopted from her brother; and Lam Lee's mother. The second apartment was rented to an unrelated family. Lam Lee, Sock Boon, and their two children lived in the third flat. Living expenses were low, and the Chans paid only S$50 to Sock Boon's mother for rent and utilities. Lam Lee also gave S$20 a month to his wife's mother for her help with the housework and child care and S$80 to his own mother out of filial duty.

Compared with women with less kin support and smaller household budgets, Sock Boon had an easy day. "Sometimes I get up at seven and sometimes at ten. I have no set routine. I cook only if I feel like it. If not, we fetch a meal of chicken and rice from the market stall. Lam Lee is easygoing and doesn't insist that I cook myself. I wash clothes at the spigot in the front yard but sometimes they pile up for a couple of days. In the afternoon I bathe the children and ask Mother to watch them while I visit friends or go downtown. Since I have a refrigerator, there's no need to worry about shopping and storing food every day, but I usually do buy fresh produce daily from the van that comes to our house. In the evenings I like to go out with Lam Lee, but usually he's too tired to go anywhere."

Lam Lee gave Sock Boon S$600 every month for family expenses, and Sock Boon admitted that she spent a lot. "Just the other day I spent seventy dollars for a couple of lengths of cloth to have a dress made. I don't like to buy things on credit. I don't feel it's ours until we've paid it off. So when we bought our secondhand car, we paid three thousand and emptied our bank account. Lam Lee's not stingy, but sometimes he accuses me of spending too much. I don't care, I just answer back, 'If you think you're so hot, you buy things yourself!' and he gives up."

Lam Lee kept his money in a drawer. "Sock Boon knows where to get money when she needs it. We don't have a budget. When we run out, that's when we start counting pennies until the next paycheck."

Sock Boon and Lam Lee had a close relationship and talked over major family issues. Lam Lee respected his father's ability to care for the home and the children. But he wanted to build a more stable family than he had had as a boy, with himself as a strong breadwinner, like his father, and Sock Boon as a more caring mother than his own. Lam Lee treated Sock Boon as a partner, with separate but complementary strengths. Sock Boon was content with this role and believed that, in contrast to English-educated Lam Lee, Chinese-educated men rarely treated their wives as partners. She termed theirs an "equal relationship." Referring to their home life, she insisted, "I control him, he doesn't control me." When Lam Lee had time, he helped her with the housework. "My husband is very helpful. He even helps me wash clothes, and you know what Chinese people think of a man washing clothes! I've asked him, 'Aren't you afraid people will laugh at you?' He just says, 'They can laugh as much as they like!' He helps me change the sheets and sweep the floor, but he can't iron or cook. I think there's no such thing as a man's or woman's job. I'm teaching my sons to help with the housework too. I even make them empty the chamberpot into the cistern, much to my mother's shock. But I just tell her, 'They must learn to care for themselves.'"

The couple's close marriage and their solid income gave Sock Boon some independence from her kin. She admitted that her mother "used to control me. She took the money I earned and told me which friends to see, but she can't anymore now that I'm married." Sock Boon also asserted herself to her mother-in-law, with whom she did not get along. When the Chans married, they rented two rooms and invited Lam Lee's mother to live with them. Sock Boon got exasperated with her mother-in-law's inability to help, and when her first child was born, they all moved into her mother's home. They also put a deposit on a three-bedroom flat and planned to send Mother Chan to a home for the aged when they moved into it. "Not the charity kind, we're prepared to pay. I just don't want Mother-in-Law around," Sock Boon said. "Mother-in-Law is a funny case. She can talk intelligently, but her behavior is peculiar. Lam Lee has no love for his mother either. When he was small, she never took care of him, never prepared good meals, never worried when he came home late in the evening. Whenever he was sick, he had to wait until his father came back from work to take him to the doctor. His mother just didn't care. She used to cook a chicken and eat the whole bird, leaving her family with the bones. Sometimes she strikes other children without a reason, although she's usually good to her own. Mother-in-Law tried to control me when I first married. If I didn't wash the dirty clothes right away, she'd say something nasty. But I put her in her place. First, she's not the one who's washing the clothes, so it has nothing to do with her. Also, if she were logical, I'd respect her, but she's not. She stays in her own part of the house now. She's not a bad person, just strange. I sure wish Lam Lee's sister would see more of her mother so she'd know what I have to put up with. If I simply tell her about the problems, she thinks I'm exaggerating."

Questioned about his wife's relationship with his mother, Lam Lee supported her position. "Well, it's not proper to say much about the old folks— they've lived a hard life. But Mother and Sock Boon are from two different generations, and it's natural that they don't see eye to eye. We're thinking of sending Mother to my sister's home for a while. Mothers and daughters always get along well."

They did sent Mother Chan to live with her daughter during the week, and brought her back on the weekends. According to Sock Boon, "Mother Chan in fact didn't want to move, but I scolded her and insisted. I'm quite bad in that sense; I don't allow anyone to control me! Lam Lee didn't object, he never cared for his mother." Lam Lee paid his sister S$30 a week for this service, but the arrangement did not last long. Soon after her return, Mother Chan fell ill, and when her care became too burdensome on Sock Boon, she was placed in an old-age home. Sock Boon's plan to send Mother-in-Law to live elsewhere was unique in my sample, though the urge to live a life of one's own choosing was common among the secure couples.

They were a close couple in their own eyes as well as in mine. Lam Lee knew most of Sock Boon's girl friends and she knew most of his fellow workers. One afternoon I found Sock Boon preparing sandwiches and Jell-o for several of her husband's friends while Lam Lee washed dishes in the kitchenette. Lam Lee explained that he always told his wife where he was going, and she did not complain. "At times my friends invite me to join them for a drink to meet some salesmen, and I call my wife to tell her I won't be back directly after work. Sometimes I come home first and she just urges me to change my clothes and bathe." Sock Boon agreed. "The only complaint I have is when he returns late after one of those drinking parties."

Although some families took their children along to parties or wedding banquets, the Chans did not. Sock Boon exclaimed, "How embarrassing it would be! My friends don't do such things. My mother looks after our kids for us when we go out." Sock Boon added, "Lam Lee joins me when I drop in on my girl friends and their families, unless it's an obvious hen thing. When one of our kids is ill, we both take him to the doctor, and we both go for appointments at the clinic to get my birth control pills. We try to do everything together."

The Chans wanted their children to study in the English school stream.

Lam Lee told me, "I'd be happy if they went to the technical stream. They'll take their O-level exams. But you know education these days. What you get in school still doesn't amount to much. If they can't study so well, I'll let them have tutors. What's a few dollars more?" He wanted them to follow in his footsteps. "My eldest son already shows some mechanical interest. Whenever I repair my car, he wants to help. A trade like mine is a good one. If a kid gets a secondary school-leaving certificate and then a clerical job, how much can he earn? Not much more than four hundred, I bet."

Lam Lee stressed, however, that he would permit his son to make up his own mind. "I don't like forcing my kids to do anything. My own character is like that. I always spurn advice, and the more someone wants me to do something, the less likely I am to do it." Lam Lee was introducing his eldest son to his line of work, as his own father had done. A man with a solid future ahead of him, Lam Lee professed not to rely on his sons for support, but he did not rule out the possibility. "I only hope the boys can support themselves. If they want to go on living with us after they marry, that's fine with us, but I don't expect it. Trouble may start with the daughters-in-law, so unless they choose to live with us, we'll live apart."

As a man who benefited from the state social services, Lam Lee agreed that the government should try to slow population growth and raise revenue. The disincentives policy, in his view, was "fifty percent right. You find people with six children or more, which is terrible. The ideal family is three or four children. It's not true that if you have more children, your chances of having filial offspring are better. If you have a boy and a girl and they're good children, naturally that's wonderful. But if they turn out bad, you just can't do anything about it, and having more children won't help."

Sock Boon agreed with government policies as well. Singapore was "just too crowded. Look at all those HDB houses, they look like bird cages, and there are so many cars you have trouble parking. It might be difficult for the children if there weren't enough school places for them to find jobs." But she felt that the hospital charges were too steep for poor parents. "It's all right when you have two sons like me, or a boy and a girl. You can penalize parents for not stopping then. But if they have daughters, it's not fair to punish them. In this way the policy is unreasonable. It's not so bad for me, because I can afford it. But what about the women whose husbands don't even earn enough to feed the family?"

Lam Lee imagined that if they had had two daughters, they would certainly have tried a third time. If they again had a daughter, "that's just too bad." We've got to stop somewhere and think about feeding our children. Girl or boy, they're still your children, and you have a duty to take care of them."

Sock Boon agreed. "Every Chinese wants sons to carry on the family name. If I had only girls, I'd have to try for a son." Sock Boon herself was ambivalent about having a third child. "I'm very lazy and don't like too many children to take care of. If I should get pregnant by accident, I hope for a daughter. My husband doesn't have any opinion about this. It's a matter of what I want. The nurse at the clinic is always after me to have a ligation, but I hear it makes people bad-tempered. When she bugs me to have one, I tell her I want a daughter. She says, 'Why are you taking the pill, then, if you want a daughter?' I just reply, 'I don't want one so soon.'"

Sock Boon had two abortions, the first a few months after her elder son's birth. She had forgotten to take her birth control pill. She went to a private clinic and paid S$150. After the birth of her second son she used the rhythm method, which a friend taught her, and found herself pregnant again. "I drank pineapple juice [considered an abortifacient because of its acidity] to induce an abortion but it didn't work. I also took herbal medicine, but when that didn't work either, I felt I had to have a D and C because I had taken so many different kinds of medicine that the baby might be born deformed or stupid. That happened to a friend of mine who tried to abort hers with self-medication." Later Sock Boon tried the injectable contraceptive but found that her period became irregular. "Sometimes it came for two days, sometimes three, and what happens if you're in town and are wearing white slacks? The period was never regular, just a little now and then." She returned to the contraceptive pill.

The Chans' rapid movement upward in the class order was attributable to the husband's place in an industry then being upgraded. Higher income followed, and other benefits flowed from there. Their actions reflected a limited amount of future planning, and in the main they relied on their current high earnings to buy the goods and social services they wanted. Lam Lee used job retraining programs, put a deposit on a public-sector flat, and relied on public education and sometimes the public health clinic to meet his family's needs. The Chans were early beneficiaries of the new industrial program.

Leong Family: Draftsman and Schoolteacher (I)

The strong economic position of the Leongs in 1975 enabled them both to take early advantage of the key government programs and to use private facilities. Thin, tanned, wearing glasses, Leong Kin Cheung was a thirty-five-year-old draftsman of Cantonese origin, employed in a core-sector American oil company. He was married to Joo Leng, aged twenty-eight, a primary school teacher of Teochew background. The couple's twins were born in 1970 and a son was born in 1973. Kin Cheung was the fourth of five children of a now-retired taxi driver. Father, aided by his wife's earnings from sewing at home, put the children through English-stream high school.

After completing his O-level examinations, Kin Cheung became a draftsman in an architectural firm. Encouraged by this milieu, he began to improve his qualifications at night while working during the day. "To tell you frankly, I was never very keen on books before I began this job. My family was always short of money. I had to begin work as soon as I left high school. But when I saw that my colleagues were all better qualified, I started to worry. Then I enrolled in a five-year night school program for draftsmen at Singapore Polytechnic. Working full-time and studying at night was really tough. I worked long and hard those five years. Now with my diploma I can earn almost as much as some university graduates. While I might join a firm at a lower starting salary, after a few years our incomes would level off. After all, ability and hard work count for something. I've returned to the Polytechnic to take a management course so that if an executive post opens up in my company, I'll be ready for it."

Kin Cheung changed jobs several times to improve his position and pay. He entered the oil firm in 1970 and in 1974 became an assistant engineer with draftsmen working under him. He designed oil refineries and gas stations for the Southeast Asian branches of his company. Kin Cheung grossed S$1,000 and thought he was underpaid. "My boss is stingy. But he was smart enough to give me my promotion. I'm doing well at my job, even though the person who held it before me was university trained. If he didn't give me this position, I might quit his company to go with another one."

In fact, Kin Cheung had turned down an offer to join another company as sales manager. He thought that sales work, although better paid, was too routine, and probably the hours would be too long. He had other ways to expand his income: he subcontracted for architectural companies (without a degree in architecture, he could not work directly for clients). These side jobs nearly doubled his monthly income. Kin Cheung got both drafting and part-time jobs "through friends, who then recommended me to friends of theirs, and so on." Most of the side jobs came from connections with classmates from his Polytechnic days. Kin Cheung felt optimistic that he could quickly climb the ladder in his firm, "Working in a private firm is better than working in the government, because working in the government means you're promoted through seniority. Whether you work hard or not doesn't really count. But in a private firm you can achieve success by your own abilities and experience. Of course, whether you have a good boss or not makes a big difference." Kin Cheung felt that his job was secure and commanded a good salary. He was pleased with his working hours and felt confident of his future: "Comparing myself with my friends, I'm one step ahead of them. I'm also better off than my younger brother. He's in a similar line of work."

A slender, well-groomed woman, Joo Leng wore a floral dress and makeup when I dropped in one evening. She recalled a childhood of some hardship as the second of three children whose mother died young and whose father remarried. Joo Leng and her brother and sister resented their treatment by Father's second wife, and so their mother's nanny became their guardian. Nanny urged them to get a good education and earn money for the family. Elder Brother became an accounting manager for a foreign electrical machinery firm and Joo Leng entered teacher's college after high school. While still a student she taught English. She believed that her teachers were less helpful to her than the actual experience of teaching. Younger Sister also became a primary school teacher.

Joo Leng believed that every woman should marry, and if she worked, she must also fulfill her family roles. She herself managed this demanding regime mainly because they could afford full-time domestic help. Joo Leng received more help than any other woman I met. For the first year after her twins were born, she hired a full-time live-in servant, who wore the traditional black-and-white uniform, to care for them day and night. After that, Kin Cheung's father, who lived nearby, visited during the day to care for them. Father Leong also went to the market for them on his way to their home. A daytime domestic servant did housework, washed clothes, and prepared meals for S$180 a month. When her son was born, Joo Leng hired her next-door neighbor to care for him during the day for S$100. Also on hand was Joo Leng's elderly nanny, who slept in the children's bedroom and kept an eye on them.

Joo Leng was responsible for managing the home and doing the "extras," such as clothes shopping. She occasionally cooked Western food, and once served me a piece of chocolate cake she had prepared from a Duncan Hines mix. She had time to attend a weekly yoga class, visit friends in the afternoon, and chat on the phone.

Joo Leng maintained that her teaching job was not a true full-time profession. She worked because she enjoyed teaching and the satisfying personal relationships. "My colleagues and I are good friends. We chat, joke, and laugh together. We have a lot of fun at work." Her income was a form of security and a means of maintaining their affluent lifestyle. "Without the extra money Kin Cheung makes from his side jobs, his earnings would be far from enough, and I'd have to put in all my income for living expenses. But now he works very hard in the office and at home too. I keep my income as savings and draw on it for special expenses." Joo Leng had a separate savings account. "I feel much more secure with my income for saving and extra things and feel free to spend the money, too."

The couple had two cars. In 1971 they bought a S$7,800 two-bedroom HDB flat in middle-class Queenstown, in which they lived, and a S$78,000 private flat as rental property. In 1974 Joo Leng traveled with friends to Hong Kong and Taiwan, and paid for the trip with her own savings. "My husband didn't mind my spending money on myself. He's all right. This year it will be his turn to go. When I go shopping, I can either ask him for money or withdraw money from my own account. We don't make it too clear whether the money is his or mine. After all, our earnings are our money. Kin Cheung's generous. Before Father died, I used to give a hundred dollars every month for his upkeep, and Kin Cheung didn't seem to mind."

Joo Leng believed that a working woman should put her family first, and saw no conflict between teaching school and being the mother of three children. "It depends on the career. There shouldn't be any problem for a woman to do her job well and be a good mother as well if she has a job like mine. As a schoolteacher I have plenty of time for the children, since I work in the morning and have the afternoons and all school holidays off. Teaching is also very easy after so many years of experience. I usually do my preparation and marking during school hours, so working gives me no pressure at all. But it would be different for a woman with a real career that demanded a great deal of her time and her mind."

She had disliked teaching at the outset, but she had had to contribute to her family. "I was only seventeen when I first started, and I thought the students were very unruly and stupid, but we had to sign a six-year contract, and after six years I was used to the job."

But she was aware that something was missing in her intellectual life: "I'm happy with what I am, yet sometimes I wish I could be like some of my old friends who had the opportunity to go to the university. They all have nice careers now. Some of them still aren't married. They're in good professions, they travel a lot, and they're really enjoying their lives. Marriage can come later, although I think that a woman eventually should get married." Joo Leng's views of the separate but complementary talents of men and women placed all women by nature in subordinate work positions. She accepted this idea, but it did not fit her feelings or information about her friends. "Men and women are equally intelligent, but men are smarter than women when it comes to moneymaking. Men are good at handling big business while women can only be good workers, working for people, like being accountants."

Joo Leng and Kin Cheung were introduced by a childhood friend of Joo Leng's, who at that time worked with Kin Cheung. English was the couple's common language, and the children spoke it at home. They still shared friends and enjoyed going out together as a couple and as a family. Before they had children, they went out quite often in the evenings. And in 1971, when their twins were a year old, they left the children in the care of their domestic servant and took a trip to Europe for two weeks. The tour cost them S$4,000. But Joo Leng complained, "Now I can't even go shopping because of the children. They're very naughty. Father-in-Law and our servants simply can't control them. I feel I must come straight home after teaching because the older children can bring the roof down when I'm not around. Although I love to go out, I stay home most of the time because of them, so the only regular activity I have away from home is my yoga lesson on Monday afternoons." Husband and wife occasionally went to the movies, and they left their door key with their neighbor, who could hear the children if they woke up. But these evening activities were less frequent than they had been in the past.

Now that their servant did not live in, they rarely went to parties together. Kin Cheung said, "It's better to have a live-in servant because I like very much having my wife going to parties with me." Their solution was to take separate vacations. Joo Leng said, "I enjoy traveling, and in fact I enjoy going to other countries with my friends even better than with my husband. He doesn't like getting up early in the morning because he thinks he has a right to sleep late when he's on vacation. But how can you get to see enough places when you get up so late? Besides, he's a fussy eater, and I think it's great fun to try all kinds of food. Really, I'd rather travel with my friends. Once I also let Kin Cheung travel without me. He and his colleagues went to Malaysia without their wives. Anyway, what to do with three little children? We have to take turns." Separate vacations had much to recommend them, but they were a choice of necessity, a short-term compromise with family demands, not a desired way of life.

They were proud of their level of communication. Joo Leng said, "We're both the talkative type. Kin Cheung often tells me what happens in his office and we usually talk a great deal to each other." Household decisions were made in accordance with their sex roles: "Kin Cheung's a very easygoing person. I have the say at home and he has the say away from home." Therefore Joo Leng decided on child care, birth control, and arrangements for servants. She took the children to the doctor and decided which doctor to see. "I guess it's more convenient for a mother to work half days instead of full days, especially if the children get sick. Because of the children, I think I'll stick to my teaching job." The pair discussed Kin Cheung's career and his business decisions, but the final word was his. "I don't interfere with Kin Cheung's work and career. That's his territory. I let him decide for himself. He's full of energy. He has confidence in his work and is quite optimistic about the future." I asked Joo Leng what they quarreled about and she thought for a few seconds, then shrugged and said, "I don't really quarrel with Kin Cheung. But sometimes if I'm tired from work, I get irritated with small things very easily. Then I don't talk to him at all. I put on a cold war until he makes an effort to make up."

The Leongs decorated their home simply, and allowed the children a free hand with their toys and belongings. A large cupboard in the living room held books, records, souvenirs from their trips, and a well-used stereo. There was a large television set, and the sofa and most of the chairs were covered with children's toys. A toy car, a tricycle, and smaller toys were scattered around. Joo Leng had relaxed homemaking standards. "We bought our sofa set from my husband's friends, secondhand. Actually I don't like it, but since the children are very young and very naughty and nothing can be kept in good shape, we'll keep on using it. After a few years, when they're a little older, I plan to buy a new set. My husband bought our TV, since I'm not fussy about those things."

This home was an investment in the future, and it was not their only investment. But despite their comfortable way of life, they felt that "all of Singapore is affected by inflation. There was a time when we could eat out any time we felt like it. We could order any dish we wanted, but we can't do that anymore."

Kin Cheung made the educational plans for their children. From his managerial position in his firm, high earnings, and wider experience in business, he reasoned that the children needed to learn Mandarin. "Neither I nor my wife speak Mandarin. When my colleagues talk in Chinese, I feel I'm one step behind them." Kin Cheung planned ahead even further. "The children should switch to an English secondary school after they've learned enough Mandarin in primary school. English-trained people have better prospects than Chinese-trained people." The public school in their middle-class neighborhood was adequate, Joo Leng said. "I'm not particular about which school, so long as the location is convenient for my father-in-law, who takes them to school and picks them up. But I wouldn't sent my children to a very bad school where they'd easily pick up dirty words. That happened once when my servant left. I sent the twins to a kindergarten next to the school where I was teaching for a short time. After just two days they came home with all those dirty words."

The Leongs were "open-minded" about their children's future careers. Yet King Cheung had a definite agenda. Asked about the kind of job he would like his sons to hold, he at first replied, "It's too early to think about that yet. Besides, we don't know what fields will be in demand fifteen years from now. Perhaps toward the end of their secondary schooling I'll try to analyze the situation and tell the children the different possibilities and let them choose the field to enter." Joo Leng interjected, "He wants his children to be architects." Kin Cheung then admitted that he had a specific idea in mind. "That's true. The future for architecture is good. Although Singapore is not very big, old buildings are being demolished, lower buildings will be changed into taller ones. An architect will never be out of work." Claiming to give their children a say in the future, they still expected to direct them toward profitable positions.

As a teacher, Joo Leng managed the children's daily activities. She supervised their home learning and opposed private tutors. She taught the three-and-a-half-year-old twins to count and read the roman alphabet. "Hiring a tutor means making the tutor do the children's schoolwork. If a normal student pays attention in class, he should be able to cope." Joo Leng was firm about the children's study time, playtime, and bedtime. She also watched over family relations. She urged Kin Cheung to give some time to his children. "Although I do admit the children are very naughty sometimes, I've advised Kin Cheung not to cane them so often. Being very busy with his work, he has very little time to spend with them." Joo Leng believed that children should be given considerable physical freedom. "I'm a very relaxed person, but my friends, seeing my baby climb up and down our sofa, get very nervous. How can a baby learn if a mother is afraid to let him try on his own? My husband also encourages the kids to be brave. When we go to the playground, we just sit on the bench and let the kids run and climb and play anywhere they like. They've learned to take care of themselves." Living in a neighborhood with ample space and helpers, the Leongs did not have to worry about their children's safety.

Concerned about her looks, Joo Leng refused to have the contraceptive pill prescribed. "Kin Cheung's slender and I'm afraid I'll gain weight if I use the pill." Therefore Kin Cheung used condoms. Their planning failed, however, and their third child was conceived. Joo Leng stated firmly she would not have a fourth. "We must take into consideration the fact that when the children grow a little older, it'll be very costly to educate them and bring them up properly." She added that the time she spent with the children made it hard to maintain her job. "Looking after the children is really killing! Although I have people to help me, I still need a lot of patience. Do you know how I spent Chinese New Year? For three days I did nothing but look after three children because my servant and babysitter were all off work."

The Leongs were informed about the population policy, but they disagreed as to whether there was a population problem. Their views flowed from their occupations. Joo Leng thought that schools were overcrowded, while Kin Cheung was keen on maintaining high demand for new building construction. He was optimistic about the future of Singapore. "I think Singapore is just right. If we can keep the two percent birth rate, we'll be just fine." Joo Leng thought that the population measures would have little effect on couples in their position. "Most of my colleagues have two children and most of them want to stop at two. I don't think they've made their decision because of these policies. If both husband and wife work, who cares about the extra delivery charges? Some of my colleagues went to very expensive private hospitals to have their babies, although they could have gone to the K.K. Hospital for much less." "Then why do you think most of them want to stop at two?" Joo Leng replied, "Child-care problems are the most important reasons I can think of, and how to bring the children up according to their economic capabilities is another." The Leongs planned good professional careers for their children, and would have no more than three to conserve and improve the quality of their family life.

The Leongs drew on the state social services for Kin Cheung's job training at Polytechnic and for their HDB flat, but they did not depend totally on these services. They bought other goods and services at high market rates, such as their private apartment, sports lessons and clubs, and cars. Help from kin and quasi-kin was a convenient supplement to their paid domestic help and gave these relatives a useful social role. Thus their high income made it possible for them to choose among sources and types of goods and services, and they devoted their energies to far-reaching family plans.

[6]

Secure Families in the
Early Development Stage

Secure couples had enough money to take advantage of the government's wide range of investment opportunities, and as the husband's earnings were accompanied by predictable career prospects, they could escape the control of their kin. This freedom was a key to the close marriages of most secure couples. The economic and social goals of these couples varied in accordance with their class backgrounds, life courses, and jobs. Some were people of modest means; others I considered truly affluent. The overall patterns reveal the dynamics of class, family, and state which shaped an identifiable secure family life course in the early industrial stage.

Work

Men's Jobs

A secure family's position stemmed primarily from the husband's job. These affluent men earned on average of S$649 a month, far above the national median for Chinese men. Only seven of the forty-two men earned less than S$347 a month. However, the average income of secure men of modest means (S$406) was less than half that of the affluent (S$849). I include them among the secure because of their educational attainment, the job status of their parents, and their wives' earnings.

Despite these differences, secure men had much in common. The fathers of most of them had had solid blue-collar occupations: tradesman, entrepreneur, proprietor (of a taxicab, a grocery store, a cargo boat), blue-collar supervisor (a shipfitter); others had held even more substantial positions (one was a hotel proprietor).[1] During the deprivations of World War II and its aftermath, one-third of the fathers died or deserted their families, a lower proportion than among the poor. As many of these absent fathers had built up strong social and employment connections, many sons still managed to enjoy a relatively stable home life, some secondary schooling, and access to higher-level jobs.

Most secure men were trained for their future careers as teenagers. Approximately three-quarters received at least some secondary education; as many as one-quarter were prepared for their A-level examinations. Moreover, many affluent men matriculated at the Singapore Polytechnic and Singapore University. Consequently, nearly all entered the labor force with good job prospects. By phase 1, they were poised to seize the best opportunities created by Singapore's initial industrialization.[2]

My investigations revealed that the earnings levels of men in Singapore's core industrial sector exceeded those in the peripheral sector by as much as 50 percent (see Table 8). The earnings of any individual, however, depended on his resources and qualifications.

The highest wages in the peripheral sector were reported by owners of a family business, such as a wholesale vegetable market. The three respondents who inherited a thriving family enterprise had received only primary-level education but had been thoroughly instructed from an early age to manage their family firms.[3] Others launched their own businesses from scratch, and many of these men had solid academic education. But no peripheral-sector entrepreneurs received formal technical training. When asked to compare their prospects with those of other men, these businessmen found it natural to choose as a reference group other small owners.

Table 8. Average earnings of secure men in peripheral and core sectors, phase 1

Sector	Average earnings[a]	Number
Periphery		
Unskilled	S$275	2
Resources[b]	619	16
Skilled	429	7
Average peripheral-sector secure male worker	538	25
Core		
Unskilled	300	1
Skilled	845	16
Average core-sector secure male worker	812	17
Average secure male worker, both sectors	S$642	42

[a]Pre-overtime monthly gross wage, before withdrawal of CPF.
[b]Occupation requires some capital, a nonindustrial skill, or an academic degree.

They felt that in comparison with these men they had a strong place in the local community, and they were optimistic about their prospects.[4]

Peripheral-sector men with nonindustrial resources included clerks and civil servants, such as the reader of household meters for the electric utility. These employees were secondary school graduates who had gotten their jobs by meeting formal employment qualifications set by government and industry. Generally, classmates or teachers or others in their circle had directed them to their first job openings, and few required family connections to get started. Their beginning salaries were above average. The men felt confident that their solid education would win them career promotions.[5] Most were in enough demand to moonlight at well-paid jobs, at which some earned enough to buy a secondhand car.

Peripheral-sector men with industrial skills learned them as apprentices or on the job. Many feared their mobility was blocked because they lacked diplomas in technical subjects.[6] Their firms produced goods for local customers or export goods with low value and fluctuating demand (the garment factory that employed the sewing machine repairman, for example). These firms had limited profit margins and could not greatly increase sales or wages every year. Men with technical skills who worked in such firms averaged lower earnings then petty businessmen.

Three men worked as unskilled laborers: two peripheral-sector bus conductors and a core-sector shipyard worker. All were downwardly mobile men with secondary schooling whose jobs did not draw on the skills or education they had obtained. Their fathers' jobs were better than their own, but they could not hold on to jobs to which their fathers had introduced them. Their earnings fell slightly below the male median wage, and hence far below the average of the secure men.

Core-sector workers earned the highest wages. We have already met the quality control supervisor who earned around S$1,000 a month as a basic wage and further raised his earnings through overtime work. He, like some others, owed his start to a family background in a closely related line of work. Yet personal connections did not ensure such men's high-level jobs. Men with technical skills first obtained a recognized certificate through formal programs of study, on the job (in special training classes or apprenticeships), or in professional institutes. Some were paid on an hourly basis, but most, like the draftsman in the oil firm, were salaried employees. These core-sector men were the early beneficiaries of the Singapore industrial program.

It was common for secure men to make efforts to upgrade their earnings. Many took courses at night—in mechanical engineering, drafting, management—to improve their chances for raises and promotions.[7] Few needed to take primary school subjects first in order to qualify. Secure men in complex organizations with orderly careers were most likely to pursue adult education.[8] These adult learners heard about such programs from workmates or

Skilled workers in a core-sector shipyard. Photo by Eric Khoo.

supervisors. And their employers rewarded them by funding the course fees, releasing them to attend class, or finding them better positions upon completion of the courses.

Secure men often changed their jobs, usually for the better.[9] Few changes were forced by layoffs, and most men looked for new work while they were still employed.[10] They could thus afford to be selective, and their new jobs usually paid more than the old.

Well-placed kin had started many on their first jobs and continued to have some say in their lives, but they exerted more influence than control. Fully 83 percent of the secure men had gotten their current jobs through a personal introduction, but the ties of nearly half of these men to the people who helped them were relatively weak.[11] Their work brought them into contact with well-placed men, and my respondents sought out such men when they considered changing jobs. Others turned to former schoolmates for job-related information. They were as likely to learn about new jobs through former co-workers as from kin. The demand for their skills permitted secure men to be selective in their choice of partners and ways to raise capital.[12] Some spoke proudly of finding work without the help of kin; the computer technician, for instance, who had found his job through a friend, interpreted the lack of relationship between them as "getting a job on my own." Still others found friends unreliable partners and then turned to kin.

Having constructed broad circles of personal contacts, secure men had considerable choice of action. Many of those who had looked to kin for help were not completely dependent on them. This sense of choice, grounded in their material and personal assets, forged an identifiable way of life for these families.

Women's Work

Twenty-seven secure women worked full-time and three others worked part-time; twelve were housewives. The majority of full-time workers worked in factories, but several were professional women. The industrial structure in which the women worked and their skill level shaped their earnings. Only two women worked for less than S$200 (the median wage of Singapore women), and both worked in peripheral-sector factories.[13] We have met one such woman—the wife of the meter reader, who worked as a recorder in a garment factory.

In general, assembly workers received much better pay in core-sector plants than in peripheral-sector firms. The majority of the better-paid factory women worked in American-financed electronics firms. Of the eleven who earned more than S$300, only two were in the peripheral sector, and both (a section leader in a textile factory and a dressmaker who taught sewing in her own apartment) had considerable training.

The several affluent women with postsecondary education worked in professional or civil service jobs and earned good women's wages. Women with high levels of education and training, such as the schoolteacher, were scarce, and so earned solid women's wages.

When I asked the secure women why they worked, their answers reflected their economic standing. Of course, wives of the seven low-paid men were compelled to earn wages: six of them worked full-time and the seventh did piecework at home, sewing seams. Most of the secure women, however, worked not from sheer economic necessity but for long-term family uplift. They used their earnings to buy social services and consumer goods: appliances and furnishings for their apartments and tuition for their children. Without their wages, few couples of modest means could buy a home of their own, and for this reason women in modest families were very likely to work.[14] Such women as the ironing section supervisor in the garment factory anchored and upgraded their families' place in society. They drew on all the resources at their command, and their wages were crucial.

Affluent women, in contrast, worked for consumer goods that the rest considered luxuries. With the wives' help these families bought stereo sets and hired private piano and ballet teachers and swimming coaches for their children. They took vacations abroad. They bought their own apartments and investment property, which further enlarged their income.

Women who did not work full-time included those who were undereducated for their class and whose past work experience had been in the peripheral sector, such as the former domestic servant. Any earnings she could get would be small, and her household was not in want. Further, the affluent standard required costly child-care arrangements and the work-related expenses of lunch and carfare. Thus no affluent woman would work for the prevailing low wage that was offered women by peripheral-sector companies.

Many wives found their home-based tasks worth more to their households than their earnings. Some ran large and complex households. Others helped husbands who ran their own businesses, such as the wholesale vegetable seller. Finally, many better-educated affluent women hesitated to entrust the complete moral and practical education of their children to poorly educated grandparents. Their husbands urged them to quit work and stay home. Thus some women decided to leave the labor force for their children's sake. The time spent tutoring and in other home education activities with their children would give their tots a spurt in the highly competitive school system.

A woman's worth was often measured by her economic contribution to the household. But affluent women who chose to work did so only if they could provide a substantial addition to their husband's wage. All three of the women who worked part-time at home had passed up the poorly paid laun-

Skilled worker in a peripheral-sector garment factory. Photo by Fred Salaff.

dering and seaming jobs as outworkers for neighborhood workshops and factories. Women were rarely required to work out of necessity in this stratum, so when they worked, they chose only the higher-paid jobs. As a result, we find that the earnings gap between the affluent couples and those of modest means was greater when both spouses worked than when only the husband's wage was taken into account.

Secure women workers earned enough to make it worthwhile for kin to undertake strenuous efforts to help them with child care and home tasks. Even if relatives were reluctant to help, well-paid women workers could often bring them around. For these reasons, women-centered transactions were crucial for the formation of the female labor force in the first development stage. Sixty percent of secure women lived with kin, and the proportion was highest among employed women.[15]

Yet, even though ties with female kin were essential to working women, few became embedded in kin ties out of desperation. Quite the contrary. Most could pay well for their kin's help and could seek help elsewhere if kin did not oblige. Further, these women can be said to work partly to loosen economic and psychological dependence on their kin. Thus the bargaining power of these better-off couples weakened the wider kin ties and strengthened the marriage.

The Marriage Bond

The marriage relationships of secure couples reflected their solid economic position. The majority of secure couples shared household tasks, leisure, and discussions. Those who did not share such joint activities felt their marriages were less than ideal. The strong marriage bond flowed from the education and job options of the husbands. Their advancement opportunities and decision-making powers on the job supported their perception that change was possible.[16] Wider circles of acquaintances and more complex social relations in the work milieu reduced the prominent role of kin on the job, while resources of their own strengthened these men's control over their families' welfare. Such assets underlay a marriage in which spouses negotiated their family tasks, from housework to child care.

Half of the secure husbands did some housework. Several, such as the meter reader, did a large share. Yet of all husbands who did a lot, the secure exceeded the poor by only 7 percent.[17] There was a difference, however. In the main, the poor women, who received little help at home, acquiesced in their lot; few secure wives whose husbands did not help liked bearing the weight of household tasks. In many secure homes, therefore, the behavior of the men did not match the ideal.[18] Most wives, in fact, expected that their husbands would help and were disappointed when they did not. The electronics factory worker married to the Tamil computer technician is but one example.

Husbands, for their part, preferred well-paid overtime work or second jobs to housework. Such men usually won, and withdrew into work or leisure. In addition, in five affluent homes, such as that of the draftsman and the schoolteacher, domestic servants lightened the burden for both spouses. These factors help to explain the sizable proportion of affluent men who did little housework.[19]

The majority of couples did things together in their leisure time. Their ability to share pastimes revealed their greater autonomy in their families of origin. Since most men looked beyond kin circles for work and career upgrading, many of them also controlled the household budget, and so had considerable bargaining power in the extended family. These husbands were able to give their first loyalty to their wives. They could enjoy outings with their wives, and leave their mothers at home.

Kin structure made a difference. The few who had no kin in Singapore forged the strongest marriage bonds. Couples who lived with their in-laws, in contrast, had to work hard for a separate sphere of social activity for themselves. As we saw in the case of the meter reader and his wife, the husband's parents tended to compete with the wife for his loyalty. Yet these two resolved this conflict in favor of the marriage bond.

Nevertheless, over half of the couples of modest means and nearly two-fifths of the affluent husbands and wives did not go out together. They had not redefined, let alone severed, their bonds with their families of birth when they married.[20] Continued close ties with kin could sometimes be traced to bonds built during childhood, especially in times of intense poverty, or to inherited family enterprises that still required kin to work together. We have seen that class differences between the natal family and family of marriage drove a wedge between the sewing machine repairman and the ironing supervisor; she preferred to join her better-off brother's family on outings.

For the most part, however, when the husband alone maintained circles of kin and friendships from which he excluded his wife, she rarely endorsed his segregated activities, and it was often hard for her to find close friends of her own to fill the gap in her marriage. Indeed, affluent wives with segregated marriages were especially sad at this turn of events.

Most secure couples talked over family matters. They planned where to work, the schools for their children, buying a home and consumer goods. Freer from binding kin ties, husband and wife viewed kin relations with the detachment needed for a full exchange of views. As most couples went to many places together, common friendships formed another realm of discourse. Such discussions contributed in turn to the partners' image of themselves as a unit.

[152]

A spouse who took the lead in making decisions usually consulted the other first. Such couples considered these consultations the main feature of their marriage, not the fact that one spouse was the major decision maker.[21] They defined their marriage as joint. Couples often discussed their purchases, for example, because they controlled their own income. When conflicts arose with in-laws over purchases, the younger set often won. In a few instances of extreme conflict in the extended affluent household, the wife wanted to break ties completely with her husband's parents, and she obtained his full support. Such a thing was unheard of in the sample of the poor.

Nearly half of the spouses did not fully confide in each other, however, and nine of the forty-two secure couples discussed very little; all but one were the very couples that did not share outings. Only some of these wives accepted the constraints on discussion. More often, when the husband deferred to his kin, his wife complained bitterly at her isolation, and did not consider her segregated marriage as ideal. The joint marriage in which wife and husband shared leisure and ideas was a widespread goal of secure couples, even if not all could attain it.[22]

A Home of Their Own

As most men held secure jobs, they could hope to buy three- or four-room flats, and many had taken steps to do so. Just over half had bought their homes, and just under half of the rest had made a down payment. But the families of modest means had little ready cash and their CPF funds were still small. Most, such as the meter reader and his wife, had only applied for but not yet moved into their homes. They expected to wait up to five years for their housing plans to mature. During that time they would save for fixtures and furnishings. But some self-employed families of modest means, such as the vegetable retailer, had no CPF funds and had scant hope of ever buying a home. All affluent couples, in contrast, could afford a home of their own and save for their retirement as well.

Couples looked mainly to the husband's earnings and his CPF to buy homes. Wives of modest means, unsure how long they would work, did not want to tie a home to their short-term earning power, while the affluent did not need the wives' earnings to help pay for their apartments.

Life-cycle stage shaped homeownership plans. Many of the young couples had not yet moved into their own apartments. The majority still lived with kin and welcomed the help with child care which allowed the wives to work. Couples also met obligations to the older folks by living with them until the next youngest son married and took their place. Such cross-generation help was found among the couples of modest means, but economic position

High-density living in Chinatown: the children are cared for by their uncle. Photo by Fred Salaff.

shaped the meaning of coresidence. Nine secure couples lived in kampung, farm, or detached houses with gardens, where they raised poultry or grew fruit to reduce their living expenses. Living with kin also reduced living costs. During their time of shared residence, they saved for their own flat and contributed steadily to the support of their elders. When they moved to homes of their own, these couples all planned to take the big step to home-ownership. An example we have seen is the sewing machine repairman and his factory-worker wife. Such modest couples especially found this period of temporary coresidence a crucial stage during which they could save to buy the home they wanted.

Affluent couples also benefited by living with kin, but because their in-comes were higher, coresidence was less often motivated by the need to economize. Rather, affluent couples stressed the need to fulfill their moral and social obligations to the elders. Indeed, usually the respondent couples owned the flat that housed their elder kin. Others owned flats that remained empty while they shared their in-laws' home. Despite the benefits of coresi-dence, affluent wives chafed at the restraints. Extended family living kept many from spending money on decor and buying consumer goods that they could afford. To keep peace in the family, daughters-in-law subordinated their felt need for living space and privacy. Several affluent women spoke of their deep wish to train their children and decorate their flats "in my own way." They curbed their wish to express their own taste in order to avoid exacerbating tensions in the household. Couples could not always, however, resolve intrafamily disputes. When the break came, they would separate their household budgets and move into a home of their own.

Education: The Pathway to Advancement

Their children's educational prospects were good, but the parents' hopes for their children varied by social background. It was true that the majority of parents of modest means had received some secondary education, and many men held jobs with a future. And although a few men's earnings fell below the median wage, the family income in each case was greatly raised by the wife's input. Nevertheless, such parents found it hard to plan far in advance for their children's education. They did not know how long the wives would work and whether they could afford to send their children as far as they could go in school. This is why many hedged their answers to the question: "What level of education do you desire for your children?" Some said, "We don't know. It will depend on their school marks and our financial situation." Still, just as many aspired to some sort of postsecondary educa-tion to prepare their children for good jobs.

Affluent parents, in contrast, from the outset had the funds and connections to draw on the best the school system offered. Most had received postsecondary education themselves. Their familiarity with the school system helped them make long-term plans for their children's education. Their confidence that they could control their children's ability to learn flowed from their own structured careers, the money that they could afford for tutors, and their often detailed information on the school system. Two-thirds wanted their children to take at least the A-level exam. Nearly half intended their children to study further.

Home study varied by class stratum as well. Some parents of modest means depended on the school to teach their children and rarely coached them at home. Those who lived with kin often could not carry out their own ideas about raising children. Others, who were confident that they could earn a solid wage, expressed greater hope for their children's higher education.[23] They also made an effort to improve their children's study habits and did not leave their children's school performance to chance or to innate ability. They sought the cause of troubles in schoolwork and visited school to learn how they could prepare their children for exams. Less well-educated parents of modest means, such as the vegetable proprietor and his wife, asked relatives with higher levels of education to help with their children's homework. Most parents of modest means had confidence in the public school system and planned to enroll their children in neighborhood schools.

More of the affluent women had secondary-level education and were keen to inculcate good study habits in their children. Few of them said that they wished their mothers-in-law to teach them how to raise their children. To these women, the older generation's ideas were old-fashioned. When conflicts over the children arose, wives usually succeeded in getting their husbands' support. Affluent mothers often sought advice on raising children in the mass media and from their friends. All but the single affluent farm family worked hard to teach their youngsters. They encouraged their children to seek knowledge, and on all occasions possible turned conversations with their children into educational opportunities.[24]

The choice of the proper school was a complex matter to affluent parents and took much time, energy, and discussion. Parents read about schools, talked about them often, and sought advice from well-connected people. A few decided to send their children to a neighborhood school, in the expectation that the school in their middle-class district would draw students from middle-income families like themselves, who spoke Mandarin Chinese or English at home and were discouraged from speaking another Chinese dialect. The majority, however, hoped to send their children to an elite public or private institution to ensure a solid bilingual academic education. They also planned a range of extracurricular activities and private lessons for their youngsters.

Five-sixths of all secure parents saved for their children's education. The few husbands who earned less than the male median wage had the most trouble setting aside such funds. But since they relied on two incomes and economized by living in extended households, even they managed to set aside at least S$50 each month toward their children's education bill. Such parents were not sure, however, how long they could spare this margin of savings. When they had to move out of the extended household into an HDB flat of their own, or when the wife stopped work to have another child, most couples of modest means would find it hard to budget this monthly sum.

Affluent parents, in contrast, never relied on cash hoarded in a drawer to meet their education bills; they could finance the children's higher education from the husband's monthly earnings. Some took out educational insurance policies. Other well-heeled professional parents in fact denied that they needed to save in order to support their children through the public higher education system. Funds for the children's schooling—for tutors, extra lessons, books, and supplies—were insulated from short-term family demands. For these reasons, two-thirds were confident that their children could study past high school.

Affluent parents educated their children for change, "to think for themselves" and adapt to the shifting job world. While they planned to take their children's interests into account, however, they still expected to mold their career choices. This combination of flexibility and career intent was consistent with the professional positions the parents themselves held and wished their children to assume. For this host of reasons, affluent parents made the highest demands on their children to study and to pass exams with high scores. Couples of modest means were more vague about their children's futures.

Planning Smaller Families

Most couples had two children and expected to have at least one more child, as Table 9 indicates.[25] Although only 10 percent had four or more children, 21 percent intended to have that many. Their long-term plans to improve the quality of life deterred the majority from wanting many children. The resources that allowed them to buy or plan for a home and to make long-term educational decisions for their children figured in their family-size goals. Few spoke of the immediate expenses of food, clothing, and shelter; most projected a family size on the basis of the long-term costs of raising children, among which education loomed largest.

Nearly all employed women were concerned that an additional child would interfere with their work plans. Others had already quit the labor force to devote themselves to raising their children. They spent considerable time on the children's homework and on activities intended to enrich the

Table 9. Number of secure couples who intended to have and did have specified numbers of children, phase 1

| Family size | Number of children | | | | |
	1	2	3	4+	Average
Intended	1	6	26	9	3.2
Actual	11	23	4	4	2.1

Note: The specified numbers of children include surviving children born to couples, children of former marriages, and adopted children; they exclude children adopted out permanently but include those temporarily living with other families as a form of child care.

children's social and intellectual skills. To them, the fourth child was not very popular. The social circles of secure couples contained diverse people with varied attitudes toward childbearing. Peers, neighbors, and kin did not know each other, nor did they express uniform views on the matter. In any case, as most of these couples were economically independent, they could ignore opinions with which they disagreed.

Over half of the couples were in accord with the spirit of the Social Disincentives against Higher Order Births, especially with the government's efforts to reduce the pressure on Singapore's limited resources. They felt that the state should limit family size for everyone. Those with reservations expressed them in ways consistent with their economic position. A few sympathized with poor parents who wished children of both sexes, though hardly any secure parents admitted they would themselves hold out for a balanced sex ratio. Opposition to the measures was not phrased in terms of the right to have as many children as they liked, either. Rather, parents had faith in the rationality of most people to limit their family size of their own accord, with no need for yet another set of state sanctions. Therefore, the overall majority claimed to take little account of the population limitation policy when they decided on the size of their own family. Those parents who did take the measures into account when they made such decisions (mainly those of modest means) saw the measures as supporting their plans for a future career.[26]

Conclusions

With relatively solid jobs and living standards, secure couples were optimistic about the future. Though many lived with kin, few depended on kin for daily support or finding jobs. The majority took steps to buy a home, set high standards for their children's education, and intended no more than three children. Most enjoyed close marriages, in which partners shared pastimes and talked things over. They were proud of their ability to plan their futures together. A minority did not have joint marriages and some were unable to plan far ahead in any respect. Most, however, took advantage of Singapore's social services to advance their family's living standard. Secure folk expressed recognizably similar goals in the main spheres of their lives as they planned for the advancement of the small family in Singapore's industrial revolution.

PART III

The Second
Development Stage

[7]

Poor Family Lives Evolve

When I spoke again with panel families of all skill levels and industrial sectors, I found them expressing increasingly similar goals as the consumer and social service society and unified market economy took hold. But within the narrowed limits of lifestyle, class, and sector, differences remained. Class position still shaped diverse family styles and plans.

Ng Family: Butcher's Helper and Homemaker (II)

In phase 1, Ng Kong Chong supported his family by the unlicensed sale of homemade cakes to customers in a downtown parking lot. When an interviewer called on the Ngs late one afternoon in the same "one-room improved" HBD flat they had occupied in phase 1, she could persuade only Wee Ping to speak with her. Kong Chong was asleep, and when Wee Ping awakened him to convey the request for a meeting, he rolled over on his pallet and went back to sleep. The interviewer surmised from Wee Ping's manner that her husband was embarrassed to talk about the family's worsened financial circumstances. Wee Ping told her that she could barely meet her S$336 monthly expenses.

Over the interphase, hawkers' licenses had become even more difficult to obtain, and despite repeated applications, Kong Chong was unsuccessful in stabilizing his petty trade. He was frequently fined for illegal vending. Soon after the Ngs' third child was born in 1977, Kong Chong decided to find another job. He switched first to heavy labor, and he continued to work part-time in construction to make ends meet. His main job, however, is now as a butcher's helper in a business owned by distant relatives. Every night at nine, Kong Chong is driven by his workmates to an abbatoir in Jurong, where they load carcasses to be sold in the market the following morning. The butcher pays Kong Chong S$250 to 300 a month. As a wage earner, Kong Chong now receives a Central Provident Fund (CPF) contribution from his employer. In addition, he can earn upwards of S$200 a month by putting in extra hours of irregular but grueling labor for construction firms.

His base wage has remained constant since 1974, and therefore its proportion of the rising national median (in nominal dollars) has declined from two-thirds to one-half. The Ng family's economic plight is attributable to Kong Chong's lack of marketable skills. As his job-finding networks are restricted to a small circle of close family and friends, he has been unable to upgrade his job category.

Wee Ping reports that her life has not changed much since she first spoke with me in 1974. She dislikes housework, but she has not entered the job market because she lacks education, experience apart from menial labor, and child care. The interviewer pursued the issue. "What kind of work would you like to get?" "A factory job, not domestic work. Any kind of factory except electronics. There I wouldn't be chosen because I lack the educational qualifications."

Her typical day as she described it reveals her preoccupation with managing the essentials of living and the closeness of her three children and her mother-in-law: "Up about six o'clock, prepare breakfast. Do household chores, wash clothes and dishes, and sweep the floors. Eldest daughter [now seven] helps. Go to the market along with youngest daughter [four]. Cook lunch for myself and the children. Nap after lunch with youngest daughter while the others are in school. Visit Mother-in-Law nearby. Prepare dinner. Have dinner with the children. Mop the floor. Son [six] helps. Make sure the children do their homework. Change the children's clothes." Kong Chong is absent from this schedule because of his long work hours and his continued habit of socializing with his friends off the job.

The poverty-stricken family cannot afford to move into less confined quarters. Their apartment is partitioned by a low screen into living and sleeping areas. Their sole acquisitions since phase 1 are a used television set, given to them by Kong Chong's younger brother after he bought a new color set for himself, and a small upright refrigerator, given to them by a friend who had just bought a new one for his family. In phase 1, monthly rent of S$40 was 16 percent of Kong Chong's basic take-home pay. (A family's basic take-home pay consists of the husband's and wife's net earnings from their main jobs, after the deduction of CPF. Overtime pay and bonus payments are excluded.) Rent and utilities payments have now risen to 30 percent of his basic take-home pay. (Housing and utilities account for 20 percent of his net income from his two jobs.)

The Ngs' educational aspirations for their children are quite limited. Like many other poor young housewives, Wee Ping said, "I don't know whether they can study or not. It's up to them. We'll see how far they can go." She claims to treat her two daughters and son equally and intends all of them to have an equal chance to advance in school.

Kong Chong, the family decision maker, chose the children's school because it was near home. The Ngs have no resources to provide for coaching with homework or other forms of educational enrichment. They have no money to bank for their children's future schooling. As she is unschooled, Wee Ping is unable to give her children any help with their homework. Nonetheless, she makes sure their lessons are completed before bedtime. While the interviewer talked with her at dusk one evening, she admonished Eldest Daughter to stop playing and finish her homework.

The Ngs have trimmed their aspirations for a better living standard, and no longer envision the operation of a thriving, home-based hawker business. They have abandoned their desire for a fourth child because of their accentuated poverty. In the hospital after Youngest Daughter's birth, Wee Ping accordingly underwent a tubal ligation.

The Ngs' marriage continues to suffer from economic and social impoverishment. Wee Ping said resignedly that she and Kong Chong do not discuss substantive matters, such as their children's educational prospects, and barely acknowledge each other's presence. They consult only about the simple necessities of household management. They seldom pursue joint entertainment activities, and Wee Ping is accompanied only by her children when she visits kinfolk. Her visits to Mother-in-Law punctuate her day with social interchange. Mother Ng, however, does not help Wee Ping with her many tasks. She has all the chores to organize and most to perform by herself. Worse still, the Ngs lost most of their support network of friends and neighbors when their associates rose in economic status and moved away. As the community of the poor breaks apart, the Ngs undoubtedly feel increasingly isolated and personally at fault. The problems of the Ng family reveal the absolute decline in living standards which still affects many unskilled workers in Singapore's peripheral sector.

Chua Family: Warehouse Worker and Electronics Factory Worker (II)

Chua Siew Gek, an assembly worker in a large transnational manufacturing firm located in her neighborhood, possesses considerable family, personal, and social resources. Her husband, Kay Yong, who was a low-paid bus conductor when I first knew him, has become a warehouseman in a Japanese computer manufacturing firm in the Jurong Industrial Zone. He still cannot inject economic surplus into the family budget. All the same, the family has prospered: Siew Gek has single-handedly advanced the Chua standard of living by her assiduous labor and social skills. In fact, when I called on the Chua family in 1981, I was impressed by their well-appointed new flat.

Kay Yong explained that he had been forced out of the Singapore Bus Service. By 1977 he had amassed seven years' seniority with the company but was being paid only S$260 a month. He and his fellow bus conductors worked long hours under punitive conditions. Most months his wages were docked from S$30 to S$50 for alleged tardiness in reporting for duty. He was assigned seven trips a day and allowed a scant five-minute rest between them. He had begun to suffer from occupationally induced gastric distress. During one crowded rush hour in 1977, he asked a passenger to move to the rear of the bus. The passenger later complained to the bus service that Kay Yong was rude. The management sent him a reprimand and a warning, and his union ignored his request for support. Afraid of losing his job, he contemplated legal action against the Singapore Bus Service and the complainant. Siew Gek, however, pointed out the improbability of winning such a suit, and he decided then to quit.

Kay Yong returned to the manual labor he thought he had escaped when he joined the bus company. Working for a succession of builders, he made no more than S$200 a month. After two years of hard labor, he again sought a job change. As his own family connections were sparse, he yielded to Siew Gek's insistence that he approach her sister's husband for help. This brother-in-law is a warehouse foreman with a Japanese firm and had once before intervened to secure unskilled work in the firm for an in-law, Siew Gek's brother. Kay Yong's starting wage as a packer in the warehouse, one of the lowest job categories in the firm, is S$320; he takes home S$30 more in overtime pay. Brother-in-Law's influence does not extend to promotions on the shop floor.

Kay Yong's income has declined in relation to the national median. In 1976 he had earned 69 percent of the national median wage for Chinese men; now, at a better-paying firm, he is making only 53 percent. Without experience he is unable to command a higher figure. He intends to remain with the Japanese firm, however. It offers training in preparation for examinations that qualify successful candidates for promotions. He commented, "Having the right connections helped me get my job, but now I must rely entirely on my own efforts to advance in the company." Five years earlier he had told us that a person in his station advanced by good fortune and pulling strings, but he now acknowledges the dead end that awaits unqualified workers in Singapore.

Siew Gek's brother-in-law told me that he had advanced through company channels beginning in 1973, in the early days of the firm, and he hoped that Kay Yong would take advantage of the same upgrading scheme: "Like Kay Yong now, I began as a warehouseman there eight years ago, and worked myself up into management. I underwent the company's training and I passed the exams set by the warehouse division. On the company job ladder, I rose to assistant technician foreman, and now I'm a senior warehouseman. I think that Kay Yong could also build a career if he's willing to improve his job habits and attend classes."

In all likelihood, however, it would be more difficult for a new employee to advance now than it was in 1973, not long after the company's establishment. Brother-in-Law told us that Kay Yong's fellow employees resent his intrusion on their usual pattern of work: "I treat all of my men the same. I don't favor Kay Yong just because he's my brother-in-law. He's somewhat stubborn and tactless and can't get along with his workmates. On several occasions I've taken him aside and told him to mend his ways, especially when teamwork is necessary to complete the operation. Otherwise our performance will suffer and Kay Yong's workmates will sabotage him."

Kay Yong is aware that his earnings lag behind the national average, and that many workers, while raising their living level, have not raised their income in real terms: "The chances for working-class advancement are the same as a decade ago. No doubt we have a house now, but rising prices make it hard to buy more than necessities. Working-class children now have the chance to attend school, but they don't perform as well as the richer children whose families can afford to hire tutors for them. So the rich keep their benefits and the poor remain at much lower levels. But workers' standard of living has generally improved and people can afford to buy more things like television sets and refrigerators. Even if a family is too poor to buy a TV set, they can watch television at a neighbor's or at a community center."

Siew Gek is less given to such sweeping statements, and busies herself with family improvement projects and social functions. The demand for experienced electronics operatives led to her promotion after eight years, from novice to category C, the highest wage grade. She regularly augments her basic S$500 monthly pay to S$569 by overtime, and to S$584 through good attendance bonuses. She is proud of her assignment as the one worker on her assembly line who applies epoxy glue to the electronic components. The speed of production depends on her.

When asked, "What do you like best about your job?" she stressed the respect commanded by her seniority. The younger women call her "auntie" and consult her about their problems. "In fact," she added, "sometimes my co-workers are jealous of my popularity." Other benefits are the proximity of the plant (she pointed out its rooftop from her balcony) and the convenience of the late-afternoon shift. Most important, however, is her ability to earn money for her household. Without her input, the Chuas would be deep in debt.

Siew Gek's limited knowledge of English keeps her from further promotion. Her supervisor asked her to join the company's quality control circle (aimed at raising production and reducing defects), but she rejected this nominal promotion because she felt she lacked the qualifications (just as her husband doubts his ability to compete for promotion). "I can converse in English, but I can't write the reports." Her supervisor has volunteered to help her, but she prefers to pursue other moneymaking ventures, and of course she has her housework to do.

Siew Gek makes extra money by helping in the homes of new mothers. While we were conversing in her apartment, one of her neighbors stopped in at her invitation. Siew Gek asked this woman, a part-time sweeper in a factory, whether she could recommend her for a similar job. Siew Gek remarked, "I prefer part-time jobs because they're more flexible, and the pay isn't too bad." Flexibility, however, is an elusive goal in factory employment. She explained that because of her pivotal position on the assembly line, it is often hard to take leave when her family needs her. Although her supervisor tries to meet the requests of an "old girl" like her, Siew Gek still finds it difficult to balance her home and work obligations. She is never certain that she can finish all of her tasks.

It was only when Siew Gek added her own S$8,000 to her husband's S$9,000 CPF contribution that the Chuas could move from their one-room rented HDB flat into a two-bedroom apartment. The purchase and furnishing of the flat were expensive, and the S$50 that she and Kay Yong each deposit every month in the revolving credit societies at their workplaces have also gone to improve the home. Siew Gek also saves a small sum in the Post Office Savings Bank for her mother-in-law as an expression of gratitude for her help with child care. Siew Gek told us candidly, "It's for emergencies, such as sickness and, you know . . . " She hesitated to mention funeral expenses. Finally, Siew Gek lends money to her younger brothers and sisters when they need cash. The Chuas do not, however, save for their children's education.

The Chuas' low income dissuaded them from applying for an HDB flat until they were desperate. Kay Yong's dignity was injured when the HDB denied his application. He told of his perseverance in using the available channels of appeal: "In 1979 the government tore down an old block of flats next to our apartment building. We were on the top floor and the wreckers made a hole in our ceiling. I complained to our member of Parliament about the unsafe living conditions we were forced to endure. I also stressed that our flat was much too crowded to house our family of five and my sick mother. This M.P. helped us. In less than three months we were awarded this new flat. And do you know, at first the housing authorities had told us no place was left in the area!"

Siew Gek is immensely proud of her contribution to her family. She beamed as she displayed the deed, known as a "land title," which she had collected that same morning at the local HDB office as evidence of the

Chuas' full ownership of their new two-bedroom flat. She replaced the certificate, along with the children's birth certificates and other vital documents, in a strongbox that she keeps locked in the teak-veneer cupboard in her kitchen.

The Chuas keep their apartment tidy despite its vigorous use by their young children. The three children, aged four, six, and ten, and Grandmother occupy one of the two bedrooms; the couple have the other.

The Chuas' front door opens into the living room; an arched doorway leads to their kitchen. The Chuas found this doorway, once rectangular, too small and inconvenient, so they enlarged it and laid tiles around the frame, for both attractiveness and ease of cleaning. The Chuas also affixed tiles to the floors and walls of the hallway and kitchen. Kay Yong hired a craftsman to design and construct a family religious altar for a designated space in their hallway. The Chuas withdrew the S$2,800 to finance these renovations from their tontines in 1979; two years later Siew Gek withdrew S$620 more to buy a set of cabinets for the kitchen. She had long intended to install these conveniences but had had to wait till she had saved the money. She plans to buy an electric oven with her next New Year's bonus.

The remainder of the Chuas' new household furnishings represent housewarming gifts from family and co-workers. They bought a set of sofa and chairs with S$270 given by their workmates and an electric standing fan and hall clock with the S$200 given by Siew Gek's brother and his wife. Her mother and sisters supplied curtains. They bought a small secondhand electric washing machine for a nominal S$100 from Siew Gek's sister, who had bought a larger unit. The teak-veneer cupboard in the kitchen is a gift from Kay Yong's workmates (the chest it replaced is now in the children's room, holding their books). Siew Gek keeps her Pyrex ovenware and other new kitchenware in this attractive new acquisition.

In common with other new householders in my panel, Siew Gek is remodeling her apartment to resemble the homes of her close neighbors. I asked her for the rationale behind the outlays on this project. "Perhaps my neighbors would look down on me if I didn't decorate this apartment well," she replied.

In accordance with their activist approach to household planning, the Chuas strive to secure what they consider the best education for their children. Siew Gek wished to enroll Elder Son, Robert, in Redhill Primary School, which she herself attended decades earlier and which she regards highly. Redhill had no vacancy for Robert, however, so in 1978 she enrolled him in Kim Seng Primary School, in the neighborhood where they were living at the time. After they moved, Robert had a long trek to school. In any case, Siew Gek was dissatisfied with the instruction at Kim Seng. She particularly objected to the high turnover of teachers. During visits to the school she discussed this and related problems with Robert's teachers, but was dissatisfied with their responses and continued her efforts to secure a place for Robert in Redhill School. Kay Yong reinforced Siew Gek's efforts by visiting their member of Parliament. The MP once again came to the family's aid, and at last Robert was enrolled at Redhill.

Siew Gek dedicates much time to shaping her children's achievement aspirations and encourages them to study. "I'm not exactly sure what the best jobs for my children will be, but I hope they won't have to take the kind of jobs their father and I have. My mother was a washerwoman and a domestic servant. When I was attending primary school I had many household tasks to perform in our home. My husband only went to school for two years, and was forced to accept manual labor. He started regular work at thirteen. So we often tell our youngsters stories of our own difficult childhood in order to encourage them to study harder. Every time I walk past a construction site with my children, I ask them whether they would like to end up like the construction workers. The children shake their heads and say no!"

When Siew Gek leaves for work at the electronics plant, she leaves a written schedule of tasks that she expects Robert to do in her absence. The boy is required to complete all of his homework each day and then to prepare for the next classroom test. Kay Yong supervises this assignment each evening after dinner. Whenever possible, Siew Gek then scrutinizes Robert's lessons the next morning. She often asks him whether he has encountered problems with his homework. She explained her methods: "I don't examine my children's school assignment books every day because I want to treat them as adults. But sometimes I do sample checking to make sure they don't hide anything from us. Once Robert failed to spell any English words correctly on a test and didn't tell us. I came across the test paper in Robert's bag. It looked like Robert was caught unawares by this test. I gave him such a severe beating that he has never since been caught unprepared. On the whole, however, Robert's work is quite good. Last year he finished second in the class." Robert proudly showed the interviewer the book that his parents gave him as a reward for this achievement.

One day the interviewer arrived just as Siew Gek was preparing to thrash Robert. Cane in hand, she explained that his performance in Chinese calligraphy had just been downgraded from B to C+. She asked the interviewer for clarification. Was C+ better than C−? Then she abandoned her attempt to discipline Robert, at least for the moment.

Poorly educated parents such as Siew Gek often send their children to better-schooled neighbors and kin for educational coaching. Thus Robert Chua is told to seek advice on his schoolwork from the children of his uncle, who are several years ahead of him in school. Siew Gek also tells Robert to consult the college-age children of the Chuas' next-door neighbors.

Siew Gek feels close to her mother and accepts her views on issues of family concern. Her mother, who has borne eight children, strongly influenced Siew Gek's decision to have a third child. "I wanted to stop after my first two because they were a girl and a boy and because we can better provide for just these two. But Mother pestered me to have a third child. Mother said that a third child would be good company for the first two, and that we'd have more support to rely on in later life. Kay Yong went along with Mother's suggestion. I don't mind having three, but I wouldn't want eight like my mother because of the hardship I experienced as the oldest child. My parents couldn't afford to send me to school beyond sixth grade. And I never had the incentive to do well because my housework and marketing errands interfered with my schoolwork. Anyway, everyone was very happy when I gave birth to a second son. Even though she lives with us, my mother-in-law isn't concerned about the number of children I have. She leaves this decision to us. She realizes that we must provide for them, not she." Siew Gek had a tubal ligation after the birth of her third child.

Her family's attitudes toward her employment have warmed gradually, from initial opposition to full support. Their help enables her to persevere. She goes to bed shortly after midnight and rises around seven for breakfast, which Kay Yong prepares for the family. Then she markets and walks her six-year-old daughter to kindergarten. She stops by the home of a neighbor who has just delivered a baby to wash the baby's diapers and the family's clothes. Then Siew Gek returns home around ten to do her household chores. Before lunch, which she or Mother-in-Law prepares, Siew Gek picks her daughter up from kindergarten. After lunch she takes a short nap before the 3:00 P.M. factory shift begins. Mother-in-Law minds the children until Kay Yong returns from work around six.

Siew Gek credits Kay Yong's introverted nature for his willingness to assist at home in the evening. Clearly, however, he acknowledges the importance of his wife's earnings to the family budget. Aside from his mother, Kay Yong has no kin to call upon, because his father's second marriage fractured the family bonds. Thus he has reluctantly acquiesced in the presence of Siew Gek's personal kin network in work and family arrangements. "My husband is cooperative and helpful. He has no choice, really, because I'm away at work evenings. Often when I'm at work or visiting friends on the weekends, he prepares and cooks the evening meals for our whole family. My husband prefers to remain at home rather than visit with me and the children. He gives the excuse that he needs to clean the walls or storage room. This is a sore spot between us. I'm unhappy that Kay Yong is unsociable, but on the other hand, I consider myself lucky that he spares me some of the housework so I can have more time for my own activities."

Kay Yong endorses the traditional precept that a woman cannot remain close to her kin after she marries. Realistically, however, he does not allow this custom to interfere with his wife's continuing close ties to her family of origin. When Third Sister celebrated the first month of their baby's life, Siew Gek spent over S$100 on a present of wine, chicken bouillon, and baby powder, with her husband's consent. "I wanted the present to look good enough because Sister's in-laws are there." Any gathering of kin is an important occasion to Siew Gek.

When her brother married, Siew Gek wanted to give him S$250, but this time Kay Yong objected that "it will create a precedent," as she has four brothers. She therefore reduced the amount of the gift to S$120, but then offered her brother a loan when he bought an HDB flat. In exchange, her brother helped her paint her own flat. Siew Gek also gets help from her sisters, who sew her clothes for her. She commented, "I'm fortunate that my sisters and sister-in-law sew my clothes free of charge. I distribute my materials so not to create a burden on any one of them, though I know that they're willing to sew for me. We know that we're all just making ends meet, and so we try to help each other out."

Kay Yong's mother has receded into the background. She tries to be helpful without asserting her own kinship demands. Mother Chua, therefore, does not provide an effective counterpoise to the more active Siew Gek.

This is a couple who have always discussed their family affairs, savings, and decisions. Their close marital bond enables them to stretch their meager resources. Most crucial is Siew Gek's ability to draw on the resources of her kin network. Although Kay Yong remains aloof from his wife's kin, the Chua family has nevertheless become fully incorporated in her network. In this case, the attenuation of the patrilineal construct allows them to pool resources with the wife's kin. The couple gain a concrete material boost as they strengthen their marital bond. As they have a modest store of resources of their own, the help they get from their kin expands their ability to use the new social services.

Loy Family: Store Clerk and Homemaker (II)

Loy Heng Yeo and his wife, Mei Po, still live with their two sons, now eight and ten, in a one-room improved HDB flat in a deteriorating section of the highrise satellite town of Toa Payoh. Before I entered, I noticed that the door was open to the hall, where their children rode to and fro on tricycles. Neighboring women often stopped in to make and receive calls on the Loys' telephone. Acquired in 1977, the phone symbolizes a modestly improved living standard. The couple have waited for a decade to upgrade their housing as well, and the time is near. The Loys' gradual uplift is a result of improvements in Heng Yeo's wage, the small shadow-economy earnings of Mei Po, and the onward flow of their life cycle.

Heng Yeo has been promoted from store clerk in the small retail outlet of his brother-in-law's stationery store to its import-export office. For ten days every month he delivers goods to customers in Malaysia; he spends the rest of his time writing invoices and overseeing the workers who load stock. I paid a visit to the two-room office of the Chung Hwa Trading Company. His desk is in an outer room filled with boxes of stationery, connected by a narrow passage to a smaller inner room in which Brother-in-Law and his secretary work. Relationships are informal. Brother-in-Law takes orders on his phone, then calls them over for Heng Yeo to fill. As the workers find Brother-in-Law's strong Hainan dialect incomprehensible, they continuously ask Heng Yeo for directions. To them, Heng Yeo is in charge. Brother-in-Law's son now works in the firm as delivery boy and his daughter clerks in the retail outlet, releasing Heng Yeo for office work. As their senior, he has authority over his niece and nephew, but he is warm toward them. When his nephew enters the room, Heng Yeo unconsciously pats the boy's shoulder. There is no apparent tension between them, for Heng Yeo is a modest man and does not feel threatened by the heir apparent.

Heng Yeo's S$540 wage has risen 216 percent over the interphase—a substantial improvement—and he holds shares in the firm. His New Year's bonus in 1981 was S$1,350 and 20 shares. But his wage is still under par. The small firm has limited capital and operates in an uncertain business climate. It not only lacks support by the state development program but appears to face relocation with the urban redevelopment of Chinatown. Heng Yeo reflected, "The firm went through bad times in the beginning, twenty years ago, but it's more stable now. In the last few years, though, our customers have decreased. We're located in a Chinatown redevelopment zone, and many of our customers have already been relocated. We may be moved, too. The future is uncertain. A new place will cost more to rent, and our customers are now all scattered. so it may not be worthwhile to set up again."

Further, his kin ties with his boss limit Heng Yeo's ability to negotiate a higher wage. "Brother-in-Law did ask me to tell him when I have difficulties making ends meet, but I'm reluctant to ask unless I can't manage at all. Having had a tough life, I feel that if I can make it, I should."

I queried Heng Yeo on his future employment prospects. It is common for subordinates in small Chinese family firms to start their own firms after they accumulate capital and experience. But he harbors no such ambition. Mei Po's parents offered a small loan to help their son-in-law start his own firm, but Heng Yeo, wary of the financial uncertainties of business, prefers to be a hired helper at low but steady pay. I asked him, "Do you plan to set up your own business?" "I'd need capital, capability, and luck. And I have none!" He punned on the words *capital* and *capability*, homophones in Cantonese. Mei Po elaborated, referring to the loan her mother has offered: "Fifty thousand dollars might make the difference." I continued, "Would you start your own business if you had fifty thousand?" He replied, "It depends on the type of business. That amount would only pay for insurance on a store like this one. It wouldn't be enough to start up an import-export firm."

"Couldn't you go into business with your wife's brother?" Mei Po's brother is a furniture maker.

"No, the natures of our jobs are too different." He is waiting out the future. Heng Yeo's tight links to this small family firm in a peripheral-sector industry limit his chances for a better life. The very connections that he has built, which are the source of his authority, curtail his alternative contacts. He is unable to construct an alternative to the family firm and has to await its fate in the second industrial stage, which promises little to firms on the periphery.

To help make ends meet, Mei Po has returned to piecework seaming at home for a neighborhood factory. The S$80 a month she grosses raises the Loys' household income above the S$600 median mark. She spends her earnings on "extras" for her sons; she therefore feels that her family life has improved greatly over the interphase. Her modest input permits her husband to bank his yearly bonus as family savings.

The Loys' telephone, the only one on their floor of their low-income house, required nearly a full month's wage as a deposit. In 1980 they bought a color TV for S$1,180 with Heng Yeo's New Year's bonus. Their other furnishings have remained the same, but the Loys look forward to moving to a new home and expect to replace their old household goods at that time.

The Loys long accepted their confined quarters as appropriate to their small income. Further, they live near Mei Po's mother, who used to help her daughter while Heng Yeo was on business trips. Now, however, Mother is elderly, her help is no longer needed, and they can afford to move. In 1980 the Loys finally applied for a two-bedroom HDB flat of their own. They expect to pay S$21,000 for it, and they already have saved over S$14,000 in Heng Yeo's CPF for installments and another S$10,000 in their savings account for furnishings. Seeing their own flat as visible evidence of achievement after their years of steady work and responsibility, the Loys feel quietly optimistic. Looking forward to the future in their new home, Heng Yeo reflected that he would like his sons to live with him after they marry. The new home is thus an ongoing investment in the family line.

I visited the Loys' Toa Payoh home one evening to discuss their educational plans. As we sat around the bridge table in their living room, the discussion was interrupted by Mei Po's efforts to extract a loose tooth from her younger son's lower jaw with her fingers. The boy squirmed and dodged until his father captured him in his lap and objected quietly that she should leave the tooth alone.

The Loys spoke of their hope that their sons would at least finish high school. Their elder boy is being tutored at a cost of S$40 a month in preparation for the primary school-leaving examination, but his grades place him near the bottom of the class. The Loys believe that he will enter a technical secondary school. The younger shows more academic promise. He will soon be tutored as well in preparation for the forthcoming primary 3 streaming examination. Mei Po checks on her sons' homework and enforces a daily hour of study. Their concentration is impeded, however, by the flow of neighbors into the small flat. Heng Yeo does not push his sons, and accepts a level of academic achievement inferior to his own. "My thinking is that if the children can learn, then let them go ahead. If not, then too bad! But of course, university is best." His younger son, still sitting on his lap, interjected, "No, high school is enough!" Mei Po added, "Then you'll have to be a street sweeper or fisherman if you don't behave!"

In response to the challenge of educating their sons and shaping their behavior, the Loys have limited their family to two children. The slight improvement in their living standard encourages Mei Po to continue piecework at home. She admitted, "I'd have liked to have a girl. Now we'll have only boys. So I plan to care for a girl during the day, as a job." Heng Yeo added his reason for lowering their intended family size from three children: "Children need discipline and knowledge these days. It's more responsibility to teach them. So we'll have only two."

Their parents have withdrawn from their former pivotal role in their lives. Mother Loy still lives with her eldest son, who has moved to a new flat some distance away. Mei Po no longer visits there nightly. Her own mother, who is no longer the vigorous woman I remember, told me, "My responsibility to my children is over, and the grandchildren are the responsibility of their own parents." She does not even concern herself with their progress in school. "My children can all stand on their own feet," Mother said proudly. Mei Po's family still gathers at Mother's every Sunday, but the tenor of the visits has changed. Whereas Mother once freely dispensed strongly held opinions and help and was the most influential force in Mei Po's life, now family visits are simply fun.

Mei Po visits daily with her neighbors, but these visits, too, have become more perfunctory as their old friends move to larger flats elsewhere. She can still gather enough players for a mah-jongg game, but she looks forward to the time when she, too, can move. The Loys spend more time together as a family now, discussing their modest plans and hopes. They feel quiet confidence in the future.

Tan Family: Tinsmith and Domestic Servant (II)

The earnings of the skilled peripheral-sector worker Tan Poh Wah have risen dramatically to 260 percent his phase 1 wage. But, like those of other poor men, his job and wage changes have taken place largely within the framework of personal bonds forged in his youth. Over the years he has worked for several small local firms. As partnerships broke up, Poh Wah would move to a new firm, and he has by now become familiar with a substantial number of owners, who tend to maintain informal relations with their workers. "At one time my bosses were all colleagues of mine. But they were lucky. With the right contacts and financial backing, they managed to set up their own company, and I became their worker." When we met Poh Wah in 1981, he traced his current job to such a link. One former employer, who bought out his partner's share and purchased machinery to upgrade production, sought him out. "Since the time I worked for my former boss, we've kept in touch. Occasionally we'd meet for coffee. So it was easy for him to find me when he needed skilled men."

He is satisfied with the terms of his employment as a lower supervisor overseeing a ten-man crew in a factory of fifty workers. His firm follows government pay recommendations, and after one year's service, workers get a week's leave; the time increases with seniority. He can earn upwards of S$500 extra each month for overtime work, and last lunar New Year received a bonus of S$650. He complains, however, of inflation. He laughed bitterly at the dilemma workers are in. "When we're given a pay raise, the government jacks up the price of daily essentials, like bus fare and provisions. So one offsets the other. I feel that the cost of living is higher, but I'm not the only one affected by it. Anyway, I can't fight back. The government regulations are law, so I just put up with them."

He enjoys the low-key atmosphere at work: "My colleagues and I get along well. Have to, being together for so long. Of course, there are a few black sheep, but generally the working atmosphere is good. Sometimes they borrow money from each other, or the boss." He has introduced his sister to the factory; as a daily rated worker she earns S$13 a day.

But there are few channels for advancement. "Is some kind of on-the-job achievement possible?" "No, just learn the hard way. No doubt I'm more familiar with the machines than a newcomer, but with so many years of practice, anyone can pick up the skill." "Which is more important nowadays, technical or academic education?" "Technical certificates are not so important, but a sound academic education in engineering is. If a man is highly educated, he's more capable of picking up new tricks fast. Like myself, I can repair some machines, but I have to do it the hard way. I dismantle the thing and try to figure out how it works. A well-educated man can just refer to books or his own knowledge and come up with better solutions. In this firm, promotion is out of the question. Maybe they can come up with the title of 'general supervisor' of the entire firm, but that's my thought, not theirs. Chinese bosses pinch pennies. My boss depends on old contacts, and for new business he acts as his own salesman. Just to save costs, I guess. Even the secretary is in charge of payroll, attendance, clerical work, and every-thing else in the office."

"Would you consider yourself a skilled blue-collar worker?" His answer reflected his insecurity. "No, it was poverty that forced me to take up this skill. It's a poor man's occupation. Now there are machines everywhere and all you have to do is press a button. Anyone can press buttons and my job could be gone in a few minutes."

Poh Wah is temporarily safe, however, in the niche carved out by his company, which takes on small orders that the larger, automated firms find unprofitable. Asked to compare his small firm with Metal Box, he showed us a color catalogue. "This is our company's line of metal containers. It's all right, but we can't compete with a big company like Metal Box. They accept contracts for tens of thousands of cola and beer cans. Can you imagine the mass use for them! Local and export consumption is very high. My company lacks the capital and machinery to compete. We're lucky if we can secure a contract for two thousand containers. The boss is too stingy to invest more and really expand the firm."

With experience and seniority he has gained authority as well. His person-al contacts direct him to alternative jobs with marginally better conditions, and he has advanced without having formally upgraded his skills. His em-ployer's former partner started up another small can factory and plans to upgrade his facilities. He invited Poh Wah to join him. But Poh Wah said, "I'm not sure if I'll move. The pay isn't much better. Besides, he's a friend, and it's hard to haggle over salary. Of course, I'd be exposed to better machinery, but I'm still not sure. The work is still the same."

Giok Bee is still a domestic servant for Japanese families, and also stays within the personal framework but without the support of the state develop-ment program. This peripheral-sector worker, the lowest-paid woman in my sample, is earning S$280 a month, 187 percent of her phase 1 wage of S$150. She believes that her pay has risen significantly, but with the current rate of inflation, she hardly feels the increment. Yet she focuses on her achieve-ments and is content. Giok Bee considers that she is working for her family. She thriftily stints on her own expenditures but is generous with her daughters. "Outings cost money, and I really can't afford to spend any," she commented in response to my questions on her leisure activities. Her job enables her daughter, who has just become a receptionist, to use her own slim paycheck on her daily expenses. Giok Bee has never given any money to her mother, who lives with a married son and cares for his children. But at last Giok Bee no longer needs to borrow money from her mother.

She estimates that it takes nearly S$1,000 to support her household, and without her input, the family would be in some difficulty. Even with it the Tans cannot save for the future, and so Giok Bee is grateful for her CPF savings.

[177]

Because of their long history of poverty, the Tans have no plans to buy a new home. In 1977, however, they rented a new, better-appointed HDB flat. The HDB authorities promote the sale of flats to families that wish to upgrade their housing, and were reluctant to rent the Tans an improved flat. Poh Wah recalled with some annoyance, "It wasn't easy to get this place, because the government rejected my application for a transfer. After many years and many visits to our M.P., they finally agreed. I disliked the old place. It was dirty and noisy and the corridor was dark and smelly. What can you expect when one row of flats faces another? In the morning, when we opened the door, the odor from the opposite row came floating in. Then my mother became very sick, she coughed all the time. So with the help of a doctor's letter, we got to move for a change in environment. We were only here a month before Mother died of cancer; she was only sixty-three." Poh Wah likes the locality and location of the flat. It is near his kin (his mother's mother and brother live upstairs) and near his in-laws' place. Giok Bee can commute easily to work and he can walk to work and save bus fare. The schools are convenient for the children.

They still have a two-bedroom flat, but the proportion of rent and utilities they pay has declined from 27 percent to 16 percent of their combined basic take-home pay. As their budget is "very tight," they have spent only $900 to improve the wiring, paint the walls, and buy a few pieces of furniture. In comparison with the homeowners in my sample, the Tans have furnished their flat simply, unwilling to invest heavily in a place they do not own. The floors are covered by linoleum, not the marble or ceramic tiles found in the flats of my homeowners.

In addition to the expense, their family structure influences them to rent rather than buy an apartment. The Tans have no son, and they do not expect their daughters to live with them after they marry. They will have to depend on their own pension to support them in later years and so cannot afford to use up their savings on a large flat. Nevertheless, they have greatly improved their home environment over the years.

Poh Wah's own negative experience nourishes the belief that a sound education is important, yet he has not provided his daughters with this advantage. Lack of money is the main problem. Though Elder Daughter's marks improved with the help of a tutor, the expense was greater than they could afford and she failed her primary 6 exams for the third time and left school. Poh Wah reconciles the importance of a solid education and their inability to pay for one by placing the burden on the children themselves. "I don't expect anything from my children. I just do the best I can as a father. If they can learn, so much the better, and I'll do all I can to support them. If they can't, like my first daughter, there's nothing I can do. It doesn't even matter what stream they choose to be in, just so they do their best."

Similarly, Giok Bee blames Eldest Daughter for her lack of intelligence.

After quitting school, the girl cared for her sisters, then went to work in a garment factory. Giok Bee said soon afterward, "I'd be glad if she became a salesgirl. With so little education, what responsible job can she hold? She's not very bright." She then arranged for this daughter to become a receptionist to her dentist. Eldest Daughter thus has a semiskilled job in the peripheral sector. The Tans' hopes have turned to their middle daughter, who they believe has potential: "I have higher hopes for her. I'd like her to become an army clerk, like my sister, or a bank clerk, like my niece. Army personnel work regular hours and their pay and promotions are good. Bank tellers have attractive three-month bonuses every New Year. But the final choice is really hers. The third girl [aged nine] has a long way to go, but I can see that she's not intelligent." The middle daughter helps the younger one and the Tans have not hired a tutor for her.

Giok Bee keeps her home neat and tidy. Although she works most of the day, she has sole responsibility for the housework. During one of my visits, she was preparing dinner for herself and her children. Now and then she rinsed out a dishcloth and wiped around the area as she cooked, keeping the kitchen grease-free at all times. She does not ask her children to help at all, despite her busy schedule.

She described her daily routine: "Early in the morning I go to the market. I bring the groceries home and then prepare breakfast and lunch for the three girls. Then I leave for work." She prefers light domestic tasks and shopping, and occasionally cooks lunch of fried rice or noodles. She leaves home early each afternoon. She has worked for three Japanese families since phase 1; when one family returns to Japan, they recommend her to another. "Since I've been working with the Japanese for so long, I manage to understand the language when it's spoken slowly. But I can't speak it too well myself. I return home after two in the afternoon, then clean and wash our clothes. My daughters are very lazy. They don't help at all. Anyway, I can't stand the way they work. Either they can't do a job properly or they waste a lot of water doing it, especially when they wash dishes. I have to do it all over again. So I might as well do everything right the first time. After that I take a nap before dinner or go to my mom's place or to my sister's place, then come back in time to get dinner. I don't like to go out. I rarely even go to wedding parties. Outings cost money and I really can't afford to attend any." "Why don't you stay for dinner in your mother's home?" "My mother is tired of cooking, and cooking for so many of us is a headache, especially on the weekend, when everybody's there. And my husband doesn't come along, he'd rather relax in front of the TV at home." Therefore she has to return before he gets there. This is her routine. Aside from visits with her grandmother, who lives upstairs, she goes nowhere else.

"Poh Wah grumbles if I'm a little lazy and let some of the housework slide, but he doesn't lift a finger to help me. I used to nag at him for coming home late and drunk. He spoke such nonsense. But he's stopped now, so there's no more friction. On the whole we don't talk much."

She spoke much more freely than she had done in 1975. I said to her, "It's easy to talk to you, you're very friendly and frank." She replied, "When the children and my husband aren't around, it's easy to talk. I don't mind confiding in another woman. Last time I couldn't because my mother-in-law was always looking over my shoulder." She says she has begun to "enjoy life" now that she has a bit more money and is no longer supervised by her mother-in-law.

With her mother-in-law dead, Giok Bee had no compunctions about ending childbearing. And in her later years her mother-in-law "did not press me for a grandson. After all, her own husband was a man and he walked out on her. As for my own mother, she had four daughters before having a son so she didn't say anything. And as you know, her husband walked out on her too. Now that the world is equal, a boy or girl won't make any difference," she concluded rather sadly.

Just before one of our interviews, Giok Bee had had a tooth extracted, and she was moaning in pain, claiming she was hungry yet it was too painful to eat. I turned to Poh Wah. "You must help out with the housework now." He replied, "No, never did that before. Don't know how to." Giok Bee's relatives visit for emotional support, but they provide no concrete domestic help either.

The friendship and kin circles of husband and wife do not now overlap, and their separate work routines are paralleled by their segregated leisure activities. Poh Wah still goes out for drinks with close friends after work, while Giok Bee visits her kin. So outside the home, their lives are separated into pieces of disconnected networks, which Giok Bee lacks the time to weave together. Poh Wah also informed us that his own kin ties have weakened with the death of his mother. For him the wider patrilineal construct has lost much of its force: "I spend most of my time in front of the TV. We don't visit relatives together or go out. On Sundays I'll be working, and after work I'm too exhausted to go out. I'm a family man, and so are my relatives. I come home to the nest after work." To him, a family man stays at home but does not necessarily take his wife out of it.

The HDB highrise tenement where the Tans lived during phase 1 had not been the center of a dense structure of neighboring relations or kin, and the move to a new apartment did not rupture a close-knit fabric of relationships. Nevertheless, Giok Bee was sad to leave it: "I had some complaints about the Malay family living opposite us in our old place. They were very untidy. They kept throwing things in the common corridor, but when we spoke to them about it, they blamed it on their children. There's no point raising the matter too often, so after a few unsuccessful talks with them, I swept the corridor myself. After they moved, a Chinese family moved in, and they were nice people. We were a little sad to leave them when we came over here, but the move is for the better. We don't keep in touch with the neighbors. They're working and we're working too, so we've never been back since we moved over here." As she has not built relations with her new neighbors, her social ties are nearly solely with kin.

The Tan family has improved their economic position by advancing largely within a framework of known ties. Their upgrading did not require them to rupture kin ties and thus their marriage bond has changed very little. As their familiar community undergoes change, however, they have to depend more on their own resources. Partly this is a matter of choice. They are fortunate to have skills that give them a material cushion so that they can reduce their dependence on their kin. But actually they have no choice. The changes in their social bonds flow from the wider processes at work in Singapore, and in their own maturing family cycle.

Lim Family: Shipyard Worker and Homemaker (II)

In a growth industry, the shipyard worker Lim Joo Koon has doubled his daily wage to S$20 over the interphase. The Lims are still very poor and have to rely on his bonus from beating deadlines for a margin of well-being. His irregular work pace and reliance on personal ties to make ends meet foster in Joo Koon and his wife, Peck Hoon, a day-to-day approach to life. The Lims can afford little of the advance planning prescribed by the Housing and Development Board, the Ministry of Education, the Family Planning and Population Board, the Post Office Savings Bank, and other state units.

Graffiti cover the walls of the house where they live and litter accumulates in the corridors. Joo Koon describes his way of life as "eat first, pay the bills later." He cannot take further courses to advance his skills, as his hours do not allow him to meet a fixed timetable. He is proud of his ability to perform the fast-paced, unskilled manual work that brings higher rewards, despite its uncertainties and many dangers. "I've been working with the shipyard for almost ten years now. Sembawang Shipyard offers a contract and my company gets it. Then I'm sent to work on the vessel. I do general painting and cleaning up. I work for several companies, all getting contracts. I work hard for my pay. Most of the time I have to work nonstop for two or three days. I've gotten used to it, though. Contract jobs are rush affairs. If the job can't be completed, the boss deducts our pay. If the contract is finished before the deadline, we get some extra money.

"Sembawang Shipyard is a tough place to work in. I'm used to it, having worked there since my teens. You can't remain on the ship once your work is done. You can't leave or enter the yard during certain hours. Once you resign, you can't go back. So many rules!" Joo Koon works around these

[181]

demanding rules. For example, he obtained permission to let his hair grow below the collar line. "I'm in mourning for my mother, so I can't cut my hair. My company wrote to the Sembawang Shipyard explaining this, so the guard lets me in now. Many accidents are not reported. Recently a Malay boy was killed by a falling crane. Everybody rushed over, but I prevented my workers from going there. I didn't want them to be scared. I saw the body myself, though. It was horrible." These risks do not blight his judgment of shipyard work. In fact, he views risk-taking as a mark of courage. He continually defends his scope of actions from encroaching control by supervisors.

He stresses his ability to make it against high odds. "I work like a dog to make ends meet. If I have a little extra, we eat better. If not, we eat the essentials. What alternative do I have? Some people just sit in an air-conditioned room and take home twice what I make. Blue-collar workers are always in demand, but it's a hard way to earn a living." He feels he cannot direct his own work future, and persists in the dream of becoming a businessman. "I'd never advise anyone to work as a contract laborer. Can't go far that way. It's better to have a little stall selling cooked food and candy. At least you're your own boss. You can't imagine the pressure we get in the yard."

"So you wouldn't have your children doing blue-collar work?" I asked him. "I can't determine their future. Even some well-educated people who can't find jobs come to work under me. It's an honest living!"

Pressures from the deadlines and the dangers both demand trust and cement close ties between workmates. Joo Koon has little authority over the workers. "We're all general workers—no need to throw one's weight around. Can't go far that way. Should treat everyone like good old friends. But you still have to keep your distance. If you're too relaxed and friendly with the men under you, they take advantage. Most of the time I hang around with senior workers like myself. They know when to play and when to work." Workers often borrow money from each other. "I borrow from my friends, and return it to them as soon as possible. We workers approach each other for small amounts, but for larger sums we have to go to the boss for an advance."

Although he clearly is proud of his newfound ability to support his family at solid working-class wages, I sense a plaintive note. Working in the elements, doing "buffalo labor," he has fallen behind his brothers, who work indoors in different sections of the shipyard. "They have easy jobs. Just clock in at nine and out at six, but I don't think their salary is very high." His job has more uncertainties but usually pays better. "During the bad weather, we have to dip into our own pockets, but when there really is work to do, the income isn't bad. Touching four figures any time."

A friendly man who believes that "nothing is impossible to the willing heart," he is easygoing but still strives hard for his family. "I just pass each day and let tomorrow take care of itself. Why think so far ahead? When I close my eyes [and die], all the plans will be for nothing, because I won't know what's happening then!"

Peck Hoon has not returned to paid employment outside the home. She cites lack of industrial skills, the heavy homemaking tasks of raising five children, and her disinterest in working under the direct control of a supervisor. "I can't go to work now, not even in the future. Who's going to look after the kids?" "How about when they're older?" I pressed her. "What work can I do? As a domestic servant or factory worker, I couldn't earn more than two hundred, and I'd be under pressure. Besides, I'm not used to it. I'd rather stay home."

And so she depends on Joo Koon. "My husband pays for everything. If I want to buy something, like a dress, I ask him for the money. The same thing with marketing. I have no bank account, because I have no money to put in it. I take everything from him."

Peck Hoon usually wakes at 6:30 to prepare breakfast for her husband and Fourth Daughter, who attends the morning session in school. Then she returns to bed and rises again to cook a noon meal for the other four children, some of whom go to afternoon session. Then she does the laundry. She usually spends her free time napping. But she has been introduced recently to industrial piecework seaming. Peck Hoon's younger sister moved in with the Lims to use Peck Hoon's electric sewing machine. Their brother delivers unfinished goods from a nearby factory and returns to fetch the stitched pieces from them several days later. Sister is also easygoing, and sews only enough to pay for her modest expenses. As she pays no rent, she helps Peck Hoon with the household chores and occasionally cooks for the family. Peck Hoon helps her sister sew but has not yet comfortably incorporated seaming into her daily routine, and resists the lure of this moneymaking opportunity. Peck Hoon remarked, "My sister and I sew together. We only sew the collars, nothing else. The pay is a dollar fifty per dozen pieces, but the material is so soft, sewing is difficult. It's not easy money! I don't know how many I can sew in a day. I haven't really put myself to the test yet."

Sister does not expect that Peck Hoon will continue to sew. "Elder Sister is rather happy-go-lucky. She's been like that since I can remember. The I-don't-care attitude." It is true that Peck Hoon allows her sister to take their joint earnings, but in the increasingly commoditized Singapore setting, she, too, is likely eventually to complete the transition to regular piecework.

The Lims moved in 1978 to a two-bedroom flat in a three-year-old highrise in Sembawang. They had earlier been offered an apartment for S$7,000 in Toa Payoh, but Peck Hoon rejected it because it was far from Sembawang, where her folks lived and she had spent her life. They were then offered this flat for S$15,000, and they took it. They paid an additional S$5,000 to renovate their place. Peck Hoon was not in favor of spending so much money, but Joo Koon persuaded her to go along because it was "once and for all."

Joo Koon, who makes the family decisions, bought the home and furnished it. "He's the one with the money." Peck Hoon estimates his total income to be S$150 a week. That is the basic wage that he gives her; he keeps his bonuses, but "I never ask him." Joo Koon paid for the home partly with gambling winnings. "Luckily, I struck a ten-thousand-dollar lottery, or I wouldn't have had the money to buy this place. I was poorly paid and had hardly any CPF. But with the prize money, I had three thousand for the down payment and five thousand for the renovations. The rest was spent on odds and ends." They are to pay S$137 a month for fifteen years plus S$45 a month for utilities. "It's a money world! But since I moved here, I've lost all my luck."

Because Joo Koon's CPF is low, he must meet the rest of the payments out of pocket. Indeed, he cannot cover the sizable cost of a home from his basic wage at all, and depends on overtime and bonus payments to do so. Their monthly bill for installments and utilities amounts to 38 percent of Joo Koon's basic take-home pay, a rise from the 22 percent he paid for rent in phase 1, although if his overtime pay is included, the proportion spent drops to one-quarter of his net pay. He has had to deepen his commitment to hard toil for years to come.

Like other homeowners, the Lims changed the shape of the kitchen doorway from a rectangle to an arch and laid white marble on the floors. They paid little for furnishings. The new long sofa was a housewarming present from Joo Koon's co-workers. Their black-and-white TV and radio-phonograph were bought secondhand from a co-worker. A large cabinet just outside the kitchen and an altar on a display cupboard cost the most. The Lims have more space now, but their new home is not much more tidy than their earlier place. Clothespins, plastic bags, and toys are scattered around. The electric sewing machine is in the kitchen, where pieces of cloth, umbrellas, and dolls hanging from the central gaspipe add an air of clutter. The Lims have moved their poverty into their three-room flat.

After paying for the flat, they have little money remaining for the education of their five children, aged six to twelve. Peck Hoon has no "expectations" for her children. I asked her, "If your children drop out of school after sixth grade, what will you do?" She laughed. "What can I do? Even if I beat them till they die, they still can't manage to learn. I don't know how to think that far, not like some mothers, who plan years ahead. I just handle one day at a time." The school persuaded the two eldest children to open a Post Office Savings Bank account, but Peck Hoon confessed, "It's just for show. There's no money inside."

During phase 1 the Lims did not hire tutors for their children, but now they can afford S$45 for a tutor for the two elder children. "They go to the tutor's home. I think it's very reasonable." But she does not think that the children will do well in school even with this extra help.

Joo Koon shares his wife's limited vision of his children's future. "It's hard to say about their schooling. If they can manage it, I'll support them all the way through. If I can't, they'll either have to work or get a scholarship. As far as I can tell, they aren't very bright and they can't learn." Joo Koon is not very well informed about their grades or stream in school. His lack of involvement in their education is due partly to his view that the children will not need postsecondary schooling for the manual jobs they are likely to get. He does not view manual labor as a sign of failure. The Lims accept the school's assessment of their children's low potential.

The Lims have bowed to the new economic demands on them by ending their childbearing with four daughters and an adopted son. Their ideal family contained a son and a daughter. As Joo Koon put it, "One of each sex is OK; after all, men and women are equal today." But he added, "It's a pity our children are all girls." "Will you have another child?" I asked Joo Koon. He joked, "I kept trying for a boy, and ended with four daughters. I admit defeat!" In another discussion, Joo Koon said, "The minute I wake up I lose five dollars." I rose to the bait. "Why?" "I have to give each of the children a dollar pocket money!" He and his wife broke into peals of laughter. Then he sobered and shook his head firmly. "No way! Can't have another. It would be one more burden. We really can't afford to."

The close ties with co-workers and kin encouraged by the shipyard and the home shape the Lims' segregated marriage. Joo Koon feels close to his workmates and former kampung neighbors. "Friends are valuable. If they can't contribute money, they contribute labor. I'll do the same for them. What's the use of having a stack of money in your pocket when nobody bothers to help you up when you fall? I go back to my old kampung home whenever I can to catch up on all the news and gossip. All my friends came to my mother's funeral. Those who couldn't afford donations came to help out. I really appreciate them."

Deep poverty, from which the Lims have barely emerged, keeps them in close dependence on kin. Now that they can make ends meet, however, Peck Hoon believes that their life is changing. "We can live from day to day now. But last year, because of the bad influence of his friends, my husband traveled to Johore Bahru to chase women. He loves to drink and smoke, and during that time we had to borrow from his elder brothers to feed the family. I could only advise him nicely and slowly. At last he listened to me and ended this nonsense. So the borrowing stopped. He has changed now, and is a better man."

The Lims do not share housework or leisure activities, but they appear to be shifting some of their activities from kin and pals to the home. Joo Koon insists that he has become a homebody. "After work I head straight home to relax. Once in awhile I go to a football game at the stadium or go for a drink with friends from work, then come straight home."

Family outings are nonexistent. Peck Hoon recalled, "I used to take the children to the beach nearby, but not anymore. Everything is expensive. Every time we go it costs us at least ten dollars. We have to save what we can." Her husband agreed. "Do I take the children out? Not very often. I can't drive, and if we go by bus, it's so inconvenient, and a cab is too expensive. Sometimes we walk to the market for a snack or movie, but that's when I have extra money."

Peck Hoon's parents live nearby and she visits them often. Apart from these outings, her life is now confined to her new flat. She never reads the newspaper and rarely watches television. She is aware neither of price changes nor of deeper societal change. She shops mainly in the provision shops downstairs, avoiding the busy market thoroughfare. She has become used to this physically limited life. I asked her, "Do you mix with your new neighbors?" "No, just exchange a few polite words. I seldom go out. But the children do play in the corridor with other children."

Like other poor families with newfound funds to upgrade their home environment, the Lims spend more time indoors than they used to. Their image of themselves as homebodies centers on their new apartment and television. They have not refashioned their marriage patterns to any great extent and do not plan far ahead. Their lives are increasingly defined by the goods they buy, the demands of the job, payments for their new flat, and the school system.

Cheong Family: Shipfitter and Electronics Factory Worker (II)

The absolute stride forward of core-sector men with skills is seen in the job history of the shipfitter Cheong Tan To, whose daily wage of S$40 at the Jurong Shipyard represents an increase of 238 percent over his phase 1 wage. Though he earns nothing when the weather is poor, with overtime pay his monthly earnings sometimes reach S$1,000. Tan To owes his wage improvement to the technical skills he gained as an apprentice in his youth and his employment in a core-sector firm at the time of the industrial take-off. He appears confident that his skills will remain in demand. He still wants to control his work pace and rhythm. "Now my pay isn't too bad, and I'm satisfied. My colleagues and I get along fine. Of course there are some junior workers who take things easy. Our work rules are posted on the shop walls and I follow them closely. So just because I work according to the rules, they think I'm trying to promote 'human relations' with the boss. But bosses aren't blind. I have every intention of making a good reputation for myself. I'd like to be called upon for work whenever they need fitters. I'm not claiming to be perfect, but I've never been sacked from a job. I work whenever I can. But my wife, Soo Hiang, wants me to work like a machine. When I wake up feeling too tired or sick and take a day off, she grumbles that I'm lazy. I'm not like her—she can't keep still for a minute, never sees a doctor unless she has to!"

Claiming he is "too old" to upgrade his skills and that his practical skills measure up to those of men with more education, he explains, "If you're an engineer or supervisor you may need a certificate to prove your worth. But as a fitter, all I need is experience. Some youngsters can read blueprints very well and explain a lot. But the actual product may not be what they expect. You can't hope to follow instructions on paper a hundred percent when you're handling metal. Even a qualified engineer might not know what to do if he was given a piece of material to fit." After work one evening, as he headed for the refrigerator for a bottle of stout, he threw over his shoulder the only complaint I ever heard about his job: "I bake easily under the sun. But what to do? When you're poor, you have to earn a living. Beggars can't be choosers." He concluded confidently, "As long as I have a bottle or two of stout every day and a pack of cigarettes, I'll just let the days go by."

Still an electronics assembler with eight years' seniority, Soo Hiang also benefits from demand for her accumulated skills. Her basic monthly wage is S$600, and overtime often raises the sum to S$800. "One time we had such a backlog that I even earned four figures with overtime, but not now."

In phase 1, Soo Hiang was my sole interviewee who held two full-time jobs. She worked all day at her factory and simultaneously managed a hawker's stall in the market near her home to help support her parents and siblings. Soo Hiang was then compelled to decline a promotion to lead girl in 1975. Her decision allowed her to continue at two full-time jobs, and thus enabled her to extend immediate help to her family, although she jeopardized any future career in the factory. "Lead girl requires one to work office hours, and at that time I had to help Mother in the morning at the hawker stall. It's said that when a person comes to a forked road, she can only take one path, so I decided against the promotion. I think it's a blessing in disguise. One of my friends who was promoted is getting so much trouble from the people over her and under her. If she complains about the people under her, they're unhappy. If she doesn't, the people over her say she's not doing her work. Eleven other girls who started work when I did are still working, and most of them have been promoted. Some to clerks, some to supervisors. I was the most outstanding of the lot. But my time is over!"

Calling her choice a blessing in disguise is her way of coping with matters beyond her control. This sort of fatalism is common among my poor respondents. Soo Hiang explained that her 1975 opportunity was opened by

[187]

the spurt in demand for experienced women in the expanding electronics industry. But now teenagers graduate from secondary school with credentials she lacks, and she no longer expects to advance on the factory floor. "Now, not a chance. Most of the newcomers are quite well educated. They pick up the work faster and can prepare impressive reports. So the management is after them. I'm content to be what I am." Nevertheless, in 1980 the management offered her a position as operator-clerk, which entails checking the attendance, performance, and pay of a number of operatives. She rejected the offer because of social competition. "No point in accepting the offer. The pay is about a hundred more than I'm making now, but the added responsibilities aren't worth it. Besides, clothes and makeup are problems. And the clerks are constantly trying to one-up you. I like what I'm doing, and I prefer the uniform of the assembly line. With overtime, the pay is about the same." Soo Hiang was referring here to the difficulties of breaking into the cliques of the better-situated office staff. Dress codes and conspicuous spending on lunch all seem forbidding to this plain woman.

With Tan To's newfound financial security, Soo Hiang's input to the family budget is less important than it used to be. Tan To now gives his entire paycheck to his wife and receives back S$5 for personal expenses each day. Soo Hiang still works "for the money," but now she can spend part of her earnings on leisure-time activities and consumer goods. "I'm against the idea of asking my husband for money all the time," she stressed. "Besides, I want to catch up with things, instead of staying at home doing nothing but gossip. I get along with my colleagues very well. And next year I'll be entitled to about two thousand dollars' worth of company shares." Soo Hiang feels free enough to enjoy window-shopping expeditions several afternoons a week after work. She introduced Tan To's unmarried sister to the factory, and the two women often eat lunch together and chat during work breaks.

Soo Hiang's work activities parallel the uplift in her family fortunes. Earlier she increased her work output when her parents, brothers, sisters, and children needed more money. Now she has dropped the second job because her brother and sisters are old enough to run their mother's hawker stall themselves and she no longer depends on them to care for her own children. At nine and twelve, her children are old enough to warm the lunch she prepares for them each morning, and then they manage unsupervised until she returns from work in the afternoon. While her burden of two simultaneous full-time jobs was somewhat unusual, Soo Hiang's interrelated family and work patterns typify the pattern of poor women's lives.

Now that their family budgets are separated, the households of Soo Hiang and her mother are no longer tightly intertwined. The Cheongs' former flat was demolished, and they were offered a replacement for sale in distant Clementi. They rejected the HDB offer and opted instead to rent a small flat near Soo Hiang's family home. Soo Hiang still visits Mother and assists at the hawker stall on weekends, but she devotes less of her time to the wider family. "We never applied to buy an HDB flat because I figured the price of HDB flats keeps going up, and by the time we got one the children would be old enough to stand on their own. Besides, after they get married and move out, who would keep the house clean for me? I shudder at the thought of managing a four-room flat all by myself. I won't have the energy to do the cleaning when I'm old and aching all over."

During phase 1, Soo Hiang expected to live with her children when they were older, but now she is sure they will want to live on their own. "Nowadays nobody wants to stay with their in-laws! This place is good enough. It's near to my mother, and my children go to Bukit Merah North School nearby."

Tan To's past history of gambling has made Soo Hiang wary of investing her CPF pension and savings in a home. Nonetheless, the Cheongs paid S$2,000 to furnish their rented flat. A floral curtain divides the room, drawn back in the daytime to let in light. On one side is a double bed, a dressing table, and a cupboard. Stacks of boxes cover the top of the cupboard. The other side of the curtain serves as a hallway, the floor covered in light-yellow linoleum. A large color TV with a turntable atop it occupies a corner. Records are stacked next to the TV. Opposite it is a showcase and altar. Every corner in the flat is fully used. The small kitchen contains a gas burner on a cement stand. A settee, coffee table, and chair are at the side of the hall, and the refrigerator is there also. Atop the refrigerator is a tank holding a couple of fish.

Soo Hiang recalled that when she married she had hoped for three children, but she settled for two when she had a son and a daughter. Her intention was firmed by her dedication to her two jobs. She was also concerned about the short-term costs of several children. When Tan To refused to undergo a vasectomy, Soo Hiang had a tubal ligation. "I was on the pill for seven years after the birth of my daughter. Then I developed pain on my left side. I had a stomach X ray and the doctor said it revealed a blood clot. So the doctors gave me another brand to dissolve the clot. But then I had second thoughts. Imagine what would have happened if the clot became womb cancer! The doctor then told me to have a tubal ligation as the final and best prevention. So I signed the form immediately. When I told my husband, he said maybe we'd have another child. I didn't agree, and he was easily persuaded. The next day he took me to the hospital, and the day after I was home again. The whole procedure cost me only nine dollars." "What did your mother-in-law say?" "Old ladies get angry at first, but after awhile the whole affair is forgotten. My mother had nothing to say. I suppose after having so many babies herself, it doesn't matter how many *I* have. Anyway, she had an operation herself long ago." The Cheongs' decision to limit their family size was based not on far-off plans for their children's education but on their wish to free Soo Hiang to work at her two jobs.

Yet the couple now believe they should devote more time to their children's schoolwork, and Soo Hiang checks it frequently. The Cheongs gave their children English names. Walter, twelve, who is repeating primary 6 for the second time, is a poorer student than Sandra, nine. He is now registered for two hours of English tutorials each week at the local PAP community center, at a monthly cost of S$8. "I have more hopes for Sandra. She can study on her own, whereas Walter is more playful. He has to be told again and again. I won't call him stupid—lazy is the word for him. He's very involved with games and school activities. He kills me with his nonsense! If Walter is still playing by the time I return from work, I make him hold out his hand and cane him on the palm. It won't injure him, and the pain will make him remember not to be too playful in the future. I don't curtail their activities in school, but I'm choosy about the children's friends. They can go out after school if I agree it's worthwhile, such as to the library."

Soo Hiang looks to her husband to reinforce their family regimen, but also complains that Tan To is too strict. "My husband wants to cane the children the minute they step out of line. I explain that the children have their own pride now, and we shouldn't destroy it too often." I saw the way the children obeyed their father on a Sunday-afternoon visit. Soo Hiang confessed, "I've been after Walter to take his bath all day. Now that his father is home, you'll see that Walter will finally obey." Seeing Tan To return, Walter rushed into the bathroom to bathe. Tan To affirmed, "I don't believe in spoiling the children. Must be strict with them. For example, most parents will complain to the parents of other children when their children fight. Not me. I just punish my own."

Like other poor men, Tan To feels close to his workmates. He rides to work every morning with his neighbor, a truck driver at the shipyard. At work he and his pals bait fishlines to drop into the water and leave untended while they work. "There are lots of fish where we work. We just throw the line down and come back for the catch at tea break. Sometimes we manage to get something, but mostly the bait is a treat for the fish!" Yet Tan To distances himself somewhat from these men, and when they gamble on work breaks, he no longer joins them. He often takes his Sony Walkman and cassettes of popular music to work. He also spends most of his evenings listening to records and tapes. He recalled, "When I was young and single I was very playful, and enjoyed going to nightclubs and to discotheques in the afternoons. No more now! I'm too old for that sort of thing. Some men relax in bars and some like the company of women, but I prefer my home above all else." Now that he has gained a modicum of economic security, Tan To really considers himself a homebody.

Soo Hiang is more content with her marriage than she was earlier, largely because of Tan To's increased sense of responsibility. "Young marriages have their advantages and disadvantages. If it were up to me, I'd still be single today. Being single means freedom and fewer responsibilities. On the other hand, when I think of my sister-in-law, still unmarried at thirty-two, I feel sorry for her. Even if she were to marry this year and have a child right away, the child would be only ten when my daughter is twenty. My husband is good to me and I really don't have anything to complain about."

The Cheongs frequently discuss family matters, but their communication does not cover advance planning. Soo Hiang commented, "Tan To doesn't even know what I earn. I tell him when my payday comes up, but he's not interested. As long as he has his daily allowance and the household runs smoothly, he leaves everything up to me. I can buy what I want without consulting him." The Cheongs spend little time on outings together and have few friends in common. The increase in their social and economic well-being over the interphase is reflected mainly in their new focus on the small flat they call home, which they now run with little help from kin, and on taking responsibility for their children.

[8]

The Lives of Secure Families

We have seen how the new state development program has reshaped Singapore's society. At the center of this program is the spreading market and the state programs that have replaced many social services once negotiated by individual families. To maintain their position in the class order over the interphase, secure families made even greater use of the state services than the poor families did. State policy, with its emphasis on capital-intensive core-sector industrial workers, has strengthened its grip on the secure families. Couples favored under the terms of the state development program vary in their use of programs and in the meaning of the policies to their way of life. Family relations are being negotiated, and social services, such as public housing, play a central part in this process. We now turn to these twin processes of extension and uniformity, variety and meaning in the uses of the new social services by the families we have come to know.

Goh Family: Meter Reader and Garment Factory Worker (II)

Goh Tee Tong, meter reader at the Public Utilities Board (PUB), heads a family that has deepened its involvement in the market and in the use of social services over the interphase. But as a peripheral-sector worker with nontechnical resources, he suffers from the loss in standing of his quasi–civil service employment. Goh Tee Tong's salary has nearly doubled over the interphase. His earnings, which earlier exceeded those of the peripheral-sector panel men, now have dropped to their average. Whereas Tee Tong was once proud of his place in government service and his contribution to society, he is no longer satisfied with his current wage of S$980. An eager worker, Tee Tong complains that the way to advancement in his job is blocked, and he feels increasingly frustrated when he contrasts his own position with those of his more rapidly advancing schoolmates in the dynamic private sector. In his catalogue of complaints, he lists lack of democracy in the workplace, his lack of authority in his position, and being overworked for low pay.

Tee Tong has left the volunteer police force, but in his workplace and at home he is still a guardian of community mores. He defends colleagues whom he feels to be unjustly accused by customers or supervisors. As a result, his work record is now studded by complaints. He believes his supervisors no longer protect him and he cannot command respect. "The supervisor told us we were expected to be polite, and that we are the first line, like an ambassador. That's nonsense! We're not paid like an ambassador, with a car. There are many difficulties with customers. There are lots of dogs in the kampungs and we get bitten. Other customers are disrespectful. One woman chased me with a cleaver. The meters are often installed at awkward heights. It's dangerous to climb up on a chair to read a hawker's meter, for example. What if we should fall? Other customers are never at home. We have a file folder with information on each customer. I put problems I run across into the folders in order to warn other workers—for instance, the woman at such-and-such an address ran after me with a cleaver. My supervisor doesn't like us to put such things in the file, he says it reflects poorly on our section.

"There must be good relations between management and workers. It's no use for management to sit in an office all day. They can't understand the workers' problems. Our relations, in fact, are not good. No communication between supervisors and workers. Graffiti on the department walls, a staff car gutted, offices being vandalized are all proof of that. So I figure we work only for the money.

"But even here we have problems. We're expected to finish all the work in our folders each day. There's no understanding if we don't get it done because it's raining or the meters are too high or they're spread too far apart and there are too many of them, like in Jurong. I make my views known to our supervisors, but then I'm penalized and don't get any incentive pay. But this is not a dictatorship! If I don't like something, I'm going to complain!"

Tee Tong is no doubt seen as a troublemaker. His opportunities to advance are blocked by his sense of being wronged and his defense of his colleagues. He had a stint in the complaints department, which could be seen as a promotion. But after several customers complained to his supervisor that Tee Tong had criticized them, he was returned to the meter department. This loss of position embitters him further.

"Would you prefer another job, then?" "Yes, in the big famous firms in the private sector. Small firms are not stable. There's no point in leaving for a small firm, and jumping here and there. I guess I'll stay with the PUB. I'll die there!" he concluded bitterly.

As Tee Tong has advanced more slowly than his friends in large private trading companies with less education, he is bitter about his limited future at a time of rising prices, expanding family needs, and new expectations. He has tried, so far without success, to obtain the help of friends in getting work. "I'm earning under a thousand a month with fifteen years of service at the PUB. They don't appreciate me, so I've taken on part-time jobs to improve my living standard. I've worked for a friend in the import-export business to try it out. No money in that. Mail sorting and delivery at the PUB gives us a hundred eighty overtime, but lots of people want that job, and you have to wait your turn. Money is so tight now with the high cost of living. I have a friend who emigrated to Australia and is doing very well there. He didn't even graduate from high school. He may sponsor me there. His two brothers have less education but have been more successful than I. One is in the well-known Guthrie's Trading Firm on Sixth Avenue here. I have another friend who claims he got eight years' salary this last New Year's as a bonus from Lee and Lee Brothers. I don't know how they made it without higher education."

"Couldn't your family help you find a better job?" "My mother's family is wealthy, true. But I can't get help from them. I couldn't even ask. The more you have, the more arrogant you become. My mother's brother is a self-made man. He set up his own business, selling door to door, and became very rich. But I couldn't get a job from him. You can't make money selling door to door anymore. People are too suspicious nowadays. At most you get one percent profit. Anyway, he plays the horses. The more he has, the more he spends. I call it 'feeding the horse.' No time for me."

Tee Tong has long been a follower of a sect of Chinese Buddhism, and in his current disillusionment over his job, his religion consoles him. In 1978 he saw visions often, and his devotion greatly increased. These apparitions direct him on family matters and give him a sense of well-being. Now he worships at the temple at River Valley four times a week and on the important days of the lunar calendar. Frustrated over his stalled career, Tee Tong seeks spiritual freedom, not a concrete return from his worship. He explains that his devotion cannot alter his fate. Thus, although he would like higher wages, he does not seek them from the gods. "If you are fated to do poorly, you will do poorly. If you're going to survive, you're going to survive." Tee Tong advocates forgiveness, and he is learning not to retaliate and to keep his temper. "I feel peaceful when I enter the temple. I make my request, and I believe the first wish will be granted. But as soon as I step down from prayer, all the pressures of money come into my head. Money is so important!"

Tee Tong also bets on the lottery. He won S$6,000 in 1980, and put this sum away for his family's use. But he knows that he cannot really depend on a lottery to strike it rich. He plays numbers mainly as a pastime. His effort to raise his status and earnings, once mainly on the job, now seem to lack direction or result. Tee Tong's fatalism has increased over the years I have known him.

Bee Tim still works at the garment factory. After nearly twenty years there, her basic wage is S$370, 185 percent of her earnings in phase 1 but still below those of core-sector women workers. She grosses S$430 when she works overtime.

Tee Tong projects an image of the breadwinner of a middle-class family. His earnings can carry the family, but only at a living standard lower than he is willing to accept. He is thus still ambivalent about Bee Tim's employment. He insists that she doesn't really need to work. Bee Tim agrees that she does not have to spend her earnings on the needs of her family. "I earn only enough to use on myself," she claims.

Tee Tong wants her to quit work and care for their son, aged seven, and daughter, aged four. "She wants to work rather than care for the children. I asked her to stop working, but she doesn't want to. She tells me that spending the whole day caring for children—washing them, cleaning their clothes, and so on—is too tiring." As Tee Tong spoke, he appeared resigned to losing this long-standing argument. But he is still torn between the desire for his wife's earnings and the hope of providing a "better environment" for the youngsters. By a "better environment" Tee Tong means mainly a more affluent neighborhood and playmates. When I asked, "Why do you want her to stop working?" he said, "A mother's care is best for children. Around here they learn all kinds of dialects playing around with the other children."

Tee Tong observes adults with children as he makes his rounds reading meters. He has catalogued numerous instances of callous and even rough behavior to back up his views that his wife should stay home and watch the children. He has overheard day-care workers object that their charges are "troublesome." "Of course they're troublesome, otherwise they wouldn't be children! These women wouldn't call their own children 'troublesome'!" Tee Tong is not afraid to act when he sees an adult mistreat a child. "I saw a mother slap her child, and so I called the police. I said to her, 'This is the government's child. You can't hit society's child.'" Yet Tee Tong still believes that "a mother's care is best."

But Bee Tim evinces even less interest in caring for her own children than before, and prefers to leave these tasks to her in-laws. Nevertheless, she may not have a choice for very long. As the children grow older, their needs become greater than Grandmother Goh can meet. Tasks related to the children's education are most crucial. Bee Tim said, "I'll work until the youngest goes to primary school. Someone has to take her there and bring her home, and Mother-in-Law doesn't have the time. The kindergarten is near Mother-in-Law's place, but the primary school is farther away. I'll see about quitting work in a couple of years."

Mother Goh shares Tee Tong's unease over Bee Tim's job but accepts a fee to watch the two children. The Goh children are joined by a three-year-old child of Third Brother. He is a low-paid bookstore clerk and his wife works as a waitress. Mother Goh admits that she is getting tired of her daily child-care duties. Her own ten-year-old son teases her nieces and nephews. On one of my visits to the Goh household I saw him thrust out his leg, trip Bee Tim's daughter, and in an injured voice cry out that she had stepped on him. The din of their play and fighting is burdensome to Grandmother. But the Gohs still seek her help and organize their housing plans around it.

In 1976 Tee Tong and Bee Tim rented a small apartment near the home of the older Gohs. They ate their evening meals together, then returned to their own flat to sleep. Their children spent the night with their grandparents. In 1977 the couple bought a two-bedroom flat of their own, again not very far from the senior Gohs' home.

Bee Tim still considers Tee Tong to be her closest companion, and Tee Tong reports that his ties with his wife are very close. Bee Tim also looks to her mother for comfort. She visits Mother every evening after she leaves the nearby factory. Apart from infrequent visits to Mother's sister on the weekends, Bee Tim participates in few other visits or outings. "I usually come right home after work. I'm tired after the daily routine. Many married women work in the factory now, but I don't see them after hours. I'm not free."

This use of separate apartments is time-consuming. Every morning the four Gohs take a bus to Mother Goh's home. The two children remain there. Tee Tong fetches his scooter, which is parked nearby, and drives Bee Tim the long distance to work. Then he himself goes to work. After work, Bee Tim walks to Mother's home and waits there until Tee Tong fetches her for the drive to the senior Gohs' for dinner. At nine o'clock at night the family of four catch a bus to their own flat. There Bee Tim puts the children to bed and washes the family clothes before retiring herself. Six days a week Tee Tong and Bee Tim follow this routine. Only on Sunday do they remain in their own new flat. Then Bee Tim does the bulk of the housework. She plainly finds this a tedious responsibility. When Mother Goh is no longer strong enough to manage the care of the several youngsters, Bee Tim will probably have to leave work. But until then, her earnings do help the family, and her quasi-clerical job has some status. She is "used to" the factory. For the time being, the benefits of Bee Tim's job outweigh the costs.

Tee Tong thinks his standard of living is "so-so." He has cut down on his purchases of clothing and other things for the home. He is trying to save on their family expenses. He gives Mother Goh S$200 every month for food costs and her child-care help. He also gives S$80 to Bee Tim's mother each month. Although they rarely eat at home, the family of four spend S$200 each month on their food, in addition to what they give Mother Goh. Tee Tong now feels that "money is tight." "We used to drink cognac at New Year's," he reported soon after the festivities. "Now we drink beer."

Nevertheless, the joint earnings of the couple provide a comfortable home for their family. They have in fact spent a large amount on housing, in order to give parents and children all the comforts that families of their milieu enjoy. In 1976 Tee Tong put pressure on the HDB authorities to rent them a flat, because of the overcrowded conditions in his parents' home. The board temporarily rented them a one-room apartment, and they spent S$2,000 to decorate it. Within a year, however, they were offered a flat of their own, and they moved again. They could not recover the money they had spent on the rented room, but Tee Tong just shrugged and smiled. "Let that be a gift to the next couple who live there." The Gohs paid S$17,600 for their new apartment, and it is fully paid for. They spent an additional S$6,000 on renovations. They laid marble slabs on the floors of the sitting room and the master bedroom (at S$4 per square) and put colored ceramic tiles on the bathroom and kitchen floors, white tiles on the walls.

The Gohs can afford to furnish their new home handsomely, even after paying for these elaborate renovations. The living room contains a large ebonized desk and two television sets. Tee Tong watches the black-and-white set when his children demand their favorite program on the color set (cost, S$1,490). The living room also contains a modern, brass-topped coffee table on a chrome stand, which Bee Tim and Tee Tong saw at a furniture display. Bee Tim chose the sofa set (S$650), but Tee Tong complained, "Bee Tim's taste isn't modern enough. The sofa isn't as comfortable as sofas made in Japan or England or other foreign countries." Tee Tong grimaced at the sofa set we were sitting on. He clearly prefers to be the family decision maker on household purchases, even though his wife helps pay for them.

The Gohs still rely on wider family support for Bee Tim's employment and Tee Tong, as eldest son, is loyal to his family of origin. These kin ties are still in tension with the couple's efforts to build a united family life. They use the HDB housing to create a separate space for their family at the same time that they obtain daily help from their kin. A separate flat is important to Bee Tim as a symbol of her close relationship with her husband. Tee Tong would have preferred a three-bedroom flat. "I'd like the children to have their own bedrooms. I think the children should be apart, and also I myself would have liked the privacy when I was a child because of the crowd of my own family. The children can also study better." A larger home might not have benefited the couple's small family at all, but instead would have enabled Tee Tong to incorporate part of his family of birth into the family formed by marriage. This is a sore point between the spouses. It was for this reason that Bee Tim preferred a two-bedroom flat. She confessed that she was afraid that Tee

Tong's brothers would stay with them if they had an extra bedroom. Tee Tong, who still hopes eventually to move to a larger flat, admitted, "We have to give way to my two brothers, who are still studying and need quiet rooms." Bee Tim, however, prefers to accept the assistance of the wider family on her own terms. The relation between the two family units is still being negotiated, and public housing plays a central part in the process for this couple of modest means.

As we strolled along the walkway that joined two towers of their housing block one afternoon, Tee Tong complained to me about the debris strewn around the area. He upholds his role of private watchdog over public morals. "It's very dirty here! The people here moved from the dockyard area nearby and don't know any better. They toss condoms and other rubbish all over the playground. People should be required to attend meetings and to learn not to destroy property. They should learn how to teach their children public cleanliness, too. They called on me to join the Residents' Committee. I don't have the time. But I'd be very strict. A condition of my joining would be to require people to attend meetings to learn good behavior." Perhaps because Tee Tong is stuck in his job, although he has followed what he thinks are the rules of proper behavior, he feels righteous in his quest for community spirit and respect for property. Throughout my visits with him he always showed concern for good deportment. Now that he cannot express his concern at work, he has transferred it to his living space.

Tee Tong once voiced the hope that his son would become a doctor. Now he is no longer specific about educational plans for his children, but he believes he should enter them in a reputable school. "There are higher standards today than before, especially in language. The school we choose for our children is important, and such a school has better and more experienced teachers." The Gohs hope to put their son in Tee Tong's former secondary school, Saint Joseph's, and their daughter in another highly regarded mission primary school. They spend no money on tutors for their son and hope that Tee Tong's old school tie will suffice to get him in if he does not do well on his exams. They have heard that tutors charge S$50 a month for each subject, and feel the expense is unjustified. They have instead put most of their money in their daily surroundings. They are not saving anything, but Tee Tong hopes later to be able to save for the children's education.

After their daughter was born in 1976, the Gohs decided to have no more children. In phase 1 they felt that a third child would make little difference to their household budget, but they have now reassessed the costs of another child. I asked Tee Tong, "How many children do you want?" "I never think about it. When I think about money, I can't think about children!" His wife added, "Two is enough." Tee Tong continued, "The idea of having a third child is ridiculous! It would undermine the savings we have to put aside for the education of the two children we have."

Tee Tong is torn between the need for his wife's continued earnings and for her "mother work" of instilling values in their children. A third child would overtax Tee Tong's mother and Bee Tim would certainly have to stop working, a forced choice that they are not yet ready to make. Thus this couple responds to new demands for their earnings and new aspirations by reducing their intended family size from three to two children.

The Goh family use the main social service goods of public housing and family planning and have educational hopes for their children. Their secure background and earnings gave them an early start. But the couple's work prospects are mixed. Tee Tong is unlikely to advance with the Public Utilities Board and cannot hope to match the pay or the status of skilled workers in private firms. Bee Tim's job, too, brings in less than workers in core-sector firms are making. The Gohs maintain their wider family relations while living apart; they provide help in return for help. Any further move toward separate living would cost more than they can afford. The Gohs' future has dimmed, and their pessimism is rooted in the declining status of Tee Tong's quasi–civil service job in the new developing order. He no longer feels that society listens to or is structured to help the little man.

Ong Family: Vegetable Stall Proprietors (II)

Also in the peripheral sector and feeling squeezed out of his former comfortable niche is Ong Nan Seng, who runs the family wholesale vegetable market. The Good Year Vegetable Market is losing customers as the old Chinatown section is torn down. Ong Nan Seng cannot expand his group of regular patrons, as a shopkeeper's convention forbids competition for another merchant's customers. This proprietor's net earnings have dropped from 125 to 89 percent of the average peripheral-sector wage among the secure men. Indeed, when I visited the Good Year Market one Sunday, I was the only patron there on an otherwise busy marketing day.

Only Nan Seng runs the business now. Father Ong has died and the brothers have found other jobs, leaving their share of the stall's profits to support Mother Ong. I asked Nan Seng if he, too, might change his line of work. "I've been in this business since my youth, and can't think of what else I could do. Besides, it's too late for me to learn a new trade or go back to school. If I do change jobs, I'll find one that will use my knowledge of vegetables and my experience in the trade."

Siew Hwa is still a homemaker. Her children are now ten, eleven, and fourteen. As their budget is tight and their savings have evaporated, she thinks about ways to earn some money. "I used to save in a rotating credit society with my sister, but I've stopped doing so ever since the government took legal action against the operators. Besides, when the children were younger, our expenses weren't so heavy and I could save a bit. Now with inflation and all three children in school, there's nothing to put aside."

To add to the family income, Siew Hwa thinks she may babysit or sew at piece rates at home when her children are older. Such work is common among women with no job experience and little education. So far, Nan Seng has objected on practical grounds. But Siew Hwa believes she has yet another option. "It's going to be hard for the children to get jobs unless they have higher education. I intend to do some hawker business, since the cost of education gets higher every year." "Why don't you work at Good Year?" I asked her. "I'm better off on my own. If I work at the store, the in-laws will gossip that we're trying to keep the business to ourselves. They wouldn't approve, because the profits from the family business are to be divided among the male heirs." A former market woman, Siew Hwa naturally thinks of returning to the work she knows. She is constrained, however, by the limited profit margin, the long hours, and the difficulty of obtaining a license. Hardship cases have little trouble securing the necessary licenses for such ventures, but her husband is the proprietor of a business.

The Ongs once expected to buy a flat of their own, but business is now so poor that they have given up the hope. In an effort to cheer up Nan Seng, Siew Hwa stresses the adequacy of their two-room flat and the importance of their ties in the area. "Never mind. We're happy here. We know all our neighbors well, and we live on the second floor, so we don't even need to take the elevator. We feel very safe staying here."

They have made only two major purchases since the mid-1970s, a color television set and a S$700 frisky Pekinese puppy. Siew Hwa washes the pup every day and feeds him on leftover rice and chicken wings. Although neighbors have complained to the HDB authorities about their dog, the children refuse to give it up and the parents are fond of it too.

As business declines, the ties that bind Nan Seng to his brothers, sisters-in-law, mother, and other kin have loosened. The Ongs increasingly devote their energies to their small household, and their children are the central focus of their daily lives. The parents proclaim their belief in the equality of their son and daughters but are raising them for distinct male and female roles. When Nan Seng makes evening business calls, he takes his son along; Siew Hwa requires household help only of her daughters.

The Ongs chose their children's schools for their proximity. Siew Hwa made the decision. "If their schools are too far away, the children will be tired by the time they come home. All schools are the same. It's up to the students themselves whether they can study hard." Siew Hwa has no special timetable for them to follow, but she does encourage the children to take ther studies seriously. Elder Daughter teaches English to her younger brother and sister, and Siew Hwa helps them with Chinese. She checks their homework and scolds and even beats them when they do not complete it. Siew Hwa believes that her daughters work harder than her son. But Eldest Daughter did not perform well enough on her exams to merit entry in the parents' first choice of schools, and in fact had to settle for their third choice. The Ongs pay S$75 monthly for their son to receive help with his lessons. They have no savings for higher education. Siew Hwa first justified her small fund of savings by saying that smart children would rise to the top and there was nothing to be done about the others. "I have just enough for daily expenses. I'll think about higher education when the time comes. There's no point in putting pressure on them if they don't have the ability to study." In other words, meritocracy becomes a justification of necessity. In further defense of her short-term educational plans, she mentioned a relative who had nine children, "all intelligent, and none ever needed pressure from their parents to study and do well." Siew Hwa grounds many of her actions in dual references to state policy and the people she knows.

Siew Hwa believes that her children are at a crucial age when they might mix with bad company. She prefers them to stay at home, though their presence increases her mothering burdens. Siew Hwa is not passive about their school experiences. She visits the schools if the children's report cards are poor and authorizes the teachers to discipline them. Once when her son fought with another boy on the school bus, Siew Hwa scolded him severely. She was critical of the fact that the mother of his adversary went to the school to complain. Siew Hwa thinks that parents should control their children themselves and that strict supervision of her own youngsters will head off future problems. "I'll tell you another example of what happens if you don't keep alert. A friend told me that her friend's son was being shaken down by a stranger who hung around the school. The man even raided the boy's house when his mother was out. The parents realized that their son had a problem only when a lot of money was missing." So, although the Ongs have few long-term goals and spend only a little more than the minimum on their children's education, Siew Hwa's days are full with the moral and educational upbringing of her three youngsters.

These two paradigms—the official world with textbook information and the personal world of the family and the farmer's market—intertwine in her perspective on having children. She draws on the strands that mesh and overlooks any contradictions. "My ideal family size was two, but I became pregnant, and I had the child because the doctor advised against abortion, and also I'd feel safer if I had another child, since the second was still so young. I know a woman who had her tubes tied after two children, and then one of them died. She asked the doctor to undo the ligation, but the doctor said it was impossible." "So then have you done it?" I asked. "I wanted to, but I was afraid of the consequences. One of my elder sisters had it done and now she's very absent-minded! The doctor also advised me not to have it done because of my condition. I continued to menstruate through the first three months of my third pregnancy. One of my friends gave birth to a retarded child because of this, and was not accepted by her old-fashioned mother-in-law. The doctor told me I was lucky my child wasn't retarded too." She concluded, "Most of my friends and relatives who have their tubes tied say it's a dangerous operation, and certain people can't do it because of bad effects." But she doesn't intend to have any more children. "Three are already quite a financial burden. I'm safe taking pills." She has withstood her mother-in-law's pressure for a second son. "I personally feel that daughters are more obedient and filial than sons."

Now that he is getting older and his customers are moving away, Nan Seng has reduced his work hours and become more of a homebody. They have a cohesive family life, which centers on the home and family store. Nan Seng has greater control of the store than before, in part because of its lack of profits. At times Nan Seng and Siew Hwa go out alone and leave Eldest Daughter in charge, but Siew Hwa is reluctant to be gone for long. Family excursions and outings are not frequent. The children spend most of their free time at home in front of the television set.

Siew Hwa still sees her in-laws more often than her own kin, although she feels closer to her own folk. She sometimes visits Mother, who lives with Elder Brother some distance away, but mainly keeps in touch with her elder sisters by phone. When Siew Hwa needs advice on a family issue, it is to her sisters that she turns, rather than to Nan Seng's relatives. She sees her older sisters as role models and combines their views with information gathered from the mass media. All of her sisters are able to make ends meet and have no need to borrow money from each other. Each is concerned mainly with her own small family. The Ongs' turn inward to their small family is a matter of choice and some financial ability. Although they are doing worse than they expected to be doing, they still earn well above the median, and they pride themselves on getting by.

I asked each of the couples, "What are the main changes in your lives since the last time we met?" Nan Seng replied dryly, "No change at all! Five years ago we lived in this flat. Five years from now we will also live in this same flat. Five years ago I was selling vegetables. And five years hence I will be selling vegetables." As Nan Seng has no retirement plan and his store's profit margin is small, the Ongs can make no further plans to upgrade their housing or work. They feel doubly left behind in the Singapore development process.

Teo Family: Sewing Machine Mechanic and Garment
Section Leader (II)

Teo Hiang Hong, mechanic in a peripheral-sector garment factory, enjoys the greatest relative wage increase of the panel. His basic wage has risen 265 percent, from S$400 to S$1,061, or from 58 percent to 86 percent of the average wage of secure men. Thus, though his earnings still fall short of their average, his options have widened considerably. He can now invest in public goods and services to an extent he did not dream of before. But a higher family income and the chance to buy into the state social service package have brought great changes to the lives of Teo Hiang Hong and his wife, Lee Kim—the life of the nuclear household, geographically isolated and physically severed from long-standing community bonds.

As Hiang Hong has always worked for one firm, whose owner treats him paternalistically, he attributes his advancement to his employer, not to a demand for his skills. Hiang Hong therefore prides himself on his loyalty. "My boss is the very best boss! Whenever I have any request to make, like taking a day off, he always tries to give me first choice." Hiang Hong has been offered somewhat better jobs elsewhere but has turned them down. He is content with his current wage and position. Indeed, he works overtime three evenings a week in exchange for meals but no overtime pay. As the firm prospered, it opened branches in two housing developments, and Hiang Hong has transferred to one near his new home. His work there is the same, although the air-conditioned new factory is more comfortable. The factory is unlikely to offer further training, and Hiang Hong turns to human relations. "There is nothing new to me in this job now. I've mastered all that I need to know. I'm happy here and have lots of friends, so I take things easy."

Younger Brother Teo has recently opened a small store selling sewing machines. Hiang Hong said, "Of all my brothers, I get on best with my youngest, because we're in the same trade. When he first started, two years ago, he asked me for a lot of advice, because I'm more experienced. I know more people than he does, and I could introduce potential customers to him. So when I have time, especially on the weekends, I go to help him. No pay, I volunteer my help. We're brothers, it's my duty to help. I don't feel forced, I offer to help willingly. And since this is what I'm interested in, I get very involved."

"Why didn't you join your brother in a partnership?" "At that time I was unsure about starting my own business. I thought it's better to stick to this job for security." But since the company requires mechanics to leave when they reach their forties, Hiang Hong is not really secure. "People who quit this firm in their middle years start their own shops that sell sewing machines, or they'll hire women to sew piecework for other garment factories. They use the contacts they make in this place to do it. I haven't thought that far ahead, though. I have lots of experience and skills, so I'm not worried. I'll just wait and see." Hiang Hong takes each day as it comes, like other men whose wages have risen with demand for their skills but whose futures in their peripheral-sector firms are uncertain.

Lee Kim resigned as ironing supervisor in 1979 because her household burden grew too great. Before 1979, the Teos lived in a kampung with Mother and Father Teo and the Teo brothers. Mother Teo minded Lee Kim's son and a neighbor cared for her baby girl. When they moved into their new apartment in 1979, the goal of her family career, Lee Kim found that it was too expensive to pay for child care so that she could continue working. Her daughter went to kindergarten for only two hours a day. Lee Kim recalled, "I'd have to pay a hundred dollars for help with each child, and I was earning only three-forty a month. It's not worth it, so I just quit."

Lee Kim does not need to work to pay the family bills. Hiang Hong shares his take-home pay of S$900 (after the CPF deduction) equally with her. She pays the bills and deposits between S$100 and S$150 monthly in a personal savings account. Her husband banks S$250 from his S$450 split of his pay in a savings account of his own.

When I asked her to compare her present and past living standards, she said modestly, "It's about the same." But "the same" in economic terms masks fundamental structural changes in their family economy. For in phase 1, the couple's joint basic wage was only S$650, and Lee Kim made a substantial contribution. Now her husband alone earns nearly twice that sum while she earns nothing. In exchange for his newfound "family wage," she has given up a productive role. I learned that although Hiang Hong did not mind giving her money and she was glad to receive it, Lee Kim felt a bit uneasy afterward. She hoped that one day she could work again. "As long as I'm not too old, there will still be employers to hire me," she affirmed, proud that she is in demand. She hoped not to have to depend on her son to support her in later years. "If I'm healthy and strong, I'd rather work hard to earn my own bread!" She further complained of boredom. "When I worked I found it easy to pass the time, I had so many friends. Now I'm bored at home. I don't see much of the neighbors and there's nobody to talk to."

"Why don't you work, then?" "Because my daughter is still young and I can't leave her at home. Also, my son has reached the worrying age, when he can be easily influenced by bad company and gangs. So I'd better stay home and look after him. In fact, if my son were a daughter, I might have kept on, because girls are easier than boys and less worrying for me." She discussed this problem with her maternal kin, who concurred. "My brother advises me against working. He said to me, 'I don't see why you should work and neglect your children when you aren't desperate for money.'" Lee Kim, who admires her brother, takes his advice seriously. She also speaks highly of her mother, who sacrificed herself for her children. She takes her as her model.

"Why don't you sew for your company at home, so that you can pass the time and earn some money besides?" "No, my husband wouldn't approve, because it would mess up the flat. Besides, I have no interest in sewing. Maybe when my kids are grown I'll go back to work." Like others who have lived with in-laws most of their married lives, she dislikes housework. As her husband works late and eats dinner out, she thinks it is a bother to cook, and often she and her children eat at a nearby hawker's stall run by her husband's second brother and his wife. Lee Kim is not highly educated and is reluctant to try to tutor her children. Clearly, time was lying heavy on her hands.

It came as no surprise, then, to learn that Lee Kim had returned to the garment factory. Her husband's supervisor, keen to have this experienced worker in the new branch in her housing development, offered her a slight raise, bringing her wage to S$400, on a par with phase 2 women's wages. She beamed when she recounted her return, and stressed that she was doing a favor for her boss. "My husband's friend [his supervisor] asked me to please come back. My husband didn't object at all."

Lee Kim takes her daughter to primary school each morning and reaches the factory by 7:00 A.M. At noon a neighbor fetches the child from school, gives her lunch, and cares for her until Lee Kim picks her up shortly after 3:00 P.M. "I pay my neighbor only seventy dollars a month because she has to provide only one meal." Her eleven-year-old son stays after school for sports and is trusted to return home by himself.

The Teos hire tutors to help the children with their homework, but the youngsters complain at the absence of family and a settled community. In the kampung of their childhood, brother and sister did not feel isolated even when Lee Kim was at work. The move away from this community has shaken the children's sense of belonging. Lee Kim may have to leave work again to give the children more personal care and mothering.

Their move from the roomy wooden kampung house to a highrise apartment provides a concrete example of the ways homeownership stimulates the market economy. When they moved, they had already undergone their first division when they added a room to the main house. Elder Brother moved his family of five into this room but still shared the family's refrigerator, stove, television, electric iron, and telephone. But when the kampung was razed for industrial development, the family split up into four flats, which they furnished with four identical sets of new appliances and furniture. The second family division was considerably more costly than the first.

Hiang Hong and Lee Kim had saved for years to pay for their two-bedroom flat, and Lee Kim's brother also helped them out. They laid elegant pink-and-white marble-chip flooring in the sitting room and tiled and remodeled the kitchen doorways. The kitchen contains built-in cabinets that surround a large stove and oven—although Lee Kim eats out often—a refrigerator, electric fan, and secondhand washing machine (gifts from Lee Kim's brother). The living room is dominated by a new sofa set, television, and stereo in a glass commode (also gifts from Lee Kim's brother). For the children's room Hiang Hong designed a space-saving modern teak trundle bed, with a bottom drawer that pulls out to form a second bed. Hiang Hong has used all his CPF (S$14,000) and Lee Kim S$1,500 of hers to help pay for the flat. Lee Kim spent her savings of S$11,000 on home decor.

Highrise housing promotes the new industrial economy, as couples must work hard to pay for their more elaborate apartment living. The dense network of kampung living, partly based on the multiple use of buildings and appliances, then gives way to dispersed homes whose appliances are underused. The virtue of sharing is supplanted by a new way of life in which high status is shown by the decor of a home of one's own. The extra cost is obvious, and these expenses stimulate the local consumer market.

The Teos give more thought now to their children's education, and Lee Kim worries that school is a lot harder than in her day. "I try to give my son extra help at home, but I find it tough to understand English, and I just about manage to help him with Chinese." She pays S$30 for group lessons for her son by a moonlighting teacher. "Without a good education you can hardly get a decent job. Competition is stiff." Hiang Hong, who leaves most decisions about schooling to his wife, simply remarked, "Of course I would like them to have a good education. Depends on how able they are. I'd like my son and daughter to have equal opportunities." "Would you like your son to do what you're doing now?" "I don't know. It depends on him. I don't think that far yet."

Lee Kim, the planner of the two, greatly admires the academic performance of her brother's children. She therefore placed her son in a boy's primary school that her nephew had attended, and later registered her daughter in a newly opened school recommended by her brother's daughter. Her son has not kept up with his classmates, however, and did poorly in the primary school-leaving examination. He will enter a technical stream in secondary school and is likely to get a certified technical education, a step only nominally higher than his father's.

Lee Kim rejects pressure by her mother-in-law to bear a second son. Hiang Hong was once willing to accommodate her, but after the household divided, Mother Teo lost her leverage over Lee Kim. Among other things, she cannot provide the help Lee Kim needs for another child. Indeed, Lee Kim has never taken care of her own babies. In response to these pressures, the Teos have reduced their intended family size from three children to two. Lee Kim says firmly, "Two is enough. I don't even dream of a third child!" She is now taking oral contraceptives. "There is no fear about the pill. If I forget one, I can make it up in the morning." In addition, Lee Kim and her husband sleep separately. She sleeps with her daughter, and her husband sleeps with their son.

The passing of kampung living reduces the Teo brothers' interchanges to occasions based on filial piety and shared interest. Hiang Hong mainly visits his mother, who lives with his younger brother, the sewing machine sales-man. He has less in common with the others and sees them rarely. "All of us brothers get on well. We never quarrel. But now that we're grown up, all absorbed in our own business and jobs and families, we seldom get to talk."

Hiang Hong keeps up friendships with fellow workers, some of whom have moved to the new branch with them. They often go out together after work without their wives. So Lee Kim and Hiang Hong rarely go out as a couple. Lee Kim's girl friends have married and moved and she seldom sees them. Occasionally she telephones her workmates to keep in touch, but most of her time is spent with maternal kin. Lee Kim visits Mother Teo "rarely, and when I do I make it brief." This distance may not last, because Mother Teo bought an apartment adjacent to Lee Kim's. Lee Kim keeps an eye on the empty flat, cleans it occasionally, and puts offerings on the altar to the dieties. She prefers the empty flat to close proximity with her mother-in-law.

The separation from her mother-in-law gives Lee Kim a chance to visit her own kin freely. Every Sunday she and her children visit her mother. Some-times Hiang Hong joins them in the late afternoon. The Teo children often spend the night with their cousins during school holidays. Sister-in-Law phones Lee Kim when she plans a special treat or outing. If Lee Kim skips a visit, Sister-in-Law phones to ask if she is all right. Lee Kim is friendly but more distant with her married elder sister, twenty-one years her senior, although Lee Kim successfully played the role of matchmaker when she introduced a younger sister of a co-worker to this sister's son. Second Sister, unmarried, lives with Brother and works in his retail outlet. Lee Kim thus sees her often.

The Teos bask in their higher earning power, which finances a home of their own and an above-average educational package for their children. But like many other folk of modest means, they look to kin to expand their personal resources. In fact, the ties maintained individually by this husband and wife divide the marriage and strain their ability to run the home jointly. Lee Kim absorbs the brunt of the new work. Finding the burden of the isolated family life heavy, she turns more often to her kin, but now she travels farther and still has less support than she enjoyed in the kampung. The Teos have thus exchanged opportunities for sharing for their greater use of the cash economy and social services. They had little choice, but they don't see it as lack of choice. They see themselves as free now to buy and consume, and to select those kin ties they wish to maintain. Nevertheless, this freedom to choose and reject ties increases the burden on the nuclear household, which Lee Kim, as wife, must take on.

Ramakrishna Family: Computer Technician and Homemaker (II)

Ramakrishna Mani, the Tamil respondent, married to Wong Far Eng, has also done relatively well and is optimistic about his recent successes. His wage of S$1,100 is 196 percent of his phase 1 earnings. He has been transferred to maintenance in the American-owned computer company and is pleased at the possibilities opened up. "I don't know how they chose me. I was lucky! An American came from the States to train me, and I read a number of books. This was not a promotion, my salary didn't change, but the work became more interesting. Before, I didn't understand what made the computer work, but now I understand more. If I ever leave this firm for another, I'll be in greater demand."

But Mani's enthusiasm wanes when he compares his earnings with those of foreign technicians and local university graduates in his firm and of employees in more dynamic firms. "What income is needed today to get ahead?" "I'd say eighteen hundred for a family like mine." "Who do you know in your firm who makes that much?" "There are several making sixteen hundred, and the chief engineer, an expat, earns ten thousand. Those kinds of people pay fifteen hundred rent for a house. They could do it for seven hundred. They just make too much money!"

He worries that his prospects depend on formal certification. He jokes about it. "When you phoned me at my office for our first appointment, they called me to the phone over the loud-speaker. Later people asked me who phoned. I said, 'They're from the university.' They asked me, 'Why did they call you from the university?' I said, 'Oh, they want me to return to school!'" He chuckles at the joke. Then, more seriously, "I can't get promoted anymore without a college degree. But I've been out so long, I can't go back to school. Now that the company is growing, they hire people right out of college. They pay them more than they pay me with long experience." "What are the greatest changes in the past five years in your work?" "This is it! Five to ten years ago, if the manager needed someone for a job, he'd look around or people could get jobs through the recommendation of their friends. You could be trained up and promoted even without a degree. But no longer."

Mani took a screening test at the Vocational and Industrial Training Board to upgrade his qualifications. "I've never taken a test like that in my life. So I brought home a lot of books on electronics and read them all. Then I sat for the test in a room full of lots of people taking all different kinds of tests—air con, radio, TV. I was so nervous, I was perspiring all over. But nothing I studied was on the test. It was so easy. I went to the coffee shop to wait to hear the results. It was a long hour. Then they came and told me that I passed."

This test qualifies him for a certifying test in electronics, but Mani worries that he will not pass. "I don't have time to go to classes because I'm on shift work, so I study on my own. I'll be taking the exam with a group of students who are trained in technical things I don't even know." "What other means do you have to advance?" "I'd have to push my way up by studying on my own. I'd also have to change companies. I'd probably choose Texas Instruments. That's a good company. They have the best computers and produce IC chips. They train you for that in their Singapore firm. They give you a chart on how the chips work, and some manuals. But since I don't know anyone there, I'd be taking a chance if I switched firms. Here I'm the most senior, and I'm unlikely to be laid off. I'm a family man, so I'm not making the effort to move." He senses the need to move onto a new career ladder, but neither his past training nor his personal connections can place him on one. He can, however, take statutory board tests to improve his bargaining power in his firm.

This affluent couple aspire to give their son, aged six, and daughter, aged four, a richer and more varied background than their own, to prepare them for higher-status jobs. These plans entail time-consuming home education. Consequently, Far Eng has left her factory job. She spends considerable time imparting social skills and knowledge by means of instructional toys and taking the children to sports and recreational events.

Mani affirmed that he called the shots. "I told her to quit work. It's better to care for your own children, because another person would be less committed and treat it as a job, not a responsibility." Mani admitted, "My wife always scolds me for not letting her work. But who is to look after the children if she works? Maybe when the kids are in secondary school she can go back to work."

In 1979, two years after Far Eng left her job and two months after the birth of their daughter, the Ramakrishnas moved to their new flat, some distance from Far Eng's family but near Mani's. Without the help she formerly received from her family, Far Eng's life is exceedingly busy. Nevertheless, she wistfully talks about a return to work. She recalls her special training as a junior mechanic, "all wasted now!" When I filled her in on news of her former colleagues, whom I also interviewed, she sighed, "Working . . . that's good! Too bad I have no chance to work!" Besides wanting to use her training, Far Eng hopes to earn money. Mani's earnings cover only their basic needs. He has paid for their $13,500 two-bedroom home and they can save nearly S$100 each month. But the lifestyle they want requires more.

[209]

Mani attributes his decision that his wife quit her job to her responsibility for their children, but is likely that her low wage in the peripheral-sector firm was also a factor. If she had been earning more, she might have been able to strike a better bargain at home. If she actually earned at the man's median level, her bargaining power would have increased further.

Mani also chose their home. They initially disagreed over its location: Far Eng preferred one near the market, whereas he wanted a quiet street. They are on a quiet street. Mani economized on the decorations by painting the flat himself. He spent S$3,000 on blue carpets for the sitting room and bedrooms and installed yellow tiles on the kitchen floor and walls. He selected the furnishings, at a cost of S$4,500, which they drew from their savings accounts. They traded in their old black-and-white television and paid an additional S$1,250 for a Telefunken color set, and bought a new small black-and-white set for S$450. A bedroom set (S$800) and stereo (S$2,000) completed their purchases; they brought the Sanyo refrigerator from their former home. The Ramakrishnas spend a lot of time in their new home, around which their family life revolves. The home is child-centered, filled with electronic and mechanical educational toys, and reflects their prime concern: a better life for their children.

The Ramakrishnas had decided before the birth of their second child that Far Eng would have a tubal ligation immediately afterward in order to obtain first preference to a school of their choice under the social disincentives measures. Mani explained, "I chose Henry Park School because it has a better class of students than the schools around here, children from semidetached and terraced houses. Those parents guide their children and pay attention to them. I hope to enroll my daughter in Raffles Girls' School."

Earlier they aimed only for secondary education for their son, Jonathan; now they hope both children will go to the university. "I want to give them what I don't have myself, so they can advance," Mani emphasized. They do not earmark their savings for their children's education, possibly because Mani earns less than his ideal income. But he turns his deficit into a moral emphasis on teaching the children the value of saving. "When they reach third or fourth grade I'll tell them it's up to them to save." Again because of his limited earnings, Mani rejects the newly popular life insurance plans." I don't like insurance at all. I want as little involvement [in credit and debt] as possible. Maybe if I had a dangerous job, I'd take out a life insurance policy. I can't even scratch my hand at my job! Anyway, I'll just support them from my wages. I can work until I'm fifty or sixty, and they'll be through with school by then."

"How can you encourage your children to do well in school?" Mani was asked. "We can't repeat the mistakes of our parents. They didn't give us enough schooling and didn't work with us on our schoolwork. Children follow you. If you teach them to study, they will. If you don't tell them to study, they won't. I don't let them outside to play much because if they start to play, they'll like it and will go on playing. My children like to read. My wife or I, when I have time, take them to the Queenstown library, where there are lots of books with simple sentences. They have their own cards. My son says he wants to be a doctor. I say, 'Yes, you can be a doctor, but you have to study.' When he sees a Mercedes, I say, 'Yes, you can have a Mercedes, but you have to study and get a good job.' They have to learn good study habits on their own. Push-button classrooms aren't far off!"

Far Eng also turns the children's play toward didactic teaching. With a stopwatch in hand, she calculates the time her daughter takes to recognize plastic shapes and put them in the holes in a Fisher-Price learning box. Mani paid S$88 for a video sports game that attaches to the television set, and plays electronic soccer, tennis, baseball, and other games with his son, who does well at them. He asked, "Do you know of the learning toy put out by Texas Instruments, 'Speak and Spell'? It can answer questions. Someone from TI came to our company to show us, and my friend bought it at a discount, only ninety dollars. Maybe I'll buy one later on."

The children take swimming lessons and Jonathan studies drawing at the community center. They showed snapshots of drawings posted during an art competition. Mani asked me to judge which picture should have won first prize, and I happened to pick his son's drawing. One of the others had won. Far Eng warmly thanked me for concurring with her own opinion. "It's not fair, is it? I don't know how the Residents' Committee chose. That other picture should be last, and the judges chose it first. My son's drawing only got second place."

Their daughter will take lessons in art and folk dancing at the community center next year. She wants to learn ballet, but it is not offered, and Far Eng thinks it would be troublesome to take the girl to private lessons by bus. When he turns seven, Jonathan will study *tae kwan do* at the center. I asked, "Why do you want your children to be involved in so many activities?" Far Eng gave both child-centered and practical rationales: "Children like to play! And he'll find it useful to know how to swim and do martial arts when he's in national service. Some rich families' children are even worse—two hours of piano lessons and two hours of ballet and two hours of private tutoring every day! The children get very tired. I don't want to load my kids with too much in one day. They have only one activity each day of the week now."

The couple's enrichment program for their children takes effort and planning. Now a single-income family, they cannot afford such a range of activities in the private sector, so they fully exploit the state's social programs. Their small family goal thus centers on their children's education. Far Eng wanted two children, although Mani was satisfied with one. When she became pregnant again, Mani imposed the condition that she quit work. Mani stresses, "I don't want to repeat my father's mistake of having too many children. I want to give my children as much as I can so they can enjoy life. With a big family, parents can't give so much care and love to all the children."

Far Eng is now completely responsible for the housework and no longer receives help from her husband. Mani has not visited the market or even walked around their housing development. Pointing to his stereo set, she joked, "He only does the recording." Pointing to the children, "They only do the eating!"

The family is close and Mani and his children tease each other. Their daughter brought out the photo album to show me. Pointing to a photograph of Mani, I asked her, "Who is that man?" The child replied, "I don't know," and she and Mani both burst into laughter. Their album contains many pictures of the family on outings, visiting pleasure spots on Sentosa Island and the zoo, and of the children's after-school lessons, which now take precedence over family outings. Mani explains, "This is better than when I was growing up. My parents never took us out. And even if they were to take us somewhere, there was only Tiger Balm Garden."

There are also snapshots of Mani's colleagues taken during New Year visits, but none of Far Eng's friends. She has lost contact with them since she quit her job. "How could I go out, with the two children?" she asked rhetorically. As these photos show, Far Eng mixes more with Mani's friends, many of whom have interracial marriages like theirs, than with her own work or school chums. Shared friends give the couple a unified perspective on their family world and plans, yet the choice of Mani's friends keeps him in control over the family's social life.

It was Mani who insisted that they raise their children in the Chinese tradition. The children speak Cantonese to Mother Wong and English at home. Far Eng has taught her children Mandarin at home to prepare them for school. In turn, Jonathan teaches his father to speak Mandarin. Mani jested, "I'd better not say much in Chinese, or else my kids will laugh at my accent." They do not speak Tamil at home, because, Mani says, "Tamil isn't spoken in business anymore." As a result, "the children can only say one or two words to my mother." Far Eng encouraged, "Better teach them how to speak a little bit to her." Nor have the children learned to pick up food with their fingers, Indian fashion, when they eat the rice and curry that their father prepares.

Mani's siblings, headed by Elder Brother, occasionally meet to discuss family problems. "For example, there are two parts to Father's barbershop, and he contracts out one part. We discuss who should receive the contract when it comes up, and usually follow Elder Brother's advice." Three of

Mani's siblings work with Father. Yet, apart from the holidays, the Ramakrishnas rarely visit relatives. Elder Brother's marriage to a Chinese Christian gives them a common bond, but they, too, visit infrequently. Every
year Mani takes his family to Elder Brother's home to celebrate Christmas;
Mani goes to Mother's for a family celebration of the Hindu autumn festival
of Deepavali, the Festival of Lights, and invites Brother to his home to
celebrate the Lunar New Year. "It's quite a joke, you know, that I, an
Indian, invite my family and office friends to come home here for a Chinese
celebration!"

Far Eng rarely visits her mother in-law with her husband, and although
they live nearby, Mani's parents do not visit them. "because they are old.
My mother has trouble walking, she has rheumatism. My parents also said
that the younger ones must visit the older ones and not the other way
around." He teased, "Since my younger brothers and sisters seldom visit us,
maybe I should tell them that the younger ones should visit the older ones,
too!"

The couple does not borrow money. "We always use our own savings to
buy things. We spent very little when we moved in, because we already had
most of the things, like the refrigerator. I do tell my brothers and sisters not
to be shy when they have problems and to come and talk things over with
me. But so far none have actually come to me."

Far Eng has strong filial feelings and is distressed that she has no money of
her own to give her mother, who has had a stroke and cannot work. It
appears that their finances are tight, and that she cannot draw on Mani's
income to support her mother, although she may make irregular donations.
"My mother now lives with Elder Sister and her family. Second Sister is still
working as a nurse, at least she can support Mother." Far Eng visits her
mother nearly every day. The visits center on emotional, not material, support. Like his wife, Mani considers himself independent of kin and friends.
He has never turned to his brother for advice. "We just take care of ourselves. It's simpler. There really isn't anyone we go to. Not my brother, he
won't know about our problems."

They base their independence on their above-average education, Mani's
technically skilled job in the computer industry, and his income, which
during the second-stage promotion was boosted above the median. The
separation of the nuclear family from the wider kin network, long one of
their aims, was accomplished during this period. Yet this newly isolated
household requires considerable sacrifice from the wife, who has given up
her job and works hard in the home. Having turned for support from their
kin to state services, they have burdened their marriage with the necessity of
meeting all the needs once shared by the wider family, and they have
ambitious goals.

Chan Family: Quality Control Supervisor and Homemaker (II)

As a core-sector worker with certified industrial skills, Chan Lam Lee has received more training in the new skills-upgrading program than any other secure man we have met so far. As a quality control supervisor he earns S$1,700, 155 percent of his wage in phase 1, and overtime work often raises his wages further. The Chans see their greatest asset as their strong marriage.

A hard worker and self-made man, Lam Lee expects to remain in the same line of work, but he is considering a move to another firm. He feels under pressure most of the time. "I'm frustrated at this job. The management doesn't have a proper working system. They push things through. They set target dates each month that are too high, and the men work till they can't work anymore. We rush, and have to work late at night to meet the goal. This may lower our quality. Then I notice that the goods sit around the yard for several weeks before they're picked up. So I wonder if this isn't just an excuse to look good with our inventory report to the States."

Lam Lee thinks a smaller firm will offer more opportunities for advancement. He recalls his past work history. "When I was young I wanted to rise fast, but I soon discovered that you have to climb step by step. My father wanted me to work in the dockyard but I didn't like it. You don't move up fast enough. In a big shipyard that has thousands of employees, if you're good and just do your job, you may not be recognized. Only 'human relations' can get you anywhere. It's really tough unless you know the person at the top. That's human nature, one person helps the other. But if you can choose a small company, you can work hard and make an honest living. You're a big fish in a little pond."

"How would you go about changing jobs?" "I'd look for another oil-drilling company. If I became a supervisor of a drilling rig, I'd earn about the same as now, so I wouldn't try to change jobs just for the salary, but for better working conditions. However, I don't hop around or take a chance. I'll wait, and if I see a job, I'll grab it. I have a family, and I don't want to be without work."

Lam Lee's problems also flow from his lower managerial position, "We supervisors are squeezed like a sandwich." He gestured toward a plate of finger sandwiches on his coffee table. "It's very difficult to be a foreman. The owner of the company wants profits, then the top manager puts pressure on us so he can answer to the boss. If we have to work overtime, I ask my workers to do it. If they don't want to, then they yell at me. All I can do is say, 'There's no point yelling. If you want to earn some extra money, then do the work. If you don't want to, then go home and I'll do it. I'll do it even if it takes me several days.' I used to say that even when I didn't receive any overtime pay. I don't like to force them. If they don't want to work overtime, we'll solve the problem ourselves."

The products manufactured by Lam Lee's firm have been in demand steadily since he joined the firm in 1972. "We had one bad year in 1977, when we lost orders. We let fifty welders go, all new employees. But after a year we hired them back and more besides. Our company is quite steady now. We have high-quality, reliable products. Buyers must pay a bit more, but the cost-cutting firm may not meet the delivery date. I think our company will still be around for years. As long as the management pays attention to the workers' problems and tries to solve them, they'll be successful."

There is a current shortage of workers in this dynamic industry. From time to time Lam Lee introduces a relative or friend to work in his firm, but in the rapidly shifting work world, he lacks control over them. "Once I recommended a friend, but he wasn't happy doing overtime. Whenever I asked him to, he always had something else on. It's difficult to push a friend. If he's a stranger it's easier. That's why, once when my boss asked if I could recommend someone for a job at a time when we needed workers, I just had to say, 'Right now, no.'"

Lam Lee has considered going into business for himself. He thought he could free himself from work pressure only if he were his own boss. In his line of work, however, this is a risky business. He has given up the idea in favor of steady advancement, "It's difficult to venture into business. Even if you do have the capital, you can still go bankrupt overnight unless you have luck too. It's safer to be an employee until you're sure the time has come to branch out for yourself."

This technically skilled core-sector worker has made good use of skill-upgrading programs. "I've taken three separate courses over the last few years. One was a course in ultrasonic nondestructive testing at SISIR [Singapore Institute of Standards and Industrial Research]. It took six weeks, three evenings a week. That course wasn't so helpful in my work because I have no chance to practice. Another was a management course at the University of Singapore. This was also six weeks long. We studied basic books. I thought it would be helpful, but my work experiences are different from those in the books. If there's an angry worker, I usually leave him alone and come back to talk with him later. I encourage him to let off steam. They have a different approach. Then I took a quality control course at SISIR for another six weeks. It wasn't really too helpful because it was for mass-production processes, such as sampling. But in our company we make one thing at a time to specification. Although it wasn't too relevant for my work, I didn't quit because the company sent me. And I do want more general knowledge."

Like other men who have worked their way up, Lam Lee says that experience is the best teacher. On a career ladder in this dynamic core-sector firm,

Lam Lee can move forward automatically without any special planning on his part. But his firm encourages him to take courses, and in the event he wishes to change firms, he can profit from his paper qualifications.

Lam Lee believes his secure wage suffices for the family. "What level income do you need for your family?" He responded, "It depends on each family's needs. It takes about six hundred a month for an ordinary family to keep up. If you have more income, you enjoy better food, movies, and so on. So I give my wife six hundred twice a month and keep the rest for my daily expenses. I also keep all my overtime pay, which was another six hundred last month."

Sock Boon, still a housewife, told us that inflation has encroached on their income. They exhaust Lam Lee's basic wage, and without his overtime pay they would have no savings. But as Sock Boon has little education and her work experience is confined to domestic service, the jobs she could command would not pay much. "Any intention to return to work this year, to break your routine?" I asked Sock Boon. "I've considered that, but if I work full-time in a factory, which is about all I can do, then my salary wouldn't justify my expenses. I'd have to send my children to a babysitter, and even if she charged only two hundred for both of them, that would be a good percentage of a factory worker's pay of around three hundred. Besides, my husband is against the idea. He says that even when I discipline them now, they still act naughty. In the care of a sitter, they'd get out of hand. No matter how dedicated she may be, she can never take the place of a real mother. But I'm looking for a part-time job to take when the children are in school. My husband wouldn't mind this arrangement because it's my own time."

Sock Boon's dilemma derives from her husband's rapid advancement in the technical core sector. His earnings overshadow any amount she could earn, and so her employment would not appreciably improve the family status. In addition, Lam Lee referred to the maternal neglect of his youth. His mother, even though she did not work, had not cared for him adequately, and was not a "good" mother. Growing children need a solid family, he affirmed. "Will your wife work when your children are older?" "No, I don't think so. I don't think I want her to work. As long as I can manage, let's leave any job she could take to others who need it more. Women who work tend to neglect the children. The children come home after school and get no attention. My mother-in-law is watching the three children of my wife's brother, and she also does sewing for a factory at home. She has no time to look after our children."

The Chan family's solid economic position and Sock Boon's lack of education shapes her homemaker career. She does not feel strong and has a thyroid condition, which she blames on her two abortions. She is afraid of closed spaces and of the dark, and does not like to be alone. During the day she sleeps long hours, does her housework quickly, then shops or visits her relatives, many of whom live nearby. She has an extensive visiting pattern, but she makes sure she is at home in the afternoons and on weekends to watch over her children.

"I wake up at about six-fifteen, after the children and my husband have finished washing. I prepare breakfast for them. This was a little difficult at first because the children attended the afternoon session last year, and I'm used to waking at nine or ten A.M. My husband went to his office for breakfast because I was too lazy to prepare it for him." She laughs. "So my husband used to say if it weren't for the children, he wouldn't have any homemade breakfast this year either. After they all leave, I go back to bed. This morning, for example, I didn't wake up till eleven. So the whole morning is gone. I'll do the laundry in the afternoon, and go to my cousin's place after that. I'll be back in the evenings. I used to knit a little now and then, but not too much because it makes me dizzy. Housework is quite interesting. I like to arrange flowers and keep the house clean. But when you're not paid for the job, you tend to put things off."

Entering the Chans' new three-bedroom home in a highrise near the Sembawang neighborhood where husband and wife grew up, a visitor walks into the large living room with windows facing a sunny corridor open to the breeze from the Malaysian causeway. The flat is neat and decorated simply. A tall vase of pussywillows rests on the window ledge next to the large color television set, in front of which the Chan boys, aged seven and nine, lie on their stomachs watching cartoons. A cream-colored carpet softens footsteps. There are a coffee table, sofa, and easy chairs. A statue of Kwan Yin, the goddess of mercy, oversees the family fortunes from her shelf on the wall. The living room has another television set and a sizable Akai stereo. Pots of plants hang in macramé baskets in kitchen and living rooms. The kitchen floor is covered by linoleum, and a cabinet of modest proportions runs along the wall. The kitchen contains a dining table and green chairs. The floors in the remainder of the flat are of a gray marble. The boys share a bedroom, and another bedroom, once occupied by Lam Lee's mother, has been turned into their study—an unusual allocation of space in my sample.

The Chans acquired this four-room flat for S$23,500 withdrawn from Lam Lee's CPF savings. They moved into it in 1976 and took ownership in 1980. Sock Boon is proud that the flat is their own possession. They saved gradually for the improvements, first paying for the floors, then installing a kitchen cabinet with Lam Lee's S$1,000 New Year bonus.

This apartment is a considerable distance from Lam Lee's firm in Jurong, but they live near Sock Boon's mother, who watches the children when they go out at night. But Sock Boon worries that her mother will spoil her sons, and does not like to leave them with her as often as she used to. She refers to her "weak" brother as an example of Mother's mistraining. Yet Sock Boon also fears that the "new way" of raising them as equals to the parents may spoil them and prevent them from being able to work steadily and to achieve. She avoids reasoning with them, as some middle-class parents do. She continues to be the disciplinarian of the children. "I am the master punisher. My husband is too soft. He laughs when he's caning the children, so of course they're not afraid of him. All I have to do is shout and they obey at once. We discuss disciplining the children, in fact we argue about it at times. I've told Lam Lee to be firm, but he turns a deaf ear. He'd rather be a friend to the kids than have a strained father–son relationship." She feels equal to this job, however. "I have a strong character and a bad temper. My mother says I should have been born a man. On the other hand, Younger Brother is timid as a mouse. He should have been born a girl."

Keen to protect the children from undesirable influences and unsure about the right way to do so, Sock Boon does not train the children for independent thinking or action. Her own considerable fears restrict her freedom of movement, and she won't permit her children much more. "I take the children outside when they have no homework. If I can't, my husband does. Sometimes we go out together. I know in this way they may not be independent, but I worry about them, and I'm afraid they'll mix with bad company. Drug abuse is everywhere. They're not allowed to play downstairs without me or to go alone to school functions. I suppose, when the time comes, I'll have to cut these ties."

The children take a public bus to the morning session of the nearby primary school. The oldest boy has a tutor who coaches him in English and mathematics and charges only S$30 a month. Sock Boon considers this son "not too bright." The younger boy is a better student. His tutorial sessions start next year, when he must take the primary 3 language-streaming exam, the first hurdle in the Singapore education system. The Chans have only now begun to speak of the great expense of educating their children in the future. Like other secure respondents, they hope their children will study hard and win a scholarship to the university. "Even if we can't send our children to the university, we must assure them Cambridge [the O-level exams]. They shouldn't be illiterate like us." They have begun to anticipate the hardship of paying for the children's education to that level, and are putting aside money for the future. In 1980 Sock Boon deposited her husband's New Year's bonus into the children's savings account.

Neither Sock Boon's health nor their income is up to another child. Sock Boon says that she does not want to have a tubal ligation because it might affect her health, but if she should become pregnant again, she would not hesitate to have an abortion. Her husband uses condoms. "I don't want my husband to be sterilized because it might interfere with his health and sex life. But two children are definitely enough."

Until recently Sock Boon cared for her mother-in-law, who was ill and nearly bedridden. Their three-bedroom apartment was large enough to permit the older woman to have her own room. But the Chans put Mother-in-Law in a retirement home when Sock Boon could no longer cope with her needs. Sock Boon complained that her husband's sister did not meet her filial obligations to her mother. "We couldn't send Mother-in-Law to a state-run old-age home because our income is too high. So I offered three hundred dollars to any kampung family who would take care of her. No one accepted it. Sister-in-Law refused to take her again. Her husband is a typical Chinese man—lord of the house. He insists that a married woman doesn't have close ties with her own family. In fact, once when I wasn't well, I asked Sister-in-Law to take care of Mother-in Law, and she refused. She suggested instead that my cousin do it. I was hurt. My cousin has offered to watch my children if I have to go to the hospital. That's enough to ask; it's not her mother! My husband was angry at his sister, too." Shortly after her mother-in-law was institutionalized, she died.

Sock Boon spends considerable time visiting her own kin. "Mother's adopted sister lives just two streets away and another cousin lives only a bit farther. It's lucky she's there, I spend most of my spare time with her. If it weren't for her I'd be really bored. If I wanted to, visiting my relatives would be a full-time occupation." Sock Boon laughed at the idea. "I have so many cousins, buying presents is always a problem! What do we talk about? With the older generation I talk with them about good and bad daughters-in-law. With the younger generation I discuss our problems with our husbands and children, fashion, and shopping trips. My relatives are fairly close, we mix well."

The husband's highly skilled job enables the Chans to live an affluent life. But Sock Boon's relatively low education limits her activities. She spends most of her time with her relatives, though she is economically independent of them. Husband and wife value their close family life and work hard to advance their family above their original working-class station, making full use of the state services to do so.

Leong Family: Draftsman and Schoolteacher (II)

Leong Kin Cheung, an assistant draftsman with an American oil company, earned the third highest wages in my phase 1 panel, and over the interphase his wage has doubled to S$2,000. His wife still teaches school. These two earn the highest family income in my panel. They easily can use state services to the full, as well as buy high-quality goods and services in the private sector.

Kin Cheung still does drafting work for architectural firms at home in the evenings and on weekends to raise his income further. He is in great demand. Indeed, Kin Cheung considers taking up this work full-time and starting a company with friends whom he met during his years at Singapore Polytechnic. Joo Leng, however, maintains that a small business might not ensure Kin Cheung a regular income, and stresses the security of his present full-time job. His core-sector position gives him a good salary and short working hours, leaving time for moonlighting. A steady career is important to both the Leongs.

Kin Cheung may in fact be moving in the direction of starting his own firm. He points out the uncertainties of employment in his private firm, where personal relationships must be maintained if a worker is to gain recognition. "Politics isn't so great in the government sector, but in the business world it's important to have a godfather if you want to rise. In a private company, it's really important whom you know. I even know people who were sent abroad to take courses, and while they were away their godfathers left the company. When they came back, they found themselves working under people they used to supervise!"

Certification is an issue for all aspiring professional men. Although currently riding a crest of demand, Kin Cheung, holding a Polytechnic diploma in drafting but no higher degree, holds mixed views on his prospects. "Right now certification isn't necessary. Someone can advance in this company as easily as the expatriates with higher degrees. But a university degree may be more important in the future, and in fact may become a minimum requirement. Then people without degrees will find it hard to advance, and those with master's or Ph.D.'s will do better. There will always be some people who can get ahead without proper qualifications, but those are the few who are exceptionally intelligent and have considerable initiative." In fact, Kin Cheung began a course in personnel administration and management which was organized by his firm, but he dropped it midway, convinced that the course was not relevant to his job. "With my part-time work, I don't have the time to take any courses now. Anyway, I don't think it's necessary for me to work for another certificate. In my field, experience is more important."

Life has improved materially for the Leongs. Kin Cheung stresses that despite inflation, his family is in a better position today than it was five years ago, because of his salary increments. "Singapore isn't democratic, but the government has done a lot of good for the people. It's not perfect, but who is?" The shortage of skilled workers in high-tech industry put men like Kin Cheung in a strong bargaining position, and accordingly he hails the economy of the second development stage.

Joo Leng maintains that she works because she can mesh her job with her family role. Since she is reasonably comfortable with this arrangement, she might as well continue working. Kin Cheung downplays the need for her income. Joo Leng therefore describes their division of labor in the family as one based on sex roles: "My husband earns the money and I spend it." The

Leongs' ten-year-old daughter quipped, "And she really does do the spending." Kin Cheung earns S$2,000 a month in his main job, which Joo Leng believes is the minimum necessary for their basic lifestyle. Then the Leongs spend his additional income and her salary, which together total about the same amount, on vacations, rental of a large flat, two cars, and a family membership in an elite sports club.

Kin Cheung and Joo Leng do not expect their children to live with them or support them in later years. "We're lucky if they do!" Kin Cheung jested. They regard their substantial pension savings as adequate for their later retirement, and so do most of the people they know. Indeed, they assume that most Singaporeans share their flush condition. "Most parents today don't expect their children to look after them. Today we have CPF to depend on. Our parents had no such savings plan. Since many husbands and wives both work today, their CPF savings are quite substantial."

Domestic chores now fall entirely to Joo Leng. Over the interphase the Leongs rented a new flat some distance from their Queenstown apartment. The move affected Joo Leng's home support system. After the move, the Queenstown neighbor who cared for their youngest son continued to mind him for only a year; she stopped when her own grandchildren came along. The Leongs' former domestic servant cannot travel so far each day, and the Leongs decided to "do the work ourselves." In practice, Joo Leng does it all. She confesses that she was "very grumpy" about this in the beginning, but "it's a matter of getting used to the arrangement." She cooks most of the meals, although the Leongs dine out at hawker stalls several times a week. The only help she gets is provided by her father-in-law, who still comes every day to look after the children. Joo Leng supervises her children's sports and other recreation and their homework. To her this home training, not housework, is the essence of running the home. So Joo Leng believes she works hard and is competent at her two roles. Now that her children are older, she feels "more at ease." She is free to take holidays and attend weekly yoga classes.

Kin Cheung perceives his wife's teaching as only half a job, and thus well paid for the time spent. He believes all women will marry. "Teaching is a good half-day job for women, and it leaves time to take care of the children. My wife is in the same school session as the children, so she's able to look after them after school lets out."

Joo Leng is also matter-of-fact about the job. For the amount of pay she receives, she considers teaching worthwhile. She is aware that other professional women, including some in private-sector firms, are better paid. Her work is worthwhile so long as she minimizes her time commitment to it and can place her role as mother in the forefront of her obligations. Joo Leng stresses her basic competence in the classroom, owing to her experience and tenure. She reduces her daily input to the minimum. "Teaching is a fine long-term career if you're getting married, but not for single women or men, because the pay isn't too good and there are too few opportunities for promotion. I'd consider taking a commercial job if I were offered one," she commented vaguely. She spoke of the time-saving strategies she devised to reduce her worktime. "I do more oral than written work, so there's little marking. My sister is different. She's always loaded with books to mark. I take things easy, I don't even care when the inspector visits my classes."

Joo Leng does not aim to move up in the school hierarchy because "it's too much work, and troublesome too." She mentioned an enrichment workshop on energy and ecology held for teachers at the Singapore Science Centre, which she had been expected to attend but did not because her father-in-law went to Malaysia and she had to look after the children. She did not seem to regret the lost exposure to new science pedagogy.

Joo Leng chafes at the restrictions on teachers embodied in the new educational reforms of second-stage development. "The ministry should have asked schoolteachers for their views." Joo Leng must now plan her classroom syllabus for the next three years in accordance with Ministry of Education objectives. She objects to such unnecessary supervision because she claims she knows her work. But she has not attempted to express her views to school authorities. Joo Leng and her sister both feel that language streaming in primary 3 is too early for some children. "There are late developers, and not all children realize the importance of the exam."

Joo Leng is close to this sister, younger by one year. Her sister is married to an architect who teaches at the university and is a high earner. Sister lives with her mother-in-law, who cares for her two children during the day. Like Joo Leng, her sister downplays the economic need for her employment, and stresses her ability to mesh paid work with child care and homemaking tasks. Her husband also stresses the children's upbringing and feels that teaching is a good career for a mother, as the children then have someone to look after them. Sister told me, "I work to avoid doing housework, which I hate. I wouldn't stop working even if I were to have another child." Like Joo Leng, Sister often takes her children to the library and to sporting events, clubs, and other recreation.

Their view of work differs, however. While Joo Leng sees teaching as "just a job" that she is used to, Sister esteems it as a "profession." Sister changed jobs three times until she found a suitable government-aided Protestant grammar school. She likes the atmosphere there. She believes the aided denominational schools have a sense of dedication and loyalty absent from the government schools, with their high turnover of staff. "The teachers in my school are mainly former students, and some of my colleagues have taught there twenty to thirty years." Sister did attend the Science Centre workshop and found it "helpful and interesting." She stresses the importance of self-improvement. "The inspectors should help us when they come around and not merely inspect teachers' work!"

Joo Leng's ability to work is predicated on the efficient meshing of hours spent in classroom teaching and preparation with raising her three children. Their educational needs will probably remain salient for her. Joo Leng contributes to the family's middle-class living standard, but her ability to define her employment commitment is limited by her gender role.

The Leongs' substantial earning power helped them obtain the major social services early on, and they continued to upgrade these services over the interphase. In phase 1 they lived in their two-bedroom HDB flat in Queenstown while renting out their private flat. Owners of private flats, however, are forbidden by government regulation to occupy an HDB flat. So in 1977 they rented the Queenstown HDB flat to another family as well. They hoped to abide by the letter of the regulation, if not its spirit. Both flats are worth large sums and bring in considerable rental income.

The Leongs' roomy bungalow, formerly a government perquisite for expatriate civil servants, rents for S$550 a month. While this rent is higher than that of an HDB flat, it is low for a house of its size in its exclusive area. It has five bright, spacious rooms, and a small building behind the main house has two additional rooms, which Kin Cheung wants to convert to a study. He plans to join the two buildings by a trellis draped with bougainvillea. They have enlarged the children's bedroom by extending it into the backyard. In their isolated compound surrounded by trees, flowers, and quiet lanes, the Leongs have approached suburban living in the heart of the city. Only one other two-career couple in my panel approaches their living standard. Although the government is slated to take back the homes in this area, the date of reversion has been postponed several times and appears to lie still far in the future. When the time finally comes, the Leongs can return to one of their other homes.

The Leongs purchased a washing machine and new furniture for the master bedroom in their rented flat but brought the remaining furniture with them from Queenstown. Because the children are still young and playful and Joo Leng is not keen on keeping house, she prefers a child-centered, lived-in home to stylish decor that takes more upkeep. Books and toys are scattered around the living room. Pictures, souvenirs, and trophies of the children's and Kin Cheung's athletic activities are on display.

Their new neighborhood, surrounded by wire fencing, is an oasis in the midst of the city. Public transportation is only a short walk away, but they felt somewhat isolated, so they bought a second car with a company loan. Both cars are fully paid for.

The Leongs enrolled their children in a private kindergarten. Then they chose a government primary school in the neighborhood for their children.

They are willing to entrust their children to a local school partly because Joo Leng supports the system for which she has worked a dozen years. Besides, the neighborhood is so affluent that Joo Leng has confidence in the moral and academic training her children will receive there.

The Leongs want their children's minds to be broadened. Joo Leng coaches the children at home in their school subjects and in others besides. They also pay S$200 a month for private Mandarin lessons. The children take private swimming lessons at their sports club, and piano and art lessons. The Leongs see these activities as equal in importance to the children's daily schoolwork, because lessons and preparation for them use the children's spare time constructively. Kin Cheung stressed, "Instead of wasting their time, they're at least learning an additional skill." Joo Leng added, "Lessons keep the children occupied and give me some peace!"

I accompanied Joo Leng and the children to their swimming lesson one steamy summer afternoon. The three children sat in the back of the car, where the twins enacted swordplay with the car tools. Mother's repeated admonishments and a slap on Elder Son's arm merely sent the children into fits of giggles. Joo Leng's attempts at discipline are so ineffective that her search for some peace by keeping her children occupied by lessons is understandable. Ambitious for their children, the Leongs need not worry about paying for the extras they wish to give them. They turn to the private sector for lessons that families of modest means obtain at the community center.

The Leongs hope for successful careers for their children. A person is "successful," according to Joo Leng, if the job pays well and offers good opportunities for promotion. The Leongs do not plan to dictate the careers of their children, but they do have strong preferences. Kin Cheung still wants his eldest son to become an architect and fulfill his unmet goals. "An architect has good prospects. The field pays well and there are good chances for promotion. That's what our son should do. For our daughters, accounting is a good career. A woman can work her way up in that job."

I asked Joo Leng whether the expense of raising children figured in their plans to have no more children. Joo Leng admitted that she and Kin Cheung were not overly worried about the basics of life. They do not even save for their children's education. "We don't need to save. We can pay the fees when the time comes for them to enroll. University fees are not so expensive." Joo Leng nevertheless confessed that their actual wants seemed continually to rise along with their ability to buy. "We need about two thousand to live comfortably. But the more one has, the better one wants to live, so that we can have cars, holidays, and other things." The main reason she will have no more children is the time required to give them quality care. "I don't want any more children. Looking after children is a lot of work!"

The Leongs' strong marriage, based on their solid earning position and relatively high education, is expressed in their desire to spend more time together as husband and wife. When their children were younger, they regretfully limited their dates as a couple. Joo Leng and Kin Cheung then took turns taking holidays away from Singapore, as the children's caretakers could not cope with them without one parent present. Now that the children are older, Joo Leng can take them along on the outings she takes apart from Kin Cheung. She plans to take the three children on a group tour to California with her sister and Sister's two children. Aside from such separate vacations, husband and wife can enjoy more frequent evenings together, leaving their children with Grandfather Leong. As a family, the Leongs enjoy holidays in Malaysia's Genting Highlands with Joo Leng's sister and her husband and children. The shared occupations (both sisters are teachers; their husbands are in architecture) adds a friendship bond to that of kinship. The Leongs thus take outings apart and together, with and without their children, with and without Joo Leng's kin. Each knows the other's friends but each spouse has specialized hobbies that involve lessons, equipment, and interests that the other does not feel it necessary to share.

The Leongs also visit other kin. Kin Cheung helps support his father. Kin Cheung introduced his only brother, a mechanical draftsman, to his oil company, where he enrolled in a three-year apprenticeship program. Kin Cheung's unmarried sister, who lives with Father Leong, occasionally visits them. Despite these visits with his siblings, which may amount to several a month, Kin Cheung says that "we are not exactly close to them." He feels independent of his kin. This perception of independence from the wider family is consistent with the Leongs' position among the affluent. They are able to underwrite a solid family future by drawing on the public and private sectors without turning to kin for help.

[9]

Singapore Society in the Advanced Development Stage: Two Families or One?

By the 1980s the Singapore development program had come to fruition. As state services and the market economy both expand dramatically, has the great class divide narrowed? Has the Singapore family evolved into a single nuclear family, with goals and activities uniformly organized around the state programs? Or have growing numbers of families remained beyond the reach of the state programs while a few enjoy unprecedented prosperity? My 1981 restudy of 45 of the 100 families studied in the 1970s sought to answer these questions. We can now look at indices of the use of goods and services by class group and the differences in the meaning of those items. I begin with the work lives of the panel men studied at two points in time.[1]

Work

Men's Jobs

The transformation from labor- to capital-intensive industrialization has not impoverished the men in my panel. Their wages have increased a striking 81 percent. The proportion of low-waged men dropped sharply, while no newcomer has joined their ranks.[2] Yet, the income gap by social-class group remains virtually unchanged. Despite the uplift of some of the poorest, poor men still average about half the wages of secure men. Thus many have edged forward, but those with class advantage retain a head start (see Table 10). Let us now turn to the poor men.

The very poor have more than doubled their wages; the semi-poor have improved their incomes to a lesser extent. Thus the ratio of very poor to

Table 10. Average earnings[a] of poor and secure men, phases 1 and 2

Socioeconomic group	Phase 1	Phase 2	Percent increase	Number
Poor				
Very poor	S$301	S$ 620	106%	8
Semipoor	374	669	79	20
Average poor male workers	353	655	85	28
Secure				
Modest means	480	957	99	9
Affluent	939	1,550	65	8
Average secure male worker	696	1,235	77	17
Average male worker, both groups	483	873	81	45

[a]Pre-overtime monthly gross wage, before withdrawal of CPF.

semi-poor men's wages has narrowed from 80 to 93 percent. This leveling follows the leap upward of wages in occupations and industries, such as unskilled construction work, undergoing expansion; these were the jobs held by many of the very poor. Meanwhile, earnings have improved less for workers in jobs and industries being phased out, such as taxi driving; these jobs were held by the semi-poor (Table 11). To show this shift in the ranking of earnings over time, I refer to the "relative wage": the ratio of the average wage of panel men with a given set of resources to the wage of panel men of their class group in each study phase.

The relative wage of poor peripheral-sector workers has fallen from 98 to 93 percent. As a group they are not doing so badly, but there are great differences among them. Worst off are the four phase 1 men without skills. Their relative wage, never high, has plunged further, from 65 to 56 percent. Such marginal men as hawkers suffer during industrialization programs in other nations, and they also fare poorly in Singapore. Although three of the four unskilled workers changed jobs, with one (the former bus conductor) entering the core sector, none earn above-median wages.[3] Lacking education and with job contacts limited to kin and close friends, such unfortunate job changers can get only low-paid work.

Those poor with nontechnical resources (academic education, a modest amount of capital) had the highest relative wage in phase 1: 122 percent of the wage of poor men. But they have since lost standing. Their wage increased only 53 percent over the interphase and is now just average. In most cases, their marginalization is not due to lack of effort. Three have changed their jobs, but they remain in peripheral-sector work that requires the same low level of skills. Some work overtime and others moonlight to make ends meet.

Table 11. Average earnings[a] of poor men in peripheral and core industrial sectors, phases 1 and 2

Sector	Phase 1	Phase 2[b]	Percent increase	Number	Earnings rank Phase 1	Earnings rank Phase 2
Periphery						
Unskilled	S$230	S$370	61%	4	5	5
Resources[c]	430	661	53	8	1	3
Skilled	304	710	134	5	3	2
Average peripheral-sector poor male worker	346	612	82	17		
Core						
Unskilled	267	567	112	3	4	4
Skilled	401	892	122	8	2	1
Average core-sector poor male worker	365	803	120	11		
Average poor male worker, both sectors	353	655	85	28		

[a]Pre-overtime monthly gross wage, before withdrawal of CPF.
[b]Men's sectoral positions are kept constant. Two poor men moved from peripheral to core positions, but no one moved from core to periphery over the interphase.
[c]Occupation requires some capital, a nonindustrial skill, or an academic degree.

Poor men with industrial skills, such as the tinsmith, have all responded to demand and changed their jobs over the interphase. Though they remain on the periphery, their wages have greatly improved. Their relative wage rose from 86 to 108 percent. Structural changes in the Singapore economy, which create a great demand for workers with certain industrial talents, are responsible for this uplift.

The relative wage of poor core-sector workers has climbed to 123 percent. Unskilled men, who benefited by the upsurge in construction and shipyard employment, now earn even more than their unskilled peripheral-sector brothers: in phase 1 they earned 116 percent of the unskilled peripheral-sector wage; in phase 2, 153 percent. Yet, because they lack a technical skill, they still earn below the Chinese male median. They depend on overtime work to make ends meet and participate more fully in the consumer society. Core-sector men with industrial skills, in contrast, have moved from third to first place. Their great improvement flows from demand for their existing skills and seniority in their place of work.

That second-stage industrialization has drawn poor workers more deeply into the wage economy can be seen from the fates of the hawkers in my sample. Ng Kong Chong, for example, has transferred to wage work. Although he still works in a peripheral service and sells the same product as before, he is an employee, not self-employed. Now he is accountable and receives regular earnings and CPF benefits. His hope for a small shop of his own is dashed and he has become a full-fledged proletarian. Of course, the hidden economy has not disappeared.[4] Many workers attempt to increase their basic wage through side jobs. Since few report these sideline earnings to the government, they become part of the underground economy. Nevertheless, the men in my sample work in the hidden economy as a second income only, to supplement their main job in the formal economy.

It is the demand for extant industrial skills, not an individual's quest for self-improvement, that raises wages among the poor.[5] Training plays little part in the process. Peripheral-sector men have few means to upgrade their skills apart from gaining more experience on the job. New in-firm courses have been launched in core-sector workplaces, and most poor men reject those that are available. They lack the necessary credentials, and since their jobs have short career ladders, they believe they will not be promoted even if they take such courses. They prefer to remain with their workmates and lack the confidence to move forward alone. All the same, their wages have risen. The shipfitter is one example. He was in the right place at the time of take-off.

Despite the increased involvement in the capitalist market, social bonds remain strong in the job search. But they are changing form. Although nearly all have kin in their place of work, these men do not in the main work among close-knit groups of relatives. They may work in the same organization but not side by side with kin. In their search for higher wages, half of the men have changed their jobs: 77 percent of these job changers got their new jobs through close personal contacts—kin, friends, co-workers.[6] (In phase 1, the proportion was 100 percent.) But help from friends, neighbors, and kin is not a particular boon. The poor do not greatly improve their wages by getting jobs through people they know well.

While more than half of the poor have found new jobs, only two of the job changers have changed their industrial sector, both from peripheral- to core-sector jobs. Instead of widespread flux, therefore, we find relative stability in structural position, partly the result of the men's practice of getting work through people they know. Because the early entrants to the new industrial program established their claims first, others later find it hard to break in. Further, as educational certification becomes the new passport to improved jobs, men without diplomas cannot compete.[7] Thus, despite the many structural shifts in the work force, few men under study have broken out of the place they established early in life.

Workers' views of the development process and their place in it are closely tied to changes in their wages over the years and the contrasts they make with others. The most pessimistic are those who, despite some efforts to improve, remain in low-paid jobs. Others who have improved their wages but remain in weak industries on the periphery hold mixed views about their positions. Skilled workers in the key core-sector firms with the chance to improve themselves in the future are the most satisfied.[8]

The new development program has reshaped relative wages within each industrial and occupational sector to emphasize technical skills for secure men as well. Because of the increased demand for industrial skills, secure men with technical skills on the periphery have improved their earnings, while those with nontechnical resources of some capital or education barely maintain their relative earning position. They now lag behind men with industrial skills (see Table 12).

As before, core-sector workers earn more than the rest. But their high average masks variation by level of education. Professional men with graduate degrees generally earn the most; technicians with diplomas follow, while those who have acquired their skills mainly on the job and lack a school certificate of any sort earn the least. Thus wages from lowest to highest are those of the computer technician, the oil-rig fitter, and the draftsman.

Though secure men with industrial skills in both sectors earn more than their counterparts with nonindustrial resources, the gap in their wages has narrowed between sectors. In phase 1, men with industrial skills on the periphery earned 43 percent of the wages of those with industrial skills in the core; in phase 2, 68 percent. This new demand for technical skills marks the spread of the development program and creates a uniformity of wage-earning profiles.

Table 12. Average earnings[a] of 17 secure men in peripheral and core sectors, phases 1 and 2

Sector	Phase 1	Phase 2[b]	Percent increase	Number	Earnings rank	
					Phase 1	Phase 2
Periphery						
Resources[c]	S$517	S$ 958	86%	6	2	3
Skilled	407	1,020	151	3	3	3
Average peripheral-sector secure male worker	481	979	104			
Core, skilled	939	1,525	62	8	1	1
Average secure male worker, both sectors	695	1,236	78	17		

Note: No secure men changed sector. No unskilled men entered the phase 2 panel.
[a]Pre-overtime gross monthly wage, before withdrawal of CPF.
[b]Men's sectoral positions are kept constant.
[c]Occupation requires some capital, a nonindustrial skill, or an academic degree.

State efforts to raise labor force productivity have focused on core-sector firms, and most of their workers have access to new training programs. Indeed, some firms virtually compel their skilled men to take courses. Such men have enough education to be eligible, and they also fear that if they fail to raise their skills, they will be passed over for promotion in favor of younger colleagues with degrees who entered the firm after them. For these reasons, core-sector men who already have technical skills and earn solid wages are the ones who make most use of job-training programs.[9] Examples among the men we have met are the computer technician and the quality control supervisor on an oil rig.

Secure men are also linked to jobs through personal ties. Half have changed their jobs over the interphase, several more than once. All have found work through personal ties, none through formal channels. They are more likely than the poor to find work through schoolmates or former co-workers than through kin or neighbors. Also, since few are unemployed when they look for a new job, they bargain from positions of strength. Their new positions invariably pay more than those they left or promise improved opportunities.

Not all secure workers view the development program positively, however. Since the earning power of all secure men remains well above the national median, none is absolutely deprived. It is their relative position in the class hierarchy that determines their sense of progress. Peripheral-sector men without technical resources (civil servants or men with small service-sector businesses) have fallen behind; they no longer expect a bright future. They have lowered their expectations and displaced their goals onto having fun with workmates. Some seek solace in religion.[10]

Peripheral-sector men with technical skills are aware of the uncertain prospects of their small firms; they know that any downturn in the market or reversal of state policy will shake their firms. Yet, conscious of their personal income gains, they feel optimistic. Nevertheless, because many lack credentials and have acquired their skills on the job, they fear that they may fall behind. And so secure core-sector men with technical skills remain the most satisfied with their place in the new society.

These comparisons show how state industrial programs draw men more deeply into the market through their labor, and as a result open them to new demands. Now men with technical skills in each industrial sector earn more than all others. A technical skill adds to the wages of workingmen, and being a skilled worker in a core-sector firm adds even more. This is the case among both poor and secure men. Demands of the market have brought about similarity in earning power, but despite these similarities, great class differences remain. We will find that these similarities and variations in market and class position determine other spheres of the lives of revisited families.

Religious procession. Photo by Eric Khoo.

Women's Jobs

Women's participation in the economy has responded to the new economic structure. For them, too, technical skills and core industrial status bring higher wages. And since these skills are linked to class, the effect of the second development phase on women depends on their social class. Nevertheless, because women are tightly bound to their family roles, their gender and family-cycle stage limit the jobs and the earnings they can get. Family demands greatly affect their ability to reach their work potential.

We find an amazing labor force continuity and wage improvement among the panel women. Only eight of the forty-five panel women have changed their positions over the interphase. Four women quit their jobs and three homemakers joined the labor force, while another changed category by acquiring a second part-time job in domestic service to achieve a full workweek.[11] I estimate the median nominal wage for women at S$400 in 1981.[12] The panel women also set S$400 as their working goal, and most earn more.

Women's labor force continuity and improved wages can be traced to Singapore's rapid industrial upsurge, which increased employers' demand for these experienced women and their families' need for their earnings. Those women who continued working through phase 1 were survivors of a cohort that had once consisted almost entirely of working women, but whose least-skilled and lowest-paid members had long before quit the labor force. Over the interphase many factories raised the quality and sophistication of their products. Few firms hire female graduates of training programs; they draw on existing hourly workers for lower-level supervisory staff.[13] The employed women of my panel, on the job when this upsurge occurred, can now command the higher women's wage. They no longer have to compete with unmarried women for the lowest-paid, unskilled positions.

But class background continues to divide women. Poor women earned 66 percent of their secure counterparts' wage in phase 1 and only 63 percent in phase 2. An underlying reason is the low education of the poor. The worst educated had quit work when they married because their prospects were so limited. The few who in recent years rejoined the labor force are again confined to inferior jobs.[14] Lack of seniority further dooms them to a low wage. Thus two of the five low-wage earners have just begun to work, and they earn no more than the mass of unmarried school leavers. Naturally, housewives are well aware of the slender opportunities for them in the labor force. Those who do not qualify for solid wages cannot command the support they need from family and kin to take up full-time employment, as we saw in the cases of the hawker's wife and the wife of the bookstore clerk.

Industrial sector also affects earning levels. The women who earn less than the median female wage work solely in the peripheral sector. Even here on the periphery, other women with sufficient experience in their firms boost their wages above the median. Nonetheless, core-sector rates of pay continue to exceed those for women of comparable seniority and education in the periphery, and no woman has changed sector.[15]

The highest-paid women are two civil servants, one of whom is the schoolteacher we have met. Although they are not in the core sector, their education gives them skills that are in demand. As no affluent woman is employed in the core sector, we are unable to learn whether core-sector wages exceed those on the periphery for affluent women as they do for men. But their very absence suggests that women find it difficult to penetrate the economic center.[16]

Women advance mainly to jobs at a slightly higher level in factories that are now improving product quality. Few women switched firms over the interphase, and of those who did, none changed her line of work. This work continuity points to the inability of poor women and those of modest means to parlay skills acquired on the job into promising new occupations. Only one factory worker completed skill-upgrading courses offered at the work site and by the National Trades Union Congress and became a section leader. It is mainly the semiprofessional affluent women, such as the schoolteacher, who continue their training and expect some form of reward. They therefore easily maintain their class lead.

With this increased demand for tenured women, I was not surprised to learn that the panel women are often considered for promotion. Six secure women had already advanced to lower-level technical or supervisory posts by phase 1. Five poor factory women have been newly offered promotions since then, and three have accepted this challenge. These salary-scale jobs carry more authority and pay slightly better than the women's former assembly positions. But in fact, some of these women declined the offer of supervisory positions, while others later resigned the posts they held in phase 1. Why is this so?

We can usefully compare the reasons that women do not reach their occupational potential with those that men give for refusing promotions. Poor women, like their husbands and brothers, have neither the education to study new techniques nor the confidence to try. They are reluctant to handle English-language forms and reporting duties. Like the men, some women prefer to augment their incomes by moonlighting. There are also women who turn down an offer of advancement in favor of staying with their peers. They fear that they will be rejected by younger and better-educated colleagues of higher social status in the new and more responsible post. True, a few affluent women have taken courses. Likewise, affluent men, encouraged by their firms, have pursued promotions. It appears that lack of education, confidence, and peer and employers' support are important for both men and women, and this influence is class-based. But here, the sexes' similarities end. Whereas men limit their concerns to earning a family wage, all women must maintain the family domestically as well. A woman's family burden is a powerful reason to refuse a promotion or abandon a superior post in the work force.

As their families are drawn into the money economy, women's earning power is increasingly attractive. Public services and goods that families once made, bartered, or did without require cash today. As families move from low-cost kampungs to high-rise flats, women are impelled into the money economy to help pay for rent, furnishings, and utilities. Extras that enter the way of life of all include consumer durables and home fixtures, school fees and tutors for the children. State policies thus indirectly encourage women to work. But the state has gone further to encourage married women to work in direct ways, beginning with its policy of putting factory units in working-class housing districts to attract women residents. Active family planning programs further enable married women to work outside the home.

Despite the family need for their earnings and the availability of work, in each household the gender-based division of labor places the burden of running the home on women. Women who have long been out of the labor force are thus taxed with many household duties and social obligations. Since reentry wages are usually low, they find it hard to enter the job market. This situation has led to a dramatic increase in part-time work. Thus ten panel women who need funds work part-time at or near home, a marked increase over phase 1. These part-time workers are all in the shadow economy. Most serve as undocumented home seamstresses for nearby factories, others as canteen assistants, a few as child minders or domestic helpers of other employed women. The rising ages of their children leave mothers time to sew at home for the pay their families now need.[17] An example is the wife of the store clerk who has resumed her home seaming for a nearby factory where she once worked. Secure women who work part-time earn much more at high-quality seamstress work on commission.

We can readily imagine the future for the large proportion of panel women who turn to the shadow economy for small sums of money. These activities will give them none of the vested pension savings or other benefits won by the organized working class. This generation of women homemakers, despite their access to some money, may repeat the fates of their seniors, who spend their later years doing informal labor in the home and community for a pittance.

The wide gender gap in wages persists throughout both phases: full-time working women earn about three-fifths of the basic wages of panel men. Although affluent women earn high wages, their husbands earn even more. Therefore, because of the higher wages of the affluent men, the gender gap is somewhat narrower in poor families than among the affluent. This fact points to the importance of women's earnings among the poor. But over the interphase, secure women's wages increased slightly faster than those of the poor. As a result, the gender gap in their class has narrowed slightly.

Women's wages, although sometimes small and earned in difficult circumstances, greatly help their families, especially at the lower income levels. Among poor families in which the wives work full-time, the average family income is 156 percent of that of couples who depend only on the husbands' earnings, while the figure in secure families is 146 percent. Women's wages also slightly narrow the class gap. In phase 2, the ratio of poor to secure couples' earnings was 53 percent for those in which the wives did not work, but 56 percent when wives worked full-time. Couples with part-time women's wages fall in between. These comparisons signify that the impact of women's wage work is felt most strongly by the poor, who need it the most.[18]

Family support, which was crucial for married women who wanted or needed to work outside the home in phase 1, has become less available. One reason is the move to new family flats. In phase 1, half of the panel lived with kin (more secure than poor couples). Coresidence has declined only slightly among the poor (from 39 percent to 36 percent) but has almost vanished among secure families (from 67 percent to 6 percent).

The new flat is not the entire reason for the drop in family support, for many panel couples who do not live with kin continue to visit. When I combine coresident with interacting families (those who live apart from kin but visit at least twice weekly, exchange domestic tasks or work with kin, or whose kin care for their children), the total shows only a moderate decline, from 87 percent in phase 1 to 78 percent in phase 2. The proportion of such families among the secure exceeds that among the poor, evidence that their close kin are still emotionally meaningful to both class groups.

Despite such continued interaction, however, women's support groups in both classes have gotten smaller. Few women now depend on their relations to release them for full-time paid labor. In phase 1, twenty panel women worked full-time, and each of them relied on kin for help with child care or homemaking. In phase 2, in contrast, only thirteen of the twenty full-time wage-earning women look to kin in order to work. Thus couples continue to see kin often, yet wives are less likely to call on them for help. The reasons vary by class group.

Even when poor working women live with or near their parents or in-laws, the older generation is now rarely strong enough to care for grandchildren. As their energy ebbs, the older folk redefine their family role. Whereas in phase 1 they helped their daughters or daughters-in-law learn mothering skills and took on part of the burden of infant care, now the older women are ready to retire. Others have died. The advance of the family cycle limits the help women receive, and poor mothers need more help than they are able to get.

Secure mothers are less likely to bewail this loss, as they have new educational values.[19] The attention that infants and toddlers need was seen mainly as custodial in phase 1. Now that they have reached school age, they require tutoring. Because of mothers' interest in raising their children the "new way," they now reject help that they might be able to receive from their seniors. Many parents consider the older generation too poorly educated to help perform this crucial task. Thus when the computer technician and his homemaker wife lost the help of an ailing mother, they rejected the help of others in raising their children.

Determined and sufficiently well-paid women can still avail themselves of new forms of child care in order to work. In phase 1 they sought figures they trusted implicitly to watch their children. In phase 2, the tots are older and can be cared for by a wider range of helpers. Many children attend school and participate in supervised sports, clubs, and other leisure activities after school, so that less care is needed at home. Part of their home care may also be provided by neighbors for pay. Higher wages enable these women to finance such alternatives. Working mothers sometimes arrange their work hours so their husbands are at home while they work.[20] Finally, some latchkey children are left unattended while mothers are at work.

Inevitably, however, many will have to cut their work load, and the four women who quit their jobs entirely did so when family support evaporated. The wife of the computer technician is again a good example. A fifth woman, the electronics assembler who doubled as a hawker stall operator, left that second job while keeping her main factory job; a sixth gave up her lead-girl position and returned to the ranks of assemblers. Thus the women who still look to kin for help are largely the poor, but a growing minority of all women must look outside the kin network for their child-care needs.

A mother's resolve to stay at work depends partly on the number and ages of her children. We have seen that the section supervisor in a garment factory quit but then returned to work for this reason. Continued employment is easiest for women who have not increased their family size over the interphase. Indeed, the four who quit their jobs over the interphase are all nurturing newborns. Conversely, the children of two of the three panel mothers who have joined the labor force are already in primary school and require only a few hours of daily care.[21] The difficulties faced by women in getting help from kin, especially when they earn low to medium wages, explain why more women who were housewives in phase 1 work in the home-based shadow economy than have joined the formal full-time labor force.

In sum, like their husbands, all women feel the reverberations of the market economy more sharply than they did in phase 1. But, unlike their men, they are constrained in their efforts to negotiate a place in the labor market by their ability to mobilize kin support. Such support, whether by kin or others, is most forthcoming for better-paid women, women who worked in phase 1 and continued to work because they found themselves in great demand, especially those in core-sector employment. In these ways, phase 1 social-class position extends into phase 2.

Public Housing

As the sole housing market for the majority, public-sector apartments are central to family life. The rising frequency of homeownership reflects improving living standards and support of public housing by state agencies. Beyond the index of homeownership, we must explore the meaning of housing as a cultural form to appreciate the profound social changes associated with the housing transformation and the extent to which they are shared by the social classes.

An impressive 62 percent of the panel moved over the interphase. Even more dramatic, 73 percent now own or have applied for flats. The proportion of poor families that have either moved or applied for a flat has risen from 15 percent to nearly two-thirds. Nearly all secure couples own flats. The gap in access to public housing by social class has greatly narrowed. In phase 1 the ratio of poor to secure owners and applicants for flats was 21 percent; in phase 2 it is 73 percent.

HDB residence has spread first because the urban renewal programs ended kampung living and compelled families to enter the state housing market. Seven panel families lived in suburban housing in phase 1, and six have made plans to move to HDB flats or have already done so. Several were keen on moving but some resisted. The views of some couples, such as the sewing machine repairman and his factory-worker wife, were divided; the husband preferred to remain in the kampung where he had lived all his life, while the wife was eager to move. In the event, the husband had no choice. Forced relocation in such cases changes family relations drastically. But it is more than compulsion and elimination of the rural sector that characterizes the Singapore housing program. Families are not passively mowed down by bulldozers. They are active participants in the housing transformation, now integral to their definitions of family living.

Let us first look at the poorest couples who have managed to buy a home. Learning how they did so is important, because the fate of such families shows how the masses are brought into a uniform way of life with development.[22] Only one of the fourteen panel men with wages under the national median in phase 1 owned a flat at that time. In phase 2 over two-thirds of those fourteen men have improved their homes: seven live in homes of their own, an eighth couple has applied for one, and three rent larger flats. This dramatic housing transformation been achieved by higher wages and steadier work. Their life-cycle advancement (more years on the job) has helped further by increasing the savings that couples can use to buy flats.

Those poor men whose wages increased most dramatically paid for their flats with their new earnings and their CPF savings, while the low earners used other resources. The shipyard construction worker, for example, has drawn on his shadow-economy earnings to buy a home: bonuses for meeting his contracts ahead of time, overtime work, and a lucky strike in the lottery. The warehouse laborer and electronics factory worker drew on her earnings to buy their home.

The proportion of homeowners among the poor does not vary by the industrial sector of the husband's job, but their reasons for failing to buy a home do differ. Core-sector husbands who have not bought flats have unstable work histories or personal habits that prevent them from saving. The husbands earn enough or could mobilize funds to buy a home, but they prefer to live each day as it comes. An example is the shipfitter who gambled. In contrast, peripheral-sector men who have not bought apartments earn wages that are far too low to finance homeownership. As several gamble in addition, these low-paid peripheral-sector men are doubly stymied by their market position and their personal difficulties in planning ahead. The husband's skill level also greatly affects wages, and consequently the ability to buy a flat. Only two of the seven unskilled men in both core and peripheral sectors have bought or applied for a new flat, whereas sixteen of the twenty-one core- and periphery-sector men with skills or resources have done so. Thus the husband's structural position in industry and his occupational skills shape a poor couple's ability to buy a flat.

Women's wages also help poor couples buy their homes. Wives in three of the twelve couples who already live in their own homes worked full-time at the time of purchase. They pledged their CPF and savings to achieve this crucial family goal. These women are all high earners in core-sector jobs, demonstrating again the importance of core-sector work in furthering family lifestyle improvement.

Given the sweep in homeownership, it is not surprising that ability to buy a flat influences couples' feelings of having "made it." Those poor families who have moved are usually optimistic even if their earnings have not improved; their move signifies to them a better station in life. Those who have improved their wages and their homes feel even more optimistic, while those with neither solid wages nor new homes feel the most deprived. The most marginalized couples lack even such public goods, and are embittered. This pattern suggests a recognition of objective social disadvantage rather than culturally transmitted feelings of fatalism and worthlessness. Clearly, the feelings of powerlessness of these alienated couples are realistic responses to limited opportunities.[23]

Secure families had a head start in homeownership, and now nearly all own their homes or have applied for one. All the core sector men have applied for or own a flat, sweeping along with them several who had earlier expected to stay out of the housing market. Indeed, the only two who have not bought homes are peripheral-sector workers, and both own their own

A family of modest means in their new home. Photo by Eric Khoo.

businesses. They lack CPF and are putting their funds into their family firms; one still hopes to buy in the future.

Working women now help their families buy a home. Ten of the fourteen secure wives who already live in their own homes worked at the time of purchase, and four contributed their CPF toward the installments. Other working women have devoted years of savings to furnish their flats.

A new trend has emerged among these better-off couples. Nine are in the process of selling at a profit the three-room flats they owned in phase 1 and moving to four- or-five room flats. Among the secure couples, most of whom already live in their own flats, the main distinction is now the size of their flats. As before, the division is along class lines, with nearly all affluent couples having opted for the larger homes, leaving families of modest means behind in smaller flats.[24] A dramatic example is the draftsman married to the schoolteacher, with a large rented house and two flats as income property.

The housing transformation furthers the penetration of the money economy by both groups. Furnishing the flat is a popular pastime for most residents. Couples who have not moved over the interphase spend the least on upgrading their homes. Most inherit castoff furniture from neighbors and relatives who improve their homes. Families that newly rent larger flats spend more on basic renovations and furniture, with expenditures of S$1,000 to S$2,000 common. Yet these figures are modest compared with the costs incurred by home buyers. Poor couples who have managed to finance a home with their own earnings have typically paid more than S$5,000 to equip it. Few low-wage couples who have bought new flats with family loans have yet bought new furniture. The largest amount spent by a secure couple was S$25,000, for renovations. Homeownership demands steady work to meet the large expenses of furnishings, installments, and down payments.

At first I had assumed that the owners would find themselves spending more of their take-home pay on their flats than the renters, but this is not the case. Normally, workers with a two-decade fund of CPF savings need pay nothing out of pocket for their new flat; only those with low CPF pay monthly installments, and the sum is surprisingly low. I call the couple's joint net earnings (after CPF is withdrawn) from their main jobs their "basic take-home pay." The proportion of the basic take-home pay that families spend on housing ranges from 2 to 38 percent, but the majority pay less than 10 percent on a place to live. Indeed, in most cases the percentage of their basic take-home pay that couples spend on what most feel is improved housing has dropped over the interphase.

The housing transformation has deep implications for the political economy. Since poor couples and those of modest means find it hard to save, CPF enables them to buy a home without having to stint on daily necessities. The low proportion of their take-home pay spent for housing frees them to spend more on consumer goods. This painless road to property ownership ties a family into debt and credit relations that require them to work steadily for years to come. But if they should lose their jobs, they will risk missing payments and losing their homes. Further, those couples with low CPF, who buy homes with the help of kin or through hidden-economy earnings, are the ones that also spend most of their basic take-home pay on housing, up to 38 percent. Moreover, only four poor couples have fully paid for their flats, and most look forward to ten more years of payment. They will have to replenish their CPF fund before they can retire. In contrast, eleven of the fourteen secure homeowners have completed their payments and have adequate retirement funds as well. In these ways homeownership contributes to changing lifestyles while reproducing class and structural cleavages in the new industrial order.

A home of one's own has been said to break apart the extended household and strengthen the bond between husband and wife. In other words, a "modern family" accompanies homeownership. In this study, we can see such a relationship. The nuclear family emerges as the primary household at the time that families move into new flats. Does this mean that the new apartment has "caused" the emergence of the nuclear household? In order to explore this process, we in fact need to examine two kinds of change separately: moving to a new flat and changing family structure.[25]

Social-class position, which so greatly shapes the spheres of family life studied so far, is again closely tied to these processes. Not only have more secure couples moved over the interphase (54 percent of poor and 76 percent of secure couples have moved); their family structure has also more frequently changed to the nuclear form (36 percent of poor but only 6 percent of secure families live in nonnuclear households). Relatively more secure couples than poor couples have moved and even more have become nuclear households.

Let us now look at how the two processes fit together. Twenty-eight couples moved over the interphase. Fifteen of these couples also changed their household structure. The majority of these fifteen are secure families; nine became neolocal when they moved. Secure families have saved for years to complete their home purchase while taking advantage of low-cost child-care help from their kin. Ultimately, secure couples formed small households when they moved. Their numbers show the link between affluence, a home, and the nuclearization of Singapore families. And the meaning of the new home strengthens the link. Most secure couples identify the nuclear family with a new home. They associate small family living and their own flat with the chance for privacy, better education for their children, and control over savings and household goods. Husbands and wives jointly discuss the purchase of goods and services, including their new home. Buying a home of their own then strengthens the marriages of those for whom economic constraints do not exist.

By itself, the new home need not negate the large household, as the stories of the six poor couples who moved and changed their family structure show clearly. Only three of them became neolocal upon moving into their own home. The same number who moved to new homes invited aging relatives who could not live on their own to join them; they expanded instead of becoming nuclear households. These poor couples are all influenced by the advance of the life cycle.[26] Therefore, few poor are found among those who both moved and became nuclear households. Clearly poor folk find moving and nuclear family living a difficult project.

Thirteen couples who moved over the interphase experienced no family change. Three of them maintained large households after they moved, and all are poor. Ten couples of both class groups were neolocal both before and after they moved.

Fifteen of the couples have neither moved nor changed their family structure—43 percent of the total poor but only 18 percent of the total secure panel. Finally, two couples have lost resident kin although they have not moved. A closer look at these two cases shows how social class defines their passage from extended to neolocal household. A very poor couple became neolocal when the husband's father (who had paid the rent for the one-room flat) died. In contrast, an affluent couple became neolocal when the husband's mother bought her own small flat. Thus the poor household lost a parent with the advance of the life cycle and the secure household lost a parent through lifestyle improvement.

New housing can thus promote a single family form. The differences between the two class groups have been greatly reduced as a result of the move to public housing. Their more secure work and higher wages enabled all of the social-class groups to attempt to purchase a home, and poor couples and those of modest means have made great advances in homeownership for the first time. Affluent couples are buying their second homes.

But social-class standing still figures in the purchase of a home, and even more in its meaning to the family. In phase 1, most poor families lived in inferior housing, and if relatives lived apart, it was because no flat was large enough to hold all those who wished to live together. Now poor folk are more likely to use their improved housing space to maintain the wider family, essentially to support their elders. Secure couples who lived with kin in phase 1 did so more for convenience than for economy. But in phase 2 they can afford two homes, one for themselves and another for their elders, and their children no longer need full-time care. Now secure folk use their home as a private space within which to develop the small nuclear family, while the old folks also have fine homes. These new social-class differences are expressed within the same public housing market rather than as differences between the haves and have-nots.

Children of the secure try out their new toys. Photos by Dominic Yip.

Education: The Pathway to Advancement

The school system draws youth into a single channel for achievement, and parents invest economically and emotionally in education. As couples increase their commitment to the school system over time, they become involved in the political economy in new ways. In phase 1 the type and level of education parents wished for their children varied greatly by their class background; indeed, few poor couples held high educational goals. However, their children were still young. In phase 2, nearly half of the panel, twenty-two couples, have one or more children aged eleven or older, the age at which they take the crucial primary school-leaving examinations (PSLE), the gateway to secondary school and a future career. Parental hopes for their offspring's education is of necessity more concrete than before, and we can assess the steps parents take to underwrite these hopes.

More poor parents now voice hopes for their children's postsecondary education. However, the proportion that retreats into vague statements about wanting their children to go "as high as possible" also has increased (see Table 13). They include those who have little interest in higher education and those who have given up earlier aspirations because they lack the funds for their children to progress along the difficult educational pathway.

Most poor parents take the school system at face value. They know that jobs increasingly demand certification, and children must go to school longer. They accept the authorities' evaluation of their children's abilities. If their children do well in school, they are "bright." If they do not get good test grades, they are "not intelligent." Few challenge this evaluation by attempting to change their children's stream or course of study. By accepting the power of the school system to determine their children's occupational future, the working class becomes further involved in the new industrial

Table 13. Percent of poor and secure couples who desired specified levels of education for their children, phases 1 and 2

Class groups	Don't know; as high as possible	Secondary	Postsecondary, university, polytechnic	Total	Number
Phase 1					
Poor	54%	42%	4%	100%	28
Secure	17	12	71	100	17
Phase 2					
Poor	74	4	22	100	27[a]
Secure	41	0	59	100	17

[a]One poor couple did not respond.

order. Nevertheless, a number of parents do not necessarily believe that they have gotten a fair deal.[27]

Use of the school system to help their children get ahead varies with the parents' own education and finances. The very poor neither aspire much nor make concrete plans for their children's educational future. Those who voice the goal of higher education are usually vague. They have little information about schools, and do not think it is possible or even important to get more. They retreat into the generalization that a comprehensive school system exists and their children, if they are bright enough, can use it fully. This abstract view of the importance of achievement cannot direct a concrete course of action.

Some with a new source of funds for paying tutors and other costs are conflicted and still cannot aspire too high. For example, men with a technical skill who have recently gotten boosts in earnings see that credentials in a technical field are important. They are most likely to ascribe to the Singapore dream of upward mobility through education. But when their children were younger, these parents had tight budgets and could not give their offspring the crucial help they needed. Now their children find it hard to make it through the competitive educational system.

Most poor parents can only hope that all of their children will attend a school in the neighborhood. Then mothers can more easily take and fetch the children, and the older children can look after their younger brothers and sisters. The mother's family tasks take priority. Only a few actively try to shape their children's progress through the school system. Taking a negotiating stance, these few distinguish the "better" neighborhood schools, where teachers "try to understand the children," from those other schools that have poor exam results. Such parents as the electronics assembler and the warehouse worker enrolled their children in a local school that promises to raise the children's exam grade. Thus the school system becomes an arena of competition for families with ambition.

Yet poor parents rarely consider placing their tots in elite schools, most of which are far from home. By the child's secondary school years, these elite schools are fully enrolled. Only those students that get very high scores on the national PSLE can win the few remaining places. But if poor children have gone to neighborhood schools in their primary years, a high PSLE score is unlikely. Only three poor couples have tried to place their children in the handful of elite government or government-aided mission schools.[28] Since no poor parents attended an elite school, none has the old school ties or the church contacts that will give their children priority admission to mission schools.

The disincentives policy, which gives priority to children of small families whose parents have undergone sterilization, provides another means of entry to a school with a good reputation. But poor parents do not limit their childbearing deliberately to upgrade their children's educational achievement. We have met the electronics assembler, married to the shipfitter, who had a tubal ligation after two children. But she did not do so in order to place them in an elite school.[29] Although a basic education is important to them, the poor do not organize their family plans to channel their children into high-status schools.

Poor parents commonly hire tutors to improve their children's grades. Half put aside funds for tutors and other costs. The monthly sum paid ranges from a nominal S$1 in a mission center to S$60 for two children twice weekly in a tutor's home, and the average is only S$38. These modest sums involve sacrifice, and some mothers take in industrial piecework to meet the cost. These parents cannot afford high-quality tutoring for their children. Parents with some secondary education may tutor their children at home, a sign of commitment to the school system as a means of getting ahead. But generally, the most such parents can do is to make sure that their children finish their homework. That half take such extra steps as seeking a tutor's help to boost their children's performance indicates their commitment to the school system as a channel toward the future. For they are not required to pay for tutors. They do so to give their children greater job benefits in the future.

Sixteen of the twenty-eight poor families have one or more children aged eleven or older, or in grade 5 or higher. My information on the school performance of the children in twelve of these families reveals that in seven families one or more children have repeated a primary school grade or dropped out altogether. Another three couples say that their children are "lazy" in school. Only two couples say that their children are "doing all right." Those who do poorly on the PSLE normally quit school, then go on to take ordinary unskilled or semiskilled working-class jobs. An example of such youthful workers is the daughter of the tinsmith and domestic servant who became a dentist's receptionist.

The below-par school results of the majority of poor children show that despite the tutors, parents cannot ensure that their children will get high marks on this crucial test. Low family educational background and income and inability to place their children in one of the elite schools contribute to their children's slow climb up the educational ladder.

Secure parents' higher hopes and their children's better school performance reflect their class lead. None believes that higher education does not matter. Indeed, keenly aware of the competition, many parents of modest means say they wish their children to go "as high as possible" in school. This statement reflects a desire for more education for their children than they can afford rather than a lack of information. The goals of many working-class parents exceed their resources. Meanwhile, the affluent remain steadfast in university-level aspirations for their children.

Many secure parents try to choose a school that has a good reputation.

Nine of the seventeen couples are trying to place their children in an elite school, and most have succeeded. We have met one of the two mothers, married to the computer technician, who, not having attended an elite school themselves, had tubal ligations after bearing a second child to make their children eligible for an elite school under the disincentive measures.

Eleven secure couples have saved some money for their children's education or currently pay from S$30 to S$200 (an average of S$80) a month for tutors. Parents of modest means, who have trouble tutoring their children at home, must rely entirely on outside help. They find this situation worrisome. Affluent parents are able to raise their children's exam scores by devoting more of their resources to this goal. They discussed and planned for their children's education at an early age, and phase 2 finds these plans coming to fruition. Affluent parents who begin to plan for their children's education when they are born thus maintain their head start in the competitive educational system.

Six of the seventeen secure families have one or more children aged eleven or older. All six sets of parents realize that this is a crucial turning point. Children in two families (both of modest means) are "doing poorly"; the parents of the rest say that their children are doing well. The two who are not doing well will be sent to the technical stream in the secondary school to get credentials. None of them will be permitted to quit school. No affluent child has yet failed to perform up to par.

In sum, measured by educational goals, the hiring of tutors, and savings, poor parents' use of the school system is greater than before and has implications for their deepening involvement in the new industrial political economy. Poor and secure families are not necessarily closer together now than in phase 1, however. Poor couples remain at the lowest receiving end, and secure couples maintain their class lead in the school system. This lead is hidden by the greater overall use of the school system by the poor in ways that I have measured, but it is put into sharper relief when we consider the meaning of the school system to poor and secure families. Thus the Singapore development strategy has made more uniform the outward appearances of family lives; but in the educational sphere, as elsewhere, their worries and concerns, their fears and hopes are shaped by distinct positions in the class structure.

Planning Smaller Families for a New Way of Living

The integration of families into the second-stage political economy has reshaped family-size goals. As the costs of raising children rise, intended family size declines, and other indicators of family size also undergo great change.[30] The meaning and place of children in family lives vary by class position, however, even as working-class parents plan smaller families in response to the new development program.

In phase 1 these young panel parents averaged 2.5 children: thirty-two had intended to bear more children, six intended no more but could still bear children, and seven had been sterilized. The panel intended an average of 3.4 children. Most intended three but seventeen intended more.[31] These goals entailed an increase of one or two children for many couples. Only five couples wanted two children, and social-class differences were substantial.[32] Now nearly all have completed childbearing.[33] Most have the family size they intended six or more years ago, but a substantial minority have fewer and none have had more. They average three children, nearly half a child less than their phase 1 intentions. It is mainly the increased popularity of the two-child family in both classes that lowers average family size, a considerable change.

Panel families in both class groups have had fewer children than they intended in phase 1, but poor parents have slightly more than secure parents, and the reasons for reducing fertility also differ by class. As the groups have distinct positions in the labor market, they also have their own views of the costs of raising children.

The new second-stage industrial society has increased the direct costs of housing, feeding, clothing, and educating children. The costs are of crucial importance to the hard-put poor. In phase 1, fourteen families intended four or more children. Of these, several ceased childbearing because of the increased costs of raising a family. The number with four or more children is now eleven. Couples who intend to have large families rarely plan far ahead. But at the point where they perceive the costs of having the next child to be too high, they avail themselves of the state's family-planning services and have one child fewer than they intended.

Eight of the twenty-eight poor couples have three children. The three-child couples take into account the direct short-term costs of raising children and also the time constraints imposed on the wives by a newborn. Time costs weigh heaviest on full-time working women, especially those who give attention to planning their children's progress through the competitive school system.

Nearly one-third of the poor parents, only two of whom had intended to stop at two children in phase 1, have stopped at two. Both early planners are economically mobile and the wives have core-sector jobs. They have since been joined by seven couples who lowered their phase 1 three-child intentions to two children. All have at least one son. Most wives work full- or part-time and prefer to continue rather than bear yet another child. They focus on their economic opportunities to buy a home and more consumer durables. The new popularity of the small family demonstrates the considerable socioeconomic change over the interphase throughout this group. These folk are all striving for an improved material living standard and fear that yet another child would jeopardize their precarious well-being. They attempt to resolve this tension between new hopes and economic constraints by limiting their family size.

Few secure couples are troubled by the short-term costs of childbearing, but their aspirations are rising. Those of modest means have started to worry about the costs of educating their children. While the affluent have always held these ideals, they are now even more concerned about the amount of time the wives must spend educating their children, a burden increased for working women. Given these reasons for wishing smaller families, four out of ten now have one less child than they had intended to have.

Three secure panel women with three children each had intended to bear a fourth, but only one did so. In phase 2, eight secure couples have three children. Six of these couples had intended to have medium-sized families and they have since achieved their goals. Two other couples had wanted four children but now are satisfied with three.

The greatest change is the increase in two-child families. Only three secure couples had earlier intended a small family, and they have attained their goal. They have been joined by five couples that have over the interphase lowered their intended family size. None stress the short-term costs of having to pay for children's food, clothing, and other daily necessities. They have long been able to afford the direct costs of having children. The sex of the child figures into their calculations: all two-child parents have a son. The parents insisted, however, that their reason for limiting their family size was influenced not by the sex ratio but by the rapid rise in the costs of educating their children. Others feel that a third child will hinder the wives from working. The indirect educational costs that they project into the future distinguish the motives of the secure families from those of the poor.

Women of both class groups find it hard to combine full-time wage labor with child care, homemaking, and other essential family tasks. In phase 1, most working women earned little more than enough to reimburse female relatives, neighbors, or other community women for care of their infants. These women now earn above the female median and intend to remain in the labor force to improve their living standard. Now, however, they face greater difficulties locating low-cost child care. They have to limit their family size in order to stay on the job.

Wives with continuous work histories thus have lower fertility than do women in the panel as a whole. Fifteen panel women entered the labor force while they were childless and have continued to work ever since, despite the births of children. They average 2.5 children, and none has a large family.

Indeed, three had intended large families in phase 1 but have since lowered their family-size goals; others dropped their goals from three to two children over the interphase in order to remain at work. These continuously employed women have no more than three children. In contrast, the homemakers and late entrants to the work force average 3.2 children and account for the twelve large families in my sample.

Five panel women entered the labor force after they had borne the children they wished. Work affects their fertility, too, but mixes with their other experiences. Two of these late entrants who planned to work when their children entered primary school kept their family size small in order to make the leap from homemaker to worker.[34] Three poor women who were late entrants to the labor force had large families at a young age when they had no intention of working. The possibility of full-time employment occurred to them mainly when their children were older. Even at this stage, one woman aborted her fifth pregnancy and then had a tubal ligation in order to remain at her newly won factory post.

The stories of the women who dropped out of the labor force over the interphase demonstrate that social class bears closely on women's work histories and childbearing plans. The sole very poor woman who quit work had hoped to continue. Her husband, an unsteady worker, gave little support to her work plans and was keen on having a large family, and over the interphase she quit her job and bore a fourth child. Poverty and lack of options overrode the wife's work plans. Three secure women, in contrast, left their jobs to devote their time to their two children's education and upbringing. They hope to improve their families' social position. We have met the former electronics technician, now a housewife. Her desire for a small family results from her overall orientation to a better life for her children, to which her phase 1 wage labor made an important contribution.

Women's labor force activity is embedded in the family context, and the ability to get what is seen as a good woman's job and to keep it throughout marriage and childbearing is crucial. Many women, especially poor women with limited education, did not remain in the labor force when they became mothers. These are the women who had large families in phase 2. The full-time, continuously working women were somewhat better educated than the rest. Fewer of them entertained thoughts of a large family to begin with. But those who did expect to have many children have had to curtail their plans or quit work. Solid work opportunities for these women strengthen their commitment to work and to a medium-sized or small family. Narrow prospects, in contrast, encourage women to remain at home, and some have borne many children to bolster the family economy or their personal social networks. Large families are incompatible with continuous participation in the work force for the women of my panel. The highly motivated working women are likely to take advantage of the government's family-planning services.

In phase 1, the household setting of part-time work encouraged mutual exchanges of goods and services in a community of kin and close neighbors. Many such women were barely involved in the money economy and intended to have large families. Now that the family economy has become deeply monetized and aspirations have risen, women perform part-time wage work to increase the money available for social services and consumer goods. Even these homebound working women can help their families gain better lives. In this new context, part-time work interacts with other family goals and can influence women to limit the size of their families.[35]

Many panel parents experience pressure from kin to have another child. The pressure affects both groups of parents, but there is also a difference in the extent and nature of the influence by social class.[36] Poor parents who began childbearing relatively early had long been under kin pressure to bear children, and many succumbed. Four couples had a third or fourth or fifth child to meet the wishes of their kin over the interphase. The fact that only three couples resisted the pressure of the older folks reflects the continued dependence of the poor on their kin.[37] Nevertheless, this influence is weakening with the improved financial circumstances of some parents and the decline in real help by their aging parents. One poor couple with two children is still trying to withstand kin pressure to have another child.

Fewer secure couples experience pronatalist kin pressure, and more resist such influence. Those who disagree with their elders' pronatalist views say that they made up their minds "independently" of their kin. Secure parents in general feel in charge of their lives and are unlikely to admit giving in to views with which they do not agree. Those who let their kin influence their childbearing plans explain that they were not coerced; they attribute the birth of an additional child in part to kin pressure, in part to their own ambivalence. They hold to the belief that they are in charge of their family planning.

Most secure couples' parents agree with them that large families are economically disastrous in Singapore today. Therefore, the majority of secure couples who were influenced by kin to have an additional child or to have one quickly were not subjected to further pressure after the birth of the third child. Secure folk view kin demands as reasonable largely because they are not urged to have very large families.

Yet kin pressure on all panel couples to have another child has declined. As the dense familial community of phase 1 dissolves or changes form, the couples have to look to their own resources. Parents also live with and interact more closely with other people of different viewpoints. There is also life-cycle change. Couples live with kin mainly during the early stages of

[253]

childbearing, and many had moved out by phase 2. Kin can provide fewer services now in exchange for an additional birth; the parents of the secure live farther away and those of the poor have aged.

Respondents felt the disincentives against higher-order births more powerfully in phase 1, when the media trumpeted the information and medical personnel routinely urged women to limit childbearing. Parents with three or more children were most pressured to undergo sterilization. Over the interphase, however, the disincentives campaign abated.[38]

Poor parents felt antinatalist government policies most strongly in phase 1. But in a broader sense, abortions and ligations are still readily available and popular. Further, multiparous women still must limit their family size or explain to medical personnel, friends, peers, and kin why they do not. Nevertheless, poor parents now tend to attribute their decision to limit their family size to economic factors. Fewer of them refer to such disincentives as hospital fees or priority for a primary school place (a popular phase 1 motive). The shift toward the economic costs of childbearing and away from state sanctions owes much to more fundamental features of the development program. Therefore, poor women who underwent tubal ligations over the interphase did not attribute these operations to government policy.

Secure parents began and ended their childbearing later than their poor counterparts. They felt the impact of the measures against higher-order births over the interphase. No secure panel woman had undergone sterilization in phase 1 but six had done so by phase 2, and four attributed this final step to the disincentives. The computer technician and his wife, for example, wished access to elite primary schools for their tots, and qualified through the disincentives.

Two secure women who had tubal ligations after a third birth in response to the disincentives belatedly regret this action. "Now the Family Planning Board has stopped emphasizing ligations," they complained. But most parents do not regret their actions. Acceptance reveals overall acquiescence in the role of the state in dictating the details of their lives. Yet most no longer perceive that their family goals are dictated by outside agencies. Couples have by now incorporated into their family plans the view that small families are in keeping with the industrial way of life.

In sum, as the second-stage development program takes hold, couples see the small family as natural. The average family size is lower in phase 2 than earlier intentions among both poor and secure. But there is still a class gap in the average family size and in the reasons parents give. Poor folk are most likely to mention the immediate costs of feeding, clothing, and educating their children. Secure parents consider the long-term demands of improving the quality of their children's lives as reasons for having smaller families than they earlier wished.

[254]

Singapore Marriage: Variations on a Theme

New economic options, state housing policy, and life-cycle advancement have had a great impact on families. How have these forces transformed couples' marriage bonds over the interphase? Is there a new Singapore family with a strong marital bond, husband and wife together, house-proud, planning for the future?[39] Or do lack of resources still divide couples? I have come to think of Chinese marriages in phase 1 as rooted in divergent family economies that gave rise to distinct styles of marriage. The two types of marriage have evolved into a single structural form with variations. They are similar because they depend on their position in the same labor market in phase 2, and they vary by their class position in that labor market.

Let us turn first to the role of kin in family lives, which figured so prominently in phase 1, when most poor couples made major decisions with reference to the wishes of kin. In phase 2 the number of panel couples living with kin has dropped from half to less than one-quarter of the overall panel, but poor couples continue to live with kin nearly to the same extent as before.[40] For these poor folk, progress through the life cycle brought the deaths of close relatives and their kin community is coming apart. It is the secure partners, keen on gaining independence from kin, who are responsible for the great drop in coresidence. They find the values of the modern family appealing. To put it another way, poor husbands and wives have lost kin; secure husbands and wives have pulled away from kin.

Of course, couples in all class groups continue to mingle with kin. But relatives who live nearby can no longer boost the living standards of the poor to the same extent as before. As couples advance in their family cycle, aging and death take their toll. The circle of those who in phase 1 had exchanged goods and services contracts. Others who enjoy a better standard of living can now pay for rather than borrow what they need. As they spend more time at home indoors in new, spacious living rooms in front of the color television, they narrow their kin circle to a few meaningful individuals, mainly their parents.

Housework remains a woman's job for poor housewives. Help from husbands has in fact declined. Poverty drives a wedge in some marriages, and the men do not help with the housework. Other men have improved their wages but have not increased their share of household chores. Indeed, these men turn their energies to new moneymaking opportunities and reduce the time spent in housework at home. Now that their children are no longer dependent infants, many husbands justify their withdrawal from regular help in the home on the basis of declining need.[41]

Women who once got help from their kin with housework find their helpers now too old to take on such chores.[42] Poor women adjust to the loss of support by turning to their older children. Several mothers have trained their children to help in the home. They expect their children to clean their rooms, and a few women obtain help in cooking meals or washing the floors after dinner. Other women find their new HDB flats cleaner, more spacious, and easier to keep up than the one-room flats they occupied in phase 1. Even luckier poor wives have basic labor-saving conveniences. All poor homes are now equipped with refrigerators and telephones and many have color televisions, which men and children enjoy, but only two have washing machines. Many women believe that washing machines do not get clothes as clean as they should be. Women remain tied to repetitive household chores.[43] Some women create new bonds with helpers to reduce their homemaking burdens. Nevertheless, housework remains their job, and fewer women (eighteen poor women, or 64 percent) obtain household help from any source now than did so earlier (twenty-two poor women, or 79 percent).

No secure husband has increased his share in household tasks, and two have curtailed their help. Many men bring work home or take courses or have attempted to start up their own firms. They say their work requires all their time, as many are rising in their careers.[44]

Secure wives, too, get less help from their kin than they used to, mainly because extended household living came to an end when they moved to their own homes. Fewer than one-quarter of the secure women get daily help with child care from their kin or dine with them so that they can work. Two households have servants, but servants are not readily available to modest earners.[45]

Few secure women call on their children for help. Their children are either too young or mothers prefer them to spend their time studying. The number of secure women who received help from any source fell from sixteen (94 percent) to eleven (65 percent). The considerable loss in domestic help has personal costs, and has compelled several to give up their jobs or resign supervisory positions. But secure women who quit work do not always express regret. They take a professional view of housework, and turn considerable energy to performing it to a high standard.

In sum, from a position some distance apart, poor and secure panel women now obtain help with household chores in close to the same proportions for somewhat different reasons. The burden of household chores is thus borne equally by women in both groups.

Leisure patterns among poor Group I couples have not changed; the same one-quarter enjoy family outings. Parents and children stroll in one of Singapore's many parks or in the marketplace, ending the outing with an evening meal in a hawker's bazaar or at one of Singapore's dozen Kentucky Fried Chicken outlets. Sometimes they go to the movies. Most parents who enjoy family outings have an above-average living standard and an interest in improving their family lives.

No poor couple go out together without their children or other kin. They describe such outings as "troublesome," since they would "have to leave their children with relatives," or selfish. "How can we ask relatives to watch our children while we go out and enjoy ourselves?" commented one couple, and this view was typical. Their responses reflect a view of marriage as linked with kinship and family affairs, not as a bond between two individuals.[46]

More men spend time in their homes in the evenings now than in phase 1. Wage gains have improved household living conditions over the phase 1 one-room apartments, crowded, hot, and ill ventilated. The larger flats that they have purchased or rented contain color televisions. Their social life has shifted indoors, in front of the television, but shared leisure with their wives is not given high priority. They watch evening family dramas with their wives but do not take them out.[47] When men claim that they have become more "home-centered" over the interphase, they have in mind the ideal Chinese family, united under one roof.[48] Poor families have in the historical and recent past been most subject to the disruption that deprived them of the prized solid family. At this stage in their life cycle and in Singapore's development upsurge, more can meet this goal. The resulting family is more a patriarchal than an egalitarian, couple-centered arrangement.

Yet as in the past, nearly half of the men are seldom home. Some still enjoy outings with their co-workers. Others work in family firms and spend more time with kin. When spouses spend little leisure time together, only separate outings with friends and kin break their daily routine. But such outings cannot cement the marital bond. While not all of the couples that have segregated leisure activities are poor and some have enjoyed a boost in earnings through core-sector employment, those couples whose earnings are low are most likely to have segregated marriages. Only one of the poor wage earners takes his wife and children out occasionally and considers it important to do so. Those who spend little time at home show the damaging effects of continued poverty on a sizable minority of marriages.

Eleven of the seventeen secure couples go on outings with their children, and they also enjoy the mass media, the shopping malls, and the other consumer pleasures that Singapore offers. They define themselves as a unit apart from their parenting roles, and this point is crucial. Ten secure couples also go out as husband and wife, leaving their children in the care of relatives. The majority are affluent couples, nearly all of whom enjoy outings with friends they have in common. Many secure couples who had gone on such excursions before their children were born were compelled to reduce their activities when their children were toddlers. Now that the children are old enough to be left by themselves, they go out more often.

In the sphere of leisure, we find that poor and secure couples have come closer together mainly by including their children in their outings. But a

[257]

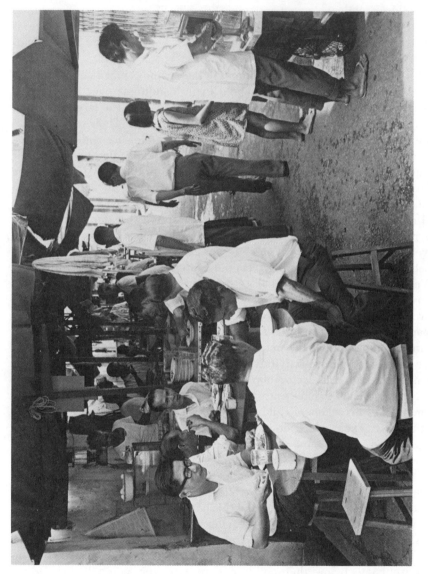

Breakfast at traditional hawkers' stalls. Photo by Eric Khoo.

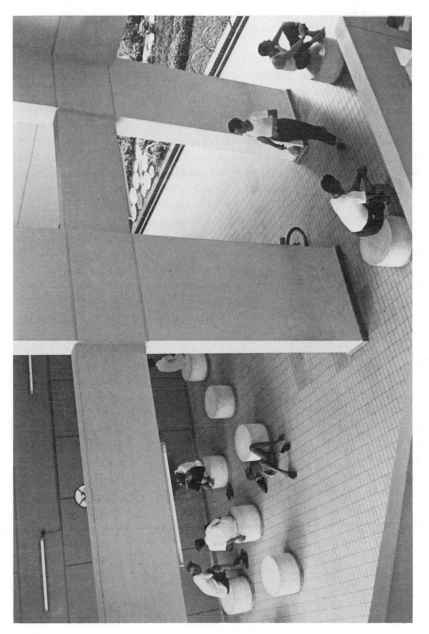

Men lounge in the shade of an HBD building to escape the afternoon heat. Photo by Eric Khoo.

bare majority of poor parents enjoy leisure excursions with their children, while the vast majority of secure parents do. Further, only secure couples define their tie as a special bond apart from the joint effort of raising the next generation.

Poor couples were unlikely to share confidences with each other, a pattern of communication set by poverty and the husband's inability to take his wife's part in quarrels with his mother; in any case, they found it hard to imagine a married couple baring their souls to each other. Now, twelve poor couples discuss few family or other matters, down slightly from phase 1. Three couples have improved their communications, mainly because of better living conditions, while continued poverty has worsened communication for two others. A decline in wider family living has hardly occurred for them, and even if it had, the nuclearization of their households would not suffice to improve the marriage bond. Thus overall communication patterns among the poor have changed little. Even the more communicative stress the limits of their discussions. Most poor couples admit that communication is limited to problems of daily living and an exchange of news. Few describe marital communication as an exchange of inner confidences.

In contrast, nearly all secure couples discuss matters, and many exchange close confidences. The proportion of couples that communicated was already high in phase 1. Secure couples remain far apart from poor couples in this crucial area of marital interaction.[49]

In sum, poor and secure panel couples are increasingly similar in some spheres, which include women's all but exclusive responsibility for household chores. New housing and consumer goods enable more poor men to enjoy remaining at home in the evening. Nevertheless, joint activities away from home are rare for the average working-class couple. Thus the poor and secure diverge considerably in their sharing of leisure outings without kin or children. Communication patterns differ even more. Class differences continue to shape the meaning of the husband-wife bond in leisure and communication patterns. Poor couples still value separate husband/wife spheres and do not define marriage as primarily a partnership. Secure couples, in contrast, view their marital bond as an important relation apart from childbearing and wider kinship activities.

[10]

Conclusion: Restructuring
an Industrial Society

Singapore's early labor-intensive export-oriented industrial economy, like those of other Third World nations, did not narrow the divide between rich and poor. Then, in the mid-1970s, the government revised its economic strategies to encourage capital-intensive industries and cultivate a technically skilled labor force. The technocratic party-state efficiently instituted deep social and economic reforms and pushed society into a full-fledged development program. The intervention of the Singapore government in molding a new family on behalf of its development program offers the best-known example in a market economy of a state restructuring society.

I sought to discover the form the new family life would take under the impulse of these programs. If equality of opportunity follows second-stage development, these social policies will then mold a two-class society into a single social organism, shaped by commitment to the market economy. If, however, the new development program further limits families' access to new opportunities, second-stage public policies may in fact polarize society. But I found that these polar choices cannot describe the nature of family change. My comparative focus on a number of Chinese families from a range of class groups over time shows clearly that policies that reshape labor and amenities can simultaneously unify families and introduce new variations.

Measured by their use of the key institutions promoted in second-stage development, poor and secure families are closer together now than they were in phase 1. Their deepening participation in wage labor has major ramifications for other spheres of family life. The number of working men and women in my sample whose earnings lift them above the poverty line has risen. Because of these economic improvements, nearly all families exploit the social services to a greater extent than before. These social services are crucial in shaping the new and more uniform way of life. All my interviewees have become proletarianized, and their commitment to the labor market determines the way they exploit the social services. The development program has most benefited new groups of workers who find jobs in the industries of the second stage, but has marginalized others who cannot. Poor couples receive the least while secure families maintain a class lead. A family's ability to buy a home in the public sector and the extent of its use of educational and family-planning programs turn on income, education, or property. Because the poor use public services more than they do private forms of goods and services (privately constructed housing, traditional medicine), the class cleavage is less visible than it was in phase 1. Yet the amount of use and meaning of these social services differs for poor and secure families.

Thus the Singapore development strategy has changed outward appearances of family lifestyle more than internal relations. Since families retain their distinct positions in the class structure and in wage labor, class position also shapes their style of interaction and their concerns, fears, and hopes. Ethnographic research indicates that the meanings attached to marriage, family building, and other aspects of life in industrial society vary by social class. My interviews of panel families of different social classes in phase 2 revealed a narrowing of differences in the many spheres of their lives specifically shaped by state policy, yet variations in goals and living standards still remain. Even though the standards and quality of life of couples interviewed over time still vary, their uses of social services are becoming increasingly similar.

The new second-stage programs root families ever more deeply in the capitalist mode of production, which opens them to control by the market and restructures them along new class lines. That the second-stage economic programs bring workers more deeply into the market economy has been seen first by the spread of wage work and the rise in basic wages earned. The proletarianization of the men and women in my sample enables policies that promote certain types of industries and occupations to reach increasing numbers of workers. The policies then force the restructuring of the labor process. Within each of the social-class groups, the earnings of workers whose skills are favored (men and women in the core-sector industries and in technically skilled occupations) have improved the most. Such a realignment of opportunities occurs throughout the class spectrum. Thus the programs of job creation, job finding, and retraining carry forward the major class divisions and inequalities.

How does the place of particular wage earners in the labor process and in the market economy at the time of industrial take-off determine their response to labor investment policies? Job training programs are highly selective. The poor, who have received little formal education and possess few industrially desirable skills owing to the lack of childhood opportunity, are least likely to upgrade their jobs through training programs. Either such programs are absent in their lines of work or people with low formal education lack access to them. The secure, who already have certificates or diplomas in technical subjects, are most likely to take retraining courses. Thus those who have skills upgrade and expand them. The secure families stay ahead of the mainstream.

But it is not only human capital that determines a worker's wage. I found that even with little additional improvement in skills, the wages of workers in state-promoted jobs rose. The wages of workers in marginalized industries, irrespective of training, did not increase so quickly. Those workers that have profited happened to be in the right place at the right time. Demand, not human capital, was the key to wage-earning power for most people over the interphase.

Finally, job opportunities are limited by the nature of the job search, which relies on informal patterns of interaction with friends and kin. The new program has reshaped, not fragmented, community, and workers retain links with others in their kin, class, and occupational and industrial circles. All of my respondents seek jobs through people they know, and social class and occupation define those to whom they turn for help. Partly for these reasons, workers remain in the same type of jobs. The compensation in these jobs, however, depends on market demands.

The new economic program sets limits to the wage-earning opportunities of panel women. Those who in phase 1 worked in the core industries or skilled occupations that gained favor in the new development program enjoyed the greatest advancement opportunities over the interphase. Other working women in jobs not advanced under the new economic regime have had lower pay increases and few mobility opportunities. Worse still, those women that were not working at the time the second-stage development program was launched have found it impossible to break into mainstream jobs. They can enter only unskilled peripheral-sector jobs or work in the hidden economy of part-time labor.

Women have been increasingly proletarianized over the interphase. Homemakers find they need to add to the family purse, and many have been compelled to work at part-time jobs. While lacking benefits and poorly paid, part-time jobs do subject women to the demands of the market economy. Whether new or old workers, through their market commitment women help bring their families more deeply into the new structures of the second-stage economy. The state social services, such as housing developments in areas where factories locate and birth control services, enable women to work. In turn, their wage labor increases their families' participation in the new state social services. Women's wages help furnish new public-sector apartments and pay for tutors for their youngsters.

[263]

Women's position in economy and society reflects their early upbringing and further contributes to the class position of the families they form. Their educational level and social class background figured in their phase 1 jobs, which then led to the work they do in phase 2. Now women's paid and unpaid labor contributes to the economic status of their families. The size of their pay packet thus makes some difference to the quality of their family life. Thus state programs that encourage women to work for a wage spread the new social institutions further among families of all class levels, while the earnings level of women may differentiate their families.

Women put even more of their energy into their family roles in phase 2 than in phase 1, efforts that limit their freedom to move ahead on the job. As women, they are also informally excluded from the key jobs of the new economy. But few in my sample struggle to overcome the gender barrier and advance in the job market, because most respondents place their home roles to the forefront of their commitments. The majority of women must maintain the family domestically, and their family burden limits their alternative activities. Indeed, much of the work of women at home also helps the families attain the new social benefits of the new economic order, such as a better apartment and a good school for their children.

The public services that structure citizens' place in the social class order shape their ideas about society. Access to new posts, higher wages, advancement opportunities, and other features of the job-creation schemes increase support for the new socioeconomic program of the state. As the worth of their jobs rises, some workers gain status at the expense of others. Their ability to enter these newly favored pursuits enhances the workers' self-image and assessment of second-stage development. The policies' true beneficiaries are core-sector men and women and especially those with technical skills, and these people lend most support to the government's development program. These workers' views of the state's economic programs thus depend closely on their relative progress in them.

The new educational programs overtly support the high-technology economy. They not only train the next generation of workers and structure their goals for the future but also bring parents at each class level more deeply into the social order in support of the second-stage economy. Parents budget money to promote their children through the school system. Families also try to encourage their children to achieve in school, and achievement is defined largely in terms of the educational system.

Despite the greater involvement of families in the educational system, a class gap remains. Under intense pressure to do well on exams and gain better school places, poor children have difficulty competing with the children of the secure. Secure families have a head start in preparing their children for the competitive exams and have better connections to good schools. But the educational system adds to a common conceptual framework that helps legitimate the class-divided nation.[1] The losers are able to redefine their loss within the dominant ideological paradigm. The ideology of the meritocracy proclaims that children with talent face no real financial obstacle to advancement in the school system. The cost of formal schooling is low and children who do well in the national competitive exams are promised state support. Many poor parents point to these factors as evidence of an open school system; few attribute their children's failure to their disadvantaged place in the class system. Borrowing from the terms of discourse of the meritocracy, they explain that their children do poorly on school tests because they lack merit or talent. Therefore, they cannot expect to get good jobs, and will always be poor.

The amenities that raise and equalize popular living standards—the public housing for sale and family-planning services—also alter living standards, reshape the popular way of life, and provide economic as well as political support for the phase 2 economic system. Owning a home of their own has become a goal for which most families strive. Writers on housing policies in developing nations argue that social policy is largely an afterthought, not conceived as an integral part of economic policy, and its aims are seldom achieved.[2] But I have found that public housing is one of the most equitable of all of Singapore's social policies. The gap in housing ownership between poor and secure families has narrowed considerably. True, three times as many poor as secure couples have no plans to obtain a flat of their own, and the size of a flat varies by class, as does its absolute cost and proportion of the worker's earnings. And the sacrifices that couples must make to fund a flat of their own, such as mortgaging their hard-gained pension funds, are greater for the poor. Come a recession, the poor will have more trouble making do on their own, without the help of their community.[3] Nevertheless, their homes integrate the poor into the market, which inexorably shapes a single lifestyle. Couples increasingly live alike.

The Singapore public housing program thus further unifies the social structure. By buying new flats, families become further constrained by the money economy. They must become involved in long-term work goals, mortgage payments, and indebtedness to their pension plans. We have seen the amount of money the members of my panel devote to their new homes. Continued market activity is necessary for Singapore homeowners, regardless of class position, even in the social service society.[4] The Singapore housing transformation has created a society of small homeowners, in fact or in aspiration. This transformation has greatly narrowed the differences in family lifestyles.

Families also may come to think alike. By providing homes and other amenities, the party-state can achieve social legitimization. A home of one's own provides the new measure of family achievement in the new society. Some can turn to the fact of homeownership as a standard of well-being, which may compensate for dashed job hopes. The poorest couples, if they lack even such a public good as a home, are embittered. They recognize they are objectively socially disadvantaged.[5] Thus public housing joins jobs and the school system in the frame of discourse for assessing the new social order.

The phase 2 social and economic development programs that have pro-letarianized the populace have also increased the costs of raising children. The programs have lowered couples' actual family size below their phase 1 intentions. The two-child family has become popular for all, but family size and childbearing motivation vary with the market position of the family. Thus the ratio of poor to secure average actual family size does not differ much from that of their intended family size in phase 1. Poor couples now plan a smaller family in order to make ends meet from day to day. Secure couples plan for somewhat fewer children to help achieve a higher living standard and to improve their children's opportunities. Parents now desire a two- or three-child family in order to attain their economic and social goals. And since their actual life options vary, they formulate these goals differently.

In recent years, the nuclear family has been seen as one of the roots of the development of capitalism in North America, Europe, and even Japan.[6] The Singapore government is not the first to embark on family reform to encourage the capitalist political economy. Let us return to the major question of my study: Has the family come to take the same form in all classes?

We have seen the several ways in which the nuclear family, structurally isolated from both close and distant kin and with independent goals and obligations, emerges as the capitalist market and the social services penetrate society. We have seen the great economic and social cleavages in the first industrial stage. Poor couples then were tightly bound to their kin by poverty, uncertainty, and job links. Secure couples also depended on their kin for mutual help, but theirs was a limited dependence, linked to the early stage of their life cycle. Both groups nourished a sense of shared responsibility in the local community.

The state, through the social services it sponsors, has pushed and even forced ties to the market and key social institutions, and the families I knew have changed. The transformation of family- and kin-based exchange of services and goods into a way of life in which families buy what they need has been largely completed during the period of study. Families can now afford to buy the everyday items they used to make by hand or exchange with kin and neighbors, as well as many other things they did not dream of having earlier. As a result, the community has changed.

By changing the source as well as the distribution of resources, the state economic and social policies restructure the fabric of community and family life. People not only become more closely integrated into a national market

Singapore, crossroads of the world. Photo by Fred Salaff.

economy, they also enter deeply into the capitalist culture. The social services, by shaping the set of ideas that people use in daily living, play a major part in their integration. In both the economic and the ideological spheres, state services commit people to a new social order. The involvement of families in the mainstream economic and social institutions can be seen in the dependence by families at all social-class levels on the money economy, public housing, the school system, and family-planning organizations. But as access to these social services and institutions varies across the class structure, the meaning of the new social order to individual families varies with social class and industrial sector.

Families in both major class groups depend on state services materially and as a source of ideas about their place in the society. But the family's position in the labor market shapes the process. The motives and meaning of reciprocal involvement with kin vary with the economic status of the family. For some, losing their kin is less a matter of choice than an outcome of the family cycle. Few poor families are economically secure, and all have a history of uncertain income. Thus economic status, coupled with the lack of crucial family support services in the public sector (day care, homes for the elderly), shapes the structure and meaning of family life along class lines. Many poor families, unable to separate from their kin for economic reasons, make a virtue of long-term reciprocity.

In comparison with the past, however, their reciprocity has narrowed. Scholars of moral economics have found that the development of the nation-state and integration into the world market economy reduces self-sufficiency. The modern state also changes interaction in regard to control of local resources, based on reciprocal sharing of risks, and the local nature of community honor and prestige.[7] In Singapore, now that sections of the formerly poor are advancing, and with the meritocracy as the overarching ideology, the community of the poor is not cohesive. Families that have bettered themselves contract their ties to a small circle. They justify their withdrawal as an effect of their stage in the life cycle. They recognize the uncertainty of their achievements and the continued need to help out those closest to them when they are called upon to do so. But as they no longer extend such help to wider circles of kin or neighbors, very poor families have lost their supportive community.

Secure folk, in contrast, were keen on separating from their wider kin links from the day they married, and now they can attain this goal. They express their better living standard by living apart, while they continue to see relatives for emotional satisfaction. If they need to support their kin materially or emotionally, they can do so while living apart. Their greater access to resources allows the husband and wife to develop a strong marriage bond. As a result of real differences in freedom from dependence on relatives, higher incomes, and their prospects for the future, the nuclear family structure and a solid husband/wife bond are more frequently found among secure couples than among the poor.

In both class groups, women's responsibility for maintaining the family has increased. Homemaking has tended to become even more the sole work of the wife. Now that families have purchased small apartments of their own, the wife has acquired responsibilities for the upkeep of new consumer items. Child rearing is also more time-consuming owing to loss of help and the deepened parental concern with the rigorous state-imposed educational standards and tests that youngsters must pass. The burden of poor women increases as the family life cycle progresses and as traditional helpers find other duties and employment, move elsewhere, or die. For secure women added burdens and a new and more substantial role flow from their decision to attenuate ties with kin.

The social services that invest in labor redraw the stratification system to bring more workers deeply into the market economy and subject them to its demands. The differences in employment situation among my worker-interviewees are large. The positions in the labor process are being differentiated, but the system offers a new ideology as a standard by which to assess their place in it—the meritocracy, with equal opportunity to advance. Their behavior varies by class, but their explanations for their positions draw on the same categories. In these ways the new development program has integrated the panel families while maintaining class divisions. It seems likely that their offspring will maintain the same class ranking in the next generation. As members of households become directly linked to the market economy as consumers, debtors, and pensioners, wider ties to the local community based on mutual aid are weakening. At the same time, these exchanges stimulate the market economy and empower the state. Thus those services that invest in labor and integrate families into the commodity economy also assist the expansion of the capitalist economy.[8] These many changes in family lives at all class levels work in concert to enable even hard-pressed families to have a more "decent" life as measured by services and consumer goods. We can readily understand why the poor and people of modest means believe that public housing, a new school system, and small families give them more freedom. Small wonder that they accept the yoke of the market economy and view the social services as tools that liberate rather than oppress them. The market and centralized services integrate the full range of families into a single industrial way of life. But within this increasingly similar lifeway, their class-based options shape their goals. The couples we have met reveal the ways in which class position elaborates meaning and social ideals. The social services can both promote the capitalist system of production and legitimate the social order. Since they perpetuate Singapore's class system, the social services contribute to new forms of unity as well as to new divisions within the society.[9]

Whereas poor and secure families formed two types of Singapore families in phase 1, now they are variations on a recognizable theme. Families in the two class groups are constrained by similar economic and social institutions. They are still divided by their market positions, which affect their behavior and the meanings they assign to their actions, but the market has claimed a tighter hold on all of them. They aim for recognizably similar goals and attempt to use the same means to attain them: the public services of the second development stage. State-sponsored public services become means to alter family lives. They provide entrance into the market and the cultural categories that become the framework within which the public evaluates the state and its socioeconomic programs.

Notes

1. Introduction: Development and the Fabric of Life

1. Folker Frobel, Jurgen Heinrichs, and Otto Kreye, *The New International Division of Labour* (Cambridge: Cambridge University Press, 1979); Peter Lloyd, *A Third World Proletariat?* (London: George Allen & Unwin, 1982).

2. For political-economic analyses of the "newly industrialized countries" of Singapore, Hong Kong, South Korea, and Taiwan, see Eddy Lee, ed., *Export-Led Industrialisation and Development* (Geneva: International Labour Organisation, 1981); Frederic Deyo, ed., *The Political Economy of the New Industrialism* (Ithaca: Cornell University Press, 1987).

3. Cheah Hock Beng, "A Study of Poverty in Singapore" (academic exercise, University of Singapore, Department of Sociology, 1977); Harold L. Wilensky, *The Welfare State and Equality* (Berkeley: University of California Press, 1975).

4. Les Howard, "Work and Community in Industrializing India," forthcoming in *Social Structures: A Network Approach*, ed. Barry Wellman and S. D. Berkowitz (Cambridge: Cambridge University Press).

5. Alex Inkeles and D. H. Smith, *Becoming Modern* (Cambridge: Harvard University Press, 1974); Myron Weiner, ed., *Modernization: The Dynamics of Growth* (New York: Basic Books, 1966); Karen Anne Miller, "Modern Experience: The Family and Fertility in Six Nations" (Ph.D. diss., Stanford University, 1976).

6. For an overview of modernization and dependency theories, see Alejandro Portes, "On the Sociology of National Development: Theories and Issues," *American Journal of Sociology* 82 (1976): 55–85, and John Walton, "Theory and Research on Industrialization," in *Annual Review of Sociology*, vol. 13, ed. W. Richard Scott, pp. 89–108 (Palo Alto: Annual Reviews, 1987). Volker Bornschier, Christopher Chase-Dunn, and Richard Rubinson conceptualize economic power dependency in "Cross-National Evidence of the Effects of Foreign Investment and Aid on Economic Growth and Inequality: A Survey of Findings and a Reanalysis," *American Journal of Sociology* 84 (1978): 651–83.

7. See, e.g., Franz Schurmann, *Ideology and Organization in Communist China* (Berkeley: University of California Press, 1966). On the role of the state viewed theoretically, see J. P. Nettl, "The State as Conceptual Variable," *World Politics* 20 (1968): 559–92. The new nations are treated in Peter B. Evans, "Transnational Linkages and the Economic Role of the State: An Analysis of Developing and Industrialized Nations in the

Post–World War II Period," in *Bringing the State Back In,* ed. Peter B. Evans, Dietrich Rueschemeyer, and Theda Skocpol, pp. 192–226 (Cambridge: Cambridge University Press, 1985). On the state and women, see Mary Ruggie, *The State and Working Women* (Princeton: Princeton University Press, 1984).

8. Larissa Adler Lomnitz, *Networks and Marginality: Life in a Mexican Shantytown* (New York: Academic Press, 1977); Terence McGee, "Conservation and Dissolution in the Third World City: The 'Shanty Town' as an Element of Conservation," *Development and Change* 10 (1979): 1–22; Alejandro Portes and John Walton, *World Exchange and Domination: Essays in the Political Economy of Development* (New York: Academic Press, 1980).

9. In October 1986, a roundtable discussion at the Social Science History Conference focused on family strategies as a useful analytic tool for assessing the dynamics of family behavior. It was generally agreed that such a concept was most useful when it took into account divergent interests based on class, gender, and generation. My approach is also akin to what is called "practice" or microdevelopmental processes. See Sherry B. Ortner, "Theory in Anthropology since the Sixties," *Comparative Studies in Society and History* 26 (1984): 126–66; Bernard S. Cohn, "Anthropology and History in the 1980's," *Journal of Interdisciplinary History* 12 (1981): 227–52. The approach used here also borrows from the insights of the sociologist W. I. Thomas, who studied family adaptation and change among Polish families in Chicago (*The Polish Peasant in Europe and America: Monograph of an Immigrant Group* [Boston: R. G. Badger, 1918–20]), and of Glen H. Elder, Jr., "Families, Kin, and the Life Course: A Sociological Perspective," in *Review of Child Development Research,* ed. Ross Parke, vol. 7: *The Family,* pp. 80–136 (Chicago: University of Chicago Press, 1984).

10. Richard Edwards, *Contested Terrain* (New York: Basic Books, 1979); Harry Braverman, *Labor and Monopoly Capital* (New York: Monthly Review Press, 1974); C. Wright Mills, *White Collar: The American Middle Classes* (New York: Oxford University Press, 1956).

11. Data are given in Harry T. Oshima, "The International Comparison of Size Distribution of Family Incomes with Special Reference to Asia," *Review of Economics and Statistics* 44 (1962): 439–45; Felix Paukert, "Income Distribution at Different Levels of Development: A Survey of Evidence," *International Labour Review* 108 (1973): 97–125. For structural theory, see Richard Rubinson, "The World Economy and the Distribution of Income within States: A Cross-National Study," *American Sociological Review* 41 (1976): 638–59; Bornschier et al., "Cross-National Evidence," find mixed results. There is evidence that effective state policies can counterbalance the negative effects of foreign investment on equality and growth; see Richard Rubinson and Dan Quinlan, "Democracy and Social Inequality: A Reanalysis," *American Sociological Review* 42 (1977): 611–23.

12. Robert Bibb and William H. Form, "The Effects of Industrial, Occupational, and Sex Stratification on Wages in Blue-Collar Markets," *Social Forces* 55 (1977): 974–86; Barry Bluestone, W. M. Murphy, and M. Stevenson, *Low Wages and the Working Poor* (Ann Arbor: University of Michigan–Wayne State University, Institute of Labor and Industrial Relations, 1973). But see Alejandro Portes and Saskia Sassen-Koob, "Making It Underground: Comparative Material on the Informal Sector in Western Market Economies," *American Journal of Sociology* 93 (July 1987): 30–61.

13. Bluestone et al., *Low Wages.* A survey of British workers, however, found intersectoral mobility: M. R. Blackburn and M. Michael Mann, *The Working Class and the Labour Market* (London: Macmillan, 1979).

14. Hagen Koo, "Center–Periphery Relations of Marginalization: Empirical Analysis of the Dependency Model of Inequality in Peripheral Nations," *Development and Change* 12 (1981): 55–76.

15. Helen Safa, *The Urban Poor of Puerto Rico* (New York: Holt, Rinehart & Winston, 1974); Lisa Peattie, *The View from the Barrio* (Ann Arbor: University of Michigan Press, 1968), pp. 40–53.

16. Janet W. Salaff, *Working Daughters of Hong Kong* (Cambridge: Cambridge University Press, 1981). For comparable trends in the West both at an earlier stage and at present, see Louise A. Tilly and Joan W. Scott, *Women, Work, and Family* (New York: Holt, Rinehart & Winston, 1978).

17. M. Mies, "Capitalist Development and Subsistence Reproduction: Rural Women in India," *Bulletin of Concerned Asian Scholars* 12 (1980): 2–15; Guy Standing, *Labour Force Participation and Development*, 2d ed. (Geneva: International Labour Office, 1981), pp. 188–89.

18. Susan C. Bourque and Kay Barbara Warren, *Woman of the Andes* (Ann Arbor: University of Michigan Press, 1981); Sidney W. Mintz, "Men, Women, and Trade," *Comparative Studies in Society and History* 13 (1971): 20–28.

19. Standing, *Labour Force Participation*, chap. 6.

20. Hanna Papanek, "Education-Employment Linkages for Women: A Comparative Analysis of South and Southeast Asian Countries and Egypt," in *Women and Work in the Third World*, ed. Nagat El Sanabary, pp. 265–73 (Berkeley: University of California, Center for the Study, Education, and Advancement of Women, 1983). For North America, see Pat Connelly, *Last Hired, First Fired* (Toronto: Women's Press, 1978); Walter B. Watson and Ernest A. T. Barth, "Questionable Assumptions in the Theory of Social Stratification," *Pacific Sociological Review* 7 (Spring 1964): 10–16.

21. Michael Young and Peter Willmott, *The Evolution of a Community* (London: Routledge & Kegan Paul, 1963); Peter Willmott and Michael Young, *Family and Class in a London Suburb* (London: Routledge & Kegan Paul, 1960); Jane Humphries, "The Working Class Family, Women's Liberation, and Class Struggle: The Case of Nineteenth-Century British History," *Review of Radical Political Economy* 9 (Fall 1977): 25–41; Jack Wayne, "The Logic of Social Welfare in a Competitive Capitalist Economy," Working Paper no. 15 (University of Toronto, Department of Sociology, Structural Analysis Programme, 1980); Jacques Donzelot, *The Policing of Families* (New York: Pantheon, 1979).

22. Donzelot (*Policing of Families*) maintains that the family, while "outside the sociopolitical field," is a "mechanism" through which doctors, educators, and other so-called representatives of the state work with the wife to regulate "images" that extol the nuclear family as the ideal. Cf. Richard Sennett, "Exploding the Nuclear Family," *New York Times Book Review*, February 24, 1980, pp. 3, 39. For the birth-control movement as ideology, with pressure toward the nuclearization of families, see Diana Gittins, *Fair Sex: Family Size and Structure, 1900–1939* (London: Hutchinson, 1982).

23. Barry Wellman, "From Social Support to Social Network," in *Social Support: Theory, Research, and Applications*, ed. Irwin Sarason and Barbara Sarason, pp. 205–22 (The Hague: Martinus Nijhoff, 1985).

24. James C. Scott, *The Moral Economy of the Peasant* (New Haven: Yale University Press, 1976).

25. Mark S. Granovetter, *Getting a Job: A Study of Contacts and Careers* (Cambridge: Harvard University Press, 1974). See also Liviana Mostacci Calzavara, "Social Networks and Access to Jobs: A Study of Five Ethnic Groups in Toronto," Research Paper no. 145 (University of Toronto, Centre for Urban and Community Studies, November 1983), p. 13.

26. Elizabeth Bott, *Family and Social Network* (London: Tavistock, 1957); Young and Willmott, *Evolution of a Community*. Christopher Turner believes that occupation, geographical mobility, education, family life cycle stage, and cosmopolitan/local orientation all affect the connectedness of networks and the strength of the marital bond: "Conjugal Roles and Social Networks Re-examined," in *Sociology of the Family*, ed. Michael Anderson, pp. 233–46 (Harmondsworth: Penguin, 1967). See also Christine Oppong, *Marriage among a Matrilineal Elite: A Family Study of Ghanaian Civil Servants* (Cambridge: Cambridge University Press, 1974); Hannah Gavron, *The Captive Wife* (Harmondsworth: Penguin, 1970).

27. Bonnie G. Smith, *Ladies of the Leisure Class* (Princeton: Princeton University Press, 1981), p. 17 and pt. 3; Mary P. Ryan, *Cradle of the Middle Class: The Family in Oneida County, New York, 1790–1865* (New York: Cambridge University Press, 1981).

28. Glenn H. Elder, Jr., "Family History and the Life Course," in *Transitions: The Family and the Life Course in Historical Perspective*, ed. Tamara K. Hareven, pp. 17–64 (New York: Academic Press, 1978).

29. Roland J. Pennock, "Political Development, Political System, and Political Goods," *World Politics* 18 (1965): 415–34.

30. Paul Willis, *Profane Culture* (London: Routledge & Kegan Paul, 1978).

31. Department of Statistics, *Census of Population, 1980* (Singapore, 1981). Singapore Chinese speech groups include Cantonese, Hainanese, Hakka, Hokkien, Shanghainese, and Teochew. In 1970 Hokkien speakers predominated among the entire population (about 33%), followed by Teochew (17%) and Cantonese (13%). Malays were fourth (13%) and Indian Tamil speakers ranked fifth (4%) in the population. Other Chinese dialects account for most of the remainder (Department of Statistics, *Census of Population, 1970* [Singapore, 1971]).

32. Ivan H. Light, *Ethnic Enterprises in America* (Berkeley: University of California Press, 1972); John T. Omohundro, *Chinese Merchant Families in Iloilo: Commerce and Kin in a Central Philippines City* (Athens: Ohio University Press, 1981).

33. No more than 5% of Singapore marriages were interracial in 1966–1975 (Eddie C. Y. Kuo and Riaz Hassan, "Ethnic Intermarriage in a Multiethnic Society," in *The Contemporary Family in Singapore*, ed. Kuo and Aline K. Wong, pp. 168–88 [Singapore: Singapore University Press, 1979]).

34. The socioeconomic measuring stick that is the basis of the classification of families as "poor" and "secure" consists of the following scores. Socioeconomic status of the couple's parents: very poor, 1; average poor, 2; affluent, 3. Couple's educational level: illiterate, 1; primary, 2; secondary, 3; postsecondary, 4. Occupation of couple: marginal, 1; blue collar, 2; white collar, 3; professional, 4. Combined monthly income of couple (in Singapore dollars): S$300, 1; S$301–600, 2; S$601–900, 3; S$901–1,200, 4; S$1,200+, 5. The range of scores in phase 1 was 4.0–7.0 for the 17 very poor couples, 7.5–8.5 for the 41 semipoor couples, 9.0–10.5 for the 19 couples of modest means, and 11.0–16.0 for the 23 affluent couples.

35. Peter S. J. Chen, "Social Stratification in Singapore," Working Paper no. 12 (Department of Sociology, University of Singapore, 1972), Table 1.1.

36. The districts are Bukit Ho Swee (very poor families), Bukit Merah (semipoor and families of modest means), Queenstown (affluent), Sembawang (poor and secure in rural and suburban homes), Toa Payoh (semipoor and secure families).

37. Between 1960 and 1971 the divorce rate for non-Muslims in Singapore averaged 14 per 1,000 marriages, with no rising trend. Compare this rate with the 1969 divorce rate in the United States of 308 per 1,000 marriages and that in Japan of 91 per 1,000 marriages. The divorce files of the Singapore Supreme Court, 1960–1971, note that 45 percent of divorce seekers cited desertion as the main reason for divorce. We cannot, however, infer rates of desertion from this statistic. See Tai Ching Ling, "Divorce in Singapore," in *Contemporary Family in Singapore*, ed. Kuo and Wong, pp. 152, 163.

38. Singapore Family Planning and Population Board and National Statistical Commission, *Report of the First National Survey of Family Planning in Singapore, 1973* (Singapore, 1974), Table 2, p. 25.

39. In phase 1, 92 husbands were interviewed. Of the rest, three men were not living with their wives and five chose not to be interviewed, saying, "These are matters for women only." In phase 2, 42 men were interviewed. Of the rest, one woman was separating from her husband, and two men, both hawkers' assistants in very poor circumstances, refused interviews. I believe they felt too down and out to wish to discuss their work conditions.

2. State, Economy, and Social Services

1. Yeo Kim Wah, *Political Development in Singapore, 1945–1955* (Singapore: Singapore University Press, 1973).

2. Philippe Schmitter, "Still the Century of Corporatism?" in *The New Corporatism: Social-Political Structures in the Iberian World*, ed. Frederick B. Pike and Thomas Stritch (Notre Dame, Ind.: University of Notre Dame Press, 1974), pp. 94–95. The other main approaches consist of Marxist analyses of the economic class basis of the modern state, or instrumentalist explanations; studies of elites, whose interests are derived less from their class than from their organizational affiliations; and the interest-group tradition, also known as the pluralist view, which focuses on the origins, prevalence, policy interests, resource endowments, and strategies of associations that seek to influence governmental policy decisions. See Edward O. Lauman, "An Organizational Approach to State Policy Formation," *American Sociological Review* 50 (February 1985): 1–19.

3. Quoted in Chan Heng Chee, *The Dynamics of One-Party Dominance—The PAP at the Grass Roots* (Singapore: Singapore University Press, 1976), p. 132. See also Chan Heng Chee, *Singapore: The Politics of Survival, 1965–1967* (Kuala Lumpur: Oxford University Press, 1971); Seah Chee Meow, "Bureaucratic Evolution and Political Change in an Emerging Nation: A Case Study of Singapore" (Ph.D. diss., Victoria University of Manchester, 1971).

4. Chan, *Dynamics of One-Party Dominance*, pp. 202–6.

5. Ibid.; Sharon A. Carstens, *Chinese Associations in Singapore Society*, Occasional Paper no. 37 (Singapore: Institute of Southeast Asian Studies, 1975); Andrew W. Lind, *Nanyang Perspective: Chinese Students in a Multiracial Singapore* (Honolulu: University Press of Hawaii, 1974); "Tapping the World Market for Good University Teachers," *Singapore Bulletin* 8 (June 1980): 1–2.

6. Schmitter, "Still the Century of Corporatism?"

7. C. V. Devan Nair, "Trade Unions in Singapore (Model of an Alternative to Futility in a Developing Country)," in *Socialism That Works: The Singapore Way*, ed. Nair (Singapore: Federal Publications, 1976), p. 99.

8. Chua Beng Huat, "Singapore in 1981: Problems in New Beginnings," *Southeast Asian Affairs, 1982* (Singapore: Institute of Southeast Asian Studies and Heinemann Asia, 1982), pp. 315–55; Frederic C. Deyo, *Dependent Development and Industrial Order: An Asian Case Study* (New York: Praeger, 1981); Michael Heng Swee Hai, "The Singapore National Trades Union Congress and the People's Action Party: A Study of Ideology and Control in an Industrial Relations System" (M.Sc. thesis, London School of Economics and Political Sciences, 1981/82); Tan Ern Ser, "A Re-Appraisal of Singapore's Development: The Ideology and Policy of the Ruling Elites" (academic exercise, University of Singapore, Department of Sociology, 1978–79).

9. Theodore Geiger and Frances M. Geiger, *The Development Progress of Hong Kong and Singapore* (London: Macmillan, 1975); Lee Soo Ann, *Economic Growth and the Public Sector in Malaya and Singapore, 1948–1960* (Singapore: Oxford University Press, 1974); Lee Soo Ann, *Industrialization in Singapore* (Perth: Longmans, 1973); Seah Chee Meow, "The Bureaucracy and the Issues of Transition," in *Singapore: Society in Transition*, ed. Riaz Hassan, pp. 52–66 (Kuala Lumpur: Oxford University Press, 1976). See the annual reports of each board.

10. Robert Gamer, "Political Parties and Pressure Groups in Singapore," in *Modern Singapore*, ed. Ooi Jin Bee and Chiang Hai Ding, pp. 197–207 (Singapore: Singapore University Press, 1969); Chan Heng Chee, "The Political System and Political Change," in *Singapore*, ed. Hassan, pp. 30–51, describes the ways medical, educational, legal, and religious circles opposed, with little effect, the Abortion Bill and the Voluntary Sterilization Bill. See, generally, Terence J. Johnson, *Professions and Power* (London: Macmillan, 1977), pp. 45–46.

11. *Singapore Undergrad,* no. 8 (November–December 1974); *Awakening (Council News),* University of Singapore, mimeo, various issues 1974–75; Marek Souris, "Malaya: The Squatters' Plight and the Tasek Mara Experience" (Singapore, n.d), mimeo.

12. Seah Chee Meow, *Community Centres in Singapore: Their Political Involvement* (Singapore: Singapore University Press, 1973).

13. Lee, *Industrialization in Singapore;* Kunio Yoshihara, *Foreign Investment and Domestic Response: A Study of Singapore's Industrialization* (Singapore: Eastern Universities Press, 1976), p. 6.

14. Department of Statistics, *Report on the Census of Industrial Production, 1975* (Singapore, 1975), p. 7, and *Report . . . , 1979* (Singapore, 1979), p. 10, Table 3; speech by Dr. Ahmad Mattar, Minister-in-Charge and Chairman of Vocational and Industrial Training Board, at the Second Term of Office of the Commercial Training Advisory Committee, December 3, 1980, *Singapore Economic Bulletin* 8 (n.s.) (January 1981): 53–57.

15. "The New Economic Direction," *Singapore Bulletin* 8 (December 1979): 4–5; Goh Chok Tong (minister for Trade and Industry), "Restructuring the Economy through Higher Wages," speech at 47th annual dinner of Singapore Manufacturers Association, June 29, 1979, typescript; "Towards Higher Achievement," budget speech, March 1981; Lim Chee Onn, "The Industrial Development Strategy—The Whys and Wherefores," *Singapore Economic Bulletin* 6 (n.s.) (November 1979): 9–15; "Trade Union Delegates Pledge Their Support (to the New Economic Program)," *Singapore Economic Bulletin* 7 (n.s.) (December 1980): 44; Lim Chong Yah, *Economic Restructuring in Singapore* (Singapore: Federal Publications, 1984); D. Lim, "Industrial Restructuring in Singapore," Asian Employment Programme Working Paper (Bangkok: ARTEP, 1984).

16. Economic Development Board, *Annual Report,* 1979–80, p. 2.

17. Data on investors' share of output value are calculated from Department of Statistics, *Report on the Census of Industrial Production, 1975,* p. 12, Table 4; Economic Development Board, Annual Report, 1979–80, pp. 3, 7.

18. Minister of Trade and Industry and the Skills Development Fund," *Singapore Economic Bulletin* 6 (n.s.) (October 1979): 39; Economic Development Board, *Annual Report, 1979/80,* pp. 2, 24–26; "Speech by Dr. Ahmad Mattar," *Singapore Economic Bulletin* 8.

19. Interviews with NTUC officials, Singapore, 1981. "Retraining is not an easy process as it is difficult to persuade workers to be retrained" (editorial in *Labour News,* quoted in *Singapore Economic Bulletin* 6 [n.s.] [November 1979]: 52).

20. Chia Siow Yue, *Export Processing and Industrialization: The Case of Singapore* (Bangkok: International Labour Organization and Asian Regional Team for Employment Promotion, 1982), p. 40.

21. Ministry of Labour and National Statistical Commission, *Report on the Labour Force Survey of Singapore, 1975* (Singapore, 1976), p. 95; *Report of the Labour Force Survey, 1979* (Singapore, 1980), p. 99. These published data are grouped in seven income categories. In calculating the median gross monthly income for Chinese male and female employees in 1975, I made the following assumptions: Employees who were earning "under S$200" earned S$200; those who earned "S$1,500 and over" earned S$1,500; the midpoint of each income interval gave the median for that earning group. I followed similar assumptions in calculating the median earnings in 1979. In 1979 the upper open wage bracket was S$3,000 and over, which accounted for only 1 percent of the total Chinese male labor force and 0.2 percent of the Chinese female workers. Basic wages are earnings exclusive of overtime and are expressed in Singapore currency.

22. My estimated *median* for Chinese men in 1981 may be compared with the *mean* income for males of all ethnic groups, as found in the 1980 census, of S$677. The census may have counted all income, whereas I excluded overtime earnings from my estimated median. See Department of Statistics, *Census of Population, 1980,* release no. 7 (Singapore, 1981), p. 4.

23. The fast-growth electronics industry hired 66,000 workers in 1979, most of them women. See Economic Development Board, *Annual Report, 1979–80*, p. 18; G. P. Lim, "Factory Workers in Jurong" (academic exercise, University of Singapore, Department of Sociology, 1974); Linda Y. C. Lim, *Women Workers in Multinational Corporations: The Case of the Electronics Industry in Malaysia and Singapore*, Occasional Paper no. 9 (Ann Arbor: University of Michigan, Women's Studies Program, 1978).

24. P. Arumainathan, *Report on the Census of Population, 1970* (Singapore: Department of Statistics, 1973), vol. 1; Ministry of Labour, *Report on the Labour Force Survey of Singapore* (Singapore, 1975, 1979). The proportion of young women with children in the full-time labor force is lower.

25. Cheah Hock Beng, "A Study of Poverty in Singapore" (academic exercise, University of Singapore, Department of Sociology, 1977).

26. In calculating the median wage of Chinese women, I drew on the *Report on the Labour Force Survey of Singapore*, 1975 and 1979, and made the same assumptions in calculating the median wage for women as for men. See n. 21, above. My estimated median of $400 for Chinese women in 1981 may be compared with the mean income for women of all ethnic groups, as found in the 1980 census, of S$430, which appears to include overtime wages (*Census of Population, 1980*, p. 4).

27. The average starting wage is 27 percent higher in foreign electronics firms than in local firms in the same field (Pang Eng Fong and Linda Lim, *The Electronics Industry in Singapore: Structure, Technology and Linkages*, Research Monograph Series no. 7 [Singapore: University of Singapore, Economic Research Centre, 1977], pp. 28–29). According to unpublished Economic Development Board data for 1974 cited in Aw Siaw Peng, "The Role of the Singapore Government Agencies in Facilitating the Transfer of Technology by Multi-National Firms" (academic exercise, University of Singapore, Department of Economics and Statistics, 1977), p. 29, daily wages in the electronics industry ranged from S$4.44 for unskilled workers to S$10.36 for skilled workers; the range in the textile and garment industry was from S$3.67 to S$6.55. Wages in the male-dominated transport equipment industry ranged from S$6.23 to S$8.05.

28. Women constitute 44 percent of employees in the manufacturing sector, but only 3.3 percent received training by employers, according to Yu-foo Shoon in a seminar, "Women in Employment," cited in *Straits Times* (Singapore), January 12, 1981, p. 10.

29. The upgraded electronics industry now handles quality control for its branch firms in the region, and no longer sends the products to North America for checking. See Lenny Siegel, "Delicate Bonds: The Global Semiconductor Industry," *Pacific Research* 11 (1980): 11; Tan Suat Keng, "The Textile Industry in Singapore" (academic exercise, University of Singapore, Department of Economics and Statistics, 1978–79), pp. 13, 46.

30. Unpublished data on the upgraded electronics industry in Singapore, 1979–80, provided by Aline Wong.

31. Department of Statistics, *Yearbook of Statistics, 1979/80* (Singapore, 1981), Table 14.2, p. 223; *Ngee Ann Technical College Annual Report, 1979/80*; Yu Yee Shoon, "The Singapore Woman," in *Socialism That Works*, ed. Nair, p. 116.

32. V. V. Banaji Rao and M. K. Ramakrishnan, *Income Inequality in Singapore* (Singapore: Singapore University Press, 1980), p. 24. In the Gini ratio, 1.00 indicates the greatest degree of inequality, with 1 percent of the population owning all the assets, while 0 indicates complete equality, with no concentration of wealth. See also Iyanatul Islam and Colin Kirkpatrick, "Export-Led Development, Labour Market Conditions, and the Distribution of Income: The Case of Singapore" (National University of Singapore, n.d.), typescript; Islam and Kirkpatrick find a decline in the Gini ratio, and hence in inequality, from 1973 through 1981, the period covered by this study.

33. In 1980, 93 percent of the female homemakers had no more than primary schooling (*Census of Population, 1980*, p. 10).

34. For the main social security schemes adopted by other nations, see International Labour Organization, *The Cost of Social Security, 1958–60* (Geneva, 1964), p. 1. On the

basis of the ILO criteria, the amount Singapore spent on social security benefits as a percentage of GDP has risen: 1975, 3.0 percent; 1979, 4.5 percent. But compare Canada, 1974–75: 14.0 percent (International Labour Office, *World Labour Report* [Geneva, 1984], 1:211–12). For a broader definition of the "social wage," which includes such items as public housing, see Peter R. Kaim-Caudle, "Social Security: Cross-National Comparisons of the Systems and Levels," paper delivered at Symposium no. 11, IX World Congress of Sociology, Uppsala, Sweden, August 17, 1978; George F. Rorlich, "Social Policy and Income Distribution," in *Encyclopedia of Social Work* (Washington, D.C.: National Association of Social Workers, 1977), 11: 1463–74. Singapore would undoubtedly rank high if the social wage were calculated.

35. Dr. Ahmad Mattar, Acting Minister for Social Affairs, quoted in *Singapore Bulletin* 8 (May 1980): 8; Toh Chin Chye, "Free Health Services Could Mean Bankruptcy," *Straits Times* (Singapore), December 10, 1976.

36. Donald V. Kurtz, "The Rotating Credit Association: An Adaption to Poverty," *Human Organization* 32 (Spring 1973): 49–58.

37. *POSB Annual Report, 1979;* Conrad Raj, "Fostering the Saving Habit," *Singapore Business* 1 (February 1977): 28–31; *Singapore Bulletin* 8 (February 1980): 9.

38. In 1976 a minimum of 15 percent of the employee's income was matched by the employers. In 1981, 22 percent came from employees, 20.5 percent from employers. The employer pays the entire sum for employees who earn less than S$200. The depositor receives 6.5 percent interest on the CPF deposit. Funds deposited with the CPF are invested in government securities; the amount so invested was S$4 billion in October 1976 (Raj, "Fostering the Saving Habit").

39. James M. Malloy, *The Politics of Social Security in Brazil* (Pittsburgh: University of Pittsburgh Press, 1979).

40. Teh Cheang Wan, "Public Housing in Singapore: An Overview," in *Public Housing in Singapore: A Multi-Disciplinary Study,* ed. Stephen H. K. Yeh (Singapore: Singapore University Press, 1975), pp. 5–6; Barrington Kaye, *Upper Nanking Street, Singapore: A Sociological Study of Chinese Households Living in a Densely Populated Urban Area* (Singapore: University of Malaya Press, 1960).

41. Yeh, "Summary and Discussion," in *Public Housing,* ed. Yeh, p. 342; Alan F. C. Choe, "Urban Renewal," in ibid., pp. 97–116; Teh, "An Overview," in ibid., p. 13.

42. Iain Buchanan, *Singapore in Southeast Asia* (London: G. Bell, 1972), p. 242. Slum dwellers paid 13 percent, HDB dwellers 30 percent of their household budgets on utilities. Seventy-one percent of 7,200 resettled families surveyed in 1968 agreed that their expenditures had "changed for the worse" (Yeh, "Summary and Discussion," p. 356).

43. Arumainathan, *Report on the Census of Population, 1970,* Table 97, 2:208.

44. However, comparison of the residentially stable kampung community of Woodlands with an HDB project found limited neighborly contacts in both areas (Chang Chen-tung, cited in *Our Home* [Singapore: HDB, December 1980], p. 6).

45. In an HDB survey in 1973, 52 percent of relocated families stated that they enjoyed increased employment opportunity for women in their new housing (Yeh, "Summary and Discussion," p. 357).

46. Buchanan, *Singapore,* pp. 189–92; Riaz Hassan, *Families in Flats: A Study of Low-Income Families in Public Housing* (Singapore: Singapore University Press, 1977), pp. 85, 145.

47. Cheah, *Study of Poverty,* p. 93; Yeh, "Summary and Discussion," Table 2, p. 352.

48. HDB Sample Household Survey, 1973, in Yeh, "Summary and Discussion," p. 333 and Table 3; Chua Wee Meng and Ho Kun Ngiap, "Financing Public Housing," in *Public Housing in Singapore,* ed. Yeh, Tables 7 and 8, pp. 71–72.

49. Teh, "Public Housing," p. 9; Housing and Development Board, *Annual Report, 1979/80* (Singapore, 1980), p. 5. Thus 40 percent of all households live in homes of their own.

50. Couples can direct five-sixths of their monthly CPF allotment to HDB home

payments. The interest rate is low (6¼ percent for a maximum of 20 years), the property tax is reduced, and owners may resell their flats at a profit.

51. HDB Sample Household Survey, 1973, in Yeh, "Summary and Discussion," Table 1, p. 331; Housing and Development Board, *Annual Report, 1979/80*, pp. 53, 55. Figures pertain to rental and purchased apartments under HDB management.

52. According to an HDB survey, the average number of income earners in resettled households in 1973 increased with the size of the rented flat, a finding that suggests different stages in the family cycle (Yeh, "Summary and Discussion," Tables 6–7, pp. 344–45).

53. Judy Payne and Geoff Payne, "Housing Pathways and Stratification: A Study of Life Chances in the Housing Market," *Journal of Social Policy* 6 (1977): 129–56.

54. Chan, *Dynamics of One-Party Dominance*, pp. 91–93; Lennox Mills, *British Rule in East Asia* (London: Oxford University Press, 1942).

55. Fifty-six percent of all schools are run by the government; the remaining 44 percent are run by religious and other groups.

56. The school system of the 1970s is outlined in Department of Statistics, *Yearbook of Statistics, 1973/74* (Singapore, 1975), pp. 155–57; Saravan Gopinathan, *Towards a National System of Education in Singapore, 1945–73* (Singapore: Oxford University Press, 1973).

57. Goh Keng Swee and Education Study Team, *Report on the Ministry of Education, 1978* (Singapore: Ministry of Education, 1979), p. 1–1. Forty percent of school leavers were minimally competent in two languages; only 13 percent could read newspapers in both languages.

58. The ratio of academic secondary school students to technical students in 1979 was 8 to 1 (personal communication, Ministry of Education spokesman, January 9, 1981); 11 students were attending an academic stream for every student in a technical and commercial stream at the secondary level in 1973–74 (*Yearbook of Statistics, Singapore, 1973/74* [Singapore: Department of Statistics, n.d.], pp. 168–69).

59. *Straits Times* (Singapore), December 2, 1982.

60. Goh, *Report on the Ministry of Education*, pp. 3-5, 3-6.

61. "A Study of Dropouts" (academic exercise, University of Singapore, Department of Sociology, 1970), cited in Cheah, *Study of Poverty*, pp. 89–91. See generally Caroline Hodges Persell, *Education and Inequality* (New York: Free Press, 1977); Raymond S. Moore et al., *School Can Wait* (Provo, Utah: Brigham Young University Press, 1979).

62. The political implications were recognized by local educators. See the exchange between the Ministry of Education and the economists Linda Lim and Pang Eng Fong in *Straits Times*, January 1–April 4, 1981; "No Dispute about Objectives, but Are Methods Right?" *Straits Times*, April 4, 1981.

63. Richard Sennett and Jonathan Cobb, *The Hidden Injuries of Class* (New York: Vintage, 1973).

64. Singapore is the only Asian country with a doctor/population ratio approaching that recommended by the World Health Organization (one physician for every 1,000 persons). The ratio in Singapore is 1,336 persons for every registered doctor (Peter S. J. Chen and James Fawcett, eds., *Public Policy and Population Change in Singapore* [New York: Population Council, 1979], p. 69).

65. Michel Foucault, *Discipline and Punish: The Birth of the Prison* (New York: Vintage, 1979).

66. George G. Thomson and T. E. Smith, "Singapore: Family Planning in an Urban Environment," in *The Politics of Family Planning in the Third World*, ed. T. E. Smith, pp. 217–55 (London: George Allen & Unwin, 1973), discuss early PAP statements at p. 232; Ministry of Health, *Population and Trends* (Singapore, 1977), p. 11; *Economic Statistics of Singapore, 1980*, p. 43; Chang Chen-tung, *Fertility Transition in Singapore* (Singapore: Singapore University Press, 1974), pp. 4, 20.

67. Singapore Family Planning and Population Board (FPPB) and National Statistical

Commission, *Report of the First National Survey on Family Planning in Singapore, 1973* (Singapore, 1974), pp. 16, 25, 54.

68. Saw Swee-Hock, *Population Control for Zero Growth in Singapore* (Singapore: Oxford University Press, 1980); James T. Fawcett, "Singapore's Population Policies in Perspective," in *Public Policy and Population Change*, ed. Chen and Fawcett; Frank Ching, "Defusing A Fertility Bomb," *Asia Magazine*, December 29, 1974, pp. 26–28.

69. In 1975, delivery charges for the first child in the least expensive government hospital ward were S$60, but charges for the fifth were S$300. Prenatal visits were free for the first two births but cost $10 thereafter.

70. According to the 1973 FPPB survey, only 18 percent of women with two children were still in the labor force. Thus the number of women at risk of losing paid maternity leave is a small proportion of the female labor force (FPPB, *Report*, Table 9, p. 30). The NTUC won maternity leave for its female members, but these rights are now annulled for multiparous women.

71. *Parliamentary Debates, Republic of Singapore, Official Report*, 1969, vol. 29, col. 322, cited in Thomson and Smith, "Singapore: Family Planning," p. 249.

72. *Parliamentary Debates, Republic of Singapore, Official Report*, 1972, 32:150–51.

73. V. G. Kulkarni, "Designer Genes," *Far Eastern Economic Review*, September 8, 1983, pp. 23–24.

3. Introducing Poor Families

1. Concubinage was a permanent relationship that was recognized by society. Although the concubine was not accorded all the privileges of a married woman, the man had obligations toward her and their children.

2. Norbert F. Wiley, "The Ethnic Mobility Trip and Stratification Theory," *Social Problems* 15 (1967): 147–59.

3. On adoption, see David C. Buxbaum, ed., *Chinese Family Law and Social Change in Historical and Comparative Perspective* (Seattle: University of Washington Press, 1978).

4. See Arthur P. Wolf and Chieh-shan Huang, *Marriage and Adoption in China, 1845–1945* (Stanford: Stanford University Press, 1980), on the custom of adopting a daughter-in-law.

4. Poor Families in the Early Development Stage

1. The median is based on the basic preovertime wage, before the CPF pension is subtracted; for self-employed men with high overhead expenses, I calculate net earnings. In giving the average preovertime wage, I follow M. R. Blackburn and M. Mann, *The Working Class and the Labour Market* (London: Macmillan, 1979). The calculation of the national Singapore median wage in 1975 is based on the Ministry of Labour and National Statistical Commission, *Report on the Labour Force Survey of Singapore, 1975* (Singapore, 1976), p. 95. My assumptions in calculating the median wage are explained in chap. 2.

2. Two percent of poor men had no formal schooling, 81 percent had primary schooling, and 17 percent had some secondary education.

3. The public service, which cannot easily make a profit or pass on labor costs to consumers, is constrained by politics and the poverty of most public sectors. In this respect it resembles the periphery. The poor and secure men and women in my sample held positions in both sectors. The core-sector industries in which they worked included construction, communications (e.g., advertising for transnational corporations), manufacture of durable goods (e.g., electrical machinery, machine tools, transportation equip-

ment), manufacture of nondurable goods (e.g., petroleum), transportation (e.g., trucking related to construction, shipbuilding, and repair). In the peripheral sector they worked in communications (e.g., Singapore Telephone and Telegraph Corporation); entertainment and recreation; manufacture of durable goods (e.g., lumber and wood products, furniture, household goods); manufacture of nondurable goods (e.g., textile mill products, apparel); personal services; printing, paper, and allied products (e.g., newspapers); public administration (e.g., civil service, teaching); transportation (e.g., Singapore Bus Service, pedicab); utilities (e.g., Public Utilities Board); and retail and wholesale trade. E. M. Beck, Patrick M. Horan, and Charles M. Tolbert II compare several classifications in "Stratification in a Dual Economy: A Sectoral Model of Earnings Determination," *American Sociological Review* 43 (October 1978): 704–20.

4. I classify among the unskilled not only laborers and service workers (e.g., night watchman, bus conductor, domestic servant, waitress) but also people who made and sold food products and rattan ware. Among nontechnical resources I include a driver's license or car, an academic degree, clerical skills, nonmovable property (e.g., a market stall), and such nonindustrial skills as tailoring. Among skilled workers I include those with mechanical skills learned on the job, in a course, by an apprenticeship, or in higher education (only secure men had such skills; see chaps. 5 and 6), and those drivers whose work entailed some degree of skill, such as crane operator.

5. The urge to become a wealthy overseas merchant stimulated Southern Chinese emigration to Singapore. See Chen Ta, *Emigrant Communities in South China* (New York: Institute of Pacific Relations, 1939); E. R. Willmott, "Review of 'Overseas Chinese in Southeast Asia—A Russian Study' by N. A. Simoniya," *Pacific Affairs* 36 (Fall 1963): 317–20; W. F. Wertheim, "East Asia," in *East-West Parallels: Sociological Approaches to Modern Asia* (The Hague: W. Van der Hoeve, 1964), pp. 39–82; John Omohundro, *Chinese Merchant Families in Iloilo* (Athens: Ohio University Press, 1981; Manila: University of the Philippines Press, 1981). Today self-employment is viewed as a form of individualism: workers trade off income for job autonomy, to avoid "alienation." Moreover, informal-sector employees may earn higher wages than formal-sector workers, who are unable to demand a family wage. See A. K. Sen, *Employment, Technology, and Development: A Study Prepared for the International Labour Office within the Framework of the World Employment Programme* (Oxford: Clarendon Press, 1975).

6. Occupational skills and resources are cross-classified with industrial sector. As my sample included no men in core-sector industries with nontechnical skills, I cannot directly compare men with real property or nontechnical skills in the peripheral and core sectors.

7. On the banding together of men with low levels of education in an all-male setting, see L. L. LeMasters, *Blue-Collar Aristocrats* (Madison: University of Wisconsin Press, 1975). Bonding is also characteristic of men with dangerous jobs; see Jack Haas, "Learning Real Feelings: A Study of High Steel Ironworkers' Reactions to Fear and Danger," in *Shaping Identity in Canadian Society*, ed. Jack Haas and William Shaffir, pp. 227–46 (Scarborough, Ont.: Prentice-Hall of Canada, 1979); Alvin Gouldner, *Patterns of Industrial Bureaucracy* (Glencoe, Ill.: Free Press, 1954). Ethnic integration is also fostered by subcontracting; see Noeleen Heyzer, "The Formation of an Industrial Workforce" (M. A. thesis, University of Singapore, 1972). On early industrializing firms, see Craig R. Littler, *The Development of the Labour Process in Capitalist Society* (London: Heinemann, 1982).

8. Only 10 poor men (17 percent) went to night school or in other ways continued their education after leaving primary school. Eight of them pursued basic courses, and only two took specialized courses in their trades.

9. In her study of the British working class, Janet Askham refers to forced job changes as "deprivation" because they never benefited the workers: *Fertility and Deprivation* (Cambridge: Cambridge University Press, 1975).

10. Many began work as helpers to self-employed venders. The informal sector is often

easy to enter, and it serves as a learning ground for entrepreneurship. But informal rules of conduct must be learned, and they may not easily be transferred to formal-sector jobs. See International Labour Office, *Employment, Incomes, and Equality: A Strategy for Increasing Productive Employment in Kenya* (Geneva, 1972); Sarah Teilhet-Waldorf, "Self-Employed of Bangkok: Urban Poor or Urban Entrepreneur?" in *Poverty and Social Change in Southeast Asia*, ed. O. Mehmet, pp. 82–99 (Ottawa: University of Ottawa Press, 1979).

11. Thirty-seven poor men were asked directly. Additional information about the rest suggests that they, too, obtained their phase 1 jobs through close ties: most were apprenticed as youths, kin were in the same line of work, or everyone in their community worked in the same industry (such as the shipyards in Sembawang).

12. The 178 very poor and 347 semipoor husbands, wives, and their siblings (including stepsiblings) whose education I was able to ascertain attained the following years of schooling:

	Primary	Secondary	Pre-university	University
Very poor	84%	15%	—	—
Semipoor	66	32	1%	2%

"Secondary" includes from one to four years of school, and may include O-level exams. "Pre-university" includes courses leading to A-level exams or the exams themselves; less than 1 percent of the very poor had taken such courses. "University" refers to work in any postsecondary school, including polytechnic and teachers' training courses.

13. See the following works by Mark S. Granovetter: *Getting a Job: A Study of Contacts and Careers* (Cambridge: Harvard University Press, 1974); "The Strength of Weak Ties," *American Journal of Sociology* 78, no. 6 (1973); "The Strength of Weak Ties: A Network Theory Revisited," *Sociological Theory* 1 (1983): 201–33.

14. Twenty-five poor women worked full-time, five part-time; twenty-eight were housewives.

15. Ten of the full-time workers earned less than S$199; thirteen earned S$200–299; two earned more than S$300.

16. See Maurice Freedman, *Lineage Organization in Southeast China* (London: Athlone, 1958); Olga Lang, *Chinese Family and Society* (New Haven: Yale University Press, 1946).

17. See Myron Cohen, "Development Process in the Chinese Domestic Group," in *Family and Kinship in Chinese Society*, ed. Maurice Freedman, pp. 21–36 (Stanford: Stanford University Press, 1970), and *House United, House Divided: The Chinese Family in Rural Taiwan* (New York: Columbia University Press, 1976); Maurice Freedman, *Chinese Family and Marriage in Singapore*, Colonial Research Studies 20 (London: Her Majesty's Stationery Office, 1957).

18. I count as isolated a wife with neolocal residence who visits kin at most once a week. The numbers of full-time wage earners and housewives who did not live with their kin were as follows:

	Full-time wage earners	Homemakers
Stem or extended family	15	9
Neolocal residence		
Isolates	2	12
Interactors	8	12
Total	25	33

19. Among the poor, 37 percent who resided in HDB flats lived with at least one elder, compared with 56 percent of families in other forms of housing.

20. On exchanges of money, services, and emotional support among poor women in North America, see Carol Stack, *All Our Kin* (New York: Harper & Row, 1974).

21. Among the very poor husbands, three shared some household tasks and 13 helped a little; none did a lot. Among the semipoor husbands, six did a lot, 18 shared some tasks, and 15 did a little.

22. See Melvin L. Kohn and Carmi Schooler, "Class, Occupation, and Orientation," *American Sociological Review* 34 (1969): 659–78, and "Occupational Experience and Psychological Functioning: An Assessment of Reciprocal Effects," *American Sociological Review* 38 (1973): 97–113; Basil Bernstein, *Class, Codes, and Control* (New York: Schocken, 1974).

23. See Joseph Pleck, "Men's Family Work: Three Perspectives and Some New Data," *Family Coordinator* 28 (October 1979): 481–88; Virginia D. Abernathy, "Social Network and Response to the Maternal Role," *International Journal of Sociology of the Family* 3 (March 1973): 86–92; Rose Laub Coser, "The Complexity of Roles as Seedbed of Individual Autonomy," in *The Idea of Social Structure: Papers in Honor of Robert K. Merton,* ed. Lewis Coser, pp. 237–63 (New York: Harcourt Brace Jovanovich, 1975); Laura Lein, "Male Participation in Home Life: Impact of Social Supports and Breadwinner Responsibility on the Allocation of Tasks," *Family Coordinator* 28 (October 1979): 489–95.

24. On the ways families transmit attitudes toward the home division of labor, see S. Hesselbart, "Does Charity Begin at Home? Attitudes toward Women, Household Tasks, and Household Decision-making," paper presented at the annual meeting of the American Sociological Association, New York, August 1976, cited in Carolyn S. Perrucci et al., "Determinants of Male Family-Role Performance," *Psychology of Women Quarterly* 3 (Fall 1978): 53–66; Jean Lipman-Blumen, "How Ideology Shapes Women's Lives," *Scientific American* 226 (1972): 34–42.

25. For a similar finding in a mining community, see Meg Luxton, *More than a Labour of Love* (Toronto: Women's Press, 1980).

26. See Lillian Rubin, *Worlds of Pain* (New York: Basic Books, 1977), pp. 86–90; Mirra Komarovsky, *Blue-Collar Marriage* (New York: Random House, 1967), p. 34.

27. Robert F. Winch, *The Modern Family* (New York: Holt, Rinehart & Winston, 1963). See also Robert A. Levine, Nancy H. Klein, and Constance R. Owen, "Father-Child Relationships and Changing Life-Styles in Ibadan, Nigeria," in *The City in Modern Africa,* ed. Horace Miner (London: Pall Mall Press, 1967), pp. 224–26.

28. Rubin, *Worlds of Pain,* p. 182. See also Glen H. Elder, Jr., *Children of the Great Depression: Social Change in Life Experience* (Chicago: University of Chicago Press, 1974), chap. 8.

29. Some studies emphasize that husbands of employed wives spend more hours a week doing housework and caring for children than do husbands of nonemployed wives. However, the number of hours is small compared with the total amount of domestic labor entailed. Joseph H. Pleck and Linda Lang found that such husbands spend about 1.8 more hours a week doing housework and 2.7 more hours a week in child care, by far the more pleasurable task: "Men's Family Role: Its Nature and Consequence," working paper (Wellesley: Wellesley College Center for Research on Women, 1978). According to exchange theory, sharing in the domestic realm increases as wives' incomes rise, or where they are "committed to work." See R. A. Berk and S. F. Berk, *Labor and Leisure at Home* (Beverly Hills, Calif.: Sage, 1979); R. Blood and R. Hamblin, "The Effects of the Wife's Employment on the Family Power Structure," *Social Forces* 36 (1958): 347–52; R. Blood and D. Wolfe, *Husbands and Wives* (New York: Free Press, 1960); C. Safilios-Rothschild, "The Influence of the Wife's Degree of Work Commitment upon Some Aspects of Family Organization and Dynamics," *Journal of Marriage and the Family* 32 (1970): 681–91. G. Farkas, however, found no relationship between the wife's wages and the husband's domestic assistance; see "Education, Wage Rates, and the Division of Labor between Husband and Wife," *Journal of Marriage and the Family* 38 (1976): 473–83.

30. Hesselbart stresses the close relationship between men's education and hours of

housework ("Does Charity Begin at Home?"). LeMasters notes that men who work in a setting that includes women are more flexible in their sex-role concepts than are men who work in male settings (*Blue-Collar Aristocrats*). See also Mary Lindenstem Walshok, *Blue-Collar Women* (New York: Doubleday, 1981).

31. Of the 17 very poor couples, 13 had little communication and none had a great deal. Of the 41 semipoor couples, 13 communicated a little, 17 some, and 10 a lot (information is lacking on one couple).

32. Seventy-one percent of the poor HDB dwellers lived in one-room or one-room-improved flats. Those who had larger flats lived with kin.

33. American working-class couples also depend on the husband's wages for home purchase even when the wives work; see Richard Coleman, "Husbands, Wives, and Other Earners: Notes on the Family Income Assembly Line," Working Paper no. 48 (Boston: Joint Center for Urban Studies of Harvard and M.I.T., 1978).

34. Kathleen Gerson, *Hard Choices: How Women Decide about Work, Career, and Motherhood* (Berkeley: University of California Press, 1985) describes the contingent nature of women's labor-force participation: its dependence on circumstances and situation.

35. Schools in industrial capitalist societies promote individual competition; the performance ethic subordinates other emotions to the desire to accumulate the society's symbols of achievement. See Herbert Marcuse, *Eros and Civilization: A Philosophical Inquiry into Freud* (New York: Vintage, 1962). See also Frank Musgrove, *The Family, Education and Society* (London: Routledge & Kegan Paul, 1960), p. 13.

36. My interviewers and I spoke with wives and husbands separately. When the interviewer noted discrepancies in a couple's answer, she discussed responses at greater length in an effort to obtain a single view. If discrepancies persisted, we coded couples on the higher level of desired schooling; when one spouse set a specific level while the other gave a vague "As high as possible," I coded the couple on the specific level of education. Of the 17 very poor couples, 7 hoped for secondary schooling, 2 hoped for postsecondary or pre-university education, only one aimed for higher, and 7 either did not know or vaguely stated, "As much education as possible." Of the 39 semipoor couples who discussed educational goals for their children, 12 named secondary school, 3 postsecondary education, 4 a university or polytechnic school, and as many as 20 held vague goals or didn't know.

37. Melvin L. Kohn, *Class and Conformity: A Study of Values* (Homewood, Ill.: Dorsey, 1969), describes comparable values in American working-class families.

38. See Mirra Komarovsky, *Blue-Collar Marriage*, p. 34.

39. See Raymond S. Moore et al., *School Can Wait* (Provo, Utah: Brigham Young University Press, 1979); Joey Noble, "Fitting the Child to the Classroom: What Mothers Do," Ontario Institute for Studies in Education, typescript (1982); Miriam E. David, "The Family-Education Couple: Towards an Analysis of the William Tyndale Dispute," in *Power and the State*, ed. Gary Littlejohn, Barry Smart, John Wakefield, and Nira Yuval-Davis, pp. 158–95 (London: Croom Helm, 1978).

40. At an early stage of British industrialization, skilled craftsmen instilled in their apprentices a drive for family uplift that was not matched by men without such training. This is a comparable group. See Peter Bailey, "'Will the Real Bill Banks Please Stand Up?' Towards a Role Analysis of Mid-Victorian Working-Class Respectability," *Journal of Social History* 12 (1978): 336–53; Geoffrey Crossick, "The Labour Aristocracy and Its Values," *Victorian Studies* 19 (March 1976): 301–28.

41. Some demographers study "desired" or "ideal" family size at the time a couple begins family building. In developing nations, this measure cannot easily be translated into a predictable fertility outcome. Many people want children of a particular sex and readjust their desired family size as the children are born. Others do not believe that fertility is under their control. See Philip M. Hauser, "Population and Family Planning Programs: A Review Article," *Demography* 4 (1967): 397–414; J. M. Stycos and Kurt W. Back, *The Control of Human Fertility in Jamaica* (Ithaca: Cornell University Press, 1964);

Elena Yu and William T. Liu, *Fertility and Kinship in the Philippines* (Notre Dame: University of Notre Dame Press, 1980), p. 76. We posed our questions on intended family size when parents had begun to bear children and made some attempt at fertility control. When husband and wife differed as to their intended family size, we questioned them further until a common figure that represented their most likely family size emerged. See Norman B. Ryder and Charles P. Westoff, "Relationships among Intended, Expected, Desired, and Ideal Family Size: United States, 1965," *Population Research* 3 (March 1969).

42. See Peter H. Lindert, *Fertility and Scarcity in America* (Princeton: Princeton University Press, 1978), pp. 181–215. In addition to the short-term or direct costs, writers refer to the costs of educating children to higher levels as long-term or economic costs, which historically increased when children's entry into productive roles was delayed. Few of the poor referred to these long-term costs of having children. See also Judith Blake, "Family Size and the Quality of Children," *Demography* 18 (November 1981): 421–42.

43. See Esther N. Goody, "Forms of Pro-Parenthood: The Sharing and Substitution of Parental Roles," in *Production and Reproduction: A Comparative Study of the Domestic Domain*, ed. John Rankine Goody, pp. 311–45 (Cambridge: Cambridge University Press, 1976); Anne K. Wilson, "Poverty and Fertility: The Role of Unemployment and Kinship Networks on Birth Planning," revised paper delivered at the annual meeting of the Population Association of America, Boston, 1985.

44. See Nancy E. Williamson, *Sons or Daughters* (Beverly Hills, Calif.: Sage, 1976); Yu and Liu, *Fertility and Kinship*, chap. 10.

45. Lack of a long-term career ladder leads many men to stress luck in their work lives. They will often chance sexual relations without expecting a birth, or a birth hoping for the child of the right sex. See Lee Rainwater, *Family Design: Marital Sexuality, Family Size, and Contraception* (Chicago: Aldine, 1965); Janet Askham, *Fertility and Deprivation* (Cambridge: Cambridge University Press, 1975).

46. The opportunity costs of bearing children rose for women when the location of productive work in factories forced a choice between wage labor and homemaking. This process is traced historically in Louise Tilly and Joan Scott, *Women, Work, and the Family* (New York: Holt, Rinehart & Winston, 1978). See also Stanley Kupinsky, ed., *The Fertility of Working Women* (New York: Praeger, 1977); Guy Standing, *Labour Force Participation and Development* (Geneva: International Labour Office, 1981), pp. 165–206.

47. See A. J. Jaffe and K. Azumi, "The Birth Rate and Cottage Industries in Underdeveloped Countries," *Economic Development and Cultural Change* 9 (1960): 52–63; J. M. Stycos and R. H. Weller, "Female Working Roles and Fertility," *Demography* 4 (1967): 210–17.

48. On family-wide fertility decisions in the Philippines, see Yu and Liu, *Fertility and Kinship*. On the importance of the *jia* (the Chinese economic family, which includes kin and may be larger than the household) in Taiwan reproductive and other decision making, see Susan Greenhalgh, "Networks and Their Nodes: Urban Society on Taiwan," *China Quarterly*, September 1984; Arthur P. Wolf and Chieh-shan Huang, *Marriage and Adoption in China, 1845–1945* (Stanford: Stanford University Press, 1980).

49. See Rita S. Gallin, "Mothers-in-Law and Daughters-in-Law: Intergenerational Relations within the Chinese Family in Taiwan," *Journal of Cross-Cultural Gerontology* 1 (1986): 31–50.

50. The couples' opinions on Singapore's population and the disincentives are tabulated below:

	Singapore overpopulated	Disincentives
Agree	42	34
Some reservation	3	13
Disagree	5	5
No opinion	8	6

51. On the ways people account for their decisions, see Hans Gerth and C. Wright Mills, *Character and Social Structure: The Psychology of Social Institutions* (New York: Harcourt, Brace & World, 1964), pp. 114–20.

5. Introducing Secure Families

1. On adoption, see David C. Buxbaum, ed., *Chinese Family Law and Social Change in Historical and Comparative Perspective* (Seattle: University of Washington Press, 1978).

2. On the Chinese concept of face, see Hu Hsien Chin, "The Chinese Concepts of Face," *American Anthropologist* 46 (January–March 1946): 45–66, and John Saari, "Breaking the Hold of Tradition: The Self-Group Interface in Transitional China," in *Social Interaction in Chinese Society,* ed. Sidney L. Greenblatt et al., pp. 29–66 (New York: Praeger, 1982), esp. pp. 33–37. On how face can cement obligations between unequal parties, see Kwang-Kuo Hwang, "Face and Favor: The Chinese Power Game," *American Journal of Sociology* 92 (January 1987): 944–74.

6. Secure Families in the Early Development Stage

1. I have information on the jobs held by 40 fathers; 36 had had solid jobs.

2. Secure men had attained the following levels of education: 2 percent, none; 19 percent, primary; 57 percent, secondary; 21 percent, postsecondary.

3. See John T. Omohundro, *Chinese Merchant Families in Iloilo: Commerce and Kin in a Central Philippines City* (Athens: Ohio University Press, 1981), chap. 6; Norbert F. Wiley, "The Ethnic Mobility Trap and Stratification Theory," *Social Forces* 15 (1967): 147–59.

4. In Robert K. Merton's terminology, these men hold "local" perspectives (*Social Theory and Social Structure* [Glencoe, Ill.: Free Press, 1957], pp. 387–420).

5. Merton (ibid.) calls men who highly value ties outside the community "cosmopolitans."

6. William Watson refers to men whose occupational mobility has ended as "blocked spiralists" ("Social Mobility and Social Class in Industrial Communities," in *Closed System and Open Minds,* ed. Max Gluckman, pp. 129–57 [Chicago: Aldine, 1964]).

7. One-third of the secure men took some higher adult education course. Only two men attended basic literacy classes.

8. See Harold L. Wilensky, "Orderly Careers and Social Participation: The Impact of Work History on the Social Integration of the Middle Mass," *American Sociological Review* 26 (1961): 521–39.

9. Secure men averaged 2.8 jobs; 19 percent had held five or more jobs by my phase 1 interviews.

10. See Mark S. Granovetter, *Getting a Job: A Study of Contacts and Careers* (Cambridge: Harvard University Press, 1974).

11. I am speaking here of the 24 secure men about whom I have information. Information is lacking on how 18 got their phase 1 jobs. The 17 men who got work without a personal introduction answered ads or made direct personal applications.

12. See Liviana Mostacci Calzavera, "Social Networks and Access to Job Opportunities," Ph.D. diss., University of Toronto, 1982.

13. Among the women who worked full-time, 2 earned less than S$199 a month, 14 earned S$200–299, and 11 earned S$300 or more.

14. Of the wives of modest means, 79% worked full-time; 52% of the affluent wives did so.

15. Of the 25 women who lived with kin, 20 worked full-time. Of the 12 homemakers, 7 had their own apartments.

16. See Melvin L. Kohn and Carmi Schooler, "Class, Occupation, and Orientation," *American Sociological Review* 34 (1969): 657–78.

17. Studies on North American families' household tasks similarly find few social-class differences. See Shelley Coverman, "Gender, Domestic Labor Time, and Wage Inequality," *American Sociological Review* 48 (October 1983): 623–37.

18. Of the 19 husbands of modest means, 3 shared "a lot" of domestic tasks, 9 helped "somewhat," 7 did "a little." Of the 23 affluent husbands, the comparable figures are 4, 5, and 14.

19. See Constantina Safilios-Rothschild, "The Influence of the Wife's Degree of Work Commitment upon Some Aspects of Family Organization and Dynamics," *Journal of Marriage and the Family* 32 (1970): 681–91; R. B. Bryson et al., "The Professional Pair: Husband and Wife Psychologists," *American Psychologist* 31 (1976): 10–16; Karen Giffin, "Opportunities and Ideologies: Women in High Status Professions in Bahia, Brazil," Ph.D. diss., University of Toronto, 1976.

20. See Peter L. Berger and Hansfried Kellner, "Marriage and the Construction of Reality," in *Recent Sociology,* ed. Hans Peter Dreitzel (New York: Macmillan, 1970), 2: 49–72.

21. Stephen Edgell argues that while the decision making of British middle-class couples appears on the surface to be egalitarian, the husband assumes the major decision-making role in matters that concern his career (*Middle-Class Couples: A Study of Segregation, Domination, and Inequalities in Marriage* [London: G. Allen & Unwin, 1980]).

22. The majority of affluent couples (22) both shared leisure and enjoyed good communication, and modal patterns were similar for couples in both social sectors: 9 couples of modest means, 13 affluent couples. The next most prevalent pattern, but far less frequent (11 couples), was separate leisure with some communication: 7 couples of modest means, only 4 affluent couples. Least prevalent overall (8 couples) was the experience of separate leisure and little communication (3 couples of modest means, 5 affluent couples).

23. Of the 19 couples of modest means, 3 hoped for secondary schooling; 1 hoped for postsecondary, pre-university education; 7 aimed for university or polytechnic training; and 8 did not know or vaguely wanted their children to have "as much education as possible." Of the 21 affluent couples who discussed the subject, 5 named secondary school, 4 postsecondary education, 10 a university or polytechnic school, and only 2 did not know or were vague ("as much as possible").

24. See David M. Schneider and Raymond T. Smith, *Class Differences and Sex Roles in American Kinship and Family Structure* (Englewood Cliffs, N.J.: Prentice-Hall, 1973).

25. Only one secure woman had undergone a tubal ligation by phase 1.

26. The couples' opinions on Singapore's population and the disincentives are tabulated below:

	Singapore overpopulated	Disincentives
Agree	27	24
Some reservation	4	6
Disagree	1	7
No opinion	10	5

9. Singapore Society in the Advanced Development Stage: Two Families or One?

1. Two points on comparisons are in order. First, the comparisons between phase 1 and 2 respondents in this chapter refer solely to the 45 panel families who were inter-

viewed in both phases; they exclude the rest of the baseline families. As the 45 panel couples form only part of the original sample, there are some differences between the entire phase 1 set of respondents and the subsample of the 45. Average income levels and homeownership differ slightly, for example, as described in chap. 1. Second, as my goal throughout has been to see how the development project has affected categories of people, I have retained the phase 1 categories of all individuals, even though a small number could be reclassified. Although some poor couples' income now greatly exceeds that of the past, they remain the group called "poor." I kept the ranking over time consistent to facilitate the comparison of changes in the fates of people of particular groups.

2. The 1975 median wage was estimated at S$319, the 1981 median wage at S$600 (see chap. 2, n. 22). In phase 1, 15 panel men earned less than the national median wage, but by phase 2 only seven of them earned under the median wage of 1981.

3. In order to trace improvements in the wages of men by their phase 1 economic position, I keep constant their position in the peripheral sector. However, only two men in the entire panel changed sector; they moved from the periphery to the core. None made the reverse shift from core to periphery.

4. John Clammer, "Peripheral Capitalism and Urban Order: 'Informal Sector' Theories in the Light of Singapore's Experience" (National University of Singapore, typescript, n.d.), emphasizes the resilience of the informal sector, despite the state strategy that opposes such activities.

5. Lester Thurow, *Generating Inequality* (New York: Basic Books, 1975), stresses that individuals' wages are based not on their own qualities but on the jobs they hold, which are assigned rates according to normative considerations.

6. I refer to the phase 2 jobs of 13 of the 16 poor men who changed jobs. Information about job contacts is lacking for three other job changers.

7. Randall Collins maintains that increased formal education since World War II has not always raised skill levels in North America, but may simply inflate and make more uniform the basic requirements (*The Credential Society* [New York: Academic Press, 1979]). See Chan Peng Fun, "The 'Diploma Disease' in Singapore: A Sociological Study of the Significance of Paper Qualifications" (academic exercise, University of Singapore, Department of Sociology, 1978–79).

8. Compare a study by Lee Rainwater, which examines the relationship between the level of earnings of Americans in 1969, views of their own deprivation, and assessments of others' status: *What Money Buys: Inequality and Social Meanings of Income* (New York: Basic Books, 1975). See also Jennifer L. Hochschild, *What's Fair? American Beliefs about Distributive Justice* (Cambridge: Harvard University Press, 1981). In W. G. Runciman's terms, workers compare themselves with others who have done better, and feel relatively deprived: *Relative Deprivation and Social Justice* (Harmondsworth: Penguin, 1972).

9. Seven secure panel men took courses as adults even before phase 1. In addition, over the interphase four men in core-sector jobs underwent skills upgrading; three of these men had never taken adult education courses before.

10. Rosabeth Moss Kanter describes the emotional solace workers get from dead-end jobs as a displacement of their goals: *Men and Women of the Corporation* (New York: Free Press, 1977). On the spread of new religions in Singapore, see Lincoln Kaye and V. G. Kulkarni, "A Queue of Christians," *Far Eastern Economic Review*, January 12, 1984; Ruth-Inge Heinze, "Coping Mechanisms in a Multi-Ethnic and Multi-Religious Society: The Case of Singapore," paper presented at the IXth International Congress of Anthropological and Ethnological Sciences, Vancouver, August 1983.

11. The experiences of the panel women over time show that the full-time workers were not likely to change their labor force position. Of the 20 panel women who worked full time in phase 1, 16 were still full-time workers and only four had become housewives. The three women who worked part-time in phase 1 continued to do so in phase 2, although one woman upgraded her earnings by taking a second part-time job. The major

change occurred in the increase in part-time workers. Of the 22 phase 1 housewives in the panel, 11 entered the labor force, only three as full-time workers. As many as eight have become new part-time workers.

12. The method of estimating the 1981 median women's wage is discussed in chap. 2, n. 26. Of the 20 full-time employed women, four poor and one secure woman earned under S$399, two poor and two secure women earned S$400 to S$499, and five poor and six secure women earned over S$500.

13. A study of electronic assemblers in Singapore in 1980 found that only 16 percent of the female labor force in this industry held lower-level supervisory posts (Aline K. Wong, personal communication). For the process of upgrading rank-and-file workers to become lower-level supervisors in Taiwan, see Lydia Kung, *Factory Women in Taiwan* (Ann Arbor: UMI Research Press, 1983). Kung also reports the relatively low wages, limited authority, and lack of security of the lower-level supervisory women workers (line leaders) in electronics factories in Taiwan (pp. 100–108).

14. Of the 21 panel women with less than primary 6 education, only six are full-time employees. In contrast, six of the ten with full primary education and eight of the 14 with at least secondary education were working full-time in phase 2.

15. The starting wages of women in the peripheral-sector textile and garment industries, for instance, were considerably lower than those of the core-sector optical instrument maker and electronics equipment assembler in both 1976 and 1980. See Chia Siow Yue, "Export Processing and Industrialization: The Case of Singapore" (Bangkok: International Labour Organization and Asian Regional Team for Employment Promotion, 1982), p. 41 (mimeo).

16. Thirugnanam Thamayanthi, "Discrimination by Race and Sex in the Labour Market: A Study of the Literature and Its Relevance to Singapore" (academic exercise, Singapore University, Department of Economics and Statistics, 1978–79), p. 65.

17. A manufacturer of quality garments for export informed me that he was able to hire home-based seamstresses to supplement his workshop staff in the late 1970s because by that time many housewives had working experience.

18. For a similar observation on Canada, see Patricia Connelly, *Last Hired, First Fired* (Toronto: Women's Press, 1978). I call the couple's joint net earnings from the main jobs of both husband and wife after CPF is withdrawn the "basic take-home pay." Because my measure of social class includes more than income variables, it may be of interest to see the impact of women's work on family income, regardless of class group, by adding together their basic monthly take-home pay (no panel men earned S$1,100–1,599):

Wife's source of income	Husband's take-home pay				Number of couples
	Less than S$599	S$600–899	S$900–1,099	S$1,600–2,000	
None	S$420	S$727	S$1,033	S$1,600	15
Part-time wages	620	732	1,081	2,500	10
Full-time wages	873	1,026	1,483	3,050	20
Number of couples	7	19	14	5	45

19. See Betsy Wearing, *The Ideology of Motherhood* (Sydney: Allen & Unwin, 1984); C. F. Hill and F. P. Stafford, "Allocation of Time to Preschool Children and Educational Opportunity," *Journal of Human Resources* 9 (Summer 1974): 323–41; A. S. Leibowitz, "Education and the Allocation of Women's Time," in *Education, Income, and Human Behavior*, ed. F. T. Juster (New York: McGraw-Hill, 1974).

20. For North America, see Harriet B. Presser, "Work Shifts of Full-Time Dual-Earner Couples: Patterns and Contrasts by Sex of Spouses," *Demography* 21 (February 1987): 99–112.

21. The third woman has fortunately enlisted her unmarried sister to care for her toddler.

22. See Lisa Peattie, *Thinking about Development* (New York: Plenum, 1981).

23. This picture differs from culture-of-poverty theory, which maintains that attitudes are transmitted unchanged despite a change in the environment. See M. Seeman, "Alienation Studies," in *Annual Review of Sociology*, ed. Alex Inkeles, James Coleman, and Neil Smelser (Palo Alto: Annual Reviews, 1975), 1:91–123.

24. No poor couple yet lives in an HDB flat of more than three rooms; only two poor couples, both living in rented flats, have applied for larger ones. Thus the practice of reselling the first HDB flat for a larger one is so far unique to secure couples.

25. Fifteen couples moved and experienced change in family structure; 13 couples moved but did not experience change in family structure; two couples did not move but experienced a changing family structure; and 15 couples neither moved nor experienced family structure change.

26. Of the six poor couples who wished to share their new and larger homes with kin, three initially moved with kin to new homes, but their kin soon died or retired to their villages. For the United States, see Juanita M. Kreps, "The Economics of Intergenerational Relationships," in *Social Structure and the Family*, ed. Ethel Shanas and George Streibs, pp. 267–90 (New York: Prentice-Hall, 1963).

27. Michael Mann distinguishes between vague lip service to national symbols of social mobility and the actual integration of these programs into working-class lifeways: "The Social Cohesion of Liberal Democracy," *American Sociological Review* 35 (1970): 423–39.

28. One couple did not succeed. A second, who lived in the neighborhood of an elite government primary school, chose it by chance as their local school. The third couple sent two daughters to live with kin, who themselves placed the youngsters in a mission primary school.

29. Several mothers, fearing that their children would be placed in a distant school, had tubal ligations to avoid this educational penalty. As they had more than three children, they would not have qualified for priority entry to an elite school even if they had thought to apply to one.

30. Indicators of family size by social class:

	Poor	Secure	Total
Number of children			
Actual, phase 1	2.9	2.0	2.5
Intended, phase 1	3.6	3.0	3.4
Actual, phase 2	3.3	2.6	3.0
Number of mothers who gave birth over interphase	9	9	18
Number of couples who reduced actual family size below intended size	11	6	17
Number of mothers with tubal ligations			
Phase 1	7	0	7
Phase 2	15	6	21

31. The number of couples who had two, three, and four or more children are as follows, by the number they had intended to have earlier:

Intended number of children, phase 1	Actual number of children, phase 2		
	2	3	4+
2	5	–	–
3	12	11	–
4+	–	5	12

32. The numbers of poor and secure couples who in phase 1 intended to have two, three, and four or more children and who actually had that many children in phase 2 are as follows:

Number of children	Phase 1 intentions			Phase 2 family size		
	Poor	Secure	Total	Poor	Secure	Total
2	2	3	5	9	8	17
3	12	11	23	8	8	16
4+	14	3	17	11	1	12
Total	28	17	45	28	17	45

33. Although most women are able to have more children, I accept their statements that they will have no more. Only two poor couples, each with two children, said that if their income improved, they might have a third child. One of these couples had two sons and wanted a daughter; the other was under pressure by the husband's mother to have a third child in case an accident befell one of the first two. In both cases, however, the youngest child was at least eight years old, and the likelihood of either woman's having another child does not seem great.

34. Judith Blake found an inverse relationship between the desire for a career and the number of children desired by high school girls in the United States: "Demographic Science and the Redirection of Population Policy," in *Public Health and Population Change*, ed. Mindel Sheps and Jean Clare Ridley, pp. 41–69 (Pittsburgh: University of Pittsburgh Press, 1965).

35. These ten part-time home seamstresses had 3.0 children in phase 1 (the panel averaged 2.5 at that time). By phase 2 they had 3.2 children, although they had intended 3.9 children. The considerable drop is owed to some extent to their home labor possibilities. Guy Standing comments that the type of employment structure crucially determines the meaning of home-based employment. Where agriculture dominates the economy, informal activities may not depress fertility; but when a rise in household income is linked to a better life for the children, home labor may help lower fertility (*Labour Force Participation and Development*, 2d ed. [Geneva: International Labour Office, 1981], pp. 168–69).

36. The numbers of poor and secure couples who felt pressured by kin to have more children, or to have them more quickly, were as follows:

	Experienced kin pressure	Accepted influence	Resisted influence	Still under influence
Poor	16	12	3	1
Secure	8	5	3	0

37. For North America, see Anne K. Wilson, "Poverty and Fertility: The Role of Unemployment and Kinship Networks on Birth Planning," paper delivered to the Population Association of America, Boston, 1985.

38. Indeed, after the study was completed, the disincentives were temporarily reversed for certain categories of elite couples; see chap. 2.

39. See Peter Willmott and Michael Young, *Family and Class in a London Suburb* (London: Routledge & Kegan Paul, 1960); Lisa Peattie, *Thinking about Development*, pp. 120, 126.

40. These are not all the same couples, as several lost kin through death and others brought kin to live with them in their new homes.

41. See Stephen Edgell, *Middle-Class Families* (London: Allen & Unwin, 1980).

42. Twelve poor women received "some help" or "a lot" of help from their husbands in

phase 1, only seven in phase 2. Such help was given by the children of only two women in phase 1 but by those of eight in phase 2. The number of poor women who received help from other people fell slightly, from 16 to 13. (Multiple sources of help are possible.)

43. See Ruth Schwartz Cowan, *More Work for Mother* (New York: Basic Books, 1983).

44. See Edgell, *Middle-Class Families*.

45. Eight secure women received "some help" or "a lot of help" from their husbands in phase 1, three in phase 2; from their children, one in phase 1, two in phase 2; from others, 14 in phase 1, ten in phase 2.

46. See Wearing, *Ideology of Motherhood*.

47. See Hannah Gavron, *The Captive Wife* (Harmondsworth: Penguin, 1970).

48. See Judith Stacey, *Patriarchy and Socialist Revolution in China* (Berkeley: University of California Press, 1983).

49. The patterns of communication among panel couples in phases 1 and 2 are as follows, in number of couples:

	Little communication	Some communication	High communication
Phase 1			
Poor	14	7	7
Secure	1	3	13
Phase 2			
Poor	12	9	7
Secure	1	3	13

10. Conclusion: Restructuring an Industrial Society

1. See Samuel Bowles, "Unequal Education and the Reproduction of the Social Division of Labor," in *Schooling in a Corporate Society: The Political Economy of Growth*, ed. Martin Carnoy, pp. 36–64 (New York: David McKay, 1972); Martin Carnoy, "Education, Economy, and the State," in *Cultural and Economic Reproduction in Education*, ed. M. W. Apple, pp. 79–126 (London: Routledge & Kegan Paul, 1982).

2. See Alan Gilbert and Peter M. Ward, *Housing, the State, and the Poor: Policy and Practice in Three Latin American Cities* (Cambridge: Cambridge University Press, 1985).

3. At the time of writing a recession in Singapore has led to some loss of jobs. The important core-sector industries of shipbuilding, ship repair, and petroleum refining are hard hit. As a result, it will become important for the government to devise means of allowing families to refinance their homes. But the ownership position of the social groups is not identical; were the economy to take a downturn, the poor would have trouble keeping up their home payments, while most secure couples have already paid for their homes. On plans for further restructuring of the economy to overcome the recession, see the report of the Economic Committee, *The Singapore Economy: New Directions* (Singapore: Ministry of Trade and Industry, 1986).

4. See Ian Gough, *The Political Economy of the Welfare State* (London: Macmillan, 1979).

5. See Melvin Seeman, "Alienation Studies," in *Annual Review of Sociology*, vol. 1, ed. Alex Inkeles, James Coleman, and Neil Smelser, pp. 91–123 (Palo Alto: Annual Reviews, 1975).

6. See John Hajnal, "Two Kinds of Preindustrial Household Formation System," *Population and Development Review* 8 (September 1982): 449–93; Arthur P. Wolf and Susan B. Hanley, "Introduction," in *Family and Population in East Asian History*, ed. Susan B. Hanley and Arthur P. Wolf, pp. 1–12 (Stanford: Stanford University Press, 1985).

7. See James C. Scott, *The Moral Economy of the Peasant* (New Haven: Yale University Press, 1976).

8. Rosa Luxemburg, *The Accumulation of Capital* (New York: Monthly Review Press, 1964), stresses the homesteading process in the North American West, which encouraged families to build a home as a spur toward capital accumulation for the new nation. For the contemporary industrial state, see Gilbert and Ward, *Housing, the State, and the Poor*.

9. See Fernando Henrique Cardoso and Enzo Faletto, *Dependency and Development in Latin America* (Berkeley: University of California Press, 1979).

Index

Abernathy, Virginia D., 283n23
Abortion. *See* Family planning
Amah. *See* Domestic servants
Anderson, Michael, 273n26
Apartments. *See* Public housing
Apple, M. W., 292n1
Aramunaithan, P., 277n24, 278n43
Askham, Janet, 281n9, 285n45
Aw Siaw Peng, 277n27
Azumi, K., 285n47

Back, Kurt W., 284n41
Bailey, Peter, 284n40
Barth, Ernest A. T., 273n20
Beck, E. M., 281n3
Berger, Peter L., 287n20
Berk, R. A., 283n29
Berk, S. F., 283n29
Berkowitz, S. D., 271n4
Bernstein, Basil, 283n22
Bibb, Richard, 272n12
Birth control. *See* Family planning
Blackburn, M. R., 272n13, 280n1
Blake, Judith, 285n42, 291n34
Blood, R., 283n29
Bluestone, Barry, 272nn12–13
Bornschier, Volker, 271n6, 272n11
Bott, Elizabeth, 10, 273n26
Bourque, Susan C., 273n18
Bowles, Samuel, 292n1
Braverman, Harry, 272n10

Bryson, R. B., 287n19
Buchanan, Iain, 278nn42, 46
Bus conductor, 46–52
Butcher's helper, 163–65
Buxbaum, David C., 280n3, 286n1

Calzavara, Liviana Mostacci, 273n25,
    286n12
Cardoso, Fernando Henrique, 293n9
Carnoy, Martin, 292n1
Car ownership, 138, 143, 146, 211, 221,
    223
Carstens, Sharon A., 275n5
Central Provident Fund (CPF), 27–28,
    112, 177, 184, 189, 204, 221. *See also*
    Public housing: and consumer financing
Chan Heng Chee, 275nn3–5, 10; 279n54
Chan Peng Fun, 288n7
Chang Chen-tung, 278n44
Chase-Dunn, Christopher, 271n6
Cheah Hock Beng, 271n3, 277n25,
    278n47
Chen, Peter S. J., 274n35, 279n64
Chen Ta, 281n5
Chia Siow Yue, 276n20, 289n15
Chiang Hai Ding, 275n10
Childbearing: expense of, 98, 129; and
    opportunity costs, 98–99, 118; and sex
    of children, 98, 158, 185
Children: adoption of, 65, 68, 74, 111–12,
    132, 158; care of, 54, 126, 128, 138–39,

Children (*cont.*)
205, 216, 221; economic dependence
on, 44, 135; education of, 42, 44–45,
57, 63, 67, 75, 94–97, 110, 116–17,
135, 141–42, 149, 156–57, 165, 169–
70, 174–75, 178, 184–85, 190, 195–96,
198, 200–201, 205–6, 210, 218, 223–
24; financial burden of, 98, 129, 178;
labor of, and household economy, 97;
parental aspirations for, 44–45, 51–52,
57, 76, 94, 97, 110, 117, 123, 128, 130,
134, 141, 155, 164, 170, 174–75, 179,
182, 185, 195, 198, 201, 210, 224; rearing and discipline of, 44, 61, 67, 76,
95–96, 109, 116–17, 128–29, 139–40,
142, 170, 175, 197, 201, 210–12, 218,
221–22, 224; work prospects of, 44–45,
57, 63, 110, 141, 198
Chinese school. *See* Children: education
of
Ching, Frank, 280n68
Choe, Alan F. C., 278n41
Chua Beng Huat, 275n8
Chua Wee Meng, 278n48
Clammer, John, 288n4
Clan ties, 20–21, 119
Clothing, 42, 107, 137
Cobb, Jonathan, 35, 279n63
Cohen, Myron, 282n17
Cohn, Bernard S., 272n9
Coleman, James, 290n23, 292n5
Coleman, Richard, 284n33
Collins, Randall, 288n7
Community centers, 211
Computer technician, 124–30, 208–13
Concubines, 43, 46, 59, 79, 114–15, 138,
280n1
Connelly, Patricia, 273n20, 289n18
Construction worker, 46, 166
Core sector. *See* Work: in core sector
Corporatism and state policy, 19–20
Coser, Lewis, 283n23
Coser, Rose Laub, 283n23
Coverman, Shelley, 287n17
Cowan, Ruth Schwartz, 292n43
CPF. *See* Central Provident Fund; Public
housing: and consumer financing
Crossick, Geoffrey, 284n40

David, Miriam E., 284n39
Dependency theory and economic devel-
opment, 5
Deyo, Frederic, 271n2, 275n8

Dialect: and children's education, 129,
141, 156, 195; and family relations, 11,
41, 46, 53, 58–59, 70, 103, 111, 118,
124, 126, 133, 136
Disincentive policy, 36–37, 100, 118; and
children's education, 210, 247; knowledge of and attitudes toward, 45, 52,
58, 64, 70, 110–11, 118, 124, 130, 135,
142
Domestic servants, 47, 50, 58–65, 84,
132, 138–40, 142, 152, 175–81
Donzelot, Jacques, 273nn21–22
Draftsmen: architectural, 136–43, 219–25;
oil company, 136–43, 219–25
Dreitzel, Hans Peter, 287n20

Economic development: and breakup of
community, 30, 165, 175, 181, 207; and
capital-intensive industry, 24–25; and
changes in childbearing stage, 10; and
changes in family structure, 5–6; and
education, 26, 35; and foreign investment, 24; and income inequality, 6, 26;
and industrial stratification, 5; and labor-intensive industry, 23–24; and local
firms, 24, 173, 202; and public housing,
30–33; and role of women, 7–8; and
social services, 10–11, 27–28; theories
of, 4–6; wage levels, 5–6, 25–26. *See
also* Urban renewal
Economic Development Board (EDB), 21
Economic recession: *1974*, 48, 72, 124;
1985–87, 265
Edgell, Stephen, 287n21, 291n41, 292n44
Education, 33–35, 94–97, 155–56; adult,
82, 137, 146–48, 167; bilingual, 34;
certification and, 208–9, 220, 263; children's dialect and, 129, 141, 156, 195;
Chinese stream, 57; and economic development, 26, 35; English stream, 57,
63, 110, 128; and meritocracy, 33–35,
201; as pathway to advancement, 33–
35; respondents' lack of, 42, 46–48, 58–
60, 101, 132, 139, 145–46, 164, 166–
68, 176, 179, 188, 200, 208, 216; and
savings, 110, 117; and work opportunity, 125, 137, 220. *See also* Children: education of
Edwards, Richard, 272n10
Electronics workers, 25–26, 46–52, 70–
78, 84, 125, 165–72, 186–91
Elder, Glen H., Jr., 272n9, 274n28,
283n28

El Sanabary, Nagat, 273n20
Employer/employee relations, 131, 193, 214
English school. *See* Children: education of; Education, English stream *and* children's dialect and
Ethnic intermarriage, 12, 124–30, 208–19
Ethnicity, 54
Ethnic rivalry, 120
Evans, Peter B., 271–72n7

Face, 131, 286
Faletto, Enzo, 293n9
Family: extended, 49, 56–57, 61, 87, 90, 93, 106, 108, 120, 122, 126, 132–33, 155, 199, 204–5; and parent–child relations, 72, 112; and social mobility, 37; women's economic contribution to, 48, 52, 60, 62, 72, 84, 86, 88, 105, 107, 119, 125, 149, 166–67, 187–88, 195, 221
Family cycle, 11, 93, 153, 239, 244
Family division of labor: and children, 43, 63, 113–14, 164, 170, 179–80; between spouses, 49, 55, 57, 61, 66–67, 86, 89–90, 106, 113, 120, 122, 126, 133, 138, 151, 164, 171, 179–80, 183, 196, 205, 212, 217
Family finances, 56, 60, 66, 72, 75, 87, 93, 108, 114, 119, 122, 126, 132, 164, 184, 188, 194, 196–97, 204–5, 209
Family firm, 53–54, 111–12, 145, 173–74, 203
Family planning, 36, 43, 45, 52, 56–58, 63–64, 69, 77–78, 97–101, 107, 110, 117, 123, 129, 134–36, 142, 158, 165, 171, 185, 189, 201–2, 206–7, 210–12, 218, 224
Family size: and economic cost, 100; average, 15–16, 97, 157–58; intended, 45, 52, 64, 69, 77, 118, 123–24, 129, 135–36, 142, 158, 165, 175, 185, 189, 198–99, 201, 206; and social mobility, 37; and state, 101
Family structure and social services, 4, 7–8
Farkas, G., 283n29
Fawcett, James T., 279n64, 280n68
Food, 41, 72; children's, 51, 128; and eating habits, 66, 106, 132, 205, 221; Western, 138
Form, H. William, 272n12
Foucault, Michel, 36, 279n65

FPPB (Family Planning and Population Board). *See* Family planning
Freedman, Maurice, 282nn16–17
Frobel, Folker, 271n1

Gallin, Rita S., 285n49
Gambling, 71, 91, 189. *See also* Lottery; Mah-jongg
Gamer, Robert, 275n10
Garment workers, 25–26, 54, 103–11, 118–24, 192–99, 203–8
Gavron, Hannah, 273n26, 292n47
Geiger, Frances M., 275n9
Geiger, Theodore, 275n9
Gerson, Kathleen, 284n34
Gerth, Hans, 286n51
Giffin, Karen, 287n19
Gilbert, Alan, 292n2
Gittins, Diana, 273n22
Gluckman, Max, 286n6
Goh Chok Tong, 276n15
Goh Keng Swee, 279nn57, 60
Goody, Esther N., 285n43
Goody, John Rankine, 285n43
Gopinathan, Saravan, 279n56
Gough, Ian, 292n4
Gouldner, Alvin, 281n7
Granovetter, Mark, 8, 273n25, 282n13, 286n10
Greenblatt, Sidney I., 286n2
Greenhalgh, Susan, 285n48
Grocers, 111–18, 199–202

Haas, Jack, 281n7
Hajnal, John, 292n6
Hamblin, R., 283n29
Hanley, Susan B., 292n6
Hareven, Tamara K., 274n28
Hassan, Riaz, 274n33, 275n9, 278n46
Hauser, Philip M., 284n41
Hawkers, 41–46, 72, 80, 163, 187
Health-care system, 36–38
Heinrichs, Jurgen, 271n1
Heng Swee Hai, Michael, 275n8
Hesselbart, S., 283–84nn24, 30
Heyzer, Noeleen, 281n7
Hill, C. F., 289n19
Ho Kun Ngiap, 278n48
Hochschild, Jennifer L., 288n8
Homemakers, 42–46, 53–58, 64–70, 124–36, 172–75, 181–86, 199, 208–19
Horan, Patrick, M., 281n3

Housing Development Board (HDB). *See* Public housing
Howard, Les, 271n4
Hu Hsien Chin, 286n2
Huang, Chieh-shan, 280n4, 285n48
Hui guan, 20–21
Humphries, Jane, 8, 273n21
Hwang, Kwang-Kuo, 286n2

Industrial sectors. *See* Work: in core sector *and* in peripheral sector
Inflation, 141, 167, 176–77, 216, 220
Inkeles, Alex, 271n5, 290n23, 292n5
Islam, Iyanatul, 277n32

Jaffe, A. J., 285n47
Johnson, Terence J., 275n10
Juster, F. T., 289n19

Kaim-Caudle, Peter R., 278n34
Kampung, 28–30
Kampung living, 87–88, 92, 121–22, 155, 205
Kanter, Rosabeth Moss, 288n10
Kaye, Barrington, 278n40
Kaye, Lincoln, 288n10
Kellner, Hansfried, 287n20
Kin: aging, 133–34, 174–75, 196; and childbearing plans, 99, 107, 123, 156, 171, 206; economic dependence on/independence from, 62, 89, 92, 97–98, 101, 111, 114, 133, 138, 163, 185, 219, 225; and homeowning, 115; and mixed marriage, 125; relations with, 50–51, 62, 120, 188, 197–98, 213; views of, on women working, 47, 49, 88, 112, 151, 195, 197, 200, 204
Kin ties: and childcare, 47, 49, 55, 60, 63, 66, 74–76, 87, 99, 105, 109, 120, 130, 132, 155–56, 196, 217–18; and work opportunity, 10, 47, 49, 59, 84, 131, 137, 146, 148, 151, 164, 166, 173–74, 176–77, 194, 203, 215, 220; women's work and maintenance of, 88, 139. *See also* Marriage: and kin relations
Kirkpatrick, Colin, 277n32
Klein, Nancy H., 283n27
Kohn, Melvin L., 283n22, 284n37, 287n16
Komarovsky, Mirra, 283n26, 284n38
Koo, Hagen, 272n14
Kreps, Juanita M., 290n26
Kreye, Otto, 271n1

Kulkarni, V. G., 280n73, 288n10
Kung, Lydia, 289n13
Kuo, Eddie C. Y., 274nn33, 37
Kupinsky, Stanley, 285n46
Kurtz, Donald V., 278n36

Labor unions, 21, 25, 105
Laksa, 72
Lang, Linda, 283n29
Lang, Olga, 282n16
Lauman, Edward O., 275n2
Lein, Laura, 283n23
Lee, Eddy, 271n2
Lee Kuan Yew, prime minister, 23, 111
Lee Soo Ann, 275n9, 276n13
Leibowitz, A. S., 289n19
LeMasters, L. L., 281n7, 284n30
Levine, Robert A., 283n27
Light, Ivan L., 274n32
Lim Chee Onn, 276n15
Lim Chong Yah, 276n15
Lim, D., 276n15
Lim, G. P., 277n23
Lim, Linda Y. C., 277nn23, 27; 279n62
Lind, Andrew W., 275n5
Lindert, Peter H., 285n42
Lipman-Blumen, Jean, 283n24
Littlejohn, Gary, 284n39
Littler, Craig R., 281n7
Liu, William T., 285nn41, 44, 48
Lloyd, Peter, 271n1
Lomnitz, Larissa Adler, 272n8
Lottery, 112, 184, 194
Luxemburg, Rosa, 293n8
Luxton, Meg, 283n25

McGee, Terence, 272n8
Mah-jongg, 114
Malloy, James M., 278n39
Mandarin school. *see* Education, Chinese stream
Mann, M. Michael, 272n13, 280n1, 290n27
Marcuse, Herbert, 284n35
Market economy, 4, 6, 203, 206
Marriage, 10, 89–92, 151–53, 255–60; arranged, 73, 91; breakdown of, 14, 125, 274n37; and friendships, 43, 48, 61–62, 68, 73, 91, 101, 106, 121, 127, 134, 138–40, 152, 180, 185–86; and homeowning, 94; and husband/wife communication, 68, 74, 107, 114, 117, 121,

Marriage (*cont.*)
127–28, 140, 172, 191, 260; and husband/wife leisure activities, 43, 49–50, 56, 61, 68, 74, 89–90, 92, 106, 121, 127, 139–40, 202, 212, 225; interracial, 12, 124–30, 208–13; joint, 10, 49, 89, 102, 153; and kin relations, 43, 50, 55–56, 61, 91, 101, 107, 113–14, 118, 127, 133, 165, 171, 180, 186, 196, 202, 207, 219, 225; segregated, 10, 89, 111, 118, 185; and sexual relations, 43–44, 56, 107; and social class, 91, 151
Marriage relationship, 43, 49–50, 62, 73–74, 92, 107, 121, 127, 133, 140, 152, 165, 175, 180, 191, 202, 212, 224–25
Mattar, Ahmad, 276n14, 278n35
Medicalization of social control. *See* Health-care system
Mee, 72
Mehmet, O., 282n10
Member of Parliament (MP) and social services, 104, 168, 170, 178
Meritocracy, 33–35, 201
Merton, Robert K., 286nn4–5
Meter reader, 103–11, 192–99
Mies, M., 273n17
Miller, Karen Anne, 271n5
Mills, C. Wright, 272n10, 286n51
Mills, Lennox, 279n54
Miner, Horace, 283n27
Mintz, Sidney W., 273n18
Moonlighting, 82, 104, 137, 152, 168, 187, 219–20
Moore, Raymond S., 279n61, 284n39
Murphy, W. M., 272n12
Musgrove, Frank, 284n35

Nair, Devan, 275n7
National Productivity Board (NPD), 24–25
National Trades Union Congress (NTUC), 21, 25, 105
National Wages Council, 24
Nettl, J. P., 271n7
Noble, Joey, 284n39

Omohundro, John T., 274n32, 281n5, 286n3
Ooi Jin Bee, 275n10
Oppong, Christine, 10, 273n26
Ortner, Sherry B., 272n9
Oshima, Harry T., 272n11

Outwork. *See* Work: part-time
Owen, Constance R., 283n27

Pang Eng Fong, 277n27, 279n62
Papanek, Hanna, 273n20
Parke, Ross, 272n9
Paukert, Felix, 272n11
Payne, Geoff, 279n53
Payne, Judy, 279n53
Peattie, Lisa, xvi, 272n15, 290n22, 291n39
Pennock, Roland J., 274n29
People's Action Party (PAP), 20
Peripheral sector. *See* Work: in peripheral sector
Perrucci, Carolyn, 283n24
Persell, Caroline Hodges, 279n61
Pike, Frederick B., 275n2
Pleck, Joseph, 283nn23, 29
Political movements and state building, 20
Political structure, 19–23
Portes, Alejandro, 271n6; 272nn8, 12
Population limitation policy. *See* Family planning; Disincentive policy
Post Office Savings Bank (POSB), 27
Presser, Harriet B., 289n20
Professional groups, 21–23
Public housing, 28–33, 153–55, 239–44; and consumer financing, 33, 62, 66, 92–94, 109, 127, 153, 168, 174, 206, 217; furnishing of, 30, 44, 48, 51, 56, 61, 65, 108–9, 115, 123, 127, 141, 155, 168–69, 174, 178, 184, 189, 197, 200, 206, 210, 213, 217, 223; ownership of, 30, 122–23, 138, 153, 183–84, 196, 205, 217; rental of, 33, 44, 51, 56, 61–62, 66, 75, 93, 115, 178, 189, 221, 223; and social bonds, 30, 240–44
Public Utilities Board, 103, 192–94

Quality control supervisor, 130–36, 214–19
Quinlan, Dan, 272n11

Rainwater, Lee, 285n45, 288n8
Raj, Conrad, 278n37
Ramakrishnan, M. K., 277n32
Rao, V. V. Banaji, 277n32
Reference groups, 145–46, 208
Religion, 67–68, 115, 126, 194, 213
Ridley, Jean Claire, 291n34
Rorlich, George F., 278n34

Rubin, Lillian, 90, 283nn26, 28
Rubinson, Richard, 271n6, 272n11
Rueschemeyer, Dietrich, 272n7
Ruggie, Mary, 272n7
Runciman, W. G., 288n8
Ryan, Mary P., 274n27
Ryder, Norman B., 285n41

Saari, John, 286n2
Safa, Helen, 272n15
Safilios-Rothschild, Constantina, 283n29, 287n19
Salaff, Janet W., 273n16
Sample: interviews of, 14–17; skills and work sectors of, 12–16; socioeconomic status of, 12
Sampling techniques, 11–16
Sarason, Barbara, 273n23
Sarason, Irwin, 273n23
Sassen-Koob, Saskia, 272n12
Savings: education and, 110, 117; family, 107, 210, 213. *See also* Central Provident Fund; Family finances; Post Office Savings Bank
Saw Swee-Hock, 280n68
Schmitter, Philippe, 275nn2, 6
Schneider, David M., 287n24
Schooler, Carmi, 283n22, 287n16
Schoolteacher, 136–43, 149, 219–25
Schurmann, Franz, 271n7
Scott, James C., 273n24, 292n7
Scott, Joan W., 273n16, 285n46
Scott, W. Richard, 271n6
Seah Chee Meow, 275nn3, 9; 276n12
Seeman, Melvin, 290n23, 292n5
Sen, A. K., 281n5
Sennett, Richard, 35, 273n22, 279n63
Sewing machine mechanic, 118–24, 203–8
Shaffir, William, 281n7
Shanas, Ethel, 290n26
Sheps, Mindel, 291n34
Shipfitter, 70–78, 186–91
Shipyard worker, 64–70, 131, 181–86
Siegel, Lenny, 277n29
Simoniya, N. A., 281n5
Singapore Family Planning and Population Board. *See* Family planning
Skills upgrading and retraining, 82–84, 125, 214–20, 222
Skocpol, Theda, 272n7

Smart, Barry, 284n39
Smelser, Neil, 290n23, 292n5
Smith, Bonnie G., 274n27
Smith, D. H., 271n5
Smith, Raymond T., 287n24
Smith, T. E., 279n66, 280n71
Social class: and child-rearing patterns, 89; and education of children, 35, 97, 155–56; and homeowning, 94; and intended family size, 100–101; and marriage relationship, 91, 151; and women's employment, 88; and work opportunity, 104, 146
Social networks, 10, 84, 180, 200. *See also* Kin ties; Work: social relations at
Social security, 27, 277–78n34
Social services. *See* Education; Family planning; Health-care system; Public housing; Skills upgrading and retraining
Souris, Marek, 276n11
Stacey, Judith, 291n48
Stack, Carol, 283n20
Stafford, F. P., 289n19
Standing, Guy, 273nn17, 19; 285n46; 291n35
Sterilization. *See* Family planning
Stevenson, M., 272n12
Store clerk, 53–58, 172–75
Streibs, George, 290n26
Stritch, Thomas, 275n2
Stycos, J. M., 284n41, 285n47

Tai Ching Ling, 274n37
Tan Ern Ser, 275n8
Tan Suat Keng, 277n29
Teh Cheang Wan, 278nn40–41, 49
Teilhet-Waldorf, Sarah, 282n10
Thamayanthi, Thirugnanam, 289n16
Thomas, George G., 279–80
Thomas, W. I., 272n9
Thomson, George G., 279n66, 280n71
Thurow, Lester, 288n5
Tilly, Louise A., 273n16, 285n46
Tinsmith, 58–64, 175–81
Toh Chin Chye, 278n35
Tolbert, Charles M. II, 281n3
Tontine, 27
Turner, Christopher, 273n26
Tutu, 41

Urban renewal, 80, 123, 173, 199, 205

Vocational and Industrial Training Board (VITB), 24–25, 208–9
Volunteer police force, 104, 193

Wages, 5–6, 25–27; of poor men, 41, 53, 59, 65, 71, 79, 163–64, 166, 173, 176, 186; of poor women, 166, 177, 187; of secure men, 104, 112, 118, 124, 131, 137, 144, 146, 193, 203, 214, 219; of secure women, 104, 119, 125, 148, 194–95, 205
Wakefield, John, 284n30
Walshok, Mary Lindenstem, 284n30
Walton, John, 271n6, 272n8
Ward, Peter M., 292n2
Warehouse worker, 165–72
Warren, Kay Barbara, 273n18
Watson, Walter B., 273n20
Watson, William, 286n6
Wayne, Jack, 273n21
Wearing, Betsy, 289n19, 292n46
Weiner, Myron, 271n5
Weller, R. H., 285n47
Wellman, Barry, 271n4, 273n23
Wertheim, W. F., 281n5
Westoff, Charles P., 285n41
Wilensky, Harold, 271n3, 286n8
Wiley, Norbert F., 280n2, 286n3
Williamson, Nancy E., 285n44
Willis, Paul, 274n30
Willmott, E. R., 281n5
Willmott, Peter, 8; 273nn21, 26; 291n39
Wilson, Anne K., 285n43, 291n37
Winch, Robert, 90, 283n27
Wolf, Arthur P., 280n4, 285n48, 292n6

Wolfe, D., 283n29
Wong, K. Aline, 274nn33, 37; 277n30
Work: in core sector, 6, 64–65, 70–72, 82, 124, 130, 136, 145–46, 165, 215, 219; men's, 79–84, 144–49, 226–32; overtime, 82, 105, 194, 203, 215; part-time, 137, 149,151, 163, 168, 174–75, 183, 200, 204–5, 216; in peripheral sector, 6, 41–42, 46–47, 53–54, 58–59, 82, 103, 111, 119, 145, 148, 163–64, 175–76, 199, 203, 220–22; social relations at, 119, 138, 182, 190, 193, 214. *See also* Moonlighting; Skills upgrading and retraining; Wages; *entries for individual occupations*
—women's, 84–89, 148–51, 233–38; and consumer culture, 88; in core sector, 148; and mobility, 48; and role changes, 50, 149; in shadow economy, 86, 149; and social activities, 88, 105–6. *See also* Wages; *entries for individual occupations*

Yeh, Stephen H. K., 278nn40–42, 45, 47–48; 279nn51–52
Yeo Kim Wah, 275n1
Yoshihara, Kunio, 276n13
Young, Michael, 8; 273nn21, 26; 291n39
Yu, Elena, 285nn41, 44, 48
Yu-foo Shoon, 277n28
Yu Yee Shoon, 277n31
Yuval-Davis, Nira, 284n39

Zero population growth. *See* Family planning

Library of Congress Cataloging-in-Publication Data
Salaff, Janet W.
    State and family in Singapore.

    (Anthropology of contemporary issues)
    Bibliography: p.
    Includes index.
    1. Family policy—Singapore.   2. Poor—Singapore.
3. Economic development—Social aspects—Singapore.
I. Title. II. Series.
HQ675.S26 1988   306.8'5'095957   87-47962
ISBN 0-8014-2140-3 (alk. paper)